LONGMAN LINGUISTICS LIBRARY

FRONTIERS OF PHONOLOGY

LONGMAN LINGUISTICS LIBRARY

General editors:
R. H. Robins, *University of London*
Martin Harris, *University of Manchester*
Geoffrey Horrocks, *University of Cambridge*

For a complete list of books in the series see pages vii and viii

Frontiers of Phonology: Atoms, Structures, Derivations

Edited by Jacques Durand and Francis Katamba

LONGMAN

LONDON AND NEW YORK

Longman Group UK Limited
Longman House, Burnt Mill,
Harlow, Essex CM20 2JE, England
and Associated Companies throughout the world.

*Published in the United States of America
by Longman Publishing, New York*

© Longman Group Limited 1995

First published 1995

ISBN 0 582 082684 CSD
ISBN 0 582 082676 PPR

British Library Cataloguing-in-Publication Data

A catalogue record for this book is
available from the British Library

Library of Congress Cataloging-in-Publication Data

Frontiers of phonology: atoms, structures, derivations/edited by
Jacques Durand, Francis Katamba.
p. cm. — (Longman linguistics library)
Includes bibliographical references and index.
ISBN 0-582-08268-4. — ISBN 0-582-08267-6 (pbk.)
1. Grammar, Comparative and general — Phonology. I. Durand,
Jacques, 1947– . II. Katamba, Francis, 1947– .   III. Series.
P217.F765   1995
414—dc20   94-27527
                                                                      CIP

Set by 15 in 10/11 Times Roman
Produced by Longman Singapore Publishers (Pte) Ltd
Printed in Singapore

Contents

Linguistic Theory
The Discourse of Fundamental Works
ROBERT DE BEAUGRANDE

The Meaning of Syntax
A Study in the Adjectives of English
CONNOR FERRIS

Latin American Spanish
JOHN M. LIPSKI

A Linguistic History of Italian
MARTIN MAIDEN

Modern Arabic
CLIVE HOLES

Frontiers of Phonology:
Atoms, Structures, Derivations
EDITED BY JACQUES DURAND
AND FRANCIS KATAMBA

Contributors

Lee Bickmore is Assistant Professor of Linguistics and Cognitive Science at the University of Albany, State University of New York. His contributions to the field include descriptions and analyses of some lesser-known Bantu languages on which he has collected the primary data. His work addresses various factors which influence the application of tone rules, especially those which are syntactic or metrical in nature.

Wiebke Brockhaus is Lecturer in German at the University of Huddersfield. She has worked mainly on aspects of the phonology of German, especially on final devoicing, about which she is now writing a book (based on her 1992 University of London PhD thesis). Having participated in a Government Phonology-based automatic speech recognition project at the School of Oriental and African Studies (University of London) in the past, she is currently involved in a similar undertaking at the University of Huddersfield.

John Coleman is Director of the Phonetics Laboratory at the University of Oxford. He has written many papers on declarative phonology, and has a special interest in developing computational implementations of non-segmental phonology and phonetics in speech synthesis. He is co-author (with J. P. Olive and A. Greenwood) of *Acoustics of American English Speech* (1993).

Jacques Durand is Professor of French and Linguistics at the University of Salford (Greater Manchester). His research work has mainly been in the areas of Machine Translation and Phonology (both general and applied to French) where he has published widely. His publications include *Generative and Non-Linear Phonology* (1990) and as editor or co-editor *Dependency and Non-Linear Phonology* (1986), *Explorations in Dependency Phonology* (1987), *Essays in Grammatical Theory and Universal Grammar* (1989). He was the Chairman of the Department of Modern Languages at Salford between 1992 and 1994, and in 1993 he became the Director of its European Studies Research Institute.

John Harris, Reader in Linguistics at University College London, writes on phonological theory, language change and the history of English. He is the author of *Phonological variation and change* (1985, Cambridge University Press) and *English sound structure* (1994, Blackwell).

Harry van der Hulst is Associate Professor in the department of general linguistics and the Holland Institute of Generative Linguistics (HIL) of the Leiden University (in the Netherlands). His publications deal mainly with issues in non-linear phonology, and in particular with stress, segmental structure and phonological aspects of sign language. He has edited over ten books on phonology and is currently Editor-in-chief of the international linguistic journal 'The Linguistic Review' (since 1990) and series editor of 'Linguistic Models' (Mouton de Gruyter).

Francis Katamba is Lecturer in linguistics at Lancaster University. He is the author of *An Introduction to Phonology* (1989), *Morphology* (1993) and *English Words* (1994). He has also written on the implications of Bantu for phonological and morphological theory. His edited books include *Bantu Phonology and Morphology* (1995).

Jonathan Kaye is Professor of General Linguistics at the School of Oriental and African Studies (University of London). The author of many books and papers on various aspects of phonological theory, notably *Phonology: A cognitive view* (1989), '*Coda' Licensing* (1990) and *Constituent structure and government in phonology* (1990, with Jean Lowenstamm and Jean-Roger Vergnaud). Along with the two last mentioned linguists, he is one of the originators of the theory of Government Phonology.

Geoff Lindsey is Lecturer in Linguistics in the University of Edinburgh's Linguistics Department. He has directed the Department's Laboratory, and has published in phonetics and phonology. He is also known for work on the semantics of intonation.

Douglas Pulleyblank is Associate Professor at the University of British Columbia. His research has centred on autosegmental representations, with a focus on West African languages. He is the author of *Tone in Lexical Phonology* (1986) and *Grounded Phonology* (with Diana Archangeli, 1994).

Draga Zec is Assistant Professor of Linguistics at Cornell University. Her contributions to phonological theory fall into three general areas: prosodic structure, lexical phonology, and the phonology–syntax interface. She is a co-editor of *The Phonology–Syntax Connection*, and her dissertation recently appeared in the 'Garland' series.

Introduction

Jacques Durand and Francis Katamba

Frontiers of Phonology: Atoms, Structures, Derivations is a collection of essays that present a selective overview of recent trends in the linguistic analysis of sound structure. During the 1970s and the 1980s a fairly radical reconfiguration of the field of phonology took place, largely against the backdrop of Chomsky and Halle's *The Sound Pattern of English* (1968), hereafter abbreviated as SPE. The need to move away from the spartan approach to phonological representations advocated in SPE is now universally accepted but the range of solutions provided within current frameworks can be quite confusing for the non-specialist. Our aim is not to attempt to provide an exhaustive, panoramic coverage of the entire field, but rather to explore theoretical issues in three core areas of phonological theory from a number of different perspectives. The questions fall into three broad categories:

1. The nature and representation of phonological features (Are they unary or binary? What is the architecture of featural representations? Is underspecification justified?).
2. The role and structure of the skeletal tier and syllable structure.
3. The competing claims of derivational and declarative approaches to phonology.

All these issues are controversial. A major objective of this book is to provide a forum for the discussion of important theoretical topics from the standpoint of frameworks such as Autosegmental and Multidimensional Phonology, Moraic Phonology, Dependency Phonology, Government Phonology and Declarative Phonology.

Not surprisingly, no one approach has found all the answers to all the questions. So, in phonology, as in many other fields of inquiry, much is to be gained from constructive criticism, debate and dialogue with those who adopt a stance different from one's own.

Further, we hope that the light thrown on these matters by dialogue will facilitate the task of judging the relative merits of the competing post-SPE models. This should be a welcome result for anyone who is sometimes left bewildered by the claims made by adherents of phonological models which are in some respects radically different and in other ways quite similar – in spite of what their proponents might say.

This book is intended for a variety of readers: advanced linguistics students and professional linguists, psychologists, speech scientists and scholars in related fields who are interested in finding out what modern phonologists are up to today. While we expect the reader to have more than a nodding acquaintance with post-SPE generative phonology, a serious effort has been undertaken to provide essays which are self-standing and do not presuppose a specialist knowledge of the issues under discussion. Readers who feel that their background is not sufficient for coming to grips with the issues discussed in this book are referred to Durand (1990a) or Katamba (1989).

Part 1 of the book deals with the atoms of phonological representation. In SPE it is assumed that segments are made up of unordered sets of phonological features and that these features are binary. Both these assumptions have been challenged within a variety of frameworks but the dust has not yet settled on these debates. In Douglas Pulleyblank's 'Feature geometry and underspecification' (Chapter 1), it is first of all argued that to account properly for assimilatory processes one needs to move radically away from the SPE model. But it is not enough to organize features in different tiers or planes as is done in Autosegmental Phonology. The best account of assimilation processes requires a geometric organization of features, i.e. that features should be intrinsically organized into a hierarchical set of a universally defined nature. Pulleyblank's Chapter then turns to the degree of specification of phonological features. While in SPE all features are fully specified as + or –, evidence is given that underspecified representations (which allow for only one feature-value to be present) can be advantageous from the point of view both of phonology and of phonetic implementation. This does not mean, however, that only unary (or monovalent) features should be countenanced. While the class nodes of geometric representations are inherently monovalent, Pulleyblank argues that the terminal features which hang from class nodes are binary in nature. Both values (+ or −) of features such as [ATR] or [voice], define a natural class and both can be manipulated by phonological processes.

In marked contrast with Pulleyblank's Chapter, John Harris and Geoff Lindsey in Chapter 2, 'The elements of phonological representation' claim that phonological primes are inherently unary. It should not be assumed, however, that the atoms of phonology (which they call 'elements') are the standard distinctive features minus the assumption of binarity. Harris and Lindsey put forward the idea that the elements are different from classical features in being independently interpretable – a hypothesis most vigorously defended within Government Phonology but also associated with Dependency Phonology and Particle Phonology. They then exemplify the theory of elements and show how phenomena assumed to require binary features can be appropriately handled with unary elements within a Government Phonology framework. The paper is also challenging in criticizing underspecification, and in tackling the question of the cognitive basis of phonological primes. In the wake of Jakobson, Harris and Lindsey argue strongly in favour of primes which are mappable in the first instance not onto articulations, but onto sound patterns. As part of the discussion, the authors offer a description of the elemental acoustic patterns which characterize a few of the primitives.

In 'Radical CV Phonology: the categorial gesture', Harry van der Hulst offers a discussion of phonological primitives from the standpoint of a revised version of Dependency Phonology. The symbols C and V in his title do not refer to the skeletal units in the sense of Clements and Keyser (1983), as used in Bickmore's article here, but to two phonological features which play a central role in his account. As in classical Dependency Phonology, van der Hulst assumes that phonological primes are grouped in hierarchical sets, called gestures, but unlike standard accounts of feature geometry (see Pulleyblank this volume) the dependency relation is seen as central to the internal structure of segments. For reasons of space, this article concentrates on the 'categorial' gesture. It includes an outline of classical Dependency Phonology proposals concerning this gesture (see Anderson and Ewen, 1987) which provides a clear point of departure for van der Hulst's own radical proposals.

Part 2 of the book is devoted to the skeletal tier and its relation to aspects of suprasegmental structure (in particular, the syllable). During the 1970s and 1980s, a lot of effort was devoted to the reintroduction of the syllable, and other units of the prosodic hierarchy, within phonological theory. It became accepted that phonological representations should be multidimensional and that the various planes should be organized around a set of timing or weight units (Cs and Vs, Xs or morae according to the framework), often referred to as the skeleton or the skeletal tier.

Lee Bickmore's Chapter 4, 'Accounting for compensatory lengthening in the CV and moraic frameworks' begins with a survey of the developments in skeletal phonology that led to the rise of moraic theory. Bickmore then goes on to present a detailed analysis of compensatory lengthening of vowels in current moraic theory. The thesis offered in this chapter is that moraic theory presents a more adequate account of compensatory lengthening phenomena than skeletal accounts formulated in terms of either Cs and Vs or Xs. In Chapter 5, 'The role of moraic structure in the distribution of segments within syllables', Draga Zec defends the idea that the mora is the unit in terms of which segments are regulated and syllable structure is projected. She advances this thesis through an explanatory account of complex nasal interactions in Pali. This chapter is also interesting in presenting an account of phonological structure in terms of Prince and Smolenski's Optimality Theory (1993). This approach is based on constraints and constraint-interactions and claims that constraints (unlike classical phonological rules) do not impose absolute requirements but vary in degrees of strength and can be ranked accordingly. Next, in Chapter 6, is Wiebke Brockhaus's committed, but not uncritical, review of Government Phonology, with special emphasis on the representation of skeletal and syllabic structures. A major claim made by Brockhaus in 'Skeletal and suprasegmental structure within Government Phonology' is that in Government Phonology, neither the mora nor the syllable is needed as a unit of phonological structure, contrary to the claims of moraic phonology and other contemporary theories of syllable structure: licensing is the motor that drives phonology. In the last chapter in this section, Chapter 7, 'Skeleta and the prosodic circumscription of morphological domains', Francis Katamba takes a different standpoint. He sees virtue in moraic phonology. However, unlike the first two moraic phonology chapters by Bickmore and Zec, Katamba's concern is not structure below the syllable, but rather the place of skeletal structures in the circumscription of phonological structures to which morphological processes apply.

In Part 3, the nature of phonological derivations is reexamined. Jacques Durand in his 'Universalism in phonology: atoms, structures and derivations' (Chapter 8) argues that a strong universalist position in phonology is the best methodological stance. After examining universalism with respect to atoms and structures, he focuses on the derivational issue. Should the theory of phonology allow for rules with transformational power as assumed in SPE and reaffirmed by Bromberger and Halle (1989) or, on the contrary, should it be structured like other components of linguistic description which in many current theories do not allow such operations? Durand argues strongly against a 'transformational' approach to phonology and surveys a number of arguments in favour of 'mirroring' between the various modules making up the language faculty.

The issue of derivation is again taken up in Chapter 9 by Jonathan Kaye's 'Derivations and interfaces'. This chapter is devoted to the notion of derivation within Government Phonology. The author discusses the lexical representation of lexical strings and their relationship to speech signals, hence the emphasis on interfaces. One of the major claims made by Kaye here is that there is no significant level of phonology as distinct from phonetics. A consequence of this claim is that, as in the other two contributors to Part 3, a derivational/transformational approach characteristic of the mainstream SPE tradition is found wanting. However, unlike Coleman who closes Part 3, the author argues that claims made in favour of notational systems such as that of *declarative phonology* do not provide the answer to the question at issue.

The final contribution to this volume is John Coleman's 'Declarative Lexical Phonology' (Chapter 10). In this chapter, Coleman criticizes the standard derivational/transformational approach to phonology and argues that many current descriptions formulated in a 'Principles and Parameters' notation (such as Government Phonology) are also close to the SPE paradigm if examined from a formal point of view. He outlines a linguistic formalism derived from unification-based grammars (cf. Shieber 1986) which does not use transformational or context-sensitive rewrite rules and yet allows for a truly restrictive, principle-based theory of sound structure. This essay is particularly interesting in offering a precise, formal description of aspects of phonological theory, a detailed critique of widely held assumptions concerning the nature of phonological derivations and a reanalysis of aspects of the phonology of English in a unification-based format.

As will be obvious from our summary of the contents of this volume, the essays offered here are wide-ranging and challenging. Many assumptions made by phonologists in their daily practice are reexamined by the contributors and debated from a variety of standpoints. We hope that the readers will gain insight into issues which are at the cutting edge of current research and, perhaps, that they will be prodded by these chapters into contributing to this debate themselves.

Lancaster–Salford, 1995

Acknowledgements

A number of people have helped us in the preparation of this book. First of all, we address our thanks to Professors M. Harris and R. H. Robins, and Longman, for supporting our proposal for a book of this kind with enthusiasm. Elaine Kelly and Joanne Leather helped us to prepare the manuscript and provided extensive secretarial support.

The Publishers are grateful to the following for permission to use copyright material: Edinburgh University Press for our Figure 8.1 being Figure 52 in *Fundamental Problems in Phonetics* by J. C. Catford (1977) and Elsevier Science for our Figures 8.2 and 8.3 from page 88 of 'Structural Analogy and Case Grammar, *Lingua* 70 by J. M. Anderson (1986).

List of Abbreviations

A&E	Anderson and Ewen
ATR	Advanced tongue root
B&H	Bromberger and Halle
BP	Brazilian Portuguese
CFG	Context-Free Grammar
CL	Compensatory Lengthening
CP	Class prefix
CS	Context sensitive
CSG	Context-Sensitive Grammar
DN	Deverbal nominal marker
DP	Dependency Phonology
ECP	Empty Category Principle
FS	Finite state
GP	Government Phonology
H&M	Halle and Mohanan
KLV	Kaye, Lowenstamm and Vergnaud
N	Nucleus
O	Onset
OCP	Obligatory Contour Principle
R	Rhyme (rime)
RCVP	Radical CV Phonology
RE	Recursively enumerable
RTR	Retracted tongue root
SPE	*The Sound Pattern of English*
UR	Underlying representation

PART 1

ATOMS

Chapter 1

Feature geometry and underspecification

Douglas Pulleyblank

1 Introduction

Phonological processes affect particular *classes* of sounds, and are triggered by other *classes*, sometimes null. A significant task for a theory of phonology is to delineate such classes, the characterization of which derives in primitive terms from a small set of subsegmental *distinctive features* (Jakobson et al. 1952, Chomsky and Halle 1968, henceforth SPE, etc.).

This chapter examines three basic properties involving such featural representations. First, features constitute a hierarchically organized set. The classes of features established by the hierarchy reflect phonetically motivated properties, and define the range of set behaviour possible in the phonological patterns attested in natural language.

Second, the phonological representation of oppositions is examined. A superficial distinction between two phonetic properties, α and β, may be most appropriately represented phonologically by assigning one member of the pair, α, some non-null phonological feature F which is not present on the second member of the pair, β. That is, representations are in many instances *underspecified*. Not only is this true of phonological representations, but such underspecification may persist right into the level of phonetic implementation.

Third, aspects of the formal relation between the feature hierarchy and underspecification are examined. On the one hand, it has been proposed that underspecification derives directly from the nature of featural primitives: if features are *unary*, or *monovalent*, then it follows from the basic structure of feature theory that phonological contrasts involve the assignment of some unary feature F to one member of a contrasting pair (α) and the absence of F on the second member of the pair (β). On the other hand, it has been suggested elsewhere that underspecification derives not from some basic property of feature theory, but from the way in which *binary* features formally combine. This apparent conflict is resolved by distinguishing between two types of features, one type appropriately characterized as unary, the second as binary. For the unary type, 'underspecified' representations are formally the only alternative and observed properties reflect this; for the binary class, representations vary in a manner that is derived from the different possibilities for feature combination. The distinction between the two sets corresponds to the distinction between class nodes and necessarily terminal nodes of the feature hierarchy.

2 Feature geometry

Non-linear approaches to feature content such as SPE viewed segments as composed of unordered sets of binary distinctive features, as seen in (1).

(1)   *Linear models*

$$
\begin{bmatrix} \alpha F \\ -\beta G \\ \gamma H \\ \delta I \\ : \end{bmatrix}
\begin{bmatrix} -\alpha F \\ \beta G \\ -\gamma H \\ \delta I \\ : \end{bmatrix}
\begin{bmatrix} \alpha F \\ \beta G \\ -\gamma H \\ \delta I \\ : \end{bmatrix}
$$

Such a linear model of segmental structure fails in numerous regards. We consider a single example here, involving *assimilation*. An assimilatory process is one whereby some segment comes to share some feature or features with some other segment. For example, a vowel may nasalize adjacent to a nasal consonant, a consonant may come to share place features with an adjacent consonant, voicing may come to be shared by the members of a cluster, and so on. Within a linear segmental model, such assimilatory processes are formally derived by changing feature values in the appropriate segmental matrices.

As a concrete example, consider the data in (2) showing the application of place assimilation to the nasal marker of the 'progressive' in Yoruba, a Niger-Congo language spoken primarily in Nigeria.[1]

(2)   *Yoruba nasal assimilation*

Simple form   Progressive form

(a)   *Labial*

bá	ḿbá	'overtake'
ba	m̄ba	'hide'
bà	m̀bà	'perch'
fɔ́	ɱ́fɔ́	'break'

(b)   *Alveolar*

tà	ńtà	'sell'
tɛ́	ńtɛ́	'spread'
dũ̀	ńdũ̀	'pain'
lɔ	ńlɔ	'go'
sũ	ńsũ	'sleep'

(c)   *Palatal*

jó	ɲ́jó	'dance'
jɛ	ɲ́jɛ	'eat'

(d)   *Velar*

kɔ	ŋ́kɔ	'write'
kú	ŋ́kú	'die'
gũ̀	ŋ́gũ̀	'climb'
wi	ŋ́wí	'say'

(e)   *Labial-velar*

gbɔ́	ŋ́mgbɔ́	'hear; understand'
kpa	ŋ́mkpa	'kill'
kpĩ́	ŋ́mkpĩ́	'divide'

In binary terms, these five places of articulation can be represented as in (3).

(3)

	Labial	Alveolar	Palatal	Velar	Labial-velar
[coronal]	−	+	+	−	−
[anterior]	+	+	−	−	−
[labial]	+	−	−	−	+

Place assimilation is achieved by causing the nasal of the progressive morpheme to acquire the values of [coronal], [anterior] and

[labial] that are found on the immediately following consonant, as seen in (4).

(4)   *Linear place assimilation*

$$
\begin{bmatrix} +\text{consonantal} \\ +\text{nasal} \end{bmatrix} \longrightarrow \begin{bmatrix} \alpha\ \text{coronal} \\ \beta\ \text{anterior} \\ \gamma\ \text{labial} \end{bmatrix} \Big/ \underline{\quad\quad} \begin{bmatrix} \alpha\ \text{coronal} \\ \beta\ \text{anterior} \\ \gamma\ \text{labial} \end{bmatrix}
$$

Such a theory of assimilation has serious drawbacks, however (see, for example, McCarthy 1988). Nothing intrinsically restricts the use of variables so as to produce assimilation rather than dissimilation – both are equally valued formally, although assimilation appears to be much more common cross-linguistically. In addition, the variable notation required in (4) can be used to produce completely unattested patterns. The rule in (5), for example, would cause a nasal to be palatal before a labial consonant ([ñ + b]) and labial before a palatal consonant ([m + j]), velar before a labial-velar consonant ([ŋ + gb]) but labial-velar before a velar consonant ([ŋm + g]), and before an alveolar consonant, the nasal would be a labialized alveolar ([ŋʷ + d]).

(5)   *Impossible place assimilation pattern*

$$
\begin{bmatrix} +\text{consonantal} \\ +\text{nasal} \end{bmatrix} \longrightarrow \begin{bmatrix} \beta\ \text{coronal} \\ \alpha\ \text{anterior} \\ -\gamma\ \text{labial} \end{bmatrix} \Big/ \underline{\quad\quad} \begin{bmatrix} \alpha\ \text{coronal} \\ \beta\ \text{anterior} \\ \gamma\ \text{labial} \end{bmatrix}
$$

Not only is such a pattern not the one found in Yoruba, but such a pattern does not occur in any known natural language. The linear model fails, therefore, to adequately account for the range of assimilatory processes actually observed in human language.

To solve these (and other) problems, the theory of autosegmental phonology developed a very different account of assimilatory processes (Goldsmith 1976, Hayes 1986, etc.). By assigning the assimilating features to a separate autosegmental tier of representation, assimilation can be represented without the use of interdependent variables. The appropriate set of features simply extends its domain to include the elements that undergo the assimilatory process. In a case such as that of the Yoruba progressive marker, the place features would appear on a separate tier and then spread as a unit, as shown in (6).[2]

(6)   *Autosegmental place assimilation*

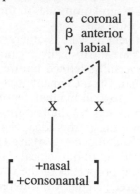

$$
\begin{bmatrix} \alpha & \text{coronal} \\ \beta & \text{anterior} \\ \gamma & \text{labial} \end{bmatrix}
$$

X   X

$$
\begin{bmatrix} +\text{nasal} \\ +\text{consonantal} \end{bmatrix}
$$

Without interdependent variables, autosegmental theory does not provide a mechanism for deriving the unattested type of process illustrated in the linear rule of (5), a welcome result. In other respects, however, autosegmental theory fails in a manner entirely comparable to a purely linear theory.

Consider the class of assimilation rules. Cross-linguistically, it is observed that some feature classes exhibit assimilatory behaviour, while others do not. The set of assimilatory classes appears not only to be finite, but also to be extremely small. Assimilation may take place with respect to individual features, to the coronal features, to the laryngeal features, to the place features, and so on. Arbitrary combinations of features, however, are not permitted. Compare the treatments of this issue within both linear and standard autosegmental theories. Within a linear theory, there are no restrictions on the classes of features that may undergo feature-changing rules of the type seen in (4). Segments are explicitly analysed as unordered, unstructured sets of binary features; any subset of this feature set can form the focus of a particular rule. As such, linear theory makes the incorrect formal claim that a cross-linguistic survey of assimilation processes should demonstrate any and every possible combination of features as a legitimate assimilation process. Standard autosegmental theory makes exactly the same (incorrect) claim. There are no inherent restrictions on the set of features that can be assigned to a particular autosegmental tier. In (6), for example, the features [±coronal], [±anterior] and [±labial] are assigned to an independent tier. Nothing prevents, however, the assignment of sets such as {[±coronal], [±anterior], [±voiced]}, or {[±labial], [±strident]}, or {H-tone (whatever the appropriate feature specification), [±nasal]}. The basic problem that both linear theory and standard autosegmental theory fail to address is that there are principled reasons for restricting assimilation rules to those involving narrowly delimited classes of feature sets.

To address this problem as well as others, much recent work has proposed that features are intrinsically organized into a hierarchical set structure of a universally defined nature (see Lass 1976, 1984, Mascaró 1983, Mohanan 1983, Clements 1985a, Ewen 1986, Anderson and Ewen 1987, etc.): individual features may spread, and those features defined as sets by the feature geometry may spread. In a particular elaboration of this idea, Sagey (1986), Ladefoged and Halle (1988) and Ladefoged (1989) argue that the features that define and play a role in phonological processes bear a direct relation to physiological properties of the vocal tract and to acoustic properties of the speech signal. Considered from an articulatory point of view, there must be features defining movements in areas such as those indicated in (7).

(7)   *Articulatory features*

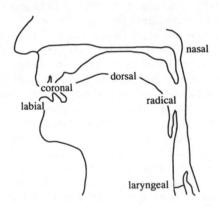

Following proposals made in Sagey (1986), the role of such articulators is directly encoded in the way features are hierarchically organized, as sketched in (8). Reference to the *root* tier involves the set of *all features*; reference to the *laryngeal* tier and the *place* tier involve *all laryngeal* and *all place* features respectively, while reference to individual articulator tiers (*labial, coronal, dorsal* and *radical*) involves all features defined for each of the individual articulators.

(8) *Place geometry*

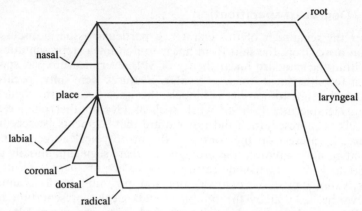

In this framework, the Yoruba rule of nasal assimilation, formulated in (9), is characterized as involving the spreading of the *place*
node.

(9) *Hierarchical place assimilation*

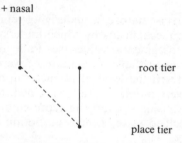

Neither of the shortcomings of linear and standard autosegmental theories arise. The actual process of assimilation results from
the simple extension of the domain of the place features; no
variables or feature-changing rules are involved. As for the characterization of the features that spread, this is determined by the
impoverished set of possibilities made available by the universally
determined make-up of the hierarchical feature structure. Note in
this regard that place assimilation can be formally accomplished by
the rule in (9) regardless of the specific place features appropriate
for a particular language. Inventories of place specifications may
vary, whether there are multiple *coronal* specifications, whether
double articulations are permitted, and so on, but whatever the
inventory permitted by a language, the entire set may be spread by
a rule such as (9).

3 Degree of specification

For the remainder of this chapter, a particular issue is discussed that arises from the shift from linear to non-linear representations. Within the standard linear theory of SPE, every feature was specified for either a ' + ' or a ' − ' value. Features were fully specified. With the shift to non-linear models, this issue became the focus of considerable attention. In work such as Goldsmith (1976), early levels of representation did not require that segments be specified for all features; on the contrary, the prototypical autosegmental configuration involved representations where segments initially unspecified for a particular feature came to acquire it as a result of derivational processes of association and spreading. It was assumed, nevertheless, that by the time a phonological representation was fully derived, it was also fully specified. This was ensured by the first clause of the highly influential Well-Formedness Condition (10) (Goldsmith 1976: 27).

(10)   *All vowels are associated with at least one tone.*

Views of the precise nature of underlying representations varied, as did the precise mechanisms by which underspecified representations received autosegmental values (see Pulleyblank 1986a), but it was typically assumed that representations were fully specified by the time they entered the level of phonetic implementation. Since representations were ultimately fully specified, a standard research strategy was to consider underlying representations as 'retreating' from a fully specified state, hence the notion of 'underspecified' representations.

The assumption of fully specified outputs, however, has been attacked on two very different grounds. First, it has been argued that a variety of features are intrinsically monovalent. They are either present or not present; they are not characterized by two values. As such, even at the level of phonetic implementation, only one value of an opposition is formally represented. Second, it has been argued that representations that constitute appropriate input to the phonetic component do not include specifications for all phonological features, regardless of whether features are binary or unary.

In the following discussion, we review certain issues raised in this debate. First, we consider implications of assuming hierarchical feature structure as regards establishing the degree of phonological specification. Class nodes are inherently monovalent, and their combinatorial properties, it is suggested, define the prototypical fashion in which distinct features cooccur. The phonetic interpretation of phonological representations is then considered, focusing on the type of evidence that has been presented in favour of positing underspecified representations at the level of the phonetics. The phonological source of such underspecification is subsequently examined.

On the one hand, phonetic underspecification could be solely due to intrinsic underspecification: if all features were intrinsically unary, then one value involved in any given surface contrast would involve an absence of specification. This approach is shown to be defective for two reasons. First, independent of intrinsic unary values, formal underspecification is necessary as a device. It is not eliminated by the adoption of unary features. Second, features are distributed between two classes with different clusters of properties, and it will be suggested that identification of the two classes falls out straightforwardly from the nature of the feature hierarchy. One of the classes is plausibly characterized by unarity, the set of hierarchical class nodes, the second by binarity, the necessarily terminal features. The discussion concludes with a brief discussion of combinatorial specification (Archangeli and Pulleyblank 1994). It is suggested that once full specification is abandoned as an output condition, phonology should focus on the features that are necessary for inclusion in a phonological representation, rather than the features that may be underspecified, or 'excluded'.

4   Unary features

Consider again the approach to *place* features laid out above. Phonologically specifying a segment for *place* involves the determination of which of four semi-independent articulators are involved in the production of a particular speech sound.[3] Consider again the figure in (7). In broad terms, the configuration found at each of the six indicated areas is independent of the configuration found at the other five. Such freedom of phonetic cooccurrence is reflected phonologically by the assignment of each articulator to an independent autosegmental tier. That is, with the formal structure of (8), the expectation is that values for difference *place* features, as well as other features such as those dominated by the *laryngeal* node, will freely combine.

As illustration, consider the cooccurrence of the *dorsal* articulator with the three other articulators. In combination with the *labial* articulator, consonants such as labialized velars [k^w, g^w, etc.] and labial-velars [kp, gb, etc.] are derived, as well as rounded vowels such as [u] and [o]. Combining the *dorsal* articulator with the *coronal* articulator can be argued to derive palatal and palatalized consonants, as well as front vowels (see Pulleyblank 1989); such a combination also derives velarized coronals such as the 'dark l' of English. Combining the *dorsal* articulator with the *radical* articulator derives uvulars (see Cole 1987), emphatic consonants such as the relevant series in Arabic (see McCarthy 1991) as well as vowels with a specified tongue root value.

Consider the same representations from a slightly different perspective. If we know that a segment is *dorsal*, this does not imply particular values for *labial, coronal,* and so on. Similarly, if we know that a segment is *not dorsal*, this implies no particular values for other features.[4] This relation of independence is reflected in the tier structure of (8). Note as well that *coronality, dorsality,* etc. are active properties that may interact and function in particular ways. There is no phonologically relevant property of *not-being-coronal,* or *not-being-dorsal.* The complement class to the *coronal* class, or to the *dorsal* class is not a natural class of segments observed to trigger or undergo phonological processes.

Combinatorial properties in conjunction with cross-linguistic patterns of natural classes, therefore, suggest that the types of class nodes constituted by articulator features are best analysed as unary nodes. A welcome result obtained through the adoption of such a hypothesis concerns the interaction of segments specified by different articulator nodes. In a sequence of segments involving, for example, coronal, labial and velar segments, coronals can be adjacent on their tier of representation even if consonants with different places of articulation intervene. Consider the schematic representation in (11).

(11)   *Articulator node transparency*

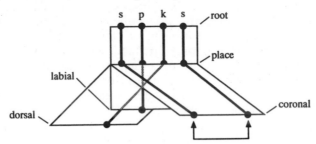

Since labials and velars are intrinsically unspecified for a *coronal* node, there is no non-null material intervening between the two coronal consonants in a representation such as (11). As a result, processes of a local type may take place between coronal segments which, on the surface, are non-adjacent. For example, in Tahltan (Shaw 1991), a process of coronal harmony affects the realization of /s/, as in the first person singular subject marker (underlined in the data in (12)).[5] Before dental consonants such as [θ] and [tθ'], /s/ is realized as [θ]; before alveopalatal obstruents such as [tš] and [dž], /s/ is realized as [š]:

(12)   *Tahltan coronal harmony*

(a) /s/

        εsk'a: 'I'm gutting fish'
        εsdan   'I'm drinking'

(b) /θ/

        mεθεθεθ   'I'm wearing on feet'
        naθtθ'εt   'I fell off (horse)'
        dεθkʷʊθ   'I cough'

(c) /š/

        hudištša   'I love them'
        εšdžıni   'I'm singing'

The harmony process is unaffected by non-coronal consonants that intervene between the trigger and target of harmony, as seen in the last example of (12b).[6]

The widely held conclusion is that features are organized in a hierarchical fashion, and that the organizing nodes are single-valued. Subject to substantive conditions on how particular nodes cooccur, such featural nodes are characterized by freedom of combination. Moreover, the locality effects defined by the intrinsic underspecification of such monovalent nodes plays a role in the phonologies of numerous languages.

Compare, however, such monovalent behaviour with that of a feature such as [±ATR]. In vowel systems employing the ATR (advanced tongue root) feature (see below), all vowels are either advanced or retracted; not having one value automatically implies having the other value. It is universally impossible to combine a [+ATR] value with a [−ATR] value.[7] Such properties describe the types of features dominated by the monovalent class nodes seen in (8); for example, the feature [±voiced] is shown in (13) as dominated by the *laryngeal* tier and the feature [±high] as dominated by the *dorsal* tier.

(13)   *The geometry of terminal features*

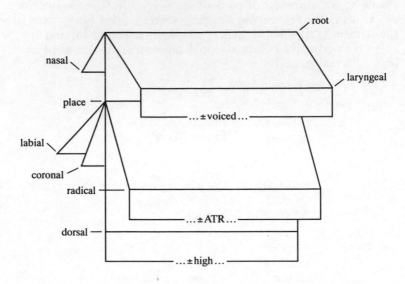

In each case, natural classes are defined by both values of the features, but the two values may not cooccur. In contrast to the representation of articulator features on independent tiers, this conjunction of properties is formally represented by assigning both values to a single tier, dominated by the appropriate monovalent class tier.

Before examining arguments for such binary features, however, we turn first to a consideration of the nature of the representations that constitute the output of the phonological component and the input to the implementational rules of the phonetics.

5   Underspecification in the phonetics

Arguments for not specifying a particular feature can be of various types: transparency effects, phonological inertness, distributional asymmetries, and so on (see Mohanan 1991, Archangeli and Pulley-blank in press, and references therein). One compelling argument has involved phonological transparency (see discussion of Tahltan above). Consider the configuration in (14):

(14)   *Transparency*

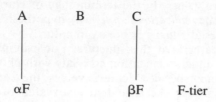

A   B   C

αF   βF   F-tier

Segments A and C are specified for values of feature F; segment B is not. It has been argued (see Keating 1988, Pierrehumbert and Beckman 1988, etc.) that such representations appropriately characterize the input to processes of phonetic interpolation and coarticulation. For example, Keating (1988) discusses cases where vowel-to-vowel coarticulation effects take place over a consonant, the consonant having no apparent effect at all on the transition. Formants appropriate for the vowel 'A' move gradually into those appropriate for 'C' without regard for an intervening consonant 'B'.

Such phonetic facts receive a straightforward explanation in a theory incorporating underspecification. Since 'B' is unspecified for feature F in the output of the phonological component, there is nothing to interfere with the phonetic coarticulation of 'αF' and 'βF'. Compare this picture with a linear, SPE mode of representation such as in (15). Since all segments are specified phonologically for all features, phonetic transparency is not expected to occur. Whatever the precise values of 'αF' and 'βF', the intervening segment 'B' is expected to have some value for 'F' itself.

(15)   *Lack of transparency in linear models*

$$
\begin{bmatrix} \alpha F \\ \vdots \\ -\beta G \\ \gamma H \\ \delta I \\ \vdots \end{bmatrix}
\begin{bmatrix} \gamma F \\ \vdots \\ \beta G \\ -\gamma H \\ \delta I \\ \vdots \end{bmatrix}
\begin{bmatrix} \beta F \\ \vdots \\ \beta G \\ -\gamma H \\ \delta I \\ \vdots \end{bmatrix} \cdots
$$

A   B   C

The value for 'F' on 'B' will be expected to create a local transition between 'B' and 'A' to its left, and 'C' to its right; coarticulation between 'A' and 'C' is not expected.

The conclusion of such phonetic investigation is that the output of the phonological component, the representation which constitutes the input to quantitative phonetic implementation, must not be fully specified. Facts of interpolation and coarticulation can only be explained if the appropriate representations are selectively assigned feature values. In the terminology of Harris and Lindsey (this volume), the *realizational autonomy* hypothesis must be correct whether features are unary or binary in nature.

Several issues arise at this juncture. For example, do phonetic arguments for underspecification correlate with phonological arguments? Are underspecified feature values the same across languages? Is it always the case that one value of an opposition exhibits the properties expected of an underspecified representation? Is it possible to predict when a representation will be underspecified? The list can easily be extended. In the following discussion, phonological arguments will be examined that bear on two related questions concerning underspecification. Is it always the same value in a feature opposition that is underspecified? Can underspecification derive from the intrinsic nature of such a representation?

6 The representation of oppositions

Conceptually, there are six basic ways of phonologically representing an opposition between two sounds, as illustrated schematically in (16).

(16) *Primary representations of an opposition*

	Binary		Unary	
+F	vs. -F	G	vs. H	
+F	vs. ∅	G	vs. ∅	
∅	vs. -F	∅	vs. H	

Assuming that each phonetic value of the opposition represents one value of a binary feature, the opposition may be represented by having both values present, $[+F]$ and $[-F]$ represented, or by having one value present and the second absent, $[+F]$ only represented or $[-F]$ only represented. An alternative is to assume that the feature in question is *unary*, that is, that it is single-valued. Under such an approach, there are again three primary ways of representing such an opposition (although see below). Two unary features could be posited, each corresponding to one value of the opposition (G vs. H), or one feature could be posited, corresponding either to the binary representation of $[+F]$ ('G') or to $[-F]$ ('H').

The choice between this range of alternatives is largely an empirical one. There are a variety of types of considerations. On the one hand, phonetic evidence such as the work on coarticulation effects bears directly on this question. Although this type of evidence will not be pursued here, it is worth noting Keating's conclusion (given in (17)) concerning the analysis of transparency and lack of transparency in Russian VCV sequences of the type given schematically in (14) above (Keating 1988, 289–90):

(17)
in Russian both members of the contrasting pairs of consonants are specified for [back], since all contrasting consonants seem to block vowel-to-vowel coarticulation. However, other data on secondary articulations also suggest the opposite: that in some languages, only half of the contrasting consonants are specified for [back].

The implications of these conclusions, albeit rather preliminary in terms of the amount of phonetic research in these questions that has been conducted to date, are important. Phonetic effects vary from language to language. In cases of a phonological opposition, the phonetic manifestation of the opposition is unary in some cases, binary in others. These conclusions are, it will be suggested below, supported in the literature on phonological representations.

To consider the manner most appropriate for the representation of an opposition, consider a concrete example. In Yoruba, the agentive prefix is realized as [o] when the first vowel of the following verb stem is [i, e, o, u] (18a) and realized as [ɔ] when the first vowel of the verbal base is [ɛ, a, ɔ] (18b) (Archangeli and Pulleyblank 1989).[8]

(18) *Agentive prefix*

(a) [o]	òjìyà	[òjìyà]	'victim'	jìyà	'to be punished'
	òṣèwé	[òṣèwĕ]	'publisher'	ṣèwé	'publish a book'
	ògbójú	[ògbŏjú]	'brave person'	gbójú	'be brave'
	òkú	[òkŭ]	'corpse of person'	kú	'die'
(b) [ɔ]	òlę	[ɔlɛ]	'lazy person'	lę	'be lazy'
	òlàjú	[ɔlàjŭ]	'civilized person'	lajú	'become civilized'
	òtọpinpin	[ɔtɔkpĩkpĩ]	'careful scrutinizer'	tọpinpin	'investigate fully'

Such alternations demonstrate that the advanced vowel [o] is in opposition to the retracted vowel [ɔ]. When the agentive prefix occurs with a vowel for which the tongue root is advanced ([i, e, o, u]), the agentive prefix is also advanced ([o]); when the agentive prefix occurs with a vowel for which the tongue root is retracted ([ɛ, a, ɔ]), the agentive prefix is also retracted ([ɔ]). The representation of this opposition is the topic of the following discussion.

6.1   Two unary features

One approach can be ruled out largely for conceptual reasons, namely the possibility of positing two unary features, one for advancement ('ATR') and one for retraction ('RTR').[9] The guiding rationale for adopting unary features (see van der Hulst 1989) is to develop a theory that is more restrictive than a theory whose features are binary. The argument is essentially the following. If features are binary, and if underspecification is possible, then there are three logically possible ways of representing an opposition in a binary theory (as seen in (16)). In contrast, if features are unary, *and if a single feature is available for any given contrast*, then there is a single way of representing an opposition within a unary theory. It should be stressed that the restrictiveness argument depends crucially on both formal and substantive factors (see Harris and Lindsey this volume).

Formally, the range of combinatorial possibilities allowed is crucial in evaluating restrictiveness. For example, it is assumed within a binary framework such as SPE that two binary features define a maximum of four contrasting outputs: (i) $[+F, -G]$, (ii) $[+F, +G]$, (iii) $[-F, -G]$, (iv) $[-F, +G]$. Two monovalent features F and G can similarly define four possible representations: (i) F, (ii) F, G, (iii) $\emptyset$, (iv) G. Supplementing these possibilities with formal notions such as headedness or dependency derives additional contrasts. For example, four forms can be doubled to eight by building in a notion of headedness (indicated by underlining) and by allowing null heads: (i) $\underline{F}$; (ii) $\emptyset$, F; (iii) $\underline{F}$, G; (iv) F, $\underline{G}$; (v) $\emptyset$, F, G; (vi) $\emptyset$; (vii) $\underline{G}$; (viii) $\emptyset$, G (see, for example, Lass 1984, Durand 1986, Anderson and Ewen 1987, Harris and Lindsey this volume). A general determination of formal restrictiveness, therefore, can be determined only by an evaluation of the full range of formal possibilities, not just whether features themselves have one or two values.

In terms of substantive considerations, the complete inventory of features must be established. If two unary features are assumed in the case of an opposition, the range of logical possibilities becomes greater than if a single feature is posited in a binary theory. Recall that the paradigm combinatorial possibility for unary features is free combination. Positing two unary features G and H would therefore predict the possibility of assigning both G and H to a single segment. As such, the possibilities of representing an opposition in some language as G vs. H, in another as G vs. $\emptyset$, and in a third as H vs. $\emptyset$ (as seen in (16)), would be supplemented by the logical possibilities of representing oppositions in appropriate languages by having one segment class specified for both G and H, with an opposing class specified as G, as H, or as devoid of specifications (see (19)).

(19)   *Additional representations of an opposition*

Unary

G/H	vs.	G
G/H	vs.	H
G/H	vs.	∅

Restrictiveness, therefore, balances formal and substantive simplicity and complexity. Formally, issues of binarity/unarity interact with issues of how such features combine. Substantively, restrictiveness depends on positing a highly impoverished set of featural primitives.

6.2   A single unary feature: retraction

Returning to the case of tongue root behaviour, no substantive properties appear to warrant combinations of putative unary ATR ('advancement') with a unary RTR ('retraction'). Conceptual reasons therefore argue against the positing of two such unary features. A unary analysis of data such as that seen for Yoruba in (18) must therefore either select the advanced value as phonologically active, 'ATR', or the retracted value as phonologically active 'RTR'. Moreover, to eliminate the possibility of combining two tongue root features in the analysis of any language, the choice for Yoruba must correspond to the choice made universally.

For Yoruba, Archangeli and Pulleyblank (1989, 1994) argue at some length that the phonologically active value must be tongue root retraction, that is, '[−ATR]' or 'RTR'. Consider the behaviour of non-mid vowels in harmonic contexts. Unlike the mid vowel prefixes that alternate according to the tongue root value of the stem, high vowel and low vowel prefixes are unaffected by the quality of a following vowel, as shown in (20) and (21) respectively.

(20)   *Abstract nominalizing prefix*

(a) [i]	ìbínú	[ìbǐnű]	'anger'	bínú	'become angry'
	ìgbédè	[ìgbědê]	'binding'	gbédè	'bind'
	ìṣòro	[isòro]	'difficulty'	ṣòro	'be difficult'
	ìdúró	[ìdǔró]	'standing'	dúró	'stand'

(b) [i]   ìbèrè   [ìbèrè]   'beginning'   bèrè   'begin'
        ìpàdé   [ìkpàdě]   'meeting'   pàdé   'meet'
        ìrójú   [ìrɔ̀jú]   'endurance'   rójú   'carry on under strain'

(21)   *Factive nominalizing prefix*

(a) [a]   àjìkí   [àjïkí]   'waking up to greet'   jí kí   'wake up to greet'
        àṣefún   [àšefû]   'doing for'   ṣe fún   'to do for'
        àbósè   [àbŏsê]   'peeling and cooking'   bó sè   'peel and cook'
        àjùlọ   [àjùlɔ]   'exceeding'   jù lọ   'exceed'

(b) [a]   àbèrèwò   [àbèrèwɔ̀]   'stooping to enter'   bèrè wò   'stoop to enter'
        àbálọ   [àbǎlɔ]   'going on behalf of'   bá lọ   'go on behalf of'
        àjọbí   [àjɔbí]   'consanguinity of persons'   jọ bí   'be a joint progenitor'

In each case, the tongue root value is redundant, derivable from the non-mid vowel's height. For high vowels, the tongue is redundantly advanced; for low vowels, the tongue is redundantly retracted. Thus if ATR is phonologically active, it could appear on high vowels, as in (22a); if RTR is phonologically active, it could appear on low vowels, as in (22b).

(22)   *Possible redundant harmonic values in Yoruba*

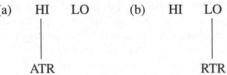

     (a)   HI   LO   (b)   HI   LO

            ATR   RTR

To test the appropriateness of one or the other modes of representation, one must look for evidence that high vowels or low vowels affect the value of an adjacent mid vowel, mid vowels being the class of vowels exhibiting alternants determined by an adjacent tongue root value. As noted in Archangeli and Pulleyblank (1989), high vowels have no effect on the tongue root value of an adjacent mid vowel. Advanced mid vowels may both follow and precede high vowels (23a); retracted mid vowels may both follow and precede high vowels (23b).

(23)   *Inertness of high vowels*

(a)   ilé   [ilé]   'house'   ìgò   [ìgò]   'bottle'
     ebi   [ebi]   'hunger'   orí   [orí]   'head'

(b)   ilè   [ilè]   'land'   itɔ́   [itɔ́]   'saliva'
     èbi   [ɛbi]   'guilt'   ɔ̀kín   [ɔ̀kî]   'egret'

With respect to vowels to their right, low vowels are comparable to high vowels in that they have no effect: when a mid vowel follows a low vowel, it may be either advanced or retracted (24a). Such inertness is in marked contrast to the active effect of the redundant retracted value when a low vowel is preceded by a mid vowel. In such a configuration, the mid vowel must be retracted (24b).

(24) *Active effect of low vowels*

(a) ate   [ate]   'hat'   àwo   [àwo]   'plate'
    àjẹ̀   [àjɛ̀]   'paddle'   aṣọ   [aʃɔ]   'cloth'

(b) ẹ̀pà   [ɛ̀kpà]   'groundnut'   ọjà   [ɔjà]   'market'
    *[eCa]   *[oCa]

The observed patterns in Yoruba are straightforwardly derived if [−ATR]/RTR is posited as the phonologically active feature.[10] If [+ATR]/ATR were the selected feature, the patterns would be anomalous.

Let us return to the general issue of feature specification. A theory with unary features should posit no more than a single feature per opposition. In the case of the advanced/retracted opposition, Yoruba must therefore be interpreted as providing evidence that the appropriate value for the phonological instantiation of the opposition is *retraction*, that is, 'RTR' or '[−ATR]'.

6.3 A single unary feature: advancement

The problem with the hypothesis that the tongue root feature is a monovalent 'RTR' is that this contradicts the actual proposals that have been made for a unary tongue root feature. In work such as Kaye et al. (1985) and van der Hulst (1989) it has been proposed that there should indeed be a single tongue root feature, but that its value should be *advancement*, 'ATR'. One type of argument that has been presented in favour of the feature ATR is based on its appearance in *dominant harmony systems*.

A large number of harmony systems are intrinsically asymmetric, exhibiting a pattern with the following basic properties. Roots and affixes may be either *dominant* or *recessive*. A word composed entirely of recessive morphemes surfaces with one harmonic value; a word containing one or more dominant morphemes surfaces with the opposite harmonic value. Crucially, a single dominant morpheme, whether a root morpheme or an affix morpheme, is sufficient to cause the entire word to surface with the dominant value.

The following examples from Kalenjin, a Nilotic language spoken in Kenya, illustrate this pattern (Antell et al. 1973). When all morphemes are recessive (25), surface vowels are retracted (ɪ, ɛ, a, ɔ, ʊ = retracted).

(25)   *Words composed entirely of recessive morphemes*

(a) kɪ-a-bar-ɪn   'I killed you (sg.)'
(b) kɪ-a-gɛr   'I shut it'

When a dominant morpheme occurs either as root or affix, then all vowels surface as advanced (i, e, ạ, o, u = advanced).[11] To illustrate the dominant pattern, the dominant root /keːr/'see' in (26a) appears with the same affixes as the root/par/'kill' in (25a);[12] as a result, *all* vowels are advanced. Similarly, the addition in (26b) of the dominant suffix /e/'non-completive' to the form in (25b) causes all vowels to surface in their advanced form.

(26)   *Words including a dominant morpheme*

(a) ki-ạ-geːr-in   'I saw you (sg.)'
(b) ki-ạ-ger-e   'I was shutting it'

As proposed by Halle and Vergnaud (1981) and illustrated in (27), an autosegmental account of such dominant harmony is straightforward. Dominant morphemes are consistently advanced, hence analysed as containing an autosegmental [+ ATR] specification as part of their lexical specification; recessive morphemes are variable, analysed as containing no such specification. The [+ ATR] value links and spreads to all vowels within its domain; vowels left unspecified surface as retracted.

(27)   *Dominant [+ ATR] harmony in Kalenjin*

'I killed you (sg.)'   'I saw you (sg.)'

(a)   (b)

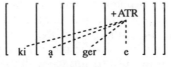

'I was shutting it'

(c)

The dilemma for a theory positing strictly unary features is that the opposition between advanced and retracted vowels requires a retracted value to be active in a language like Yoruba, but an advanced value to be active in a language like Kalenjin. The dilemma is compounded by the fact that patterns of dominant harmony are not restricted to languages with an advanced active value.

6.4 Dominant harmony: retraction

In languages like Nez Perce (Hall and Hall 1980, Song 1990) and Chukchee (Bogoras 1922, Archangeli and Pulleyblank 1994, etc.), dominant harmony systems exist where the dominant value is [−ATR] and the recessive value if [+ATR]. The phonological behaviour of such systems is entirely comparable to that seen above for Kalenjin, except that the dominant tongue root value is inverted.

Illustrating with Nez Perce, roots such as in (28) are recessive, surfacing with advanced vowels.

(28)   *Recessive roots*

(a) mæq   'paternal uncle'
(b) cæqæːt   'raspberry'

In combination with recessive affixes such as *næ?* 'first person possessive' and *æ?* 'vocative', the resulting words continue to exhibit uniformly advanced vowels, as seen in (29).

(29)   *Recessive affixes*

(a) næ?-mæx   'my paternal uncle'
(b) mæq-æ?   'paternal uncle!'

In combination with a dominant morpheme like *tuːt* 'father', however, recessive affixes surface with retracted variants (30a, b); similarly, with a dominant affix like *?ayn* 'for', a recessive root surfaces as retracted (30c): [13]

(30)   *Dominant morphemes*

(a) na?-tuːt   'my father'
(b) tuːt-aʔ   'father!'
(c) caqaːt-ʔayn   'for a raspberry'

Just as the Kalenjin pattern of harmony is accounted for by positing dominant, morpheme-level [+ATR] specifications that link and spread, so is the Nez Perce pattern accounted for by a comparable analysis involving [−ATR], as shown in (31).

(31)   *Dominant [− ATR] harmony in Nez Perce*

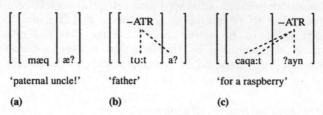

(a) 'paternal uncle!'   (b) 'father'   (c) 'for a raspberry'

6.5 Two values in one language

Languages such as Kalenjin argue for postulating an active phonological feature of tongue root advancement; languages like Yoruba and Nez Perce argue for postulating an active phonological feature of tongue root retraction. The clear prediction in a theory allowing both such values is that a third language type could exist, one employing the two values actively. One example of such a language type is Lango, a Nilotic language of Uganda (Woock and Noonan 1979, Archangeli and Pulleyblank 1994).

Although a detailed discussion of Lango harmony goes beyond the scope of this chapter (see Archangeli and Pulleyblank 1994), two sub-patterns of the overall harmonic system illustrate the importance of positing both [+ ATR] and [− ATR] values. Lango has a basic five-vowel system [I, E, A, O, U] crosscut by ATR. This gives ten surface vowels, as seen in the stem column of (32).

(32)   *Advancement harmony*

Stem			Stem + suffix	
[i]	píg	'soup, juice'	píggí	'your juice'
[e]	ém	'thigh'	émí	'your thigh'
[ə]	ñə̀ŋ	'crocodile'	ñə̀ŋŋí	'your crocodile'
[o]	dòk	'cattle'	dòkkí	'your cattle'
[u]	búk	'book'	búkkí	'your book'
[ɪ]	yíb	'tail'	yíbí	'your tail'
[ɛ]	dɛ̀k	'stew'	dɛ̀kkí	'your stew'
[a]	màc	'fire'	mə̀ccí	'your fire'
[ɔ]	kɔ̀m	'chair'	kòmmí	'your chair'
[ʊ]	lòt	'stick'	lùttí	'your stick'

The second person suffix seen in the stem + suffix column of (32) is underlyingly advanced. As can be seen by its interaction with the set of underlyingly retracted vowels, the second group of five in (32), the [+ ATR] value of the suffix spreads regressively back onto the stem vowel. Such regressive harmony takes place only from high vowels. Compare, for example, the absence of regressive advancement harmony in the cases in (33) involving an advanced mid-vowel suffix:

(33)   *Absence of regressive harmony from a non-high argument*

[i]	riŋŋo	'to run'
[e]	ketto	'to put'
[ə]	(no example in Woock and Noonan)	
[o]	pwoddo	'to beat'

[u]	rucco	'to entangle'
[ɪ]	lɪmmo	'to visit'
[ɛ]	nɛnno	'to see'
[a]	wayo	'to pull'
[ɔ]	lwɔkkɔ	'to wash'
[ʊ]	lʊbbɔ	'to follow'

That the mid vowel of the suffix is advanced is clear from the three examples *lɪmmo* 'to visit', *nɛnno* 'to see' and *wayo* 'to pull'. Since the root is retracted in these cases, there is no source for the suffixal [+ATR] value other than the suffix itself. But with this in mind, the last two examples need to be considered: *lwɔkkɔ* 'to wash' and *lʊbbɔ* 'to follow'. In these cases, the back vowel of the root triggers the spreading of [−ATR] from left to right onto the suffix vowel.

We observe, therefore, that the focus of the regressive assimilatory process seen in (32) is [+ATR], while the focus of the progressive assimilatory process seen in (33) is [−ATR]. Such behaviour is consistent with the hypothesis of a binary feature governing tongue root oppositions, [±ATR], but is inconsistent with positing either a unary ATR or a unary RTR to the exclusion of the second feature value.

Empirical considerations are therefore inconsistent with the view that all oppositions are to be characterized by the positing of unary features. The opposition between advanced and retracted tongue root requires the postulation of phonological values for both advancement and for retraction. It would of course be possible to posit two unary features to express the two poles of the tongue root opposition, but this would have the result of weakening, not strengthening, the theory for the reasons discussed in section 6.1.

7 Voicing oppositions: another binary contrast

One might ask, of course, whether the binary behaviour of the feature governing the tongue root is special in some way. Is it the only feature whose properties are binary? There appear, in fact, to be numerous binary features governing oppositions. Still considering vowels, cases have been made for both values of features like [±high] and [±back] (see Archangeli and Pulleyblank 1994). For consonants, LaCharité (1993) argues that both values of [±continuant] are required; both values of [±anterior] have been used for the description of various consonant harmony systems (see Poser 1982, Shaw 1991). Theories of *contrastive underspecification* (see Clements 1987, Steriade 1987) have argued for the analysis of numerous phonological patterns in terms of binarily represented oppositions. In this section, one additional case of a binary feature is briefly addressed, a case that is of some interest since it has been proposed recently that the feature is actually unary.

Many languages exhibit an opposition between voiced and voiceless consonants. In binary terms, this contrast is standardly represented in terms of the feature [±voiced] (see Chomsky and Halle 1968). Recently, however, it has been suggested that the feature should be considered to be unary, its phonologically marked value being [+voiced] (Mester and Itô 1989, Rice and Avery 1990).

Evidence for the phonologically active status of [+voiced] is uncontroversial; consider, for example, the case of Russian voicing assimilation (Hayes 1984, Kiparsky 1985, etc.). Cases involving assimilation to voicelessness also exist, for example English *loose/lost*, but it has been suggested that these cases, like the widespread phenomena of syllable-final and word-final devoicing, actually involve the delinking of a phonologically specified [+voiced] specification (Mester and Itô 1989).

Other patterns, however, are not straightforwardly amenable to such manipulations of a [+voiced] feature. In a recent paper, Peng (1991) discusses one such case from Kikuyu. Dahl's Law affects velar consonants in a large number of related Bantu languages (Davy and Nurse 1982). The rule voices velar stops (which subsequently and independently spirantize) when they are morpheme-initial and followed in the next syllable by a voiceless obstruent. In the examples in (34), Dahl's Law applies to voice the initial velar stop of *ko* because the initial consonant in the syllable following the prefix is voiceless.

(34)   *Voiceless obstruents*

(a) go-tɛm-a   'to cut'
(b) go-ku-a   'to die'
(c) go-θɛk-a   'to laugh'
(d) go-cuuk-a   'to slander'

In (35) and (36), on the other hand, Dahl's Law does not cause voicing of the prefixal [k] because the root-initial consonant is voiced.

(35) *Voiced obstruents*

(a) ko-gat-a   'to cut'
(b) ko-βaβat-a   'to pinch'
(c) ko-gor-a   'to buy'

(36) (*Voiced*) *sonorants*

(a) ko-rug-a   'to cook'
(b) ko-mɛñ-a   'to know'
(c) ko-niin-a   'to finish'

Strings of velar stops undergo the rule, as illustrated by examples such as in (37).

(37) *Sequences of velars*

(a) ge-ge-ge-θok-a   'and thus it was spoiled'
(b) a-ge-go-tɛng-a   'he met you'
(c) ga-ge-gaa-ge-go-θɛk-a   'before it goes and laughs at you'

The analysis of this pattern depends crucially on basic assumptions about the phonological representation of voicing. If the theory allows for the active specification of [– voiced], the analysis is straightforward: a [– voiced] specification is lost from a velar consonant when the following syllable begins with a [– voiced] segment (see (38) below). Considered in these terms, Dahl's Law is formally a dissimilation process, as it has been traditionally characterized.

(38) *Dahl's Law in Kikuyu – Delinking* [– voiced]

–vd –vd	–vd –vd –vd –vd –vd	–vd	–vd
(a) ko – ku – a	(b) ke + ke + ke + θok + a	(c) ko – gor –a	(d) ko – rug – a

An analysis is not so straightforward if phonological theory allows only for the specification of [+ voiced]. Within such a theory, two basic analyses are possible, depending on assumptions about the underlying representation of the k/g segment. If prefixes exhibiting the k/g alternation are analysed as underlying unspecified for voicing, then Dahl's Law must insert a [+ voiced] specification, as in (39). The problem for such an analysis is how to characterize the class of environments that conditions such insertion.

(39)   *Dahl's Law in Kikuyu – Inserting* [+ voiced]

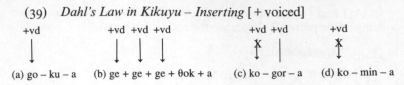

(a) go – ku – a   (b) ge + ge + ge + θok + a   (c) ko – gor – a   (d) ko – min – a

Insertion of [+ voiced] must take place with the prefix of (39a), as with the series of prefixes in (39b); insertion must be blocked with (39c) and with (39d). While blocking of [+ voiced] insertion in (39c) could be attributed to the [+ voiced] specification of the root-initial voiced obstruent, there is no explanation for the absence of insertion in (39d): since the voicing of sonorants is completely redundant (see Kiparsky 1982b, Pulleyblank 1986a, Archangeli 1984, Clements 1987, Steriade 1987, etc.), sonorants would not be expected to bear a voicing specification, hence would not be expected to block the insertion of a [+ voiced] specification. Note in this regard that Dahl's Law applies at the very earliest level of Kikuyu phonology, applying as a Morpheme Structure Condition (Pulleyblank 1986b). Moreover, even if one were to allow the presence of [+ voiced] on sonorants, there would be no plausible account for the absence of blocking in the series of velars in (39b). If Dahl's Law is blocked by the presence of a [+ voiced] value on a root-initial consonant (39c), then it should be similarly blocked by the presence of a [+ voiced] value on a prefix-initial consonant (39b) – but such is not the case.

An analysis of the alternating prefixes as underlyingly [+ voiced] is similarly problematical (40). Under such an account, it would be necessary to have a root-initial [+ voiced] specification trigger delinking (40c), while an affix-initial [+ voiced] specification would not (40b). As with the other account involving [+ voiced], sonorants would be required to trigger the process in spite of a complete absence of motivation for a [+ voiced] specification on such a class of segments.

(40)   *Dahl's Law in Kikuyu – Delinking* [+ *voiced*]

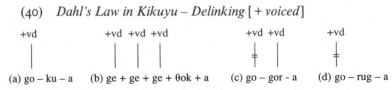

(a) go – ku – a   (b) ge + ge + ge + θok + a   (c) go – gor - a   (d) go – rug – a

As a final point concerning Dahl's Law, Peng (1991) argues that the feature involved in the process is indeed [voiced], not some other feature such as [spread glottis], citing phonetic evidence that the voiceless stops of Kikuyu are unaspirated; note also relevant discussion of the 'lenis' fricative [θ] in Davy and Nurse (1982). The conclusion is that reference must be made to the feature value [−voiced]. A theory that makes it impossible to refer to this value forces complications in the formulation of rules like Dahl's Law as a direct result.

8 Binary features and underspecification

One might ask whether binarity implies full specification at any level of phonological representation. Clearly such is not the case. The dominant harmony systems considered above, for example, depend crucially on positing a single harmonic value, whichever of the two binary possibilities such a value corresponds to. Similarly, for asymmetries of the type exhibited by Yoruba, it is important that only one value of the binary feature [±ATR] be specified phonologically (see Pulleyblank 1988).

Like unary features, binary features *when underspecified* may participate in long-distance processes. For example, the Japanese forms in (41) illustrate a process referred to as Rendaku whereby the initial consonant of the second member of certain compounds is voiced (Itô and Mester 1986).

(41) *Rendaku*

(a) iro + kami   [irogami]   'coloured paper'
(b) mizu + seme   [mizuzeme]   'water torture'
(c) yama + tera   [yamadera]   'mountain temple'

Of interest, application of Rendaku is blocked by the presence of a voiced obstruent anywhere in the member of the compound undergoing the rule (Lyman's Law). The initial consonant therefore remains voiceless in examples like (42).

(42) *Lyman's Law*

(a) kami + kaze   [kamikaze]   (*kamigaze)   'divine wind'
(b) siro + tabi   [sirotabi]   (*sirodabi)   'white tabi'
(c) onna + kotoba   [onnakotoba]   (*onnagotoba)   'feminine speech'

As noted by Itô and Mester (1986), to account for Lyman's Law, it is crucial that voiceless obstruents be underspecified for voicing since if only [+voiced] specifications are present (43a), Lyman's Law can be attributed to a constraint prohibiting the insertion of

[+voiced] adjacent to an existing [+voiced] specification: * [+voiced] [+voiced]. If [−voiced] were specified (42b), there would be no violation of such a constraint in cases like *onnagotoba (42c) and Rendaku would erroneously be expected to apply.

(43)   *Lyman's Law in Japanese*

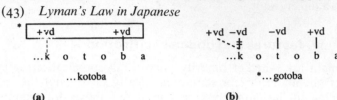

(a)	(b)

In a later paper, Mester and Itô (1989) note that the required underspecification could be due to the intrinsic unarity of a monovalent [+voiced] feature. If, as argued by Peng (1991) however, voicing is necessarily binary, then cases such as Rendaku clearly argue for the possibility of underspecifying a binary feature. Moreover, in the absence of positive evidence to the contrary, such underspecified representations are perfectly adequate to serve as input to the quantitative implementation of the phonetic component.

9 Conclusion

To recapitulate, it was first demonstrated that features do not constitute an unordered set. On the contrary, features group together in a highly restricted fashion to determine the attested range of classes that function in phonological processes of natural language. It was demonstrated that oppositions may be phonologically characterized in two ways. Monovalent class nodes establish unary representations of oppositions: the presence of such a node contrasts with its absence. Such unary specifications are characterized by their relative freedom of combination: the presence of one feature does not imply the absence of the other. It is precisely the range of combinatorial possibilities that establishes the basic diversity of phonological systems. It can be noted as well that different class nodes appear on distinct phonological tiers, the formal expression of their ability to function independently in phonological processes. Finally, it should be noted that the complement class of a set defined by a monovalent class node is not a natural class. For example, in a system that includes labials, coronals, velars and pharyngeals, while *dorsal* defines the natural class of velars, this does not mean that the complement class, labials, coronals and pharyngeals, constitutes a similarly natural class.

In marked contrast to the above range of properties, unary class nodes dominate terminal features that are binary in nature.[14] The opposing values of binary features like [±ATR] and [±voiced] may not cooccur; their combinatorial possibilities are governed by the types of constraints that govern combination of their dominating nodes. With binary features, the presence of one value implies the absence of the other value. Both values of such features, in contrast with class nodes, appear on the same phonological tier. Finally, and importantly, both members of a binary opposition constitute natural classes, and both define classes of elements manipulated and referred to in phonological processes.

Both unary and binary feature types exhibit properties of under-specification. For class nodes this is a necessary property, inherent to the theory of feature structure itself. For binary features, lan-guages vary as to the feature value that is phonologically active, variously exhibiting properties characteristic of underspecified repre-sentations and properties of representations that are more fully specified. This might appear to be an unfortunate result: while underspecification is an intrinsic part of a theory of unary features, it must be stipulated for binary features.

In fact, however, such a negative evaluation is inappropriate for at least two reasons. First, even the active value of a unary feature can be underspecified, hence underspecification as a formal prop-erty is independent of such intrinsic underspecification. For exam-ple, sonorants are clearly unspecified for [+voiced] in Japanese since they do not invoke the blocking characteristic of Lyman's Law: /haɪa + kuro/ 'stomach + black' → [haraguro], *[harakuro] 'wicked'. Nevertheless, in a language like Zoque (Kenstowicz and Kisseberth 1979, Sagey 1986), stops voice after nasals; that is, the [+voiced] value spreads from nasals: tatah 'father' vs. ndatah 'my father'. At the relevant stages, therefore, Japanese and Zoque differ in that Japanese is underspecified for even a hypothetically monovalent [+voiced] specification, while Zoque nasals are redun-dantly assigned a voicing specification by the time the rule takes place. Whether features are unary or binary, it is therefore neces-sary to include underspecification as a property of phonological theory.

As a second point, it should again be noted that to 'underspecify' implies a research strategy of beginning with full specification and retreating from that position to the extent that there is evidence for such a retreat (a strategy that reflects the history of generative work on the topic since SPE). But since phonetic work suggests that the goal of full specification is ill-founded, the research strategy based on such retreat must also be reconsidered. An alternative research strategy is to posit only those feature specifications required to establish the oppositions attested in a particular language, filling out such representations with redundant specifications to the extent that there is positive evidence for such (see Archangeli and Pulleyblank 1994). The expectation of such a strategy is that the specification of all features, whether unary or binary, will be relatively sparse, at least at initial stages of representation. In the case of unary features, some class nodes are more commonly involved in establishing oppositions than others; for example, the tongue root is less commonly employed than the tongue dorsum, laryngeal oppositions are common but not universal, and so on. The same is true of values for binary features; invoking values like [+ back], [+ voiced], [+ high] is very common, while invoking a feature value like [+ ATR] is much less so. Both values of a binary feature would not normally be invoked in a single language to establish an opposition since one value is sufficient to establish the opposition. Where motivated by patterns of distribution or alternation, adding a second value establishes redundancy, not opposition.

Notes and Acknowledgements

Thanks to Jacques Durand and Pat Shaw for discussion of this article. This work was supported by a Social Sciences and Humanities Research Council of Canada grant, No. 410-91-0204.

1. In the following transcriptions, [j] represents a palatal stop, [ɱ] represents a labio-dental nasal, and tone-marked nasals are syllabic.
2. Note that the variables in (6) are completely different from those in (4) and (5). In (6), the variables simply mean, 'spread *whatever values* of [coronal], [anterior] and [labial] are found after a nasal consonant.' In (4) and (5), the variables indicate interdependency; one matrix is assigned a particular value of a feature in a manner that is sensitive to the value of a feature in some other matrix.
3. Characterizing the nodes dominated by PLACE as purely articulator nodes may be an over-simplification (see Gorecka 1989, McCarthy 1991).
4. In a specific case, for example in a language where there are no labialized velars, no palatals and so on, one might be able to make predictions on the basis of the presence vs. absence of a DORSAL specification. This, however, cannot be true in general.
5. For a detailed discussion of Tahltan as well as for discussion of consonant harmony systems in general, see Shaw (1991).
6. Note that a small class of coronal consonants may also intervene without interrupting harmony. For discussion, see Shaw (1991).
7. Setswana and Sotho may constitute counter-examples to this claim; see Khabanyane (1991), Dichabe (in preparation).
8. In Yoruba orthography, 'ẹ' represents [ɛ] and 'ọ' represents [ɔ]; 'ṣ' represents [š], while 'p' represents [kp]; a 'Vn' sequence indicates a

nasalized vowel. The symbol/letter 'j' represents a palatal stop in both orthography and transcription.

9. For a contrary view, however, note Anderson and Ewen (1987).

10. See Archangeli and Pulleyblank (1989, in press) for detailed arguments to this effect.

11. Not discussed here are three opaque morphemes that interrupt the harmonic domain. See Antell et al. (1973), Halle and Vergnaud (1981) and Archangeli and Pulleyblank (in press) for discussion.

12. Obstruents are underlyingly voiceless in Kalenjin, becoming voiced between sonorants.

13. In Hall and Hall (1980), the retracted back vowel [U] is transcribed as [o]. Nez Perce exhibits a three-vowel system [I, A, U] crosscut by the ATR distinction. The vowel in question is the retracted counterpart of /U/, transcribed as [U] here so as to avoid the suggestion that it is an advanced mid vowel rather than a retracted high vowel. For relevant discussion of problems in the transcription of ATR systems, see Archangeli and Pulleyblank (1994).

14. *Terminal* here means *necessarily terminal*. Class nodes may or may not be terminal while binary features like [±ATR] and [±voiced] must be terminal.

Chapter 2

The elements of phonological representation

John Harris and Geoff Lindsey

1 Introduction[1]

What size are the primes of which phonological segments are
composed? From the standpoint of orthodox feature theory, the
answer is that each prime is small enough to fit inside a segment, and
not big enough to be phonetically realized without support from
other primes. Thus, [+ high], for example, is only realizable when
combined with values of various other features, including for
instance [− back, − round, − consonantal, + sonorant] (in which
case it contributes to the definition of a palatal approximant). This
view retains from earlier phoneme theory the assumption that the
segment is the smallest representational unit capable of independent
phonetic interpretation.

In this chapter, we discuss a fundamentally different conception
of segmental content, one that views primes as small enough to fit
inside segments, yet still big enough to remain independently interpretable. The idea is thus that the subsegmental status of a phonological prime does not necessarily preclude it from enjoying stand-
alone phonetic interpretability. It is perfectly possible to conceive
of primes as having autonomous phonetic identities which they can
display without requiring support from other primes. This approach
implies recognition of 'primitive' segments, each of which contains
but one prime and thus reveals that prime's autonomous phonetic
signature. Segments which are non-primitive in this sense then
represent compounds of such primes.

This notion – call it the *autonomous interpretation* hypothesis –
lies at the heart of the traditional notion that mid vowels may be
considered amalgamations of high and low vowels. Adaptations of
this idea are to be found in the work of, among others, Anderson

and Jones (1974, 1977) and Donegan (1978). Anderson and Jones' specific proposal is that the canonical five-vowel system should be treated in terms of various combinations of three primes which we label here [A], [I] and [U]. Individually, these manifest themselves as the primitive vowels *a*, *i* and *u* respectively (see (1a)). As shown in (1b), mid vowels are derived by compounding [A] with [I] or [U].

(1)

    (a) [A] a   (b) [A, I] e
        [I]   i   [A, U] o
        [U] u

Not all work which incorporates this type of analysis has maintained the notion of autonomous interpretation. In current Dependency Phonology, the direct descendant of Anderson and Jones' (1974) proposal, the view is in fact abandoned in favour of one in which primes such as those in (1) ('components') define only the resonance characteristics of a segment and must be supplemented by primes of a different sort ('gestures') which specify manner and major-class properties (see Anderson and Durand 1987, Anderson and Ewen 1987 and the references therein). A similar line has been followed in van der Hulst's 'extended' dependency approach (1989, this volume).

Nevertheless, the principle of autonomous interpretation continues to figure with varying degrees of explicitness in other approaches which employ the primes in (1). This is true, for example, of Particle Phonology (Schane 1984a) and Government Phonology (Kaye et al. 1985, 1990), as well as of the work of, among others, Rennison (1984, 1990), Goldsmith (1985) and van der Hulst and Smith (1985). Although the use of the term *element* to describe such primes is perhaps most usually associated with Government Phonology, we will take the liberty of applying it generically to any conception of subsegmental content which incorporates the notion of autonomous interpretation. The analogy with physical matter seems apt in view of the idea that phonological elements may occur singly or in compounds with other elements. Moreover, to the best of our knowledge, Government Phonology is the only framework to have explicitly pushed the autonomous interpretation hypothesis to its logical conclusion – namely that each and every subsegmental prime, not just those involved in the representation of vocalic contrasts, is independently interpretable.

In this chapter, we explore some of the consequences of adopting a full-blooded version of element theory. This entails a view of phonological derivation which is radically different from that associated with other current frameworks, particularly those employing feature underspecification. One significant implication of the autonomous interpretation hypothesis is that phonological representations are characterized by full phonetic interpretability at all levels of derivation. This in turn implies that there is no level of systematic phonetic representation. Viewed in these terms, the phonological component is not a device for converting abstract lexical representations into ever more physical phonetic representations, as assumed say in underspecification theory. Instead, it has a purely generative function, in the technical sense that it defines the grammaticality of phonological structures. In the following pages, we will argue that these consequences of the autonomous interpretation hypothesis inform a view of phonology and phonetic interpretability that is fully congruent with current thinking on the modular structure of generative grammar.

The various element-based and related approaches share a further theoretical trait which distinguishes them from traditional feature theory: they all subscribe to the assumption that phonological oppositions are, in Trubetzkoyan terms, *privative*. That is, elements are single-valued (monovalent) objects which are either present in a segment or absent from it. Traditional feature theory, in contrast, is based on the notion of *equipollence*; that is, the terms of an opposition are assigned opposite and in principle equally weighted values of a bivalent feature.

It is probably fair to say that, of the various facets of element-based theory, monovalency is the one that has attracted the closest critical attention. The empirical differences between privative and equipollent formats continue to be disputed, and the debate is hardly likely to be resolved in a short chapter such as this. Since the arguments have been well aired elsewhere (see especially van der Hulst 1989, den Dikken and van der Hulst 1988), we will do no more summarize the main issues (Section 2). Our intention here is to shift the focus of the comparison between features and elements to the fundamental conceptual differences that centre on the issue of autonomous interpretation, a matter that up to now has received only scant attention in the literature. In Section 3, we discuss the place of the autonomy hypothesis in a view of phonology which at first blush may seem paradoxical but which is in fact fully in tune with a modular theory of language. On the one hand, the view is 'concrete' to the extent that phonological representations are assumed to be phonetically interpretable at all levels of derivation. On the other, the representations are uniformly cognitive; the primes they contain, unlike orthodox features, do not recapitulate modality-specific details relating to vocal or auditory anatomy. We then go on to show how this view is implemented in the specification of elements involved in the representation of vowels (Section 4) and consonants (Section 5).

2 Monovalency

Phonological oppositions, it is widely agreed, are inherently binary, rather than multivalued or scalar. That is, each phonological prime defines a bifurcate partition of segments into classes. One question that arises in connection with this observation is whether the two terms of an opposition are equal, in the sense that both have a role to play in phonological processing. If they are, the opposition is said to be equipollent; that is, the prime in question is deemed to have two values, usually expressed as a plus vs. minus co-efficient, both of which are potentially addressable by the phonology. In the case of a private opposition, on the other hand, only one term is considered phonologically significant; the relevant prime is then monovalent, being present in one class of segments and absent from the complement set.

The issue of how the valency of phonological primes is best expressed impinges only indirectly on the issue of whether or not they should be credited with autonomous interpretation. The assumption that features are not independently interpretable is compatible with both monovalency and bivalency. In SPE, all oppositions were treated as equipollent. Direct descendants of this tradition, however, incorporate varying degrees of privativeness. In feature geometry, for example, non-terminal class nodes are inherently monovalent (e.g. Clements 1985a, Sagey 1986). Within the latter model, there is some disagreement about whether the terminal nodes of the hierarchy, the features themselves, are uniformly bivalent, uniformly monovalent, or mixed. (For competing views on this matter, see for instance Avery and Rice (1989), Mester and Itô (1989) and Archangeli and Pulleyblank (1994).)[2]

It is not immediately clear whether adherence to the notion of interpretational autonomy necessarily entails a commitment to privativeness. In practice, however, all approaches based on the autonomy principle subscribe to uniform monovalency.

Drawing direct comparisons between available privative and equipollent models is not at all straightforward, for the reason that other theoretical variables are typically implicated, some of which interact with how the valency of primes is treated. A completely level playing field would require concurrence on such matters as the basic set of phonological operations (spreading and delinking, for example), the universal set of primes, and the question of whether or not primes enjoy interpretational autonomy. The nearest we get to such controlled conditions is within feature theory itself, where it is possible to isolate privative versus equipollent versions of the framework which differ minimally in most other respects. (Compare, say, Avery and Rice's 1989 monovalent feature approach with the bivalent approach of Archangeli and Pulleyblank 1994.)

Nevertheless, one thing we can be certain of is that, all other things being equal, a full-blown privative model of phonological oppositions has considerably less expressive power than one based wholly on equipollence. This weaker generative capacity naturally favours the privative approach, unless it can be shown to be significantly empirically underpowered. Assuming for the sake of argument that the controlled conditions mentioned in the last paragraph are in place, we can compare how the two models treat the possibilities of spreading involving an opposition defined in terms of the prime [round], such as might be observed in vowel harmony. The equipollent approach predicts three types of harmony system: one in which [+ round] spreads, one in which [− round] spreads, and one in which both values are active. In a privative framework, the only expressible spreading pattern is one involving [round]. There is no possible way of defining a complementary system of nonround spreading, since there is no object equivalent to [− round] to which the spreading operation could have access.

A strictly privative model makes the strong prediction that all phonological oppositions will rigidly display this sort of asymmetry. That is, only one term of each distinction, the one possessing the relevant element, has the potential to participate in phonological activity. The element is available for, say, spreading or for blocking the propagation of some other element. By contrast, the complement set of segments, those lacking the element in question, is predicted to be phonologically inert; they will fail to trigger spreading and will be transparent to it.

There is little doubt that asymmetries of this type exist. Markedness theory and its implementation in. underspecification frameworks represent attempts to graft this insight onto the equipollent approach (Kiparsky 1982a, Archangeli 1984 and Archangeli and Pulleyblank 1994). According to this notion, only one value of an opposition is specified underlyingly and is thus accessible to phonological processing at the outset of derivation. In the normal case, it is the marked term that is lexically present, while the unspecified value is filled in by universal default rule. Again in the normal case, the latter operation does not take place until the final stage of derivation, with the result that the unspecified value remains invisible to phonological processes. Thus far, underspecification theory resembles a privative model. However, the power of the former is greatly increased by allowing supposedly universal markedness conventions to be overturned in individual grammars, something that can be achieved in two ways. Universal specification preferences can be reversed such that it is the marked value of a feature that is represented underlyingly. Moreover, an underlyingly unspecified value is permitted to be filled in at any stage of derivation, at which point it is free to become no less phonologically active than the underlyingly specified value.

When coupled to a bivalent feature theory, the set of markedness conventions constitutes an independent look-up table against which the marked/unmarked status of individual feature values is gauged. Within a uniformly privative framework, in contrast, a more radical alternative is adopted whereby markedness relations are built directly into phonological representations. Thus, while the privative and equipollent-underspecification approaches are united in acknowledging the skewed nature of phonological oppositions, they part company on the issue of how the universality of this asymmetry is implemented. According to the equipollent account, the asymmetries are relative; the favouring of one distinctive term over its complement is a matter of preference, potentially reversible on a language-specific basis. In a genuinely privative approach, by contrast, the universality of distinctive imbalances is absolute. Viewed from a bivalent perspective, the monovalency of the privative position implies that one value of each prime is *inherently* underspecified (Archangeli 1988).

Potential counter-evidence to the more restrictive privative model comes in the form of any equipollent analysis which refers to a feature value for which there is no direct privative equivalent. And it has to be acknowledged that such accounts are myriad – hardly surprising, considering the almost unchallenged ascendancy that the equipollent view enjoyed during a period which included the publication of SPE. In some cases, such examples can be straightforwardly reanalysed in terms of the opposite feature value. In other words, they turn out not to constitute counter-evidence at all but rather reflect one of the recurring maladies that is symptomatic of over-generation – the possibility of analysing a single phenomenon in more than one way. For example, McCarthy's (1984a) account of the height harmony system of Pasiego Spanish involves spreading both values of the feature [± high]. Vago (1988) shows how the spreading process can be reanalysed so as to access only [+high]. An element-based treatment of the same facts, to be briefly outlined below, need refer only to a single monovalent element ([A]).

Nevertheless, there no doubt exists a corpus of more robust equipollent accounts that need to be reassessed on a case-by-case basis. It is clearly beyond the scope of this chapter to tackle such cases one by one. What we can do, however, is provide a brief illustration of the more general issues that arise when particular examples such as these are re-investigated from an element-based perspective.

Let us return to two of the factors cited above as potentially disruptive of any attempt to undertake a direct comparison between the privative and equipollent approaches to phonological analysis. First, disagreement on the issue of autonomous interpretation probably removes the possibility of complete agreement on what constitutes the universal set of phonological primes in the first place. It often seems to be taken for granted that there exists an ultimate level of systematic phonetic representation defined in terms of traditional features (see, for example, Kaye et al. 1985, Pulleyblank, this volume). However, any such presumption immediately queers the pitch in favour of an equipollent account. Segments defined in terms of SPE-type features cannot be considered pre-theoretical entities. For example, in the version of element theory to be presented below, strict adherence to the principle of interpretational autonomy means there is no equivalent of (traditionally bivalent) features such as [consonantal], [strident] or [sonorant].

Second, there is the challenge of pinning down the particular phonological operations that are deemed to manipulate primes in individual phenomena. This issue may appear reasonably straightforward in view of the emerging consensus that phonological processes should as far as possible be reduced to a small set of formal operations. These days, most phonologists, whether of equipollent or privative persuasion, would probably subscribe to the view that all processing should, ideally at least, be reducible to two fundamental operations – linking and delinking, or perhaps more generally composition and decomposition (Kaye et al. 1985, Mascaró 1987). Composition involves the fusion of primes, achieved through spreading or OCP-triggered coalescence. Decomposition describes either the active rupture of associations between primes, achieved through delinking, or the failure of compositional potential to be realized. The complicating factor in any privative–equipollent comparison, as we will see presently, is that we cannot assume prior agreement on which of these basic operations is at work in a particular phenomenon.

With these provisos in mind, we will try to illustrate some of the theoretical variables that need to be controlled for in a comparison between bivalency and monovalency by contrasting the feature [±high] with the element [A]. Although the segment classes defined by these two primes are clearly not isomorphic, the sets of phenomena to which they are applicable overlap sufficiently for at least some degree of close comparison to be possible. The phenomena to be focused on here are two kinds of height harmony, one a 'lowering' type, the other a 'raising' type. Elsewhere these have been analysed as the spreading of [−high] and [+high] respectively. This particular comparison is especially instructive, since it has been alleged that an element-based approach is unable to express the raising pattern (Clements 1991a).

Lowering harmony is widely represented in the central Bantu languages. In the typical case, mid vowels are lexically absent from certain types of suffix and only appear in such positions during derivation as a result of high vowels lowering under the harmonic influence of a mid vowel appearing in the root. This is the pattern encountered in, for example, Luganda (Katamba 1984), Yaka (van den Eynde 1968) and Chichewa (Mtenje 1985). Compare, for instance, high (2a) and mid (2b) suffix vowels in Chichewa (Mtenje 1985):

(2)

		Causative	Applied	
(a)	pind-a	pind-its-a	pind-il-a	'bend'
	put-a	put-its-a	put-il-a	'provoke'
(b)	lemb-a	lemb-ets-a	lemb-el-a	'write'
	konz-a	konz-ets-a	konz-el-a	'correct'

In earlier feature accounts, this type of system was treated in terms of the rightward spreading of both values of [±high] (Katamba 1984, Mtenje 1985). Within an underspecification framework, it can be reanalysed in such a way that only [−high] spreads (from mid root vowels), with [+high] being filled in by default (Harris and Moto 1989).

In element-based analyses, there is nothing akin to fill-in treatments of harmony (or of any other type of phenomenon for that matter). The nearest equivalent is a situation in which one set of harmonic spans within a system remains unaffected by spreading and simply manifests the identity of lexically present elements. Exactly this state of affairs can be shown to hold in the central Bantu case. Alternations between mid and high vowels are treated in terms of the presence versus absence of the element [A] in other

than low vowels. In the central Bantu pattern, mid vowels in
harmonically recessive suffixes arise through the rightward spreading of [A] from a mid vowel in the root nucleus (see Goldsmith
1985, Rennison 1987).[3] As shown in (3a), fusion of [A] with the [I]
of a suffix such as -il- produces the mid-vowel alternant -el- in
Chichewa.

(3)

(a) *lemb-el-a*   (b) *pind-il-a*

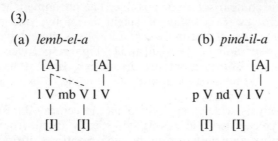

In the complement set of harmonic spans, illustrated by the form
in (3b), a high-vowel nucleus in the root lacks [A], and no spreading
occurs. The *i* reflex of -il- in such cases is then simply the independent realization of the lexically present element [I].

Thus far, [A] and [– high] are roughly equivalent in their coverage of height harmony. The challenge to the element-based
approach would now seem to come from feature analyses of
harmony which invoke the complement value [+ high]. Just such a
case is presented by the treatments of Pasiego Spanish mentioned
above.

Very briefly, harmony in Pasiego is controlled by the vowel in
the stressed syllable of the word; if it is high, then all non-low
vowels to its left are also high. Hence alternations such as the
following:[4]

(4)

Infinitive	Future first person singular	Future second person plural	
bebér	*beberé*	*bibirí:s*	'drink'
komér	*komeré*	*kumirí:s*	'eat'
koxér	*koxeré*	*kuxirí:s*	'take'

McCarthy's (1984a) account of this phenomenon actually incorporates two operations: delinking and spreading. According to the
first part of his analysis, a lexically present [±high] value in a
harmonically recessive nucleus is delinked under the influence of a
harmonically dominant nucleus bearing a value for the same fea-

ture. Any vowel affected by this process then picks up the dominant value through spreading. Under Vago's (1988) reanalysis, only [+ high] is lexically represented; this spreads from a dominant nucleus to any harmonizing vowels in its domain. In the complement set of harmonic domains, [− high] is filled in by a later default rule.

The element-based analysis of Pasiego to be sketched here retains McCarthy's (1984a) insight that lowering harmony involves delinking (cf. van der Hulst 1988a). On the other hand, it parts company with both types of feature analysis in dispensing with spreading altogether (Harris 1990a). The analysis makes appeal to the licensing relations that obtain between vowels within harmonic spans. A nucleus which determines the harmonic category of a span can be said to license the other nuclei within that domain. The specific proposal is as follows: [A] is sustainable in a licensed nucleus only if it is sanctioned by an [A] in the licensing nucleus. Any [A] that fails to receive such a sanction is delinked. In (5a), the occurrence of [A] in the two recessive nuclei is supported by an [A] in the stressed nucleus. (The arrows indicate the directionality of the licensing relation.)

(5)

(a) *komeré*   (b) *kumirí:s*

In (5b), in contrast, there is no [A] in the licensing nucleus to sustain the lexically present [A]s in the licensed positions. Delinking (indicated by =) ensues. Each of the residual elements independently defines a high vowel.

Under this analysis, Pasiego harmony is expressed in terms of a single generalization governing the appearance of [A] in adjacent nuclei. Moreover, the mechanism it invokes, inter-nuclear licensing, is motivated by a wide range of facts, most of which are quite independent of height harmony (Kaye 1990a, Charette 1991). These include vowel syncope and metrical phenomena, as well as harmony involving other elements. In a still wider perspective, this mechanism is itself subsumed under the general notion of phonological licensing, the fundamental principle by which all segmental material and constituents, not just nuclear positions, are integrated into the phonological hierarchy (Itô 1986, Kaye et al. 1990).

The process illustrated in (5b) manifests a type of complexity agreement whereby complex vowels in licensed positions undergo reduction if a simplex vowel occupies the licensing position. This is but one instance of a much more general principle according to which the elemental complexity of a licensed position cannot exceed that of its licensor (the Complexity Condition discussed in Harris 1990b). The generality of this principle is reflected in its applicability to an apparently disparate range of contexts that goes beyond the inter-nuclear relation at issue here. Other domains displaying similar complexity effects include those formed by branching onsets and coda-onset clusters.

The delinking analysis of harmony is further supported by the observation that it parallels the treatment of vowel reduction under weak stress. That is, the single formal operation of delinking is invoked as a means of deriving the curtailed distributional potential of prosodically recessive nuclei, irrespective of whether this manifests itself harmonically or metrically. In the Pasiego example, the two aspects of prosodic weakness happen to cooccur: harmonizing nuclei appear in unstressed positions.

Our comparison of height harmony analyses illustrates the more general point that *harmony*, like its hypernym *assimilation*, is a descriptive term with no formal status (see Mascaró 1987). The notion, it is sometimes assumed, can be directly equated with the formal operation of spreading, and this was certainly the state of affairs envisaged in early autosegmental research. In classic (i.e. feature-based) autosegmental treatments of vowel harmony, for example, all harmonic spans in a given system are derived via spreading. That is, both values of the harmonic feature are deemed to spread, as illustrated in several of the feature-based analyses referred to above. (The original example is Clements' 1981 treatment of Akan ATR harmony.) However, in the light of more recent proposals, the claim that assimilation uniformly reduces to spreading is no longer tenable. As shown in our discussion of Pasiego Spanish, two other operations have been invoked: delinking and, in underspecification approaches at least, blank-filling redundancy rules.

The immediate relevance of this point to the treatment of height harmony is that the deployment of [− high] in some feature-based accounts and [+ high] in others does not imply that the monovalency of [A] must be abandoned or that some additional height element must be posited. The nearest privative equivalent of spread-[− high] (lowering) is spread-[A]; the effect of spread-[+ high] (raising), on the other hand, is achieved by delink-[A].

The absence of a unitary formal treatment of assimilation has a significant impact on how we assess whether each term of an opposition is phonologically active or inert. And this in turn has a direct bearing on how we weigh up the merits and demerits of the equipollent and privative approaches. At the beginning of this section, we noted that bivalency predicts three types of process for each harmonic feature, involving the spreading of either or both values. In fact, taking account now of two possible operations in harmony, spreading and delinking, we find the number of expressible systems increases to six, illustrated in (6) for some given prime [P]. This is in contrast to the two types of system generated by the equivalent monovalent model.

(6)

Equipollent		*Privative*	
Spread	[+ P]; [− P]; [± P]	Spread	[P]
Delink	[+ P]; [− P]; [± P]	Delink	[P]

Including the blank-filling operations of underspecification theory, together with the different orderings these permit, actually multiplies the possibilities defined by bivalency still further. Admittedly, the trend in more recent equipollent work has been to eschew harmonic analyses which manipulate both values of a feature simultaneously. Nevertheless, within this framework the intersection of the two terms of a bivalent feature with the formal operations of spreading, delinking and ordered blank-filling increases the likelihood of more than one analysis being available for a particular harmony system.

To do full justice to the whole issue of monovalency would take up more space than is available here. Nevertheless, we believe that the discussion of the analyses outlined in this section, however brief, illustrates the care that needs to be exercised in comparing the performance of the equipollent and privative models. Given the inherently more constrained nature of the privative approach, the onus is on proponents of equipollence to prove the need to compromise on the universality of markedness asymmetries by showing that both terms of phonological oppositions are potentially phonologically active. The equipollent game-plan should thus be to force advocates of privativeness to admit the necessity of recognizing two monovalent elements for any given bivalent feature. (In the height harmony case, the extra privative element would be ['counter-A'].) If completely successful, the strategy would lead to a situation in which the privative model contained exactly twice as many primes as the equipollent model. At this point, all notion of the absoluteness of universal markedness asymmetries would be relinquished, and the two models would be to all intents and purposes indistinguishable. However, as the foregoing comparison of harmony analyses suggests, any such concession to the equipollent viewpoint should not be made too hastily.

3   Phonetic interpretation in generative grammar

3.1   There is no level of 'systematic phonetic' representation

Recognizing the interpretational autonomy of phonological primes gives rise to a view of phonological representations and derivations which is fundamentally different from that associated with ortho-dox features. Within the latter tradition, it has long been usual to suppose that only a subset of the feature specifications appearing in final representation is present at the outset of derivation (Halle 1959). Underlyingly absent values, those that are non-distinctive or predictable, are filled in during the course of derivation by redun-dancy rules or phonological rules proper. This view achieves apotheosis in Radical Underspecification Theory, in which all predictable feature values are stripped from underlying representation (Arch-angeli 1984, 1988, Pulleyblank 1986a). There has been a slight retreat from this extreme position in recent descendants of the theory. In the Combinatorial Specification approach of Archangeli and Pulleyblank, for example, a criterion of representational simplic-ity, which favours maximal despecification of lexical representations, may be overridden in certain cases where otherwise non-distinctive values can be shown to play an active role in underlying association patterns (1994: 88–9).

Coupled to the assumption that features lack interpretational autonomy, the classic underspecification arrangement implies that any non-final representation containing blank feature values is phonetically uninterpretable. The realization of lexically repre-sented values is contingent on the support of non-distinctive or predictable values; and the full complement of mutually supporting feature values is not mustered until the final stage of derivation, the level of systematic phonetic representation. This view too has been modified somewhat in more recent underspecification ap-proaches. As a result of work by Keating (1988), Pierrehumbert and Beckman (1988) and others, it is now assumed that fragments of underspecification may persist into phonetic implementation (Arch-angeli and Pulleyblank 1994: 43, Pulleyblank, this volume). This situation supposedly arises in certain instances of what used to be termed *sequence redundancy*, where the phonetic interpretation of a segment with respect to a particular feature is entirely predictable on the basis of the value this feature has in neighbouring segments. In a sub-class of such cases, it has been argued, the intervening sound fails to be assigned a value for the feature in question and is thus submitted to motor planning without an inherent articulatory target. The relevant articulatory dimension then allegedly manifests itself through simple linear interpolation between the motor targets associated with the specified values of the flanking segments. (Reservations about the allegedly targetless nature of such segments have been expressed by, among others, Boyce et al. 1991). Even when adapted to allow for sporadic instances of persistent underspecification, it nevertheless remains true of this overall approach that a significant proportion of feature values, particularly those which are predictable from other values within the same segment (*segment redundancy*), must be specified in phonetic representation before phonetic interpretation is possible.

According to this line of thinking, one of the main jobs of the phonological rule component is to transform abstract representational objects into ever more physical ones. This mismatch between underlying and surface representations is sometimes justified on the grounds that the two levels allegedly perform quite different functions: underlying representations, it is sometimes claimed, serve the function of memory and lexical storage, while surface representations serve as input to articulation and perception (Bromberger and Halle 1989). The validity or otherwise of this view hinges on a number of considerations, only some of which we have space to consider here.

One issue concerns the degree of circularity that is inherent in the strategy of stripping lexical representations down to the distinctive bone, a problem fully discussed by Mohanan (1991). In many instances, the presence of a given pair of phonological properties in a representation may involve balanced mutual dependence. That is, in such cases there is no non-arbitrary way of determining the directionality of the relation whereby one property is deemed lexically distinctive and the other predictable and hence derived. A well-known example concerns the relation between syllable-structure and segment-structure information. As observed by Levin (1985), Borowsky (1986) and others, it is often the case that the former can be extrapolated from the latter with a facility equal to that with which the latter can be extrapolated from the former.

Another issue concerns the desirability of having underspecified representations as addresses for lexical storage and retrieval. The despecification of lexical feature values may be viewed as a type of archiving programme which compresses information for compact storage.[5] As noted by Lass (1984: 205), Mohanan (1991) and others, one of the motivations for proposing redundancy-free lexical representations in generative phonology seems to have been the assumption that long-term memory constraints prompt speakers to limit storage to idiosyncratic information and to maximize the computing of predictable information. This view has never been seriously defended in the psycholinguistic literature.[6] But if underspecification is not justified by storage considerations, nor does it constitute a particularly plausible model of efficient lexical access. The goal of maximal economy of lexical representation can only be achieved at the expense of greatly increasing the amount of computation to be performed at retrieval (Braine 1974). Just as an archived computer text file has to be de-archived before it can be accessed, so would a speaker-hearer have first to 'unpack' the condensed, underspecified form of a lexical entry before submitting it to articulation or recognition.

This last point leads on to perhaps the most fundamental objection to the notion that the function of phonological derivation is to prepare cognitively represented objects for phonetic implementation. Bromberger and Halle (1989: 53) express this notion quite succinctly when they make the claim that systematic phonetic representations 'are only generated when a word figures in an actual utterance'. It is as well to be quite clear about how this view relates to the Chomskyan dichotomy between I-language and E-language. In equating the notion of generation with speech production, it immediately places the phonological component outside the domain of grammar proper. It is not just that the systematic phonetic level constitutes a buffer between the representation of internalized phonological knowledge and its articulatory or perceptual externalization; the phonological component as a whole is geared towards fulfilling a goal which is essentially extragrammatical, that of turning out utterance-bound phonetic forms.

The validity of this view cannot be taken for granted. In what follows, we will consider the consequences of adopting an alternative position, in which phonology remains on the competence side of the competence-performance divide. According to this view, phonological processes, in line with general principles, do no more than capture generalizations holding over alternations and distributional regularities. This function can be served quite independently of any provision that needs to be made for articulation and perception. That is, processes can be construed as purely generative in the technical sense of specifying the membership of the set of grammatical phonological structures in a language. Under this view, initial and final representations in phonological derivation are isotypic: processes map phonological objects onto other phonological objects rather than onto phonetic ones. Such a view places phonology firmly in the grammatical camp.

If phonological processes map like onto like, it follows that initial representations should be no less phonetically interpretable than final representations. In fact, initial representations can in principle be envisaged as being wholly indistinguishable in kind from final representations. Such an arrangement is of course impossible if non-final representations are subject to underspecification. But it is perfectly consistent with an approach in which phonological primes enjoy autonomous interpretability. In a full-blown element approach, there is no sense in which a final representation is any more physical or concrete than an initial one. There is thus nothing corresponding to a systematic phonetic level, since any representation at any stage of derivation is directly mappable onto physical phonetics.

It is necessary to bear this point in mind when comparing the empirical content of element theory with that of feature underspecification. As noted in the last section, it is sometimes assumed that the two approaches somehow share the same realizational outcome, namely a systematic phonetic representation consisting of fully specified matrices of bivalent features. In the light of the foregoing discussion, it is clear that this opinion is mistaken. The assumption gives the incorrect impression that one theory is directly translatable into the other, an impression that has hardly been discouraged by the occasional practice of explicitly spelling out the phonetic exponence of elements in traditional feature terms (Kaye et al. 1985, Rennison 1990). These researchers are quick to point out that features employed in this way serve no more than a phonetic implementation function and as such are not accessible to the phonology. However, it seems to us better to return to Anderson and Jones' (1974) basic proposal that features have no place in element theory whatsoever. Not only does invoking features muddy the water as far as presentation of elemental phonology is concerned; in several respects, it actually hamstrings attempts to provide an accurate account of how elements are mapped onto physical phonetics, a point we will return to below.

3.2 Jakobson *redivivus*
This last point introduces yet another motive for dispensing with references to orthodox features in specifying the phonetic expo-

nence of elements. The use of SPE-type features entails acceptance of the notion that phonological primes are mapped in the first instance onto the articulatory dimension, in spite of what is usually claimed about a generative grammar being neutral between speaker and hearer. This orientation is perhaps most vividly illustrated in the close congruence that exists between current conceptions of feature geometry and Browman and Goldstein's (1989) gestural model of speech production (Clements 1992). To the slight extent that researchers working within this tradition have concerned themselves with the hearer side of the equation, it has been assumed that the primarily articulatory features can be mapped, albeit indirectly, onto acoustic and perceptual dimensions. (For a recent proposal along these lines, formulated within feature geometry, see Clements and Hertz 1991).

It would perhaps be unfair to speculate that the articulatory slant of much feature theory is not entirely unconnected to the clear articulatory bias of most introductory courses in phonetics. Nevertheless, it is worth pointing out that a belief in the centrality of speech production, however tacit, implies varying degress of commitment to the motor theory of speech perception, the notion that the listener decodes speech by some species of internal articulatory synthesis. The theory, in various guises, has met with rather less than general agreement in the phonetic literature (see Klatt 1987 for discussion). Many phoneticians and phonologists remain to be convinced of the wisdom of abandoning the Jakobsonian insight that the phonetic exponence of subsegmental primes should in the first place be defined in acoustic terms.[7] The speech signal, as Jakobson was wont to point out, is after all the communicative experience that is shared by both speaker and hearer (Jakobson et al. 1952: 13). Its primacy in phonetic interpretation should hardly be in question, at least if we are to pay more than lip service to the idea that generative grammar is neutral between production and perception.

It is for this reason that the specifications of elements provided in the following sections are couched in primarily acoustic terms (an orientation long associated with Dependency Phonology). That is not to say that elements should be construed as acoustic (or articulatory) events. They are properly understood as cognitive objects which perform the grammatical function of coding lexical contrasts.[8] Nevertheless, continuing the essentially Jakobsonian line of thinking, we consider their phonetic implementation as involving in the first instance a mapping onto sound patterns in the acoustic signal. Viewed in these terms, articulation and perception are parasitic on this mapping relation. That is, elements are internally represented pattern templates by reference to which listeners decode auditory input and speakers orchestrate and monitor their articulations.

4 Elements for vowels

This section covers four main topics: the specification of [A], [I] and [U] (Section 4.1), the headedness of compound segmental expressions (Section 4.2), evidence supporting the existence of a 'neutral' element which defines the resonance baseline on which the other elements are superimposed (Section 4.3), and the representation of ATR (Section 4.4).

4.1 Elemental patterns: [A], [I], [U]

The phonological evidence supporting recognition of the elements [A], [I] and [U] is reasonably well established. For example, we may refer to the pivotal role played by the independent manifestations of these elements in the organization of phonological systems. The 'corner' vowels *a*, *i* and *u* figure with much greater frequency than any other segments in the vocalic systems of the world's languages (Maddieson 1984). Moreover, there is a substantial body of distributional and alternation evidence supporting the conclusion that primes of this nature are individually accessible to phonological processing. Thus we find harmony processes, for instance, which address natural classes identifiable with dimensions such as 'palatality' (characterized by presence of [I]), 'labiality' ([U]), or, as illustrated in the last section, 'height' ([A]). (For examples of all three types of harmony process, see van der Hulst and Smith 1985, van der Hulst 1988b.)

As suggested by representations such as those in (3) and (5), we are following current thinking in assuming that each prime resides on its own autosegmental tier. (The question of whether these tiers are hierarchically organized is something we take up in Section 5.3.) A compound segment thus involves the co-registration of elements on separate tiers. This is illustrated in (7), which shows

(7)

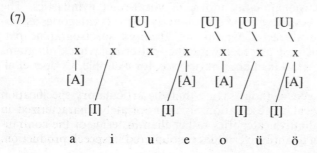

not only the five canonical vowels already given in (1) but also *ü* and *ö*, the two other segments derivable by possible [A]-[I]-[U] combinations of the type we have been assuming up to now.

Of course, not every language opts to exploit the full range of combinatorial possibilities presented by this fully autosegmentalized model. According to Kaye et al. (1985), such systems can be derived by means of parameterized tier conflation. The effect of collapsing two tiers is to prevent the relevant elements from fusing with one another. For example, as depicted in (8), a system in which [I] and [U] take up residence on the same tier is one lacking front rounded vowels.

(8)

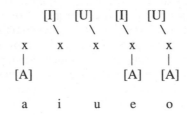

a   i   u   e   o

In what follows, we will only indicate autosegmental structure where the discussion demands it.

How are [A], [I] and [U] to be defined, and how do we derive the results of their combination? For reasons explained in the previous section, we begin by proposing for them definitions which may be mapped rather directly onto the acoustic signal. Before embarking on such an exercise, it is as well to ensure that we disabuse ourselves of a common misconception – the idea that quantitative values specified with reference to waveforms or spectrographic displays are to acoustic phonetics what qualitative categories specified in terms of vocal tract diagrams are to articulatory phonetics. In fact, a more apt proportion is one that relates a spectrogram to a three-dimensional X-ray movie of vocal-tract gymnastics. The closest acoustic analogues of the relatively abstract categories associated with vocal-tract diagrams are idealised spectrographic patterns. (The nearest precedents are the 'pattern-playback' diagrams pioneered by Haskins Laboratories; see, for example, Cooper et al. 1952.)

It usually goes without saying that the articulatory specification of phonological representations is appropriately characterized in terms of qualitative categories rather than in terms of the continuously varying quantitative values encountered in speech production.

By the same token, the specification of the acoustic signatures of phonological categories should be couched qualitatively in terms of overall quasi-spectral shapes, and not quantitatively. It would therefore be misguided to express the resonance characteristics of elements such as [A], [I] and [U] as quantitative values relating, say, to formant frequencies. Rather it is necessary to determine the gross quasi-acoustic shapes – what we may call elemental *patterns* – which constitute these categories, and for which symbols such as [A], [I] and [U] are no more than shorthand notations (Lindsey and Harris 1990). The grossness of these patterns should presumably be related to their interpretational autonomy, which they exhibit regardless of whether they appear alone or in compounds.

In Figure 2.1 we diagram the elemental patterns which, we have proposed elsewhere, characterize [A], [I] and [U] (Harris and Lindsey 1991). We display each pattern in a frame mimicking a spectral slice in which the vertical axis corresponds to intensity and the horizontal axis to frequency. The latter coincides with what we may term the *sonorant frequency zone*, the frequency band containing the most significant information relating to vocalic contrasts (roughly speaking between 0 and 3 kHz).

The elemental pattern of [A], shown in Figure 2.1a, is appropriately labelled *mAss*. The signal specification of the vowel *a*, the element's independent manifestation, is a spectral energy mass in the middle of this zone, interpretable as the convergence of Formants 1 and 2;

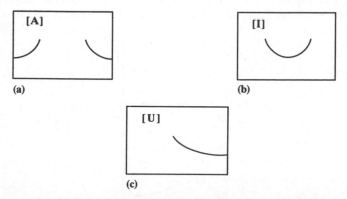

(a)   (b)

(c)

FIGURE 2.1 Elemental patterns: [A], [I], [U] (from Harris and Lindsey 1991). The contours are schematic spectral envelopes, plotted here in frames which map onto acoustic spectral slices (vertical axis: amplitude, horizontal axis: frequency (ca. 0-3kHz)). The solid lines specify regions of low energy. The energy contained within the blank regions is at a higher level than the specified minima, but its precise envelope is not criterial to the definition of the patterns.

that is, crucially there are energy minima at top and bottom of the zone. In the diagram for [A], the precise structuring of the massed energy in the middle of the frequency range is not a criterial part of the pattern's definition and is thus left blank.

The spectrum of *i* contains a low first formant coupled with a spectral peak at the top of the sonorant frequency zone, the latter peak being relatable to the convergence of Formants 2 and 3. This configuration, with energy lower in the middle of the zone than at either side, may be taken to correspond to a *dIp* elemental pattern characterizing [I] (see Figure 2.16).

The signal evidence relating to *u* indicates what we may term a *rUmp* elemental pattern for [U]. The vowel displays a spectral peak at the lower end of the sonorant frequency zone (produced by a convergence of the first and second formants); that is, there is no significant energy above the middle of the zone. The corresponding elemental pattern is displayed in Figure 2.1c; here the lower portion of the contour is left blank, since the precise structuring of the higher-amplitude energy in this part of the frame is not criterial to the pattern's definition.

In summary, the elemental patterns associated with the three resonance elements under discussion are: [A] mAss (energy minima at top and bottom), [I] dIp (energy minimum in middle), and [U] rUmp (energy minimum above middle).

The effects of compounding elements are derived by overlaying elemental patterns on one another. The two complex profiles depicted in Figure 2.2 result from fusing pairs of patterns shown in Figure 2.1. Figure 2.2a shows *e*, the outcome of fusion between [A]

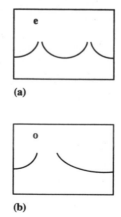

FIGURE 2.2 Compounded elemental patterns: (a) [A, I] *e*, (b) [A, U] *o* (from Harris and Lindsey 1991).

and [I]. The profile here, which might be described as 'dIp within a mAss', can be viewed as an amalgam of two patterns: (i) energy minima at top and bottom, indicating the presence of [A]; and (ii) energy minimum in middle, the pattern associated with [I]. In *o*, a compound of [A] and [U] (Figure 2.2b), we see a pattern that might be dubbed 'mAss at the rUmp'; that is, we have both (i) energy minima at top and bottom, i.e. [A], and (ii) energy minimum above middle, i.e. [U].[9]

Elemental patterns are templates which hearers endeavour to detect in speech input and speakers endeavour to match in the production and self-monitoring of speech output. When a given element is input to speech production mechanisms, the speaker will marshal whatever articulatory resources are necessary or available for the spectral realization of the target elemental pattern. For example, the desired acoustic effect associated with the mAss pattern [A] can be achieved through maximal expansion of the oral tube and constriction of the pharyngeal tube. Note that the imaginary point of maximal height of the tongue body, long cited in impressionistic phonetics (at least since Sweet 1877) as the crucial reference point in the definition of articulatory categories such as 'high' and 'low', has no particular importance in the specification of how [A], or indeed any element, is produced. As is well known, a single vowel sound can be produced with widely varying tongue body contours by different individuals and even by the same individual on different occasions. (See for example, Ladefoged et al. 1972 and the results of bite-block experiments of the type reported by Folkins and Zimmerman 1981.) It is by manipulating the overall shape of the vocal airway that the speaker targets particular acoustic effects. Nor is any elemental specification required to determine that the vocal cords should vibrate. Indeed, if anything, such specification would be undesirable, since the speaker may, depending on circumstance, choose whisper rather than voice as the acoustic source.

The articulatory incarnation of dIp [I] calls for maximal expansion of the pharyngeal cavity and maximal constriction of the oral cavity. The articulatory implementation of rUmp [U] involves a trade-off between maximal expansion of both the oral and pharyngeal tubes. Labial activity (rounding and/or protrusion, for example) is but one of the factors that contribute to the overall size of the oral cavity. One implication of this is that lip rounding is not an articulatory prerequisite in the production of vocalic expressions containing [U].[10]

Consideration of the articulatory implementation of elemental patterns helps underline the distinction between element-based and current feature-based approaches to the specification of phonetic detail. Feature *under*specification refers to the lexical suppression of properties that are phonologically represented at later stages of derivation. As noted earlier, this notion is incompatible with the autonomous interpretation hypothesis, since specified properties are in most instances uninterpretable without support from temporarily suppressed properties. Implicit in element theory, on the other hand, is the conclusion that certain properties assumed by feature theory are *non*-specified. The non-specification of a property implies that it has no representational status whatsoever, either lexically or during derivation. In fact, some such properties, it can be argued, do not even exist as independent entities in physical phonetics. Note that non-specification, as understood in this sense, in no way impairs the interpretational autonomy of elements. The element [A], for example, has a direct and independent physical interpretation that can be defined without so much as even a passing reference to features such as [± back], [± low], [± sonorant], [± consonantal], or whatever. Recognition of this point in recent element-based research is reflected in the abandonment of the earlier notion (outlined in Kaye et al. 1985, for example) that phonetic implementation involves the translation of each element into a traditional distinctive feature matrix. Such a featural halfway house, it is now acknowledged, is both logically and empirically redundant.

A further consequence of this view is that there is no place in element theory for anything resembling the featural interpretation of the traditional phonemic notion of contrastivity. A familiar feature matrix includes values whose primary function is to distinguish the sound it specifies from other sounds with which it is in opposition. The matrix for *a*, for example, might include [− round] (whether lexically present or filled in by redundancy rule), which helps differentiate the vowel from a round vowel such as *u*. In element theory, on the other hand, *a* is identified solely on the basis of the only element of which it is composed, namely [A]. To be sure, there is a descriptive sense in which a sound may be viewed as entering into Saussurian relations of contrast with other sounds in a given system; but this does not necessarily imply that each such distinction is directly coded in representation as a particular unit of segmental content. In element terms, the definition of *a* does not include reference to properties that identify other vowels with which it happens to be in contrast, such as the [U] present in *u*. That is, *a* is **non**-specified with respect to the pattern characteristics that are relevant to the definition of *u* (acoustically, concentration of energy in the low frequencies, typically realised in articulation by lip rounding). No specification of [U]-related characteristics ('non-rUmp', 'non-round', or whatever) ever enters into the identification of this vowel. Not being *u* is no more a criterial property of *a* than not being an orange is a criterial property of a banana.

4.2 Elemental weightings in compound expressions

Most element-based approaches incorporate some means of representing the notion that the phonetic manifestation of a compound segment reflects the weighting of one element over others occurring in the same expression. The precise implementation of this idea varies from one theory to another.

In Particle Phonology (Schane 1984a), preponderance is formalized by allowing multiple occurrences of the same element to be stacked within a single expression. The relative openness of a vowel, for example, can be reflected in the number of [A]s it contains. The sum of [A]s contained in the expression of a particular vowel is a language-specific matter, varying according to the number of distinctive heights exploited in the system. The same object, *a* say, then receives different representations in different grammars; it might consist of two [A]s in one system and only one in another. The relativism that is implicit in this arrangement clearly represents a retreat from the view that elements are universally defined and uniquely interpretable.

In other versions of element theory, preponderance is represented through relations of headedness between elements occurring within the same expression. In Dependency Phonology, a pair of primes α and β can enter into one of three relations: (a) α dependent on β, (b) β dependent on α, and (c) mutual dependency (Anderson and Jones 1974, Anderson and Ewen 1987). In Kaye et al. (1985) and van der Hulst (1989), on the other hand, only relations (a) and (b) are recognized. Assuming the latter mode of representation, let us compare two [A, I] compounds, one headed by [A], the other by [I]. Informally, we can think of the [A]-headed expression as a palatalized version of an essentially open vowel; the [I]-headed expression meanwhile can be considered an open version of an essentially palatal vowel. These asymmetric fusions are assumed to define the vowels *e* and *æ* respectively, as shown in (9a) (head element underlined).

(9)

(a) [A, I̲]	e	(b) [A, U̲]	o
[A̲, I]	æ	[A̲, U]	ɒ

As shown in (9b), the contrast between *o* and *ɒ* is treated in parallel fashion. (The contrast between ATR (advanced tongue root or tense) e/o and non-ATR (lax) $\varepsilon/ɔ$ has also to be character-ized somehow, a matter we take up in Section 4.4.)

In terms of its effect on the signal, intrasegmental dependency is reflected in the predominance of one elemental pattern over an-other. The compounded profile of [A, I̱], for example, can be interpreted as a relatively less salient mAss pattern located in the middle of a relatively more salient dIp. The expression [A̱, I], on the other hand, is realized as a preponderantly mAss pattern with a less salient dIp at its centre. These two elemental profiles simulate the spectral characteristics of e and $æ$ respectively.

The fusion asymmetries illustrated in (9) provide a straightfor-ward means of representing widely attested processes of raising and lowering involving low and mid vowels.[11] Take for example the raising of $æ$ to e and of $ɒ$ to o. (As attested in one portion of the English Great Vowel Shift, for example; see Schane 1984b and Jones 1989 for element-based analyses.) In terms of their elementary make-up, the inputs and outputs of each of these raisings are isomers (Kaye et al. 1985). That is, the elements of which they are composed are identical but are arranged in different ways. Viewed in this manner, the raising of low vowels involves neither the loss nor the addition of elements; it consists rather in a switch in the headedness of the relevant segmental expression. Lowering of mid vowels presents the inverse operation, in which [A] in a compound switches from dependent to head status.

The introduction of intrasegmental relations, it has to be acknowl-edged, adds to the expressive power of the theory. One way of preventing this power from getting out of control is to take compen-sating steps towards reducing the number of primes. In fact, much work in this area has been directed towards striking a balance between structural and elementary modes of representation. The enrichment of intrasegmental structure has enabled Dependency Phonologists to reduce the manner dimension of segmental con-trasts to two fundamental primes or 'gestures'. This avenue has been most thoroughly explored by van der Hulst (this volume), who reduces all segmental content to two such gestures. This is balanced by an elaborated model of dependency relations, in which segmental contrasts are represented in terms of X-bar structure. This contraction in the role played by segmental primes comes at the expense of sacrificing the notion of autonomous interpretation. Under this view, stand-alone units such as [A], [I] and [U] are derived from syntactic configurations of two primes which do not enjoy independent interpretability. There is apparently a minimum set of primes below which it is impossible to maintain the interpreta-tional autonomy principle. That is, below this point primes become 'too small' to be independently interpretable. On current assumptions, the threshold is somewhere around ten elements (a total not much smaller than the number of primes proposed by Jakobson et al. 1952).

When we turn our attention to compounds containing three or more elements, two issues arise which have a significant impact on the generative capacity of element theory. One has to do with whether or not the fusion of elements occurs in a pairwise fashion. If it does, as assumed by Kaye et al. (1985) for example, then multiple element compounds can be compiled with different patterns of embedding. For example, a three-element compound composed of [X], [Y] and [Z] could be constructed as [X, [Y, Z]], [Y, [X, Z]], or [Z, [X, Y]]. Second, there is the issue of whether any expression may form the head of a compound, irrespective of whether it is itself simplex or complex. In the three-element example [X, [Y, Z]], either [X] or [Y, Z] could in principle act as head of the expression. Together, the possibilities of pairwise fusion and free directionality of headedness greatly inflate the generative power of the theory to an extent that is empirically unjustified. And the expressive potential of course increases exponentially as more elements enter the equation.

These issues are fully discussed in a series of exchanges between Coleman (1990a, 1990b) and Kaye (1990c), in the light of which it seems prudent to abandon the notion of pairwise fusion. In the simpler model that results, one which has no recourse to nested compound structures, an unbounded relation exists between the head element of an expression and any dependent elements that may also be present. This is the model we will assume in the remainder of this chapter, although we will only indicate the headedness of a compound expression where the context demands.

Before leaving this topic, we should note that the free combinability of elements is further constrained by quite general and independent principles. One of these is the Complexity Condition referred to in Section 3, which has the effect of severely restricting the number of elements that can appear in adjacent positions.

4.3   The neutral element
Occurring singly or in combination with one another, [A], [I] and [U] help define the basic set of vocalic contrasts given in (7). Additional elements are necessary for the definition of other dimensions of contrast, including that of peripherality, to which we now turn.

The spectral peaks associated with a, i and u are inherently large and distinct. From an articulatory point of view, this is a reflection of the fact that these vowels, the universally limiting articulations of the vowel triangle, represent extreme departures from a neutral position of the vocal tract. The supralaryngeal vocal-tract configuration associated with the neutral position approximates that of a uniform tube and produces a schwa-like auditory effect. The resonating characteristics of this configuration are such that the first three formants are fairly evenly spaced, with the result that it lacks the distinct spectral peaks found in *a*, *i* and *u*. Most researchers within the element-based tradition accord this neutral quality some special status, either by treating it as a segment devoid of any active elementary content or by taking it to be the manifestation of an independent element, which we will symbolize here as [@]. Broadly speaking, this corresponds to the centrality component in Dependency Phonology (Lass 1984, Anderson and Ewen 1987), to the 'cold' vowel of Government Phonology (Kaye et al. 1985), and to an 'empty' segment lacking any vocalic content in Particle Phonology (Schane 1984a) and in the work of van der Hulst (1989).

The element [@] may be thought of as a blank canvas to which the colours represented by [A], [I] and [U] can be applied. From a production point of view, this metaphor reflects the point just made that [A], [I] and [U] are realized by means of articulatory manoeuvres that perturb the vocal tract from its neutral state. From a signal point of view, this implies that the dispersed formant structure of [@] constitutes a base line on which the elemental patterns associated with [A], [I] and [U] are superimposed.[12]

The idea that [@] is signally blank may come as a surprise to those who assume that the phonologically relevant *dramatis personae* of vocalic acoustics are formants. To be sure, schwa-like vowels exhibit formants just as much as other vowels. However, in the light of what was said in Section 4.1, it is an assumption we should have no truck with. It is elemental patterns that are the phonologically relevant actors to be detected in vowel signals. Their absence from the dispersed acoustic spectrum associated with [@] indicates a stage on which the phonetic sound and fury of [@]'s formants phonologically signify nothing.

In phonemic and quasi-phonemic transcription 'ə' is frequently employed as a cover symbol to designate a vowel-reduction reflex. The range of phonetic qualities indicated by the symbol in the literature is quite impressive; in terms of the traditional vowel diagram, it covers varying degrees of openness, backness and roundness. (In transcriptions of Catalan, for example, it symbolizes a relatively open value, in Moroccan Arabic relatively close, and in French front rounded.) Some aspects of this variability are phonologically insignificant, but others evidently involve distinct phonological categories. In the former case, variability across languages can be taken to reflect indeterminacies in the fixing of the base line on which other resonance components are superimposed. From a speech production viewpoint, this variability is sometimes characterized in terms of different articulatory or vocal settings. (For a review and discussion of the relevant literature, see Laver 1980.)

In element theory, the independent realization of [@] may be understood as covering that area of the traditional vowel diagram which is non-palatal, non-open and non-labial. Non-peripheral categories that are potentially distinct from this base line can then be thought of as displaced versions of the neutral quality. In terms of their segmental make-up, these different reflexes can be characterized as compounds in which [@] is fused with some other element(s). The relatively open ə of Catalan, for example, can be represented as a combination of [@] and [A].

The idea that [@] defines the base line on which other resonances are superimposed can be implemented by assuming that it does not reside on an independent autosegmental tier. Rather it is omnipresent in segmental expressions but fails to manifest itself wherever it is overridden by any other element(s) that may be present. Viewed in these terms, reduction to a centralized vocalic reflex does not involve the random substitution of one set of elements by [@]. Rather it consists in the stripping away of elementary content to reveal a latently present [@].

One of the advantages of viewing centralization in this way is that it unifies the representation of the process with that of certain processes of raising and lowering which, although not involving reduction to non-peripheral reflexes, nevertheless occur under the same prosodically weak conditions. A widespread phenomenon in the world's languages is a tendency for mid vowels to be banished from prosodically recessive nuclear positions. In metrical systems, recessiveness refers to positions of weak stress; in harmony systems, it refers to nuclei whose harmonic identity is determined by an adjacent dominant nucleus. Under such conditions, it is common to find neutralization of vocalic contrasts in favour of either non-peripheral reflexes or the 'corner' vowels *a, i, u* or some mixture of both. The height harmony systems reviewed in Section 3 are uniformly of the peripheral type. Non-harmonic cases exhibiting similar patterns of neutralization include Bulgarian and Catalan, in which raising and centralization cooccur. In Bulgarian, the stressed five-vowel system (*i, e, a, o, u*) contracts to three vowels under weak stress, with the mid vowels raising to high and *a* undergoing centralization (Petterson and Wood 1987). The stressed seven-term system of Catalan (*i, e, ɛ, a, ɔ, o, u*) gives way to three terms under weak stress: the *a-ɛ-e* contrast is neutralized centrally, the *ɔ-o-u* contrast is neutralized under *u*, and *i* remains as it is (Palmada 1991: ch. 2).

The fact that the processes just mentioned, raising or lowering of mid vowels and centralization, all potentially occur in the same general recessive context indicates that we are dealing with a single phenomenon. Although this commonality has long been recognized, it has not always been clear how it should be captured formally. In terms of element structure, however, the processes in question are uniformly expressible as decomposition; all involve the total or partial suppression of segmental material.

Summarizing the foregoing discussion of [@], we may identify two main respects in which it differs from other elements. First, it lacks the distinct peak-valley patterns of [A], [I] and [U]. Second, it is latently present in all segmental expressions. One question that remains is how the latter notion is to be accommodated in the mechanism of element fusion. According to Kaye et al. (1985), the desired result can be achieved by assuming that the only circumstances under which [@] contributes anything to the phonetic interpretation of a compound segment are when the element acts as the head of the expression. It will thus fail to make its presence felt in any expression in which it occurs as a dependent. The only circumstances under which latent [@] can become audible are when it is promoted to headship as a result of other elements in the expression undergoing suppression or relegation to dependent status.

4.4   ATR

Let us now turn to ATR, another dimension implicated in peripherality contrasts, most famously those associated with some kind of harmonic alternation. The treatment of ATR harmony remains a hotly disputed topic (one that is potentially bound up with height harmony, since, for some researchers at least, the two dimensions are of a piece). Issues on which there continues to be rather less than general agreement include the following. What are the relevant primes? Is there evidence to support the recognition of retracted tongue root harmony systems? How are transparency and opacity effects involving ATR to be represented? It is not part of our brief to examine these points in detail. All we can do is make some very general observations about the status of ATR in element theory.

Broadly speaking, there have been two element-based approaches to the representation of ATR. One is to posit an independent [ATR] element, the solution preferred by Kaye et al. (1985). Another is to derive the distinction between ATR and non-ATR vowels structurally, by means of different combinations of [A], [I], [U] and [@]. One version of the latter approach resorts to the element-stacking device mentioned in Section 4.2. According to Smith (1988) and van der Hulst (1989), ATR i, for example, contains two instances of [I] (with differing dependency status), while non-ATR ι contains only one. (In Dependency Phonology, ATR is represented both structurally and in terms of an independent prime; see Anderson and Ewen 1987.)

There are at least two factors weighing against the positing of a privative [ATR] element. For one thing, it detaches the theory from the original insight that the bounds of vowel space are defined by the extremes represented by i, a and u. It implies that non-ATR vowels are less complex than their ATR congeners. The independent manifestations of [I] and [U] are thus taken to be non-ATR ι and υ respectively – not i and u, which are now represented as [I, ATR] and [U, ATR]. (The realization of [A] remains as a, which is non-ATR in any event.) The prediction inherent in this arrangement – that the unmarked three-vowel system is a-ι-υ – fails to tally with the empirical record.

There is a further, this time theory-internal, reason for being suspicious of an independent [ATR] element. As Kaye et al. (1985) acknowledge, it is anomalous in being the only element whose contribution to the make-up of compound expressions must be considered constant, irrespective of whether it is a head or dependent. According to these authors, the ability of elements to combine within a compound is controlled by their 'charm' values. (In brief, elements of opposite charm attract, while those of like charm repel one another.) The overall charm value of an expression is determined by the head element. This is assumed to hold of all cases – except those involving [ATR], which anomalously imposes its charm value on an expression even as a dependent.

There are reasons for supposing that ATR can and should be derived by exploiting otherwise well-established properties of the theory rather than by adding to the pool of elements. The question is whether a purely structural definition of ATR is achievable without sacrificing the principle of interpretational autonomy through recourse to element stacking. One proposal is that non-ATR high and mid vowels, unlike their ATR counterparts, contain an active [@] (Lass 1984: 277 ff). Given the recessive behaviour of this element in compounds, this implies that such vowels are [@]-headed. Thus, as before, the basic set of non-low vowels is assumed to be ATR i, u, e, o, as shown in (10a). The non-ATR set is then represented as in (10b).[13]

(10)

(a) ATR		(b) non-ATR	
[I̲, @]	i	[I, @]	ɪ
[U̲, @]	u	[U, @]	ʊ
[A, I̲, @]	e	[A, I, @̲]	ɛ
[A, U̲, @]	o	[A, U, @̲]	ɔ

Besides representing the unmarkedness of *i/u* *vis-à-vis* ɪ/ʊ (Maddieson 1984, Lindsey 1990), this arrangement makes sense from a signal point of view. In non-low vocalic space, each non-ATR vowel is characterized by an attenuation of the well-defined peak-valley pattern that is associated with its ATR counterpart. This is consistent with the mode of representation of ɪ, ʊ, ɛ, ɔ given in (10b). This allows us to view the elemental patterns contributed by the active resonance elements [A], [I] and [U] as being muffled as a result of their being subordinated to the neutral pattern defined by head [@]. It should be emphasized that it is not formants but the patterns of other elements that are attenuated by [@] under such circumstances. The autonomous realization of [@] as some schwa-like object constitutes 'pure' attenuation, the absence of other elements' patterns.

The question now is whether this treatment is capable of representing processes involving ATR, particularly those harmonic cases which have been analysed in feature terms as the autosegmental spreading of [+ ATR] or [− ATR].[14] In the absence of an independent privative [ATR] element, we have to assume that all such cases conform to the non-spreading pattern illustrated in the analysis of Pasiego discussed in Section 3. That is, they involve changes in the internal representation of harmonizing vowels, triggered by particular conditions obtaining in the dominant vowel within the harmonic span. ATR alternations take the form of switches in the headship of vocalic expressions, with [@]-headedness in non-low vowels representing non-ATR. Note that this does not involve the insertion or spreading of [@]. Given the latent presence of [@] in all segments, such alternations are entirely isomeric. That is, the manifestation of this element within a particular vocalic expression is simply a reflection of its promotion to head status. ATR harmony is thus a matter of what might be termed *head agreement*; that is, the head elements of all vowels within a given harmonic span are aligned (Lowenstamm and Prunet 1988, Charette and Kaye 1993). In Akan (Clements 1981), for example, the head elements of non-low vowels are aligned as in (11).

(11)

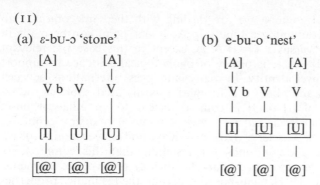

(a) ɛ-bʊ-ɔ 'stone'   (b) e-bu-o 'nest'

Either all vowels within a span are [@]-headed, in which case a non-ATR domain is defined (as in (11a)), or they are headed by an element on the [U/I] tier, in which case an ATR domain is defined (as in (11b)).[15]

5 Elements for consonants

In this section, we focus almost exclusively on the resonance characteristics of consonants (Section 5.1) and on the dimension traditionally referred to as 'manner' (Section 5.2). Lack of space precludes us from discussing laryngeal contrasts in any detail, and we will abstract away from this dimension in much of what follows. (On the nature of independent laryngeal elements, see Kaye et al. 1990 and Brockhaus 1992.) Nor will we have anything to say about nasality; given the current state of our knowledge, it is not clear whether this should be represented by an autonomous nasal element or is more appropriately subsumed under one of the laryngeal elements. (On the phonological evidence supporting a laryngeal–nasal connection, see, for example, Piggott 1992.) We conclude the section with a consideration of the applicability of segmental geometry to element theory.

5.1 Resonance elements

It is now widely acknowledged that the resonance/cavity characteristics of consonants and vowels are represented in terms of the same set of primes, rather than in terms of separate sets as assumed in SPE (e.g. Smith 1988, Clements 1991b). This commonality is most obviously illustrated in the case of glides, which are segmentally identical to vowels and differ only in terms of their syllabic affiliation. The transcriptional distinction between *u* and *w*, for example, records the difference between occupation of a nuclear head and occupation of any other type of position (such as an onset). In terms of segmental content, we are dealing with the same object – an expression containing a lone [U]. A similar point can be made in respect of *i* versus *y* (= IPA *j*), except in this case the relevant element is [I]. There is plenty of phonological evidence to support this glide-vowel identity. In many languages, alternations between high vowels and glides are straightforwardly analysable as the re-assignment of [I] or [U] from a nuclear to an adjacent onset position, as in French *avu* – *avwe* < avoue – avouer > 'confess', *si* – *sye* < scie – scier > '(to) saw' (Kaye and Lowenstamm 1984).

There are good grounds for assuming that this commonality extends to the resonance characteristics of non-vocalic segments. According to one element-based proposal, the resonance properties contributed to consonants by [A], [I] and [U] vary according to their status as heads or dependents (Smith 1988, van der Hulst 1989). Our more optimistic assumption, following Jakobson, is that the elements in question maintain relatively stable, albeit gross patterns. So, for example, the rUmp elemental pattern [U], besides inhering in labial vowels, also shows up as a spectral associate of labial consonants (what Blumstein and Stevens 1981 identify as a 'diffuse-falling' spectral pattern).

[I] is present in palatal and palatalized consonants, while [A] is present in uvulars and pharyngeals. According to one view, coronal-ity requires an additional element ([R]), on which more presently. The exponence of [@] can be informally described in articulatory terms as non-coronal, non-palatal, non-labial and non-low, which suggests that it should be considered the resonance element in velar consonants.

The assumption that the resonance elements are shared by all types of segments, vocalic as well as non-vocalic, is supported by a range of assimilatory processes showing consonant-vowel interactions. These are straightforwardly treated in terms of ele-ment spreading, as in the palatalization of consonants before front vowels, where the active element is [I]. In similar fashion, [U] is implicated in labialization ([U]), while [A] is active in the lowering of vowels in the context of a uvular or pharyngeal consonant.

Non-assimilatory processes, particularly those involving lenition, provide further support for the notion that the resonance elements inherent in consonantal segments are identical to those in vowels. One class of lenition process takes the form of vocalization, the reduction of a consonantal segment to its homorganic vocalic counterpart. (In the case of a plosive target, the process historically passes through a fricative stage, as in *b* > *β* > *w*.) Typical vocaliz-ing outcomes include the following:

(12)

	Residual element
(a) p → w, m → w	[U]
(b) č → y, λ → y	[I]
(c) k → (γ →) θ	[@]
(d) t → r	[R]

Each of these is exemplified in the following representative alternations: [16]

(13)

(a) Korean: *ki:p-t'a − kiw-ə* 'sew'
    Irish: *mo:r − wo:r* (fem.) 'big'
(b) Arbore: *gerrač − gerray-me* 'thief'
    Spanish: *vaλe − vaye* 'valley'
(c) Turkish: *inek − ine[ø] − i* 'cow'
    Welsh: *garð − (ei* 'his') *[ø]arð* 'garden'
(d) English: < a[t]omic > − < a[D]om >
    Korean: *si:t-t'a − sir-ə* 'to load'

Processes of this type are straightforwardly represented as the suppression of all elementary content save that relating to resonance (Harris 1990b). In each example in (13), the residual reflex reflects the primary resonance property of the leniting segment. Each of these properties can be equated with an element, as shown in (12).

Vocalization of velars (13c) typically results in reduction to zero, sometimes via γ. This development is not unexpected, given the assumption that velar resonance is associated with the element [@]. Independently, [@] manifests itself as approximant γ (non-syllabic i), but the lack of an active resonance component in this element is predicted to make it particularly likely to be eclipsed when not supported by other elementary material.

It would be consistent with the line of reasoning pursued thus far to consider the tapped *r* reflex in (13d) to be the independent realization of a coronal element, [R]. This is indeed the position taken, for example, in Kaye et al. (1989) and Harris and Kaye (1990), and it is the one we will simply assume here without further argument. However, certain considerations suggest that this view is probably in need of reappraisal. For one thing, a single pattern signature for [R] has proved somewhat elusive. (Some attempt at a definition is made in Lindsey and Harris 1990.) For another, there is a growing body of evidence indicating that specific representational provision needs to be made for the special status of coronals among the resonance categories of consonants. (The issues are conveniently summarized in Paradis and Prunet 1991a.) Among the well-known peculiarities are the following: coronals are more prone to assimilation than other classes; consonant harmony exclusively affects coronals (at least in adult language); and coronals, unlike other resonance classes, behave transparently with respect to many processes.

Facts such as these have prompted a variety of analyses in which coronals are represented as 'placeless' consonants. In Dependency Phonology, for example, it has been suggested that they lack a place component (Anderson & Ewen 1981). According to various feature-geometric analyses, coronal is deemed the default place category, underlyingly unspecified for the PLACE node. (For a selection of examples, see Paradis and Prunet 1991b.) In this way, it is possible to account for the propensity for coronals to assimilate: they are underspecified at the point where spreading of the PLACE node takes place. For the same reason, they can be transparent to vowel-harmony processes involving the spreading of PLACE.

Treating coronality as an independent [R] element, on a par with any other, fails to capture the special properties of coronals. Following the lead of the analyses just mentioned, we might suggest that coronality has no elementary representation. However, the implications of such a move for element theory would be much more radical than anything countenanced in current underspecification approaches. It would banish coronality from phonology altogether. That is, *coronal* would be similar to *glottal* in being an exclusively articulatory detail. (This line of enquiry has recently been pursued by Backley 1993.) The question is whether this move can be made without jeopardizing the insight that glottal segments are the classic 'placeless' reduction consonants.

5.2 'Manner'

From the perspective of element theory, vocalization is on a representational par with the lowering and raising of mid vowels discussed in Section 2. All of these processes take the form of decomposition – the dissolution of compound segmental expressions resulting from the suppression of elementary material. The significance of such processes is that their outcomes allow us to identify the independent manifestations of individual elements. The same principle can be applied to the task of determining further elements implicated in consonantal contrasts, for example those that are suppressed in the vocalization processes illustrated in (13). An obvious place to start looking in this case is debuccalization, the process by which the resonance properties of consonants are stripped away. Lenitions of this type can reasonably be expected to lay bare those elements that are associated with the 'manner' dimensions of consonants.

As far as obstruents are concerned, there are two types of

weakening process that can be considered to have this disclosing effect. These occur on two lenition trajectories, which may be schematized as follows (cf. Lass and Anderson 1975: Ch. 5):

(14)
   (a) Spirantization   > 'aspiration' > deletion
       plosive > fricative > h   > ∅

   (b) Loss of release   > glottalling > deletion
       plosive > unreleased stop > ?   > ∅

Lenition trajectories such as these are established on the basis of cross-linguistic observations of the directionality of diachronic change. There is no implication that every lenition process inexorably culminates in elision. Historical progression through the various stages on a particular path may be arrested at some point, with the result that two or more stages on a particular trajectory may be retained within the same phonological grammar as stable alternants or distributional variants. Typical alternations involving the 'opening' types of lenition schematized in (14) include the following: [17]

(15)
   (a) Central American Spanish: *mes* − *meh* − *me* 'month'
   (b) Tiberian Hebrew: *malki* 'my king' − *melex* 'king'
   (c) Malay (Johore): *masak-an* − *masaʔ* 'to cook'
   (d) English: < ge[t] no > − < ge[t⁻] no > − < ge[?] no >

The weakest sounds on a lenition path are those occupying the penultimate stage; they represent the last vestige of a segment before it disappears altogether. Combining the autonomous interpretation hypothesis with a view of lenition as segmental decomposition leads us to conclude that the penultimate stages in (14), namely *h* and *ʔ*, are primitive segments; that is, each is the independent embodiment of a single element. The recognition of these two elements, [h] and [?] (Kaye et al. 1989), is strongly reminiscent of Lass and Anderson's (1975) insight that the segments in question are the 'reduction' consonants *par excellence*. Elsewhere we have explored the consequences of taking [h] and [?] to be the main 'manner' elements in consonantal contrasts (Harris 1990b, Lindsey and Harris 1990).

The elemental pattern associated with [?] may be described as *edge* or *stop*. In signal terms, it manifests itself as an abrupt and sustained drop in overall amplitude. This effect is achieved by a non-continuant articulatory gesture of the type that characterizes oral and nasal stops and laterals. The independent manifestation of [?] as a glottal stop is due to the fact that the element lacks any inherent resonance property. In element theory, glottal place is thus non-specified in the sense described in Section 3.1. The use of glottal location to produce the independent manifestation of [?] is a purely articulatory affair: it is the only articulatory means of orchestrating the amplitude drop of the relevant elemental pattern without introducing resonance characteristics into the signal.

This point underlines the care that needs to be exercised in making sense of the notion that elements are, as is sometimes claimed, individually *pronounceable* (Kaye et al. 1985: 306). To say that each element is independently interpretable is not to say that it can be targeted by executing a unique articulatory gesture. The performance of a particular elemental pattern typically involves the arrangement of one or more of an ensemble of gestures.

In compound segments, the constriction necessary to produce the edge pattern of [?] will be located at whatever place produces the acoustic effects associated with a resonance element occurring in the same expression. For example, fusion of [?] with [U] implies labial constriction. Stops with other places of articulation are formed by fusion of [?] with [A] (uvular), [I] (palatal), [@] (velar), or, if such an element is recognized, [R] (coronal).

The elemental pattern of [h] may be identified as 'noise', manifested in the speech signal as aperiodic energy. The articulatory execution of this effect involves a narrowed stricture which produces turbulent airflow. Noise defined in these terms is present in released obstruents (plosives, affricates, fricatives) but is absent from sonorants and unreleased oral stops. Just as with [?], the absence of any supralaryngeal gesture in the independent articulation of [h] is entirely a function of the fact that it lacks its own resonance property. In compounds with other elements, however, the location of the noise-producing gesture will be determined by whatever resonance element may also be present.

The contrast between strident and non-strident fricatives can be expressed in terms of different relations of headedness involving [h] and those elements which contribute supralaryngeal resonance. Strident fricatives, in view of their relative noisiness (in the sense of displaying higher-intensity aperiodic energy), may be assumed to be [h]-headed, unlike their non-strident counterparts:

(16)

[h̲, U]	f	[h, U̲]	ʍ
[h̲, R]	s	[h, R̲]	θ
[h̲, I]	ʃ	[h, I̲]	ç
		[h, @̲]	x
[h̲, A]	χ	[h, A̲]	ħ

Treating all types of lenition as segmental decomposition implies that movement along any of the trajectories in (12) or (14) takes the form of decomplexification – a progressive depletion of the stock of elements contained in a segment. Let us pursue the consequences of this view for the various stages on the opening trajectory in (14a). If *h* is the least complex segment, the plosive input must be the most complex and oral fricatives of intermediate complexity. An oral fricative differs from *h* by one degree of complexity: as indicated in the last paragraph, the former contains a resonance element that is absent from the latter. By the same token, the internal structure of a plosive includes whatever elementary material is present in a homorganic fricative but is more complex than the latter by virtue of the presence of an additional element, the stop property represented by [?].[18] This line of reasoning leads us to conclude that [h] inheres in all released obstruents, both plosives and fricatives. Thus weakening along trajectory (14a) may be expressed as the progressive suppression of elementary material, here illustrated by labials:

(17)

Spirantization/aspiration	p	[h, U, ?]
	f	[h, U]
	h	[h]

Spirantization is frequently preceded by affrication, as illustrated in the High German Consonant Shift: *p* > *pf* > *f*; *t* > *ts* > *s*; and *k* > *kx* > *x* (the *kx* reflex is only attested in some dialects). We make the standard current assumption that affricates are contour segments consisting of stop and fricative expressions attached to a single position. In element terms, this implies that [h] and [?] are not fused in such structures. Thus the [U] that is present in, say, *pf* is separately fused with [?] and [h].

The difference between released and unreleased oral stops is represented in terms of the presence versus absence of [h]: plosive *p* is [h, U, ?], whereas unreleased *p⁻* is [U, ?]. Suppression of [h] is thus one stage on the lenition trajectory in (14b), while debuccalization of an unreleased stop to *?* results from the suppression of its resonance element:

(18)

Loss of release/glottalling	p	[h, U, ?]
	p⁻	[U, ?]
	?	[?]

Vocalization of a plosive consists in the suppression of both [h] and [?], leaving a lone resonance element:

(19)

Vocalization   p   [h, U, ?]
              w   [U]

Vocalization of a true voiceless obstruent also implies the suppression of the relevant laryngeal element. (No such change accompanies the vocalization of so-called 'partially voiced' or neutral obstruents, since they already lack a laryngeal element.) By its very
nature, a vocalic segment is produced with physiological voicing.
But it would be misguided to attempt to represent vocalization as
the acquisition of an active laryngeal prime (such as [+ voice]). The
phonetic voicing of a vocalized reflex, being of the spontaneous
type, is simply a secondary effect of the phonological process
which strips away the segment's obstruent-defining properties.[19]

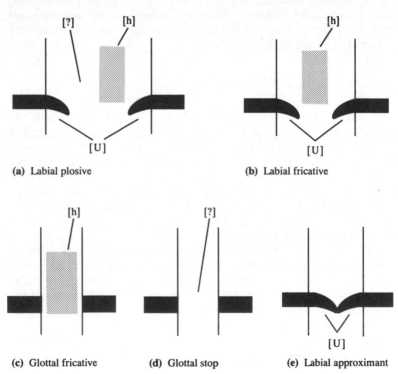

FIGURE 2.3 Stylized spectrograms showing various combinations of the elements [?]
(edge), [h] (noise), and [U] (rUmp). Different types of lenition are defined by the
suppression of particular elemental patterns: (b) spirantization, (c) 'aspiration'
(debuccalization to h, (d) glottalling (debuccalization to ?, and (e) vocalization.

Elsewhere, we have demonstrated how the various effects of lenition can be simulated by excising certain portions of the acoustic signal associated with plosives. Each of these portions can be taken to instantiate a particular elemental pattern (Lindsey and Harris 1990). The results relating to the various stages in (17), (18) and (19) are illustrated in the stylized spectrograms shown in Figure 2.3.

The term *fortition* or *strengthening* is usually applied to processes which turn approximants or fricatives into homorganic stops. That is, they represent the converse of a subset of the lenition processes schematized in (12) and (14). The classic fortition cases are assimilatory in nature. For example, a fricative may be hardened to a plosive in the context of a nasal consonant, as in Sesotho *fa* 'give'— *m-phɛ* 'give me'. The strengthening effect commonly displayed by nasal stops indicates that they, just like oral stops, contain [?]. Fortition in such cases is thus straightforwardly treated as the spreading of [?] from the nasal into the fricative. Fusing [?] with [U, h] (= *f*) yields [?, U, h], a labial plosive.

Different head-dependent configurations in expressions containing [?] enable us to capture various types of manner and resonance contrasts among non-continuant consonants. Labial-velar stops, like their approximant and fricative congeners, can be assumed to be [U]-headed. This leaves plain labial stops as [?]-headed. On theory-internal grounds, velars must be considered [@]-headed. This follows from the assumption that [@] is unable to make an active contribution to the resonance profile of a segment unless it occurs as the head of the expression.

The contrast between laterals and coronal stops, it has been argued, is also a matter of headship (Kaye et al. 1989). According to this analysis, *l* is [R, ?], while coronal stops are [R]-headed. The phonological plausibility of the relation that is predicted by this arrangement is based on frequently observed alternations between *l* and *d/t* (e.g. Sesotho *bal-a* − *bad-ile* 'read/count'). It also has a certain phonetic plausibility: whether or not [R] is the head of an expression might be expected to be reflected in the degree of lingual contact associated with the closure contributed by [?]. The [R]- headedness of coronal stops is consistent with full contact, both medial and lateral. The partial (medial) contact required for the production of laterals is consistent with the relegation of [R] to dependent status.

5.3 Elements and geometry
Together with nasality, the elements [?] and [h] allow us to represent all the major manner contrasts among constricted segments. The nearest corresponding feature values might be taken to be [− continuant] and [+ continuant] respectively, but the equivalence

is only very rough. For one thing, [h], unlike [+continuant], inheres in plosives. Note, moreover, that the version of element theory presented here lacks anything equivalent to the features [sonorant] or [consonantal]. These categories are becoming increasingly anomalous within current feature theory in any event. It is quite possible that, like the now-abandoned feature [syllabic], they represent obsolescent throw-backs to pre-linear theory. That is, the major class distinctions they were originally designed to express are more appropriately represented not in terms of primes but in terms of prosodic constituency. (This may not seem quite so obvious in the case of [sonorant], particularly in view of the widespread process of final obstruent devoicing, the phenomenon perhaps most often cited as evidence in support of the feature. However, this argument is no longer persuasive, in view of the increasing acknowledgement that only obstruents bear a distinctive (non-spontaneous) voice feature and are thus the only segments susceptible to this type of devoicing (see, for example, Rice and Avery 1990, Brockhaus 1992).)

In recent feature theory, [sonorant], [consonantal] and other manner features, particularly [continuant], have had something of a chequered history. This is reflected in ongoing disagreements over whether an independent manner node needs to be recognized in the hierarchical arrangement of features that is assumed in most current research. This mode of representation is motivated by the insight that primes, no less than segments, pattern into natural classes. If we are to maintain the constraining principle that each phonological process can access only one unit in a representation, then we need to make the assumption that primes are hierarchically organized into classes (Clements and Hume, forthcoming). The by-now familiar geometric model in which this assumption culminates

(20)

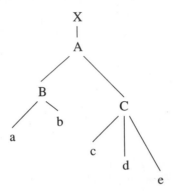

is illustrated in (20), where upper-case letters stand for class nodes, while the terminal nodes in lower-case represent primes (Clements 1985a, Sagey 1986, McCarthy 1988, Pulleybank, this volume). Under this arrangement, each process may address either an individual prime or a class node. In the latter case, the whole class of primes dominated by that node is automatically also affected.

The class nodes for which there is the firmest empirical support are those shown in the geometric fragment in (21).

(21)

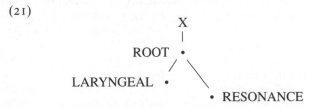

Each of these nodes can be shown to correspond to a particular recurrent grouping of primes. Under the RESONANCE (or PLACE) node are gathered those primes which can be observed to pattern together, for example, in place assimilation processes. The LARYNGEAL node is motivated by the independent and unified behaviour of primes involved in tonal and phonation-type contrasts. Both of these class nodes are grouped under ROOT, the matrix node which defines the integrity of the melodic unit. The latter concept is justified on the basis of the potential for segments to be spread or delinked in their entirety.

The nodes in (21) have a purely organizing function; that is, they are devoid of any intrinsic phonetic content. In element geometry, this can be assumed to be a defining property of class nodes; in keeping with the autonomous interpretation hypothesis, only elements themselves are independently interpretable. In this respect, feature geometry is quite different, in part a reflection of the articulatory bias of the theory. Particular organizing nodes in the feature hierarchy are deemed to have 'intrinsic phonetic' content (Sagey 1986). Of this type are the so-called articulator nodes, e.g. [coronal], under which may be grouped, depending on the version of the theory, such features as [anterior], [distributed], [lateral] and [strident].

If there is more or less general agreement on the class nodes given in (21), this can certainly not be said of nodes which have been posited for grouping manner and major-class distinctions. Even among phonologists who assume there is evidence to support such a view, there is considerable disagreement about where such nodes should be located in the geometric model and about whether these dimensions are themselves subdivided into further class nodes.

(For competing views on this matter, see, for example, Clements 1985a, Sagey 1986, McCarthy 1988, Avery and Rice 1989 and the articles in Paradis and Prunet 1991b.) Take the features [sonorant], [consonantal] and [continuant] for example. According to one proposal, the first two of these are lodged in the ROOT node, which directly dominates [continuant] (among other things) (e.g. McCarthy 1988). Another approach assumes the same relation between ROOT and [continuant] but posits an independent SUPRALARYNGEAL node dominating [sonorant] and PLACE (e.g. Avery and Rice 1989). In their gestural analogue of feature geometry, Browman and Goldstein (1989) suggest a third arrangement, under which separate specifications for [constriction degree] (roughly equivalent to [continuant]) are attached to each terminal node in the hierarchy specifying place.

Whichever of these solutions is adopted, none is able to represent the lenition processes discussed in the last section in a unified manner. Debuccalization to *h*, for example, calls for the simultaneous delinking of PLACE and a change from [−continuant] to [+continuant]. Vocalization of plosives requires simultaneous changes in [sonorant] (minus to plus), [consonantal] (plus to minus) and [continuant] (minus to plus). In both cases, arbitrary conjunctions of features and nodes have to be manipulated, in clear violation of the principle that each phonological process should only be allowed to address a single representational unit. And in the first case the two independent operations are of different types: delinking and feature-change.

These particular problems, we believe, are ungainly artefacts of the articulatory pre-occupation of orthodox feature theory. More gener-

(22)

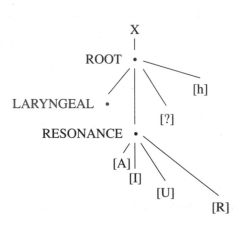

ally, this bias can be considered ultimately responsible for the lack of agreement on the featural representation of manner contrasts.

Freed of articulatory bias, element theory is able to represent lenition in a uniform and direct manner. Assuming the rather simple geometric arrangement in (22), we can express each step along a weakening trajectory as the delinking of a single element or node. Given the notion that lenition is uniformly expressed as decomposition, the number of weakening processes to which a segment is susceptible is logically limited by the number of elements of which it is composed. Debuccalization involves delinking of the RESONANCE node (and thus any element it dominates). In spirantization, it is [?] that is delinked. Subsequent vocalization implies delinking of [h], resulting in a loss of release burst. None of these operations needs to make reference to anything resembling major-class features. In keeping with the autonomous interpretation hypothesis, the outcome of any decomposition process is automatically defined by the independent manifestation of any element that remains present in the representation. Once a given element is delinked, no auxiliary operations are needed to adjust the representation to ensure that remaining segmental material can be phonetically interpreted.

6 Summary

The elements of phonological representation are monovalent entities which enjoy stand-alone phonetic interpretability throughout derivation. This conception of phonological primes informs a view of derivation which is in the strict sense generative and which dispenses with a systematic phonetic level of representation.

Elements are cognitive categories by reference to which listeners parse and speakers articulate speech sounds. They are mappable in the first instance not onto articulations but rather onto sound [sic] patterns. They constitute universal expectations regarding the structures to be inferred from acoustic signals and to be mimicked in the course of articulatory maturation. No phonological process, we claim, requires modality-specific reference to auditory or vocal anatomy. In particular, we deny any need to recapitulate the latter in the manner of feature-geometric biopsies.

Notes and Acknowledgements

1. Our thanks to Outi Bat-El, Wiebke Brockhaus, Phil Carr, Jacques Durand, Edmund Gussmann, Doug Pulleyblank and Neil Smith for their helpful comments on earlier drafts.
2. Some versions of Dependency Phonology permit segment classes to be identified by means of the Boolean operator $\sim$ (e.g. $\sim$ [A] 'not [A]'), a move which immediately reclassifies an opposition as equipollent (Anderson & Ewen 1980).
3. The low vowel *a* in Chichewa and related systems does not trigger lowering harmony, e.g. *bal-its-a* 'give birth (causative)' (* *bal-ets-a*). Moreover, it blocks the rightward propagation of harmony, e.g. *lemb-an-its-a* 'write (reciprocal-causative)' (* *lemb-an-ets-a*). In an element-based approach, this effect is derived by specifying that [A] is harmonically active only when it occurs as a **dependent** within a segmental expression (Harris and Moto 1989). (On the notion of intra-segmental dependency, see Section 4.2.) [A] is thus active in *e* and *o*, where it has dependent status, but is inert in *a*, where it is the head of the segment.
4. For the purposes of this comparison, we may set on one side the treatment of low vowels, which exhibit neutral behaviour in this system. An element-based analysis of this phenomenon (see Harris 1990a) exploits the notion of intrasegmental dependency, in a fashion similar to the Bantu height analysis just discussed.
5. We owe this analogy to Jonathan Kaye (personal communication).
6. This issue is not addressed in recent psycholinguistic applications of feature underspecification (e.g. Lahiri and Marslen-Wilson 1991, Stemberger 1991).
7. There have always been at least some dissenting voices against the Gadarene rush from acoustic to articulatory features, Andersen's being a particularly eloquent example (1972, 1974: 42–3).
8. As Phil Carr has pointed out to us, this means that phonetic events cannot be considered *tokens* of element *types*. Assuming such a relationship of instantiation would imply that the two sets of entities were of the same ontological status. This view is incompatible with the notion that elements, unlike physical articulatory and acoustic events, are uniformly cognitive.
9. Precise modelling of the computations by which the speaker-hearer detects such patterns in acoustic signals is of course no trivial matter. But we assume it is no easier, and probably more difficult, to model detectors of [high], [low], [back] and [round] in X-ray movies of natural speech articulation.
10. This means that our occasional labelling of [U] for convenience as 'labiality' must be taken with an especially large pinch of phonetic salt. Jakobson's term *flatness*, regrettably out of fashion except among Dependency Phonologists (Anderson and Ewen 1987), is much to be preferred.

11. Again, precise modelling of the cognitive computations by which headedness can be detected in acoustic signals is hardly likely to be a simple research programme. (For a preliminary element-based attempt, see Williams and Brockhaus 1992.) But there is no reason to suspect that the challenge is in principle any more difficult than the corresponding one of modelling the detection of assorted values of [high], [low] and [back] in articulatory movies.

   It should be noted that taking relative and gradient signal preponderance as the phonetic interpretation of phonological headedness does not entail a gradient conception of headedness itself. The number of ways in which multi-element compounds may be headed is constrained by purely phonological considerations.

12. By analogy with the terms mAss, dIp and rUmp, we might dub the element [@] **neutr@l**.

13. As noted above, inherently non-ATR *a* is still to be taken as simplex [A]. The neutral behaviour this vowel typically exhibits in ATR harmony systems is then related to its representational distinctiveness *vis-à-vis* non-low vowels, which are either [@]-headed (non-ATR) or headed on the [I/U]-tier (see the discussion of Akan below).

14. Not all harmony systems that have been analysed in terms of the feature [±ATR] should automatically be submitted to the treatment outlined here. A subset of such systems can be shown to involve the spreading of other elements. For reanalyses of some allegedly ATR patterns in terms of [A]-spread, see for example van der Hulst (1988b) and Anderson and Durand (1988).

15. The participation of *a* in a more restricted form of harmony in Akan requires a separate analysis. For the arguments, see Clements (1981) and Archangeli and Pulleyblank (1992: 186).

16. Sources for the data in (13): Sang Jik Rhee and Yong Heo (personal communication) (Korean), and Hayward (1984) (Arbore).

17. Sources for the data in (14): James Harris 1983 (Spanish), Leben 1980 (Hebrew), Farid 1980 (Malay).

18. The notion that the relation among plosives, fricatives and *h* involves a progressive loss of closure is made explicit in the description of opening provided by Lass and Anderson (1975).

19. For this reason, Lass and Anderson's (1975) term for this phenomenon, **sonorization**, seems more appropriate than **voicing**.

Chapter 3

Radical CV Phonology: the categorial gesture

Harry van der Hulst

1 Goals

'Radical CV Phonology' is a variant of Dependency Phonology (Anderson and Jones 1974, Anderson and Ewen 1987). The symbols C and V do *not* refer to skeletal units in the sense of Clements and Keyser (1983), but to two phonological features, which play a pivotal role in this chapter and in the theory I develop here. Radical CV Phonology shares with Dependency Phonology most of its 'leading ideas' and tries to further develop the execution of these in specific domains. In this chapter the domain I focus on is *segmental structure* and, specifically, non-place properties.

The organization of this chapter is as follows. In Section 2 I will offer an overview of the framework of Dependency Phonology as presented in Anderson and Ewen (1987), henceforth AE, limiting myself to the segmental domain.[1] In Section 3 I will then present a critique of AE's model and in Section 4 I proceed with outlining the Radical CV alternative. Section 5 contains a summary of the main points of my proposal and specifies areas for further research.

2 An introduction to Dependency Phonology

The most fundamental principle of Dependency Phonology (henceforth DP) is the idea that units (or constituents) which are combined to form higher level units (or constituents) enter into a head – dependency relation. With specific reference to the level of segmental organization, we can formulate further leading ideas of DP as follows: the primes of phonology ('features') form constituents *within phonological segments*, which are called *gestures* (comparable to 'feature classes dominated by a class node' in

Clements 1985a, but not to the 'gestures' in Browman and Goldstein 1989 which are defined in their model as the primitive
actions of the vocal tract articulators). A further central claim is that
the features are *privative*, and are called *components* (comparable
to 'unary features'). The term *component* will not be used here,
however, and instead I will use the term *element* (cf. Kaye et al. 1985,
Harris and Lindsey this volume, Brockhaus this volume).

DP recognizes two major gestures, the *categorial* and the *articulatory* gesture, and, in addition, a *tonological* gesture. Both major
gestures contain two sub-gestures and all four sub-gestures contain
a number of elements. The topic of this chapter will be on the
categorial gesture, which in standard DP contains a *phonatory*
sub-gesture (for elements expressing manner or stricture properties)
and an *initiatory* sub-gesture (for elements expressing airstream
properties and glottal states). The articulatory gesture contains the
locational sub-gesture (with elements for place properties) and an
oro-nasal sub-gesture containing just one element (viz. nasal), as in
(1) below.

(1)   *Anderson and Ewen (1987)*

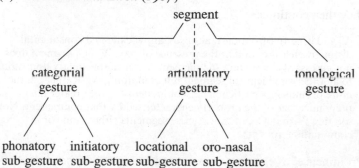

The relevance of feature grouping has long been recognized in DP.
Already in Lass and Anderson (1975) and Lass (1976) a number of
specific arguments are put forward that support the view that the
matrix characterizing the segment should be split up into at least
two sub-matrices, or gestures, the phonatory and articulatory gestures of Lass and Anderson (1975), or the laryngeal and oral
gestures of Lass (1976). This subdivision into phonatory/laryngeal
and articulatory/oral feature sets reflects the fact that phonological
rules and processes can refer precisely to (e.g. delete) either of these
gestures, the other gesture being unaffected (cf. the so-called 'stability effects' of Autosegmental Phonology). Lass (1976) discusses
cases of reductions of full consonants to the glottal consonants [h]

and glottal stop, [?], as occurring for instance in many varieties of Scots (cf. also Lass 1984: 113–5), which show the independence of the laryngeal features *vis-à-vis* the oral features, a proposal also made in Thrainsson (1978) on the basis of Icelandic preaspiration data and subsequently in various versions of Feature Geometry (cf. Pulleyblank this volume). It is these two gestures which, together with the latter added initiatory and oro-nasal sub-gestures, and the recently introduced tonological gesture, are the primary ingredients of the most recent DP feature tree, defended in AE, and represented in (1).[2]

The proposals which AE make for the tonological gesture are sketchy; I will return to them below (AE 1987: Section 7.5). First, let us have a look at the content of the four sub-gestures which have been more fully developed, starting off with the phonatory sub-gesture. This gesture contains two elements, |V| and |C|, which AE define as follows (recall that AE use the term component instead of element):

|V|, a component which can be defined as 'relatively periodic', and |C|, a component of 'periodic energy reduction'. (p. 151)

They then continue:

|V| and |C| differ from the [Jakobsonian] vocalic and consonantal distinctive features in that the presence of, say, |V| in a segment does not necessarily imply that the segment is in a simple binary opposition to an otherwise identical segment not containing |V|. Rather . . . the more prominent a particular . . . component . . . the greater the preponderance of the property characterised by that component. Notice too that |V| and |C| can characterise segments either alone or in combination. (p. 151)

'Prominence' of elements is expressed in terms of a head-dependent relation. In DP, elements can not only be joined by simple, symmetrical combination, but they can also enter into a relationship in which either element is more important, the other element being dependent on it. In addition, two elements can even entertain a relation in which neither feature is dominant, a relationship which DP call 'mutual/bilateral dependency'. Thus we arrive at the set of dependency relationships in (2).[3]

(2)

(a) $\{|X; Y|\}$ or $\{|X \Rightarrow Y|\}$: Y is dependent on X
(b) $\{|Y; X|\}$ or $\{|Y \Rightarrow X\}|$: X is dependent on Y
(c) $\{|X: Y|\}$ or $\{|X \Longleftrightarrow Y|\}$: X and Y are mutually dependent

These dependency relations hand DP the tools to express a number of major segment classes in terms of combinations of |V| and |C|, as in (3), where 'vcl' is 'voiceless', 'voi' is 'voiced' and 'fric' is 'fricative':

(3)

        {¦ V:C ¦}
        vcl fric

{¦C¦}   {¦ V:C ⇒ V¦} {¦ V ⇒C¦} {¦ V ⇒V:C¦} {¦V¦}
vcl stop   voi fric   nasal   liquid   vowel

      {¦C⇒V¦}
      voi stop

Underneath the actual representations I have indicated what classes of segments they represent. AE argue that the representations reflect a sonority ranking, going from left to right, in which the classes of voiceless fricatives and voiced stops are claimed to have equal sonority. Further distinctions (leading to separate representations for laterals, strident fricatives, etc.) will be discussed in Section 3.

We see here that, as stated in the above quote, the precise phonetic interpretation of the elements |C| and |V| is determined by their status in a structure. Roughly, the phonetic impact of the dependent occurrence of an element is less than the impact of that same element as a head. Note also that we can, if we wish, associate traditional feature names to these interpretations. For example, in the above array of structures, an ungoverned |V| can be glossed as [(+)sonorant], whereas a governed |V| forms the equivalent of [(+)voice]. This particular example reveals that DP manages to express distinct but clearly related phonological categories in terms of a single primitive appearing in different structural positions, where traditional feature systems must stipulate a relation in the form of redundancy rules like [+ sonorant] − > [+ voice]. In DP [+ sonorant] and [+ voice] are manifestations of one and the same element, viz. |V|. Thus the relation between these two phonetic events is 'built in' into the basic vocabulary.

In order to characterize the same segment classes in a feature system of the SPE (Chomsky and Halle 1968) type we would need the features [voice], [consonantal], [continuant] and [sonorant] (Clements 1990), where DP uses just two single-valued features, the elements |C| and |V| and their interdependencies. However, pure reductionism has not been AE's primary motivation for replacing major class and manner features by CV-complexes. Their foremost claim is that their approach is more adequate than traditional binary theories in at least three respects.

First, by replacing binary features with structures of varying complexity, representations more adequately reflect the relative markedness of phonological major class and manner categories. In (3), the categories *vowel* and *voiceless stop* are the least complex which reflects their relative unmarked status. Fricatives are more complex than stops, and voiced obstruents are more complex than voiceless obstruents. This again reflects well-known and widely accepted claims regarding the relative markedness of these categories.

Second, as stated earlier, AE also claim that the array of structures provides an adequate characterization of the notion of relative sonority. Degree of sonority corresponds to the amount of 'V-ness' that a representation contains. We could likewise define *strength* in terms of the amount of 'C-ness'.[4]

Third, the structures composed of |C| and |V| provide a more adequate basis for the expression of phonological processes. With reference to (3) AE note that these structures reflect an asymmetry in the behaviour of 'voicedness', as opposed to 'unvoicedness'. If we assume (as most phonologists do) that phonological rules can only cause phonetic events by manipulating phonological units, the structures in (3) express that languages can spread 'voicing' but not the absence thereof. If this is empirically correct, representations as in (3) are superior to binary feature systems in which [+ voice] and [– voice] have the same status.[5]

I now turn to the second sub-gesture of the categorial gesture, viz. the initiatory sub-gesture. This sub-gesture contains the 'glottal opening' element |O| and two elements used for the description of different types of airstream mechanisms, |G| (for 'glottalicness') and |K| (for 'velaric suction'). These three elements can each enter into a dependency relation with an element or elements of the phonatory sub-gesture, as in (4), in which the contrast between aspirated and unaspirated voiceless stops is represented in Dependency terms (cf. Ewen 1980: 9.4, Ewen 1986: 204).

(4)

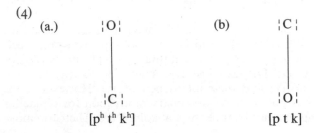

(a.)   ¦O¦   (b)   ¦C¦

            ¦C¦   ¦O¦

         [pʰ tʰ kʰ]   [p t k]

I emphasize here that DP allows, then, that representations of the two sub-gestures display variable dependency relations. A similar relationship can also be observed between the |G| element of the initiatory sub-gesture and the |C| of the phonatory sub-gesture, used to differentiate between glottalic ingressive ({|C; G|}) and egressive ({|G; C|}) sounds. Below we will see that dependency relations between sub-gestures are also allowed in the articulatory gesture between the nasality element |n| and the features of the locational sub-gesture (cf. 6). So in addition to dependency between individual elements DP allows dependency between representations of sub-gestures belonging to the same gesture.

Proceeding with this sketch of DP, let us turn to the daughters of the articulatory gesture, which are the locational sub-gesture and the oro-nasal sub-gesture. The place elements, listed in (5), belong to the former:

(5) *DP place elements*

|i|	'palatality, acuteness/sharpness'	|l|	'linguality'
|u|	'roundness, gravity/flatness'	|t|	'apicality'
|a|	'lowness, sonority'	|d|	'dentality'
|@|	'centrality'	|r|	'retracted tongue root'
|T|	'Advanced Tongue Root (ATR)'	|L|	'laterality'

The heart of the set of place elements is formed by the familiar 'aiu' subset, which plays a key role in the representations of vowels and consonants. Two further elements are added for vowels, centrality and ATR, as well as a set of elements which are mainly or exclusively used for consonants.

It is irrelevant for our present purposes that DP uses precisely these elements for the representation of the place of articulation of the vowels and consonants. I refer to AE (Chapter 6) for details and to van der Hulst (1993, 1994) for an alternative in the spirit of the present chapter.

Then, finally, there is the oro-nasal sub-gesture, which contains precisely one element, |n|, for 'nasality'. Recall that there also is a phonatory characterization of nasality: {|V ⇒ C|}. One might wonder whether DP really needs a nasality element, or, if it turns out that such an element is necessary, whether this element should have a sub-gesture entirely for itself. With respect to the first question AE argue that nasal consonants not only form a natural class with other sonorant consonants by sharing certain characteristics in their categorial (particularly phonatory) representations, they also form a natural class with nasalized segments, which may have different specifications in the categorial gesture. In order for this latter natural class to be reflected by the DP representations of the segments in question, Dependency Phonologists argue that we need a separate element, |n|.

The oro-nasal sub-gesture falls under the same gesture as the locational sub-gesture. AE claim that there is at least one language in which the nasality element shows dependency relations with elements of the locational sub-gesture, viz. Chinantec (cf. Ladefoged 1971: 34; Catford 1977: 138). In this language there appears to be a distinction between two different degrees of nasalization, to be represented in DP terms as in (6) (cf. AE 1987: 250):

(6)

$$
\begin{array}{ccc}
\mathrm{|\,a\,|} & \mathrm{|\,a\,|} & \mathrm{|\,a\,|} \\
 & | & | \\
 & \mathrm{|\,n\,|} & \mathrm{|\,n\,|} \\[2mm]
/\,a\,/ & /\,\tilde{a}\,/ & /\,\tilde{\tilde{a}}\,/
\end{array}
$$

The question as to whether the nasality element should occupy a (sub-)gesture of its own, is rather more difficult to answer. In DP phonetic considerations have always played a central role in the justification and motivation of its primitives and hierarchical organizations. Although Catford (1977) recognizes only three functional aspects in the specification of speech (correlating with DP's phonatory, initiatory and locational sub-gestures), Ladefoged (1971) distinguishes four aspects required in speech specification; he adds the oro-nasal aspect. On the basis of Ladefoged's sub-classification into four aspects, AE (1987: 148) conclude that 'it seems possible, then, to account for the oro-nasal process as a distinct sub-gesture within the articulatory gesture', and that hence a subdivision into two sub-gestures, just as in the categorial gesture, 'is perhaps not inappropriate for the articulatory gesture'. Notice, though, that the motivation for a separate oro-nasal sub-gesture does not appear to be overwhelming.

Proposals within Feature Geometry (cf. Pulleyblank this volume) have sometimes also adopted a separate node for the feature nasal (cf. Sagey 1986, 1988). Piggott (1990, 1992) proposes a 'velic class node' dominating only [nasal]. In addition, he adopts a node 'spontaneous voicing', which also may dominate a feature nasal. The duplication of nasality in Piggott's model clearly bears a resemblance to the way DP treats nasality.

Finally, we briefly look at AE's proposals for the tonological gesture. In their excursus on representations for tonal distinctions, AE (1987: 273) make the intriguing suggestion that the elements |i| and |u| (as part of the tonological gesture) could be employed for high and low tone, respectively:

> we propose that the appropriate representations for the two tonal components are . . . |i| and |u|. In other words, we are suggesting that |i| and |u| in the tonological gesture bear the same relation to |i| and |u| in the articulatory gesture as |V| in the categorial gesture does to |a| in the articulatory gesture . . . That is, |i| involves (relatively) 'high frequency' and |u| (relatively) 'low frequency'; whether this is interpreted as high (or low) F_0 or as concentration of energy in the higher (or lower) regions of the spectrum depends on the context – i.e. gesture – in which it occurs.

What is most noticeable in this proposal is the idea to use the same elements, viz. |i| and |u| in two different gestures. In my own proposals I will make quite crucial use of this strategy. To emphasize that this strategy can be traced back to AE's own proposals, I will here also quote AE (1987: 215) on their suggestion concerning the identity of |a| and |V|:

> there is clearly a relationship between |a|, as a component within the articulatory gesture, and |V|, as a component of the categorial gesture. Consider the acoustic glosses which we have given the two components: |V| corresponds with maximal periodicity, and |a| with maximal sonority. Vowels, by virtue of their periodicity are the most sonorous of the categorial segment-types, while open vowels are the most sonorous within the class of vowels . . . The open unrounded vowel, then, might have {|V|} both as the representation of the categorial gesture and of the articulatory gesture.

The importance of these quotes is to show that AE themselves suggest the strategy to employ the same elements in different (sub-)gesture, thus deriving similarities in phonetic interpretation, while attributing the differences to the fact that the '(sub-)gestural location' of an element has a bearing on the phonetic interpretation as well. Thus elements are interpreted taking into account not only their position in the head-dependent relation but also taking into account the sub-gesture they are part of. It is precisely this line of reasoning that I fully explore in my own alternative.

3   A critique of classical Dependency Phonology

3.1   Inter- and intrasub-gestural dependency

We have seen that DP explores the possibility of allowing sub-gestures to enter into dependency relations. The possibility of entering elements of the initiatory and phonatory sub-gestures into a dependency relationship is not, however, fully exploited: while it is apparently necessary for |O| and |G| to be able to entertain dependency relations with |C|, |K| cannot 'look beyond' the initiatory sub-gesture, there being no DP representations in which (combinations of) |C| and/or |V| entertain non-symmetrical relations with |K| alone. In addition, intrasub-gestural relationships are not exhaustively employed either, since we do not find dependency relations between the features contained in the initiatory sub-gesture. Schematically, all this is summarized in (7); a '*' indicates that no dependency relations are proposed between the units connected by the bidirectional arrow:

(7)

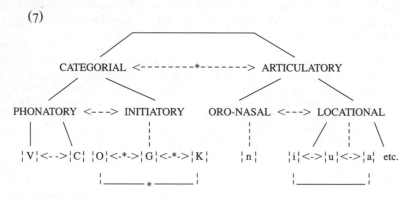

In (7) I also encode that there are no dependency relationships between the two main gestures: there are no circumstances under which segment-types are distinguished by means of a difference in the dependency relation holding between the elements of the categorial and articulatory gestures.

It is unclear why AE use precisely the dependencies illustrated in (7) and no others. In an attempt to restrict the DP model, Davenport and Staun (1986) have argued to dispense with *inter*sub-gesture dependency. They show that once the glottal opening element |O| is assigned to the phonatory sub-gesture and a new element |I| ('initiator velocity', expressing the direction of airflow) is assigned to the initiatory sub-gesture, no need remains for dependency relations between the phonatory and the initiatory sub-gestures. In the present chapter, I do not want to discuss the specifics of Davenport and Staun's (1986) modifications of the DP framework, but my own proposals agree with theirs in disallowing variable intersubgestural dependency.

AE also exploit the possibility of allowing variable dependency between the two sub-gestures of the articulatory gesture (cf. 6). I tend to look upon two distinctive degrees of nasalization with great suspicion, but apart from that, it is very questionable whether there is any need for an articulatory sub-gesture containing the element |n|. If, as I argue in the next subsection, no such sub-gesture is postulated, it follows, for that reason alone, that no intersub-gestural dependency relations can be postulated within the articulatory gesture.

The upshot of the above points is that in my own model I will dispense with variable dependency relations between sub-gestures. In the next subsections I will offer critical remarks concerning the various DP sub-gestures and mention some alternatives proposed by others which anticipate my own proposals. I will not, however, discuss the locational sub-gesture since this is treated separately in van der Hulst (1994).

3.2 The oro-nasal sub-gesture

First, although there is abundant evidence for suggesting that nasality can spread autosegmentally, and can hence function independently of other elements, this does not in itself suggest that the element expressing nasality should occupy its own (sub-)gesture. Since the oro-nasal sub-gesture dominates precisely one element, it is impossible to make out on empirical grounds whether, in a case of nasal harmony, it is the oro-nasal sub-gesture that spreads or rather the |n| element individually: in either case we derive the same result. Hence some other argument should be found that could support the relevance of the oro-nasal sub-gesture. We have seen that AE only provide a general phonetic line of reasoning based on suggestions of Ladefoged.

Another question that comes up is why, in the tree in (1), the oro-nasal sub-gesture should be grouped together with the locational features under the articulatory gesture. Perhaps, intuitively, this assumption makes some sense in that the feature [nasal] can only apply to place of articulation features, and cannot have scope over the elements grouped under the categorial gesture. Yet, there does not appear to be any phonological evidence from the area of assimilation processes that could corroborate or disconfirm the constituent-hood of the velic and locational features.

Noting that DP expresses nasality in two ways, Davenport (1993) proposes to dispense with the element |n| altogether. This implies that the categorial characterization of nasality 'survives', although Davenport's proposal is that nasality is not expressed in the phonatory sub-gesture (i.e. not in terms of specific |C|/|V| combination), but as a separate element |N| in the initiatory sub-gesture. So, in a sense, Davenport's proposal is a compromise between the two 'old' ways of expressing nasality in DP. I refer to Davenport who shows that the dual representation of nasality leads to unsatisfactory results in DP, but whatever these arguments are, it will be clear that if we can demonstrate that a single expression for nasality (in whichever sub-gesture) is sufficient, one of the ways nasality is expressed in DP must be eliminated, whether the dual representation creates 'problems' or not. My own proposals regarding nasality are in agreement with Davenport's. As becomes apparent in the next subsection, nasality will be represented only once in the Radical CV model.

3.3 The initiatory sub-gesture

Davenport and Staun (1986) maintain an initiatory sub-gesture, which contains elements for airstream distinctions: |I| 'egressive airflow', |G| 'glottalicness' and |K| 'velaric suction'; |O| which forms part of this sub-gesture in AE has been moved to the phonatory sub-gesture in their model. Furthermore, we have just seen that Davenport (1993) proposes to add an element |N| 'nasal' to the initiatory sub-gesture. In my own proposal the equivalent of Davenport's initiatory sub-gesture contains no elements like |I| and |K|, but it agrees with his proposals in expressing glottal and nasal/ oral distinctions in a single sub-gesture.

3.4 The phonatory sub-gesture

I will now turn to a more extensive evaluation of the organization of the phonatory sub-gesture and argue that the 'syntax' of CV combinations is not clearly defined in AE's version of DP, a point also emphasized in den Dikken and van der Hulst (1988), who offer an alternative which can be seen as the earliest predecessor of the proposals I advance in the next section. For convenience I repeat here the set of distinctions built from |C| and |V| which AE propose as a kind of core set:

(8)

	{|V: C|} vcl fric				
{|C|} vcl stop		{|V: C ⇒ V|} voi fric	{|V⇒ C|} nasal	{|V ⇒ V: C|} liquid	{|V|} vowel
	{|C ⇒ V|} voi stop				

Given the combinations which are employed one may wonder why many other possible combinations of |C| and |V| are *not* used in AE's model, e.g.:

(9)

{|C ⇒ V: C|}   {|V: C ⇒ C|}   . . .

As AE do not fail to observe themselves, |V: C| represents [continuant] and it would seem therefore that DP has three and not just two categorial features, and, we might add, redundancy statements ruling out combinations of [consonantal] (|C|) and [continuant] (|V: C|), for which there seems to be no use (cf. 1987: 9).

AE do add a number of additional, more complex representations to capture further distinctions:

(10)

{|V: C ⟺ V|}   {|V ⇒ V: C ⇒ C|}   {|V: C ⟺ V ⇒ C|}   {|V: C ⇒ C|}
fricative   lateral   voiced lateral   non-sibilant
trill   fricative   fricative

The argumentation that AE provide in favour of these representations is crucially dependent on the representations in (8) which form the starting point. Fricative trills may pattern with voiced fricatives in conditioning phonological processes for which AE discuss 'Aitken's Law' as an example. Given the representation in (10), the relevant natural class can be represented as {V: C ⇒ V} (cf. 1987: fn. 3). Lateral liquids, of course, must be distinguished from r-sounds, which motivates the second structure in (10):

> laterals are phonetically unique, as far as the phonatory sub-gesture is concerned, in having effectively two manners of articulation. While there is a stricture of open approximation at one or both sides of the mouth (at least for sonorant laterals), there is also closure in the centre of the oral tract. . . . Essentially, then, the |C| node characterizes a secondary . . stricture type within the phonatory sub-gesture. (AE 1987: 163)

The extra dependent |C| in the third representation, then, also adds laterality to the fricatives (p. 164).

The fourth structure reflects the distinction between sibilant and non-sibilant fricatives:

> /s/ may be interpreted as the optimal fricative phonetically; acoustically it shows the 'simplest' combination of consonantal and vocalic properties, while the other fricatives involve energy reduction in various frequency bands. In comparison with the sibilants, then, the other fricatives display extra /C/-ness. (p. 166)

Even though AE are careful in motivating the structures in (8) and (10), one starts having serious doubts concerning the restrictiveness of their approach. Assuming that a theory of segmental structure aims at characterizing a closed set of well-formed representations which matches the set of attested phonological distinctions, I must conclude that classical DP does not do very well in this respect. The 'syntax' underlying combinations of elements (and sub-gestures) is not explicitly defined, i.e. we do not know what the total set of possible dependency structures is. This implies that AE make no serious attempt to come to grips with the notion 'possible phonological segment'.

Despite this criticism, I believe that the basic ideas of DP as well as the specific proposed structures are extremely interesting, even though some of the perhaps most fruitful ideas (like using the same elements in different sub-gestures) are left unexplored. At the same time, due to the absence of restrictions and explicit hypotheses, the theoretical status of DP as a research programme is rather weak. This is perhaps the main reason why this model has not been taken up by many phonologists who now, independently, develop ideas which are quite similar to those characteristic of Dependency Phonology (cf. den Dikken and van der Hulst 1988, van der Hulst and van de Weijer 1994 for a discussion of this point).

3.5   Summary and preview

In the next section I will propose a different architecture for the categorial gesture, arguing that this gesture comprises three sub-gestures which I will call: *Stricture*, *Phonation* and *Tone*; I use capital letters when referring to the sub-gestures in Radical CV Phonology. Thus (for the moment ignoring details concerning the internal organization of the sub-gestures), I refer to Anderson and Ewen's 'phonatory sub-gesture' as the Stricture sub-gesture. I then use the term Phonation sub-gesture for some of the properties they express under their 'initiatory sub-gesture' (abandoning the latter term), and I incorporate their tonological gesture into the categorial gesture as the Tone sub-gesture.

I will only deal with Anderson and Ewen's articulatory gesture where I am concerned with the representation of nasality. In standard DP, nasality has a dual representation, as we have seen. It is represented in terms of a categorial (more specifically, phonatory) characterization (for nasal consonants) and as a separate element |n| under the oro-nasal sub-gesture of the articulatory gesture (for nasal consonants and nasal vowels). I will propose to represent nasality in categorial terms only, expressing it in the Phonation sub-gesture. Thus I arrive at the position that the articulatory gesture deals exclusively with locational or place distinctions (cf. van der Hulst 1993, 1994)

(11)

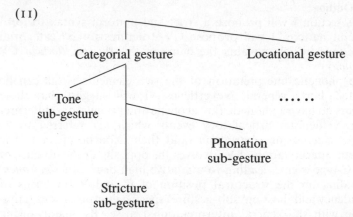

We have seen that in standard DP, sub-gestures, like elements, may enter into dependency relations with each other, such that different dependency relations give rise to different segment types. Apart from rearranging its content, a second aspect of my proposal for the categorial gesture is that its sub-gestures enter into a *fixed* dependency relation: the Stricture sub-gesture is the head and the other two sub-gestures are dependents.

A third aspect of my proposal concerns the choice of elements. In standard DP, each sub-gesture has its own set of elements. The use of the same elements in different sub-gesture is hinted at but by no means fully explored. In the proposal advanced here I claim that *all* sub-gestures contain exactly two elements. A logically independent claim will be that in each case we are dealing with the same pair: |C| and |V|. In van der Hulst (1993, 1994) I discuss how this works out for the Locational gesture. In this chapter I will demonstrate that not only Stricture distinctions, but also Phonation and Tonal distinctions can be represented in terms of |C|, |V| and a fixed set of CV-combinations. The main goal of this exercise is not to arrive at a totally new set of distinctive categories but rather to *re*construct the more or less accepted set of distinctive features in such a way that (a) the set is not a random list but instead a well-defined subset of the logically possible |C|/|V| combinations and (b) relations between separate features are not arbitrary since they turn out to involve (partially) identical |C|/|V| combinations occurring in different sub-gestures.

4   An alternative approach: Radical CV Phonology

4.1   Outline

In this section I will propose a strict and uniform syntax to form
CV-combinations. I will propose CV-structures for *all* categorial
distinctions (which explains the name of this theory: *Radical CV
Phonology*).

The phonetic interpretation of the two elements is, as can be
expected, fairly general. Nevertheless, I will suggest that these
elements do have a phonetic (i.e. acoustic and articulatory) interpretation: C denotes articulatory events which are referred to as
closure, stricture or *contraction* (and their acoustic effects). The
phonetic interpretation of V involves the opposite or the absence of
these C-type events, leading to a relative high degree of *sonorancy*.
Depending on the structural position of C and V (in terms of
dependency and 'hosting' sub-gesture) specific interpretations (compatible with the general interpretations) arise. By mainly using
articulatory glosses I do not intend to disagree with Harris and
Lindsey (this volume) who claim that the primary meaning of
elements is a mental acoustic image. I do not, however, subscribe
to their view that all elements are independently pronounceable.
This may be true of locational elements in so far as they occur in
vowel structures, but that is simply a result of the fact that pure
vowels (i.e. a, i, u) have no categorial elements in them. A discussion
of this issue would take me beyond the scope of the present
chapter, however.

I will propose that the categorial gesture consists of three sub-
gestures which enter into a fixed dependency relation:

(12)

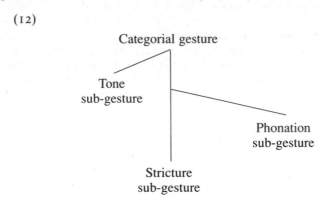

In each of these we find the four simplest structures which can be
composed from C and V:

(13)

(a) $\{|C|\}$ $\{|C \Rightarrow V|\}$ $\{|V \Rightarrow C|\}$ $\{|V|\}$

(b) C C_v V_c V

(13a) is the standard DP notation, while (13b) gives a simplified notation which I will henceforth use. I will assume, then, that elements do not enter into a dependency relation with themselves within a sub-gesture, since it will turn out that the four-way distinction in (13) is sufficient for all sub-gestures, given that within each sub-gesture we allow instead combinations of the four structures in (13) can occur. I will represent these combinations as in (14):

(14)

C-headed				V-headed			
C	C	C_v	C_v	V_c	V_c	V	V
$\mid$	$\mid$	$\mid$	$\mid$	$\mid$	$\mid$	$\mid$	$\mid$
V	V_c	V_c	V	C	C_v	C	C_v

I will refer to the structures in (13) as simple structures and to those in (14) as complex structures. I assume that complex structures consist of two simple structures with non-identical heads. It will turn out, however, that the distinction between C- and V-headed complex structures is distinctive in the Stricture sub-gesture only. For the other two sub-gestures a total of four complex structures will be sufficient.

In van der Hulst (1993, 1994) the current approach is extended to cover place distinctions. It is argued that the place gesture is composed of two sub-gestures. The categorial and the place gestures, as we may expect, enter into a (fixed) dependency relation in which the categorial gesture is the head:

(15)

The argumentation for taking the categorial gesture as the head is based on the fact that categorial distinctions (and specifically stricture distinctions) determine the distribution of segments in the syllabic organization. Being head properties we expect them to be 'visible' in the root node. A further indication comes from spreading behaviour. I assume that the head-dependent asymmetry is manifested in spreading processes in such a way that dependent properties can spread independently, while heads can only spread together with their dependents. It is well known that stricture properties do *not* spread, while place properties do. This confirms the head status of the categorial gesture. Notice, however, that I do not claim that the dependent categorial sub-gestures Tone and Phonation are incapable of spreading. In fact, the two layers of dependency in (12) are meant to reflect that Tone properties are more likely to be 'prosodic' (i.e. autosegmental) than Phonation properties. Tone elements form, so to speak, the outermost shell of the categorial gesture.

The diagram in (15) is *not* meant to express *linear order* of elements within the segment. I will assume that linear order is only specified at the root level, but in this chapter I will not discuss 'supra root' gestures (cf. van de Weijer and van der Hulst, in preparation).

Concluding this section, let me note that a structure as in (15) is not unlike the kinds of structures which have been proposed within *Geometrical Phonology* (Clements 1985a, Sagey 1986, 1988, McCarthy 1988, Pulleyblank this volume). My approach differs from that line of work in that I assume that the adoption of structural relations can, and if possible *must*, be counterbalanced by a reduction of the number of phonological primes. Implicit to this point is of course the criticism of Geometrical Phonology that this approach has taken for granted that the hierarchical relations must simply be *added* to the set of features which stems from the SPE tradition. This criticism is not undermined by the fact that certain changes *vis-à-vis* the SPE system have been adopted, since it seems that these changes are not at all determined by the adoption of (a specific) hierarchical structure.

The addition of structure to the segment allows us to recognize different traditional features as 'allofeatures' of the same 'featureme'. Obviously, in order to explore the reduction strategy that I suggest, we need independent support for the particular grouping we assume and both phonetic and phonological constraints on assigning 'allofeatures' to a single 'featureme'. I suggest the following criteria. First, the two features must be in complementary distribution in the sense that they occur in different sub-gestures. Second, one might argue that the two phonetic events corresponding to allofeatures must be *similar*; this would be the phonetic constraint.

Third, we must be aware of (historical) phonological processes which reveal their affinity; this is the phonological constraint.

For a phonologist, the reduction strategy and the constraints I mention here must have a familiar ring. After all, it is common practice to argue along similar lines when we try to establish the minimal set of phonemes for a particular language. Two sounds will be attributed to a single phonological category (a single phoneme) if they occur in complementary distribution (i.e. occur in different structural positions) and if, in addition, there is phonetic similarity, and, furthermore, both are involved in phonological alternations.

In the next subsection, I will discuss whether there is a reasonable match between the structures allowed by our syntax and the distinctions which are generally considered contrastive in the analysis of segment inventories. In this enterprise, I must rely on a certain consensus with respect to which phonetic properties are potentially distinctive. Such a consensus is apparent from the fact that certain features appear to be widely accepted, or that certain relations between features have been taken to be well-established. Despite consensus there is, of course, a lot of uncertainty as well. In the model proposed here I will be forced to make decisions which await further empirical underpinning.

4.2 The proposal

The following diagram anticipates most of my proposals regarding the match between the elements in the Categorial gesture and traditionally recognized distinctive features:

(16)   Categorial gesture

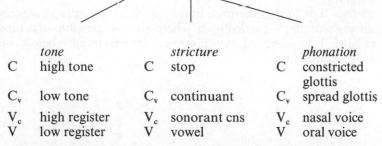

	tone		*stricture*		*phonation*
C	high tone	C	stop	C	constricted glottis
C_v	low tone	C_v	continuant	C_v	spread glottis
V_c	high register	V_c	sonorant cns	V_c	nasal voice
V	low register	V	vowel	V	oral voice

In each sub-gesture I will create further distinctions in terms of the combinations given in (15). I will now discuss the sub-gestures one by one starting with the head sub-gesture: Stricture.

4.2.1 The Stricture sub-gesture

The elements C and V, when part of the Stricture sub-gesture, correspond to the following articulatory events and their acoustic effects:

(17)

C = relatively high degree of stricture (as in obstruents)
V = unimpeded outflow of air (as in sonorants)

A dependent C differentiates between two types of 'high degree of stricture' and a dependent V between two types of 'unimpeded outflow of air':

(18)

C = absolute stricture (as in stops)
C_v = non-absolute stricture (as in fricatives)
V = unimpeded outflow of air (as in vowels)
V_c = unimpeded outflow but not necessarily centrally or uninterrupted (as in sonorant consonants)

Both V and V_c express what has been called *spontaneous voicing*. In (18) we express directly that stops and oral vowels are unmarked with respect to their stricture: stops are unmarked obstruents (as opposed to fricatives) and oral vowels are unmarked sonorants (as opposed to nasal vowels); the *oral* outflow is clearly the default option. This is in accordance with the fact that the prototypical unmarked syllable consists of a stop followed by an oral vowel, as well as with many other well-known generalizations stemming from the study of language acquisition, language change and aphasia (cf. Jakobson 1941 for this line of reasoning).

I now turn to the interpretation of complex stricture structures, starting with the V-headed ones. There are four possible structures (cf. 19). I have added the proposed interpretations below the complex structures:

(19)

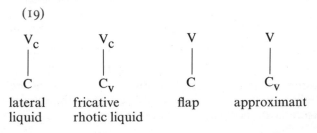

V_c	V_c	V	V
|	|	|	|
C	C_v	C	C_v
lateral	fricative	flap	approximant
liquid	rhotic liquid		

In the first complex structure, the dependent C expresses 'the secondary central stricture' which lateral liquids have: the governed C stands for (central) closure. In (18) we have seen that ungoverned C represents stops. To say that the same stricture occurs in laterals (and nasals, which I will represent below as 'nasal liquids') allows us to capture the natural class of stops, liquids and nasals: 'bare' C (whether head or dependent). In general terms we expect all classes denoted by a common substructure to be natural. In this particular example, traditional feature systems can only succeed in grouping stops, nasals and liquids by attributing the redundant [− continuant] to laterals and nasal consonants.[6] At the same time, since the bare C occurs in different structural positions in stops as opposed to lateral and nasal sonorants, we can 'choose' to differentiate between stops and sonorants by assuming that processes can make reference to bare C *as a head*, i.e. to stops alone. It is reasonable to expect that the reverse is excluded, i.e. that one cannot refer to a property in a 'weak' (i.e. dependent) form and ignoring its stronger manifestation, but this is a point that needs further investigation.

There is of course a phonetic difference between stops and nasals on the one hand and laterals on the other hand: the oral stricture is *total* in the case of stops and nasals, and *partial* (i.e. central) in the case of laterals. This does not take away that an element such as C has a constant phonetic interpretation, viz. *contact stricture* (as opposed to non-contact stricture). The reason why in nasal consonants C is realized as a total closure is that nasals, but not laterals, allow the air to escape through the nasal cavity. Hence nasals are sonorant in having free outflow of air, but since the nasal escape route is chosen, the oral closure is 'free' to be optimal. In laterals there is no nasal outflow of air and the oral stricture must therefore be partial.

The class of rhotics is very diverse. Still, phonologically, there appears to be a single category (cf. Lindau 1980), except when we find a so called fricative rhotic next to a 'normal' rhotic (as in Czech). A system opposing a normal rhotic to a lateral can be represented as having both V_c (the rhotic) and $V_c \Rightarrow C$ (the lateral). In systems which have no lateral/rhotic contrast, the liquid can often vary from rhotic to lateral depending on contextual factors. The precise factors which condition this allophonic variation are not always clear (cf. Bhat 1974). In some cases the choice depends on the manner properties of surrounding segments: the rhotic occurs in intervocalic position and the lateral elsewhere. This suggests that rhotics have a weaker constriction than laterals since the environment V-V counts as a weakening or lenition context (cf. 21(c)). The structures in (19) are adequate in this respect. In other cases the rhotic appears in a post-coronal context (Ewe, Ganda; cf. Halle and Clements 1983) which implies that place factors are involved. (Cf. van de Weijer 1993b for a study of this type of allophony.)

The second structure in (19) will be taken as the representation of a fricative /r/, which AE also argue for (cf. above). This r-type shares with continuants obstruent the substructure C_v and may thus be expected to pattern with (voiced) fricatives, as, in fact, it does in Aitken's law (cf. above).

For the third structure I propose the interpretation 'flap' or 'tap'. I follow Maddieson (1984) in the claim that taps and flaps (although different from an articulatory point of view) do not involve distinct phonemic categories. The taps or flaps have clear consonantal properties in that they involve a contact stricture, but they fall in the class of sonorants in being spontaneously voiced. Below, I demonstrate how a flap can be seen as an expected natural weakening of stops, just like approximants are weakening products of fricatives.

Finally, for the fourth structure I propose to interpret this as *approximant*, assuming that approximants may be categorially different from vowels and not just positionally different (i.e. in terms of syllabic position). The approximants /y/ and /w/ in Dutch, for example, have traditionally always been analysed as sonorant consonants and the phonology of Dutch seems to offer no reason to treat these sounds as vowels at any level of representation. Another classic case where a lexical distinction must be made between a vocalic and consonantal labial approximant is found in French in the pair *l'oiseau, le whisky*, where the shape of the definite article reveals that in the former case the initial approximant is a vowel, while in the latter case it must be analysed as a consonant.

The representations in (19) predict that rhotics are more sonorous than laterals, because the latter have an additional C. Hankamer and Aissen (1974: 137–8) discuss this matter and conclude that the relative ordering of laterals and rhotics on the sonority scale is not universally fixed. In certain cases rhotics are clearly more sonorous than laterals, e.g. syllable final -*rl* is allowed but -*lr* is not (for example in German), but sometimes, at least according to Hankamer and Aissen, it is the other way around. I tentatively suggest that in that case the 'lateral' is not a liquid but a weaker sound falling in the category of flaps. Example (20) represents the full sonority scale for sonorants, showing increasing sonority going from left to right:

(20)

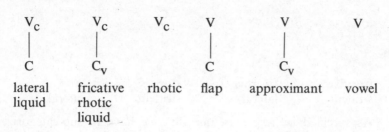

V_c	V_c	V_c	V	V	V
|	|	|	|	|	
C	C_v	C	C_v		
lateral	fricative	rhotic	flap	approximant	vowel
liquid	rhotic				
	liquid				

The representations proposed here for taps/flaps and approximants provide a good basis for dealing with lenition processes:

(21)

(a) stop → flap   (b) fricative → approximant

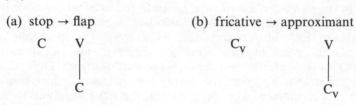

$$\begin{array}{ccccc} C & V & & C_v & V \\ | & & & & | \\ C & & & & C_v \end{array}$$

(c) *Weakening*

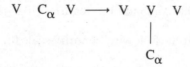

$$V \quad C_\alpha \quad V \longrightarrow V \quad V \quad V$$
$$| $$
$$C_\alpha$$

In this view, then, weakening is interpreted as an assimilatory process. Another view is expressed in the version of element theory found in government phonology, where lenition is seen as the loss of complexity (cf. Harris and Lindsey this volume).

A further advantage of our sonority scale (when compared to that of AE) is that nasal consonants have no place on it. This is preferred because nasals never occur as steps in weakening chains, as Davenport (1994) observes, who, as we have seen, also removes nasality from the stricture sub-gesture.

We will now turn to obstruents. The table in (22) specifies the four possible complex structures, differing from those in (19) by being C-headed:

(22)

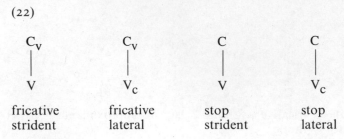

| fricative | fricative | stop | stop |
| strident | lateral | strident | lateral |

As specified in (22), I assume that we have to sub-categorize stops and fricatives in terms of *stridency* (or sibilancy) and *laterality*. To claim that strident and lateral(ized) are relevant categories for fricatives is not controversial, but I would like to suggest here that the same two categories apply to stops as well: both the third and the fourth structure can be taken to represent *affricates*. The fourth is a *laterally released stop*, also referred to as *lateral affricate*. The third structure is a 'simple' affricate, which Jakobson et al. (1952), in fact, also characterize as a *strident* stop. From an articulatory point of view stridency seems to involve an extra barrier creating greater turbulence of the outflowing air. Dependent V represents the high acoustic energy (i.e. stridency) which results from this turbulence. This suggests that we must interpret V-ness not simply as sonority, but as something more abstract, viz. acoustic energy. Sonority adds to acoustic energy and so does the extra noise associated with stridency. Lombardi (1990) and van de Weijer (1994) offer other views on the representation of affricates, which involve the use of combination features like [stop] and [continuant].

We thus arrive at the following sonority scale for obstruents:

(23)

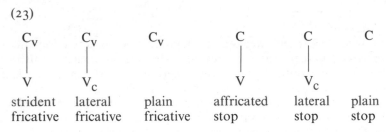

| strident | lateral | plain | affricated | lateral | plain |
| fricative | fricative | fricative | stop | stop | stop |

We note that the finer distinctions in (20) and (23) (i.e. the ones represented by complex structures) are mainly relevant for coronal place. This fact, however, finds no formal expression in this model. It is not obvious that this correlation *must* be formally expressed. Geometrical proposals which make features such as [lateral] and

[strident] formally daughters of the feature coronal run into problems anyway, as has been pointed out in various studies (e.g. Shaw
1990, Rice and Avery 1991). In this model, where the Location
gesture is formally dependent on the Categorial gesture, we expect
the latter to determine the former, but this geometrical relation
does not exclude the other possibilities. Hence (as pointed out in
van de Weijer 1993a) the implication (formulated in Shaw 1990): if
lateral then coronal, or if tap/flap then coronal, reflects the dependency relation which I posit between the Categorial and the Locational gesture.

4.2.2   The phonation sub-gesture

We now turn to the 'complement' sub-gesture: Phonation. The
proposal is that the elements C and V, when part of the Phonation
sub-gesture, correspond to *glottal stricture* and *voicing*,
respectively:

(24)

C = glottal stricture (as in glottal stop, glottalized consonants
and ejectives)
C_v = glottal opening as in aspirated obstruents and 'voiceless'
sonorants
V = oral voice (as in sonorants and voiced obstruents)
V_c = nasal voice (as in nasal consonants and nasalized vowels
and approximants)

In (24) I express the fact that glottal (stop) and oral voice
are unmarked. This is supported by the fact that the glottal stop is
the most widely attested hiatus filler or default consonant and by
the clear fact that nasal vowels are more marked than oral vowels.

By specifying C and C_v on obstruents I characterize aspirated
and glottalized obstruents. I assume that glottalized stops and
ejectives fall in the same phonological category. This point follows
from the survey given in Ladefoged (1973) which tells us that these
phonation types never contrast in a single language. Lombardi
(1991, 1993) draws the same conclusion. C and C_v, then, represent
two opposing glottal states which may be found on both obstruents
and sonorants.

An advantage of the proposal I make here is that the 'features'
stop/continuant and constricted/spread are considered to be instances of the same elements, i.e. C and C_v, respectively. This
allows us to find a formal expression for the well-known phenomenon that stops reduce to *glottal* stop and fricatives to [h], if we
assume that stops and fricative when losing their place acquire a

phonation type which 'mirrors' their original stricture type; another instance of enhancement perhaps (cf. Padgett 1991 who disputes the empirical basis for this point.)

Like C and C_v, V and V_c may also occur on both obstruents and sonorants. Added to obstruents they represent *voice* and (*pre*)*nasalisation*, respectively. On this view, then, (non-spontaneous) voice is a privative property, a claim which has both been supported (Mester and Itô 1989, Cho 1991a, 1991b, Lombardi 1991, 1993) and rejected (Pulleyblank this volume).

Attributing the C-phonation types to sonorants leads to glottalized and 'voiceless' sonorants. The glottalized category is obviously needed, whereas the second will be taken to lead to aspirated sonorants. This latter claim is also made in AE where they use |O| (aspiration) to represent voiceless sonorants. Cho (1990) and Lombardi (1991, 1993) make the same claim in a different model and provide a number of relevant examples.

If we say that both V and V_c may occur on sonorants as well, we allow that oral vowels and liquids have simple V. This adds, redundantly one might say, non-spontaneous voicing to these sonorants. The fact that vowels and liquids are V-headed in the Stricture sub-gesture already accounts for their spontaneous voicing.

If we can specify sonorants redundantly with the Phonation elements V we predict that they may trigger voicing assimilation. Yet, it has often been pointed out that even though sonorants are voiced, they do not trigger voicing assimilation processes. Rice and Avery (1989), however, mention the case of Sanskrit where sonorant consonants do in fact cause voicing on preceding obstruents. This shows that we should, in fact, allow sonorants to carry the element expressing (non-spontaneous) voice in specific cases.

Nasalized vowels and nasal sonorant consonants have V_c in the Phonation sub-gesture. More specifically, I will say that a lateral liquid structure, if provided with V_c phonation, *is* a nasal consonant. This predicts that /l/'s, when nasalized, turn into the nasal consonant /n/ which is an attested alternation type (cf. 29).

Notice that whereas nasal vowels are more marked than oral vowels, it is commonly assumed that the unmarked sonorant *consonant* is the nasal consonant. Perhaps this is so because in nasal consonants the phonation type V_c enhances the stricture type V_c. As Stevens and Keyser (1989) point out: enhancement (i.e. more of the same) is a common phenomenon, which may outweigh economy.

With the proposed interpretations we arrive at the following combinations of Stricture and simple Phonation structures (C_a

stands for bare C or C_v; V_a stands for bare V or V_c) for obstruents and sonorants, respectively:

(25) *Obstruents*

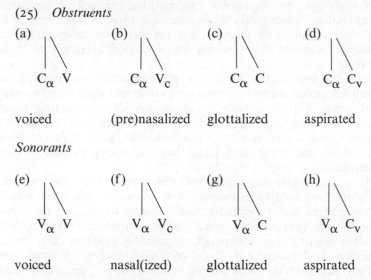

(a)

C_α V

voiced

(b)

C_α V_c

(pre)nasalized

(c)

C_α C

glottalized

(d)

C_α C_v

aspirated

Sonorants

(e)

V_α V

voiced

(f)

V_α V_c

nasal(ized)

(g)

V_α C

glottalized

(h)

V_α C_v

aspirated

The fact that voicing and prenasalization on obstruents are represented as closely related elements finds support in the observation that (pre)nasalized obstruents are sometimes interchangeable with voiced obstruents or function as such in forming the 'voiced' counterpart of a voiceless obstruent series. We can say that in such cases the dependent phonation element is bare V, where, in the absence of a contrast with V_c, its interpretation varies between voicing and prenasalization.

Steriade (1991) suggests that fricatives cannot be *pre*nasalized because they have no 'stop phase'. This, however, does not require us to exclude nasality on fricatives, as Steriade points out herself. The result of this is simply a fully nasalized fricative.

I now turn to the interpretation of *complex* phonation structures. Complex phonation types can, in principle, be V- or C-headed, as in the Stricture sub-gesture, leading to eight different possible structures (cf. 20, 23). In actual fact, however, we need at most four:

(26)

V_c & C	V_c & C_v	V & C	V & C_v
nasal	nasal	creaky	breathy
glottalized	aspirated	voice	voice

The first and second structures represent glottalized and 'voiceless' nasals. Technically speaking, we expect to find these complex structures also on obstruents, leading to glottalized or aspirated (pre)nasalized obstruents. Such cases are rare, at best, and it is therefore tempting to suggest that the first two cases prefer to 'enhance' segment types which are V-headed in terms of their stricture.

Breathy and creaky voice are phonologically represented as combinations of aspiration plus oral voice and glottalization plus oral voice. This is a very common way of representing these glottal states, going back to Halle and Stevens (1971). Recent support for this view is offered in Lombardi (1993). In this case we may note that these two cases have a strong preference for obstruents.

If we need just four categories this means that the dependency relation holding between the two simple structures which are combined is not distinctive. This is why I represent the combinations in (26) without specifying a dependency relation. We are not denying that a dependency relation holds in every combination (a fundamental claim of DP), however. Instead, we simply say that the dependency relation is not distinctive and therefore not phonologically specified. There may be reasons for choosing one way or the other on the basis of more phonetic considerations.

Another way to go would be to encode the 'bias' of these structures in terms of the dependency relation. If the first two are only relevant for sonorant consonants (i.e. because there are no prenasalized glottalized or aspirated obstruents) we may encode this by their V-headedness, assuming, as before, that in the unmarked case structures in the different sub-gestures are in an enhancement relation (i.e. have the same head type). If we take this option we will want to represent the two other cases in (26) as C-headed, since creaky and breathy voice appear to be distinctive on obstruents only. This matter needs further investigation.

Following Ladefoged (1973), Lombardi (1991, 1993) proposes to regard *implosives* as falling in the same phonological category as consonants with creaky voice, which also includes *preglottalized* and *laryngealized* consonants (cf. Greenberg 1970). This is a welcome move. Ejectives have been analysed as glottalized sounds and in van der Hulst (1994), it is proposed (inspired by Traill 1991) that clicks are complex segments (more specifically 'double root segments', cf. van de Weijer and van der Hulst in preparation, van de Weijer 1994). Finding a place for implosive *within* the current system, then, makes it unnecessary to look any further for 'airstream features'. To eliminate such a category was also the goal of Halle and Stevens (1971) and the present proposal shares some characteristics with their feature system. Interestingly, Greenberg reports that in Mayan languages implosives may have a *nasal release*. Greenberg also notes that implosives cannot be directly preceded by nasals, which then typically show up as plain voiced obstruents. This shows that the phonation of implosives is, as it were, 'absorbed' by the nasal voice of the preceding nasal. Implosives may also be in contrast with prenasalized stops as in Kambera (Marian Klamer, personal communication), showing that it would be wrong to attribute both to the same category. Precisely how such phonetic effects and cooccurrence restrictions must be expressed forms a topic for further research.[7]

Summarizing, I have proposed to represent six oral and three nasal phonation types:

(27)

(a)

V	voiced
C	constricted glottis
C_v	spread glottis (i.e. aspirated)
V $\Rightarrow$ C	creaky voice, laryngealized, implosive
V $\Rightarrow C_v$	breathy voice, murmured

(b)

V_c	nasal
$V_c \Rightarrow$ C	glottalized nasal
$V_c \Rightarrow C_c$	aspirated nasal

Lombardi (1991, 1993) supports these types as phonological categories even though she does not count nasality among phonation.

Although in this chapter I will not investigate the formulation of processes, it is clear that in most cases we are dealing with the 'unification' of structures; for the notion of unification employed here, cf. Scobbie (1991) and Coleman (this volume). I will illustrate this with some examples taken from Rice and Avery (1989).

Nasalization of stops (as a process) may apparently give rise to plain nasals. In Korean, for example, stops assimilate to nasals:

(28)

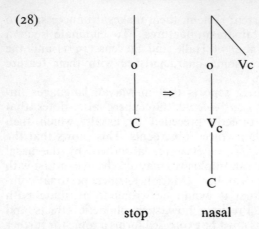

stop   nasal

The nasal structure subsumes the stop structure. Note that we must allow, then, that the addition of CV-information may involve demoting a C to dependent status.

Another case I made reference to above was the alternation between /l/ and /n/, the latter occurring in a nasal context. This, for example, occurs in Yoruba (cf. Akinlabi 1992: esp. fn. 6):

(29)

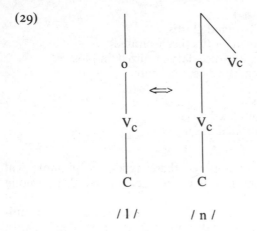

/ l /   / n /

This is a case which shows the appropriateness of representing /l/ as being subsumed by /n/. Rice and Avery (1989) propose exactly the opposite, i.e. laterals have more structure than nasals. This, I would claim, makes it more difficult to deal with /l/ – /n/ alternations of this type.

Rice and Avery also discuss the case of Kuman where /l/ is changed into /t/ before /n/:

(30)

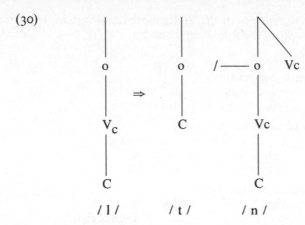

We can view this as a dissimilation phenomenon, since /l/ and /n/ share the substructure V_c, which is lost for /l/.

In this Section I have suggested various areas which call for further research. This implies that the representations and their associated interpretations must be taken as tentative. Yet, the main point, i.e. that we *derive* a set of structures representing a set of distinctive phonological categories which all other phonological models simply enumerate in the form of a distinctive feature list, should not be obscured by the fact that we, like all other writers on the subject, currently have insufficient data involving inventories and phonological alternations to decide on the precise set of phonation categories and their phonological representation.

4.2.3 The tonal sub-gesture

We finally turn to the 'specifier' sub-gesture Tone. Current proposals in the area of tonal phonology distinguish two 'ingredients': tone (proper), sometimes called 'melody' (Yip 1989), and register. This view goes back to Gruber (1964), and has been extensively supported in Yip (1980, 1989, 1993), Snider (1988, 1991), Inkelas et al. (1987), Hyman (1993), Bao (1991) and Duanmu (1991). In this section I will show that in this case too, such proposals fall out rather straightforwardly from the general principles which, in our view, underlie the inventory of distinctive categories. I propose that the elements C and V, when part of the Tone sub-gesture, can be taken to represent *tone* (proper) and *register*. What we have to decide is whether V represents tone and C register, or vice versa.

To find the right correlation, let us take a look at one example which involves the interplay between phonation and tone/register.

In his work on the genesis of the Vietnamese tonal system, Haudricourt (1954) proposes the following scenario:

(31)
I. *First phase* (1st century)
   pa   pas > pah   paT > pa?   (T = stop)
   ba   bas > bah   baT > ba?

II. *Second phase* (6th century)
   mid   falling   rising
   pa   pah > pà   pa? > pá
   ba   bah > bà   ba? > bá

III. *Third phase* (12th century)
   mid   falling   rising
   pa   pà   pá   high register
   pa   pà   pá   low register

The first phase is an automatic result of debuccalization, i.e. loss of
locational elements. Then, the loss of final aspiration and glottal
stop produced a tonal distinction and the loss of the voice distinction (in the onset) produced a register distinction. We thus find the
following correlations:

(32)

aspiration C_v → low tone
glottalization C → high tone
oral voice   V → low register

If we assume that Tone sub-gesture structures prefer to be in an
enhancement relation with Phonation, we may choose for the
following interpretations for our simple Tone structures:[8]

(33)

C   = high tone
C_v = low tone
V   = low register
V_c = high register

Note that, whereas low register derives from voice in this view,
high register comes into being as a consequence of having low
register. I am unaware of evidence for or against correlating high
register with nasality.

Phonetically, tone results from vocal cord vibration. The correlation between tone and glottalization/aspiration, then, has a clear
physiological basis in so far as both aspects involve vocal cord
activity.

In my view, register does not involve vocal cord activity. Rather register involves a more global characteristic which refers to a resonating cavity, the pharyngeal cavity, which is relatively small in case of V_c and relatively large in case of. V. Likewise, V as part of the Phonation sub-gesture also refers to a resonating cavity, the oral cavity. The action of increasing or decreasing the volume of the pharyngeal cavity may involve a whole collection of articulatory activities. This interpretation of register is familiar from studies on Asian languages (cf. Matisoff 1973, Trigo 1991).

Simple tonal systems with a two-way 'H/L' opposition may be represented with either tone or register. In view of the fact that low 'tone' is usually regarded as unmarked, one is tempted to interpret this as an indication that register is used to express the opposition in those cases.

I now turn to the interpretation of complex phonation structures. Again it would seem that we need just four possibilities and we therefore have not specified a dependency relation (cf. 26):

(34)

V_c & C	V_c & C_v	V & C	V & C_c
high	high-mid	low-mid	low

What we arrive at here is simply a reconstruction of the current view on tonal representations.

Again it seems possible to assume that a three tone system (like a two-tone system) can be represented in terms of register alone. I do not want to exclude, however, the possibility of register *and* tone playing a role in three-tone systems. In that case the mid tone would either be specified with a low or with a high tone, depending on whether it is part of the high or the low register. Such differences appear to be empirically motivated (cf. van der Hulst and Snider 1993 for a discussion of relevant cases). Of course, most current feature systems for tone have all the 'flexibilities' that we encounter here (cf. Duanmu 1991). In four tone systems, tone and register *must* both play a role and such systems are no longer ambiguous like the more impoverished systems.

There are, in addition, tonal systems which have more than four distinctive tones *per tone bearing unit* (especially in East-Asian languages), but it is usually claimed that the additional distinctions *must* involve *tonal contours*, i.e. *two* tones per tone-bearing unit. Hence such cases do not call for more tone structures, but rather for the possibility of one tone bearer being associated to more than one tone structure.[9]

A question that must be addressed at this point is whether the

possibilities in (33) and (34) can be used contrastively. Implicit in
the preceding discussion was the point that once register and tone
are active, the absence of neither can be used contrastively with
the options in (34). Hyman (1993) makes a proposal which is
similar to the one proposed here, allowing, however, precisely this
contrast. He argues that tonal distinctions are made by specifying
H, L or HL (which for him gives a mid tone). He then allows either
of these possibilities to combine with high, low or *no* register.
Hyman, then, allows the *absence* of register to be contrastive with
the presence of both low and high register. I refer to his study for
motivation of the resulting set of contrasts. I doubt whether we
must reckon with the *contrastive* absence of register-specifications.
Formally, there seems no reason why the presence or absence of
tone (in our case) cannot be used distinctively. In the Phonation
sub-gesture, after all, we do allow (24) and (26) (which correspond
to (33) and (34) respectively) to be contrastive. This issue, then,
needs more investigation.

A final question I will address is whether we wish to say that the
tonal structures may be combined with both V-headed and C-
headed stricture. This boils down to the question whether we want
to say that obstruents may bear tone and/or register. Kingston and
Solnit (1988) argue in favour of a tonal node for obstruents (or
rather consonants in general) based on empirical evidence coming
from case studies of tonogenesis in a variety of East-Asian
languages.

As I have demonstrated in (30), the loss of certain consonantal
phonation types may produce tone and register distinctions on
neighbouring vowels. In our view this could be represented in two
steps. First, we could 'move' the structures in (33) from the Phonation to Tone sub-gesture. In that phase, then, consonants (including
obstruents) acquire a simple copy of their phonation type under
the Tone sub-gesture. Subsequently, in the second phase, the phonation type gets deleted and the tone structure spreads to the neighbouring vowel. Kingston and Solnit strengthen the argument for
assigning tones to consonants by showing that consonantal tone
structure cannot always be regarded as simple copies of their
phonation properties. Here, as in a number of cases involving tone
and phonation, further study must shed more light on this
question.

Finally, let us observe that the distinctive use of headedness for
complex structures is only necessary for Stricture; we have not used
it for phonation and tone (cf. 26 and 34). Given that Stricture is
the head sub-gesture, we would indeed expect that this sub-gesture
makes use of the largest variety of structures.

5 Conclusion

In spoken languages, most morphemes have a phonetic form, an acoustic event brought about by a complex articulatory activity. This phonetic form of morphemes is represented as a structured set of discrete categories, organized in a particular way. These categories correspond to mental representations of the phonetic 'sub-events'.

Virtually all theories of phonological structure are based on the assumption that there is a universal set of such categories which are basic, i.e. which cannot be decomposed in smaller sub-events and which are called *distinctive features* or *elements*. From this set languages employ a subset to make lexical distinctions.

Currently, there is no full consensus with respect to the extension of the set of elements, but the general view is that whatever the set is, its members must be enumerated. The extension of the set, then, is essentially random from a theoretical phonological point of view. The elements which are currently postulated have been established inductively, i.e. on a case-by-case basis. Whenever some language appears to make distinctive use of a previously unattested phonetic 'sub-event', a new feature is added to the list. In Feature Geometry models the claim has been made that features are organized in 'second order' categories (like a laryngeal feature category, a place feature category and so on), but the number of such categories, and their extension, is again random, from a theoretical point of view (cf. Clements 1985a, McCarthy 1988, den Dikken and van der Hulst 1988, to appear).

The central thesis of this chapter is that the set of features and feature classes is random in one specific respect only, viz. with respect to the choice of the phonetic dimensions from which the discrete categories are derived. For example: from a theoretical point of view it is random that there are tone features, phonation features and stricture features. What is considerably less random, in my view, is the specific constellation of discrete categories which is 'extracted' from these domains and perhaps it is not random either that categories are selected from *three* domains, since this produces the typical '[spec[head complement]]' pattern. Taking as a point of departure a common core of distinctive features which emerges from roughly half a century of phonological research, including more recent proposals regarding ways in which these features are organized in second order categories (i.e. place, manner, laryngeal, etc.), I have shown that the set of 'phonological features' has a quite specific structure. The above proposals for the representation of non-place properties, especially those for phonation types and tonal distinctions, are still rather tentative. I believe, however, that the claim that the distinctions in these various sub-gestures do *not* call for three sets of totally independent phonological primes is convincing. Our approach may not be entirely successful in neatly characterizing the set of allowed combinations, yet it does succeed in deriving the specific set of 'features' and a fair amount of the relations which the tradition posits between these features. In other feature models these feature sets and the relations among the features have to be stipulated. 'Redundancy rules' of the following sort are quite typical:

(35)

    (a) [+ son] → [+ voice]
    (b) [+ voice] → [+ low register]
    (c) [+ lateral] → [− continuant]

In our model these rules find no equivalent, since in all cases we are dealing with different interpretations of the same primes.

Implicit in our approach is the claim that there is *no* innate set of features. Rather what is innate is a capacity to parse a limited set of discrete categories from the available phonetic 'scales', and a limited syntax for combining these categories.

There are two obvious lines for further research. First, the present proposal needs to be tested against a richer body of data involving both segmental inventories and phonological processes. The proposal advanced here accommodates a lot of claims in the area of non-place properties, but it also leaves a number of issues undecided. Second, the approach outlined must be applied to the place dimension as well. A third area of investigation concerns the relation between categorial features, specifically stricture features, and syllable structure. It will be clear that the current approach embodies interesting perspectives, especially if we decide to represent the syllable organization itself in terms of C and V (for onset and rhyme, respectively).

The first and third task form part of research in progress (cf. van der Hulst 1993, in preparation), whereas an attempt to perform the second task can be found in van der Hulst (1994).

Notes and Acknowledgements

This chapter is an extraction from a longer work, *Principles of Radical CV Phonology*, which contains work in progress (van der Hulst 1993). In a paper, which forms the complement of this chapter, I discuss the representation of place properties (van der Hulst 1994; cf. also van der Hulst to appear). Earlier versions of van der Hulst (1993) have circulated under the title 'Book of Segments'. During the period 1980–93 I presented a number of talks based on this material, using subtitles such as 'The molecular structure of phonological segments' and 'On the nature of phonological primes and the structure of segments'. I received useful comments on these oral presentations from Mike Davenport, John Harris, Rob Goedemans, John McCarthy, Michael Kenstowicz, Jacques Koreman, Aditi Lahiri, Simone Langeweg, David Nessly (who suggested the name of this model), Iggy Roca, Wendy Sandler, Keith Snider and Moira Yip. I am grateful to Marcel Den Dikken, Colin Ewen, Helga Humbert, Norval Smith and Jeroen van de Weijer who discussed with me some of the material presented here. I would like to thank Marian Klamer, Jeroen van de Weijer, Rint Sybesma and the editors of this volume for their comments on a prefinal version of this chapter.

1. This section draws on a similar section in den Dikken and van der Hulst (1988).
2. The tree in (1) is the, at present, final stage of a discussion within the DP framework about featural hierarchitecture, beginning with Lass and Anderson (1975), whose phonatory gesture was later renamed categorial gesture, and whose bipartite division was extended with a third main gesture, the initiatory gesture, introduced in Anderson and Ewen (1980) and Ewen (1980):

(1)

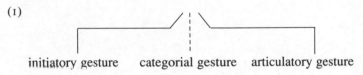

   initiatory gesture   categorial gesture   articulatory gesture

This tripartite split was not felt to suffice either, however, essentially because it was considered to be 'somewhat understructured' (Ewen 1986: 205). As a result, DP introduced sub-gestures within gestures, and eventually developed the tree in (1).
3. In the notational system of DP, an element enclosed between vertical lines represents just the element in question, while the representation {|x|} is used to exhaustively characterize a particular sub-gesture of a segment. DP also employs the notation {x}, which is used to express that the segment class in question is characterized by the element |x|, but not exhaustively so. A DP representation such as x;y denotes that |x| governs |y|, or that |y| is dependent on |x|. This representation is equivalent to the alternative representation with double arrows or the vertical notation used, e.g. in (12), below, so that x;y equals x ⇒ y as well as x.

   x
   |
   y

4. In the next section I will call this claim into question with respect to the representation of nasals.
5. This discussion gets more complicated once we allow rules which may delete elements.

6. In most traditional accounts (cf. Clements 1985a, Levin 1988, Hegarty 1989) it has been argued that nasals and laterals are [– cont] just in case they pattern with stops. Such an *ad hoc* strategy is clearly superfluous in this model.

7. On the phonology and representation of implosives in a feature geometrical framework, see Lloret (1992).

8. Interestingly, C and C_v, used here for H and L tones, are also the representations for coronal and labial in the locational gesture. In a sense I therefore agree with AE's proposal to use |i| (coronal) and |u| (labial) for H and L tone, respectively.

9. Duanmu (1991) claims that tonal contours always involve two tone-bearing units.

PART 2

STRUCTURES

Chapter 4

Accounting for compensatory lengthening in the CV and moraic frameworks

Lee S. Bickmore

Introduction

The process of compensatory lengthening (CL) is probably best introduced by observing examples which illustrate the phenomenon. Consider the following examples, taken from Chilungu, a Zambian Bantu language (CP = Class Prefix; DN = Deverbal Nominal marker).

(1)

(a) /ma-ino/ → miino 'eyes'   (cf. ma-tama 'cheeks')
    CP eye   CP cheek

(b) /ka-eleka/ → keeleka   (cf. ka- koma 'one who kills')
    'one who cooks'   DN kill
    DN cook

In both examples above the underlying /a/ which immediately precedes a vowel initial root is deleted. The resulting form, however, is not simply the sum of the two morphemes minus the deleted vowel; instead the member of the two vowel sequence which survives becomes lengthened. This can be thought of as a *compensating* or filling in for the elided material. To put it another way, the number of vowel *positions* has not changed during the transition from underlying to surface form. In (1a) the Chilungu word began with three vowels and, despite the application of Vowel Deletion, surfaced with three vowels (two of them being identical of course).

The goal of this chapter is to examine the means by which examples such as those in (1) can be accounted for insightfully in modern generative phonology, and more specifically in moraic theory (see also Zec and Katamba, this volume). The organization of the chapter will be as follows. First, we will summarize the historical developments which led to the formulation of moraic theory. This will include a brief summary of two other theories of timing units, the CV theory and the X theory (see Brockhaus, this volume). We will outline in some detail the version of moraic theory presented in Hayes (1989), which itself is based on proposals made by Hyman (1985) and McCarthy and Prince (1986). Next we will examine various typological manifestations of CL, and account for each in terms of moraic theory, while at the same time comparing the moraic analysis to previous analyses. The results are then summarized.

Two final points should be made. First, it should be pointed out that the process of CL is not a universal one. For example, many languages have a vowel deletion rule whereby one vowel in a two-vowel sequence is elided. In some languages, e.g. Chilungu (see (1)), this type of deletion triggers a CL of the surviving vowel. There are other languages, however, which have the same type of deletion rule, but where there is no CL of any other segment. Thus, while one might claim that the presence of CL in a language represents the unmarked case (due to what seems to be a statistical preference), this is certainly a parameter along which languages differ. Second, we can insightfully talk about CL from both a synchronic and diachronic perspective, and examples of both will be presented below.

1   Timing units

1.1   The CV tier

The model of phonology presented in *The Sound Pattern of English* (Chomsky and Halle 1968) suggested that phonological representations were a sequence of matrices which contained values for distinctive features. In such a model the phenomenon of CL as illustrated in (1) finds no natural account. One cannot simply apply Vowel Deletion and then Vowel Lengthening. Because of a prohibition on globality (looking back into the derivation of a word) it would be impossible to formulate a Vowel Lengthening rule which only lengthened vowels which formally were adjacent to another vowel. The only possible way, then, to account for this CL process would be to first apply Vowel Lengthening to a vowel which follows another vowel, and then apply Vowel Deletion which would delete a vowel before a long vowel. This is illustrated below.

(2)

ma-ino	Underlying Representation
maiino	Vowel Lengthening

miino   Vowel Deletion

As no Short Vowel–Long Vowel sequences ever surface, such a solution seems somewhat contrived.

With the advent of autosegmentalism (Goldsmith 1976) came the realization that there was more structure in a phonological entity than simply a string of feature matrices. Tonal processes, for instance, were much more insightfully accounted for if one assumed that the tones are sequential units on a *tier* of their own. These tones could then be associated to segmental material via association lines. It quickly became apparent that not only tones, but many other features as well should be thought of as having an independence from other features which formally meant putting them on their own tier.

One important development in this regard was to put syllabicity on its own tier. The formal implementation of this involved the establishment of a CV tier, where C is a consonant (i.e. [– syll]) slot and V is a vowel (i.e. [+ syll]) slot (see McCarthy 1979, Clements and Keyser 1983). These Cs and Vs, also referred to as *skeletal slots* or *timing units*, were then grouped into syllables. Below is an example of the formal representation of the form [triidayu].

(3)

```
     σ           σ   σ      Syllable Tier
   //|\        /\  /\
   C C V V     C V C  V    Skeletal Tier
   | | \/      | | | |
   t r  i      d a i  u    Segmental/Melodic Tier
```

Two comments are in order. First, the IPA symbols represent the conglomeration of distinctive features for these sounds, minus [syllabic], which can be inferred from the linkage to either a C or V slot. Thus an *i* linked to a V slot is syllabic and realized as [i], while an *i* linked to a C slot is non-syllabic and hence realized as [y]. (The use of *i*, rather than *y* in (3) is completely arbitrary.) The second comment has to do with the long [ii]. In a CV framework a long vowel or consonant can be represented as a single unit on the segmental or melodic tier, linked to two units on the CV tier. It is in this sense that the CV tier can be considered a *timing* tier. The *i* in (3) is linked to two timing slots while the *a* and *u* are linked to only one.

Furthermore, just as a long in this model is represented as one melodic segment linked to two skeletal (in this case V) slots, a

geminate consonant is represented as one melodic segment linked
to two C slots, as illustrated below.

(4)   *Representation of* [*makko*]

It should be borne in mind that the introduction of the skeletal
tier introduced a whole new layer of structure in phonological
representations. This increase in generative power and complexity
could only be justified by a considerable boost in descriptive and
explanatory adequacy in the phonology. It turns out that the
process of CL was used as a justification of the existence of a
skeletal tier. Let us consider the derivation of (1a) in this model.

(5)

(a)   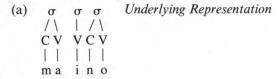   *Underlying Representation*

(b)      *Vowel Deletion*

In (5) we see the effect of Vowel Deletion on the underlying
representation: the /a/ is deleted on the segmental tier. What is
crucial, however, is that the V slot to which the /a/ was associated,
does *not* delete. This falls out naturally if the Vowel Deletion rule is
written such that it only affects elements on the segmental tier.
Such a rule could be written as follows:

(6)

$$\alpha \rightarrow \emptyset / \underline{\quad} \beta$$

with V V above the slash, each linked by | to positions.

The rule is interpreted as follows: delete an element α on the
segmental tier linked to a V position, when that V is followed

immediately by another V slot (linked to some melodic unit β). When writing rules in this framework, it is thus important to bear in mind that a 'V' in the rule does not mean a feature matrix containing [+syll], as it did in SPE, but rather, 'V' indicates a position on the timing tier.[1]

Next, we will assume that when the /a/ is deleted, the syllable node which was associated to it (via the V slot) also deletes, as a syllable must always have a segmental nucleus. Hayes (1989) has defined this process as 'Parasitic Delinking'.

(7) Parasitic Delinking (Hayes 1989): Syllable structure is deleted when the syllable contains no overt nuclear segment.

This yields the following structure:

(8)

<pre>
    σ σ   Vowel deletion
    | /\
  C V V C V
  | | | |
  m   i n o
</pre>

If we now stipulate as part of the Well-Formedness Conditions on the language, that every skeletal slot must be associated to some segmental element, then we have a very natural account of compensatory lengthening. The V slot becomes associated to the /i/ on the melodic tier as shown below. (In languages where no compensatory lengthening occurs following vowel deletion, we might assume either that (a) the deletion rule removes both the vowel on the melodic tier as well as the V slot it is associated to, or (b) there is no Well-Formedness Conditions which necessitates that stranded timing units must be reassociated.)

(9)

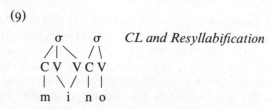

<pre>
    σ   σ   CL and Resyllabification
   /|\   /\
  C V   V C V
  | \/ | |
  m i   n o
</pre>

Several additional comments are in order. The empty vowel slot in (8) could not associate with the /o/ segment due to the prohibition on crossing association lines. Next, the fact that the V slot does not associate with the /m/could be due to one of several reasons. First, the language could stipulate that V slots can only be associated with [− cons] segments (although this is usually *not* the case as we will see below). Second, the language might have a general constraint which prohibits the formation of geminate consonants (i.e. the linkage of a [+ cons] segmental element to two or more skeletal slots) or a more specific constraint that would prohibit geminates in initial position.[2] Finally, the language might have a general rule that free V or C slots are always filled by a melodic unit on the right, or conversely, on the left (cf. Hayes 1989). Finally, we will assume that the general principles of syllabification (to be made more precise below in Section 2.0) reapply every time a structure is altered. These principles will associate the word initial CV slots to the first syllable node.[3]

1.2 The X tier

A subsequent approach to the skeletal tier was to remove the distinction between C and V, and have timing units represented uniformly as Xs (see Levin 1985, Lowenstamm and Kaye 1986, Brockhaus this volume). Under this approach additional syllabic structure is needed. Consider the representation below of [triidayum], where O = Onset, R = Rhyme, N = Nucleus, and C = Coda.

(10)

```
         σ    σ   σ
        /|\   |\  |\
       / R | R | R
      /  | / | | |\
     O O N O N O N C
     | | /\ | | | | |
     X X XX X X X X X
     | | \/ | | | | |
     t r i  d a i u m
```

Let us make a few points of comparison between (3) and (10). In both representations the segmental content of [i] and [y] is identical. Whereas in (3) the difference was linkage to a V or C node respectively, in (10) the difference is linkage to an N versus an O or C node. With regard to vowel length both theories treat vowel length as one segmental unit linked to two timing units. We will have occasion to discuss additional aspects of the X tier again later.

1.3 Moraic theory

With the discussion of the developments of the CV and X timing tiers as background, we can now fruitfully describe and discuss moraic theory. The first obvious formal difference in moraic theory is that the timing tier consists not of Cs, Vs, or Xs, but μs, where μ represents the traditional concept of mora. The major theoretical departure of moraic theory from the theories of timing units just described is that only certain segments are associated to elements on the timing tier. In this regard we will discuss the status of both onsets and codas.

The traditional concept of the mora involves syllable *weight*. In languages that make a weight distinction, *heavy* syllables are said to have two morae (or moras) while *light* syllables have only one. This weight distinction is typically made use of in the assignment of stress. Consider a language (e.g. Latin) where a syllable with a short vowel (V) is light, while syllables with either a long vowel (VV) or a coda consonant (VC) are heavy. One way to formalize the fact that light syllables are monomoraic while heavy syllables are bimoraic is simply to link the appropriate number of morae to melodic elements. This will accurately reflect syllable weight. Consider, as an example, the moraic representations of the syllables [tra], [tra;], and [trad].

(11)

```
   (a)   σ       (b)   σ        (c)   σ
        /║\           /║\            /║\
       / ║ μ         / ║μ μ        / ║ μ μ
      /  ║ |        /  ║| /        / / | |
     t   r  a      t   r a        t r  a  d
```

The difference between a short vowel and a long vowel in this theory is simply the linkage to one or two morae respectively. Thus the syllable in (11a) is straightforwardly interpreted as monomoraic (= light), while (11b) is interpreted as bimoraic (= heavy). The syllable in (11c) receives its second mora due to the presence of a coda consonant, which in moraic theory is simply a segmental unit which is tautosyllabic with a previous vowel.

While a long vowel is represented by linkage to two mora nodes, a long or geminate consonant is simply one which is the coda for one syllable while being the onset for the next one. Such a configuration is shown below for [tragga].

(12)

```
           σ   σ
          /║\ /|
         / ║ μ/ μ
        / /| |/ |
       t r a  g  a
```

As was the case in CV theory, in moraic theory it is also possible to completely dispense with the feature [syllabic]. The difference between a vowel and its corresponding glide is interpreted by noting what part of the syllable structure it is linked to. Consider the examples below:

(13)

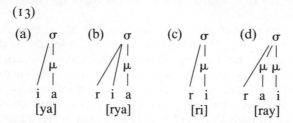

(a) σ   (b) σ   (c) σ   (d) σ

     μ   μ   μ   μ μ

     i a   r i a   r i   r a i
     [ya]   [rya]   [ri]   [ray]

The /i/ on the melodic tier represents a tense high front vocoid. If it is linked directly to the syllable node (13a)–(13b), then it is realized as non-syllabic, being part of the onset. If it is linked to the sole mora of a syllable as in (13c) then it is realized as fully syllabic. If it is moraic, but tautosyllabic with another moraic segment, then the sonority rules of the language will determine the precise phonetic realization of the resulting diphthong. The example in (13d) represents the typical case of a high vocoid becoming an offglide after a more sonorous element.

We can now return to our comparison of moraic theory with the CV and X accounts. One striking aspect of the representations in (13) is that certain segmental elements are not linked to any element on the timing (in this case moraic) tier. In particular, it is the onset segments which are associated directly to the syllable node. This is a departure from both the CV and X accounts where each melodic unit was linked to an element on the timing tier. Why is moraic theory different in this regard? Since the traditional concept of mora is inextricably tied to syllable weight distinctions, the only elements which can be moraic are those which help to determine syllable weight. It turns out cross-linguistically that while languages do vary somewhat in what constitutes a heavy versus light syllable, onsets do not play any role in this determination; only rhyme elements do.[4] For that reason, onsets will not be mora-bearing. We will see later that the lack of morae in onsets bears directly on the question of CL.

The next point of consideration is the aforementioned difference or variability in what a language considers light versus heavy. While onsets do not play a role in this regard, rhyme elements do. For example, in some languages (e.g. Lardil) a syllable with a long vowel (VV) constitutes a heavy syllable, while a syllable with a short vowel (V) and a syllable with a short vowel and a single coda consonant (VC) constitute light syllables. In moraic theory this is directly reflected in the number of morae assigned to the syllable. Thus, while (13a) and (13b) would be represented identically in a language like Lardil, a word such as [rid] would have the representation given in (14).

(14)

$$
\begin{array}{c}
\sigma \\
| \\
\mu \\
r \; i \; d
\end{array}
$$

In the representation above the coda element /d/ simply does not receive its own mora. The stress system will then correctly interpret the syllable in (14) as light (= monomoraic). This then is a parameter along which languages differ. The assignment of an additional mora to a coda consonant (e.g. 11c) has been termed 'Weight by Position' by Hayes (1989).

2   The formal assignment of syllabic and moraic structure

Let us now consider one way in which syllabic and moraic structure would be formally assigned to a string of segmental units (adapted from Bickmore 1991).

(15)   *Mora and syllable construction:*

   (a) Certain segments may be underlyingly associated to two μ's (= phonemic length)
   (b) Associate any sequence of two tautosegmental morae to a single σ.
   (c) Assign a μ and σ node to syllable nuclei.
   (d) Maximal onset principle: associate as many segments as possible as onsets of every nucleus.
   (e) Any remaining free segmental units will be associated leftward to a μ node. If the language is [+ weight by position], then a free segmental unit will receive its own mora, and that mora will associate leftward to σ.

Given these principles, consider the following sample derivations:

(16) (a)   μ μ   (b)   μ   (c)   *UR*

        \ / | (15a)

  t r a p u k   b i g o   i o r l e i

      σ   (15b)

     / \

    μ μ

    \ /

  t r a p u k

   σ   σ   σ   σ   σ σ   σ σ   (15c)

  / \ | | | | | | |

  μ μ μ   μ μ μ   μ μ μ μ

  \ / | | | | | | | |

  t r a p u k   b i g o   i o rl e i

   σ   σ   σ   σ   σ σ   σ σ   (15d)

  // \ | /| /| | | /| |

 / μ μ μ   / μ μ/μ   μ μ / μ μ

 / /\ / | | | || | |/ | |

  t r a p u k   b i g o   i o rl e i

   σ   σ   σ   σ   σ σ   σ σ   (15e)

  // \ /| /|\ /| | | /| |

 / μ μ / μ μ   / μ μ/μ   μ μ / μ μ

 / /\ /\| | | || | |\ / | |

  t r a p u k   b i g o   i o rl e i

Principle (15a) is relevant for languages which have phonemic length (either in Vs or Cs or both). A vowel which is phonemically long will be assigned two μs in UR (16a). A consonant which is long will be assigned one (16b). Principle (15b) then insures that both morae of a long vowel are tautosyllabic.

Principle (15c) then assigns μ and σ to all melodic units which can act as a syllable nucleus, and is thus very language-dependent. In some languages (illustrated by the forms above) this may be all vocoids (elements which result phonetically as vowels); in other languages this may include nasals as well; in still other languages this may include vocoids, nasals, and liquids.

Principle (15d) then associates to a syllable node the greatest possible onset. What can constitute an onset is language-dependent. In some languages this is straightforwardly calculated on the basis of the sonority of the melodic units (e.g. 'elements in an onset must increase in sonority'). In other languages the algorithm is somewhat more complex, parts of which may simply be stipulated (e.g. 'if the first segment of the onset is x, then the next segment can be y or z').

Principle (15e) then associates leftover melodic units into the syllable. (16a) illustrates the case of a language in which codas are moraic, (16b) illustrates the case where they are not.

There may then be language specific rules which will modify the structure built by (15a–e). For example, a sequence of two moraic segments might combine to form a diphthong and hence become tautosyllabic. For example, the word in (16c) might become [jorley]. Similarly, the language might have a rule of gliding (to be discussed further below) which might, e.g. alter the syllabicity of the first segment in (16c), yielding [yorlei] or [yoːrlei].

Now that we have examined syllable structure in a moraic framework, let us reconsider the case of compensatory lengthening in (1a). We saw in (7)–(9) above that the CV model was certainly adequate to handle such cases (as would the X theory for precisely the same reasons). Below, we account for this example in moraic theory.

(17)

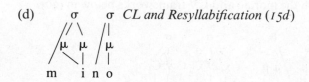

(a) σ σ σ *After Mora and Syllable Construction* (15)
      μ μ   μ
      m a i n o

(b) σ σ σ *Vowel Deletion*
      μ μ   μ
      m   i n o

(c)   σ σ *Parasitic Delinking* (7)
         μ μ   μ
         m   i n o

(d)   σ   σ *CL and Resyllabification* (15d)
         μ μ   μ
         m   i n o

The derivation in (17) is much like the one in (7)–(9) in all relevant respects. One segmental unit deletes, leaving a mora node temporarily stranded. In (17c) the stranded mora node reassociates to the /i/. (See the discussion in Section 1.1 for reasons why the μ must associate to /i/ and not any other segment.)

In moraic theory the Vowel Deletion Rule could be formalized as in (18)

(18)

The precise formulation of the rule, however, would depend on the phonemic inventory and syllable structure of the language. For example, if every mora bearing unit was a vowel, and never, say a consonantal coda (e.g. in Polynesian languages which lack codas), then the syllable nodes in (18) could be dispensed with.

We are now in a position to examine other, often more complex, cases of CL.

3   More cases of CL

We begin by examining cases like the one above in (1) in which one sound lengthens due to the deletion of an adjacent sound. The Chilungu case showed CL following vowel deletion. The Latin examples below (taken from Hayes 1989) illustrate CL due to the deletion of an adjacent consonant.

(19)

(a) *kasnus → kaanus 'gray'
(b) *kosmis → koomis 'courteous'
(c) *fideslia → fideelia 'pot'

In each case above, a rule of s-Deletion has applied. CL then applies, lengthening the preceding vowel. The derivation of (19a) is given in both the moraic and CV frameworks below in (20).

(20)

(a)

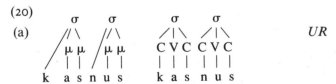

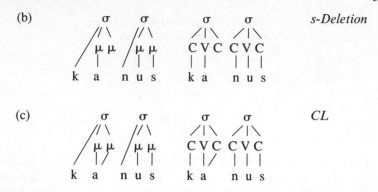

(b)   *s-Deletion*

(c)   *CL*

Although at first glance both theories seem to be able to straight-forwardly account for the compensatory lengthening, there are several important differences in the two approaches. First, consider the structure of the compensatorily lengthened [a:]. In the moraic framework the [a:] is formally identical to the structure of an underlying long /a:/ (cf. 11b). This predicts that any rule involving long vowels (which takes place after CL) will treat underlyingly long and derived long vowels identically, as their structure would be identical. Such is not the case in CV (or X) theory. Compare the vowel in the first syllable in (20c) above with the underlying long /i:/ in (3) and (10). In the case of (3), the melodic unit is associated to two V slots, while in (20c) it is associated to a V slot and a C slot. In (10) the melodic unit is associated to two X slots immediately dominated by an N node, whereas a compensatorily lengthened vowel would be associated to one X slot dominated by an N node, and another X slot dominated by a C node as shown below:

(21)

(a)   *Underlying Representation*

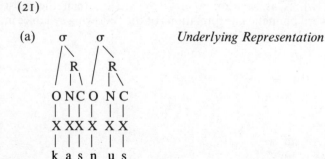

(b)   *s-Deletion and CL*

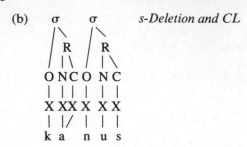

Therefore, both the CV and X theories, unless somehow modified, make a prediction that moraic theory does not, namely that the phonology of a language has the potential to treat underlyingly long vowels differently than those derived by CL. No such cases, however, appear to have been found. It is possible, of course, to modify the CV and X theories such that they make the same prediction as moraic theory. In the CV theory one alternative would involve changing the C node to a V node after CL. In X theory this would involve deleting the C (= Coda), after which the X slot would be associated to the N node to its left. The second alternative would be to set up underlyingly long vowels as a melodic unit linked to a V and a C slot. While this makes underlying long vowels structurally identical to long vowels derived by CL after consonant deletion (as in 19), long vowels derived by CL after vowel deletion (as in (9)) will have a different structure (viz. linkage to two V slots). Therefore in a language which exhibits CL of a vowel before a following deleted vowel or consonant, some change from C to V, or V to C, would be required to maintain an isomorphic representation of long vowels.

One further point can be made in this regard. Since the sole distinction between a vowel and a corresponding glide (e.g. [i] vs [y]; [u] vs. [w]) is association to a C or V slot, then the most straightforward phonetic interpretations of the following syllables in a CV framework are given below.

(22)

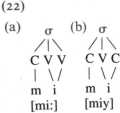

Assuming that the phonetic realization of both underlying and derived long vowels is identical (i.e. either 22a *or* 22b), then a language

which generates both types will presumably either need a patch up
rule or some stipulation in the phonetic component to insure that
the phonetic pronunciation of both of these structures is identical.

There is a second, and perhaps more important difference between the skeletal timing theories and the moraic one illustrated by
the derivations above. Recall that the original motivation for mora
assignment was to straightforwardly formalize the traditional distinction between heavy (= bimoraic) and light (= monomoraic)
syllables. In order for CL to apply in the Latin example in (21) a
mora needed to be assigned to the coda consonant /s/ in the
underlying representation. As mentioned above, there is independent
evidence in Latin for a heavy vs. light distinction, namely in the assignment of stress. Both CVV and CVC syllables are considered heavy,
while CV syllables are considered light. Thus, two different aspects of
the Latin grammar (viz. stress assignment and CL) converge with
regard to the moraic status of consonantal codas. Since the same
formal elements (viz. morae) are used to determine both syllable
weight for stress and potential for CL, moraic theory makes a strong
prediction in this regard that the segmental timing theories do not.
Moraic theory predicts that no language will have a stress system
which interprets a syllable with a VC nucleus as light (e.g. for stress
purposes) while exhibiting CL of a vowel after the deletion of a coda
consonant. For a VC syllable to be light, the coda C must *not* be
moraic. If coda consonants are not moraic, however, their deletion
cannot induce CL as there will be no stranded mora subsequent to
the deletion. This is illustrated below using the Latin example in (23).

(23)

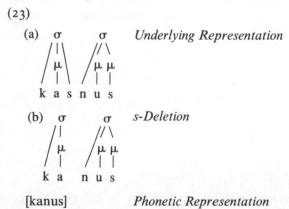

(a)   σ   σ   *Underlying Representation*

                        k a s n u s

(b)   σ   σ   *s-Deletion*

                        k a   n u s

      [kanus]   *Phonetic Representation*

The skeletal timing theories (both CV and X versions) make no such
prediction in this regard. Since each melodic unit is underlyingly
associated to a timing slot, the potential for CL is always present

regardless of how the light vs. heavy distinction is being made for stress purposes. Therefore, while the existence of a language which interprets VC syllables as light while exhibiting CL after the deletion of a coda C would be a major problem for moraic theory, the lack of such cases is a credit to its more constrained approach.

It should be noted that the converse of the aforementioned prediction of moraic theory does not hold. The propositions involved in the above logic are as follows:

(24)

   (a) Deletion of consonantal coda induces CL of previous vowel

   (b) For stress purposes, a syllable with a -VC rhyme is interpreted as bimoraic (= heavy)

The logical statement 'if a → b' is true (as 'if not b → not a'). Let us now examine why the converse: 'if b → a' is not true. As was previously mentioned, not all languages exhibit CL. Formally, a language which exhibits CL is simply one which preserves the integrity of the moraic tier, i.e. phonological rules may delete melodic units without affecting timing positions. It is equally logically possible, however, for a language to have, say, deletion rules which delete not only the melodic unit but also the timing slot associated with that melodic unit. This is possible in all of the timing tier theories examined thus far, and will have the effect of preempting any CL, as there will be no stranded mora.[5] This is illustrated below.

(25)

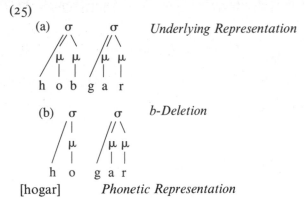

   (a) σ   σ   *Underlying Representation*

        h o b g a r

   (b) σ   σ   *b-Deletion*

        h o   g a r

  [hogar]   *Phonetic Representation*

The b-Deletion rule (which, say, deleted a /b/ before a /g/) could be formalized as follows:

(26)   μ

      | ⟶ ø /

      b   _ g

In the example above the /b/ in (25a) is moraic because CVC syllables in the language are treated as heavy. What makes this case different from the Latin one (cf. 20) is that the consonant deletion rule (in its structural change) not only deletes the consonant but the mora it is linked to as well. This correctly predicts that no CL will ensue.

As a final refinement of (24), if deletion of a coda C induces CL of a previous vowel in a language, it is not strictly necessary that there be positive evidence that – VC rhymes are interpreted as heavy. What is crucial is that they are not interpreted as light. Thus a language exhibiting the CL effects while not having a heavy vs. light contrast (i.e. a 'quantity insensitive' stress system) would not be a counterexample to moraic theory. This would simply be a case where evidence for moraic structure came solely from one component of the grammar (viz. the CL facts).

Up to this point CL has always had the effect of lengthening a vowel. There are also cases where a consonant becomes lengthened (i.e. becomes a geminate). Consider the following historical changes in verbal and nominal roots from Proto Bantu to Luganda (Clements 1986)

(27)

    (a) *-jima → -mma 'refuse'
    (b) *-jiba → -bba 'steal'
    (c) * jika → -kka 'descend'
    (d) *-tuiga → -tugga 'giraffe'

First, there is an independent rule which deletes the initial *j in (27a)–(27c). The relevance of these examples here is that in each case the elision of a vowel (viz. /i/) has had the effect of lengthening the following consonant. Let us consider the derivation of (27d) in a moraic and CV framework.

(28)

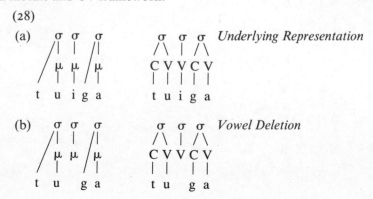

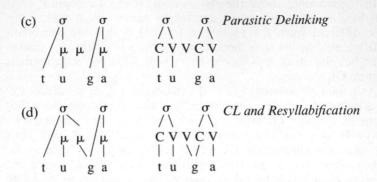

As is evident, both theories are capable of insightfully handling this type of CL. We saw above in (20) that after CL a long vowel was represented structurally as VC. In the example above, the first syllable [tug] is represented as CVV. It is becoming apparent that in CV theory the important aspect of the representation is the number of slots a melodic unit is linked to (which determines its length) and not the actual type of slot it is (C vs. V).

Below is the derivation of the above example in X theory.

(29)

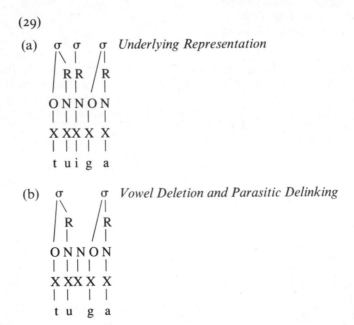

(c) σ   σ   *CL and Resyllabification*

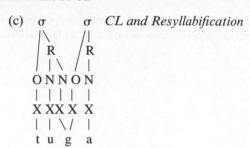

If we make the minimal number of changes in the syllabic structure after CL, then the structure in (29c) results. In order to have the coda of the first syllable dominated by a C node instead of an N node, some additional rule or stipulation in the syllabification algorithm would be necessary.

To summarize, then, we have examined several instances of CL of one sound due to the deletion of an adjacent sound. Specifically we have seen the following subcases:

(30)

(a)   σ   σ
         | |
         V_1 V_2 ⟶ Ø V_2 ⟶ [V_2:]   (cf. (17))

(b)   σ
        ╱ \
        V C ⟶ V Ø ⟶ [V:]   (cf. (20))

(c)   σ σ
         | |
         V C ⟶ Ø C ⟶ [C:]   (cf. (28))

On the basis of the above examples one might be tempted to assume that languages which exhibit CL will, whenever a sound is deleted, lengthen an adjacent sound. Such, as we will now see, is not true; only certain deletions will trigger CL. Let us investigate this more fully. One thing that holds true for all the cases in (30) is that the deleted element is in the rime of the syllable.[6] It turns out that typologically this is the crucial factor which determines the potential for CL, i.e. membership in the rime. To put it another way, the deletion of a syllable onset does not induce CL. This distinction of onset vs. rime, as discussed above, is one which has traditionally been employed in determining syllable weight. While the structure of the rime is crucial in determining any heavy vs. light distinction for stress purposes, onset structures are irrelevant.

Let us consider the predict deletion the various frameworks make regarding a derivation where the onset of a syllable is deleted.

(31)

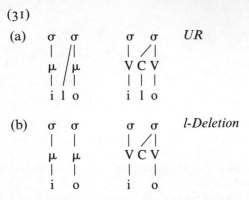

In the moraic derivation, since the onset /l/ was never moraic, no CL is predicted. The decision not to assign a mora to the /l/ underlyingly is not simply an arbitrary or language-dependent decision. In moraic theory no onset will be mora-bearing. This has a twofold effect: first it accounts for the fact that onsets never determine syllable weight, and second it makes the prediction illustrated in (31) above that the deletion of an onset will never induce CL.

Let us now discuss the CV case. The question is what happens next to the final structure shown in (31b). Recall that the l-Deletion rule must not automatically delete the C slot as well, as presumably the deletion of a coda /l/ *would* induce CL (e.g. /ilko/ → [i:ko]). Prima facie it seems like the requirements for CL are met as there is an empty skeletal slot, predicting that CL should apply. Note that the fact that it is a C slot does not inhibit CL. While we have not seen any examples of long vowels as CV entities, we have seen a case (20) where a long vowel is represented as VC. In order to prevent CL from applying here (linking the /i/ to the free C slot) we would need to stipulate that a melodic unit cannot spread to C slot which is an onset.[7]

Consider next the possibility: the deletion of a consonant in a word initial cluster.

(32)

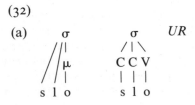

(b)   σ   σ   *s-Deletion*

Note that the two theories make very different predictions here. In moraic theory, since the /s/ was part of the onset it will not be moraic. The /s/ in the CV approach, however, will be assigned a C slot. Moraic theory predicts that, even in a language which permits word-initial geminates, no CL (e.g. in this example of the /l/) will ever occur. In contrast, the prediction of CV theory seems to be that (in a language which permits word-initial geminates) the /l/ could spread to the initial C slot, yielding [llo]. I know of no such cases where these differing predictions can be tested, but it seems to be an empirical issue.

While the only example presented above of geminate formation involved the spreading of a C to a V position (28d), there are ample cases of the type /asta/ → [atta]. To permit this type of CL, while excluding the type shown in (32) above one would have to form a constraint along the lines of: a consonant cannot spread leftward to a C slot which is tautosyllabic to the C slot to which it is presently linked.

Let us now move to a discussion of cases of CL caused by phonological changes other than the deletion of an adjacent segment. One common trigger for CL is gliding. Consider the following examples from Kinyambo, a Bantu language spoken in northwestern Tanzania (cf. Bickmore (1991)).

(33)

(a) o- mu-rimi 'farmer'   (cf. a- ba- rimi 'farmers')
    PP CP farmer   PP CP farmer

(b) /o- mu-ana/ → omwaana   (cf. a- ba- ana 'children')
    'child'   PP CP child
    PP CP child

(c) /o- mu-isiki/ → omwiisiki   (cf. a- ba- isiki 'daughters')
    'daughter'   PP CP daughter
    PP CP daughter

Nouns in Kinyambo are formed by combining the Preprefix (PP), the Class Prefix (CP), and a root. This is straightforwardly observed in (33a). The examples in (33b) and (33c), however, are different in two important respects. First, the Class Prefix is realized as [mw] instead of [mu], and second the vowel which follows is long. These cases then differ from those presented in Section 1.1 in that the CL is not due to the outright loss of a segment. Let us consider the derivation of (33b) in both a moraic and CV framework.

(34)

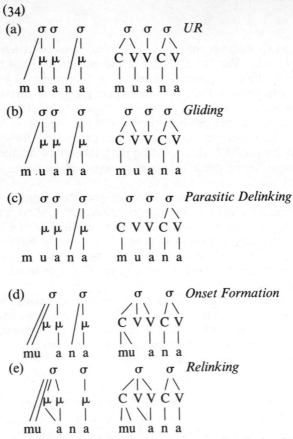

The important thing to remember in the derivation above is that the syllabicity of a melodic unit is determined by what it is linked to (cf. 13). In the moraic framework a rule of 'gliding' is simply a rule which deletes the association line between a melodic unit and a mora (34b). This is shown below:

(35)

Gliding

$$\mu \atop [+high] \longrightarrow \mu \atop [+high] \Big/ \underline{\quad} [\quad]$$

The principle of maximal onset (15d) will then automatically link both the /m/ and the stranded /u/ directly to the syllable node (34c). This leaves a stranded mora which will then associate with the /a/ making it long. In the CV framework gliding is also a matter of deleting an association line, this time from the melodic unit to a V slot (34b). The /u/ will reassociate to the C slot to become part of the onset (34c) after which the stranded V slot associates with the /a/.

Although the two derivations are quite similar there is one small difference between them having to do with the structure of onsets. In the moraic theory, the final representation shown in (34d) would most straightforwardly be interpreted as having multiple segments in the onset, i.e. [mw]. If the result is not a complex onset, but rather a complex single segment, i.e. a labio-velarized bilabial nasal [mʷ], then a further phonological or phonetic rule would be necessary.[8] The CV case seems to be just the opposite. The most intuitive interpretation of the structure in (34d) would be to assume that the onset of the first syllable is one complex segment [mʷ] as it is representationally distinct from a structure in which both the /m/ and the /u/ are linked to individual C nodes as shown below:[9]

(36)

```
           σ
        ╱╱│╲╲
       C C V V
       │ │ ╲╱
       m u  a
```

If a language does not distinguish between onset clusters (e.g. [mw]) and corresponding complex segments (e.g. [mʷ]) in the phonology, then the structures in (34) and (36) will simply receive a uniform phonetic realization in the phonetic component.

Consider the gliding in the Chilungu examples below:

(37)

(a) /u- ik- e/ → [wiike]   (cf. ik-a 'put!')
2 sg. put SUBJ
'that you put'

(b) /u- ikal- e/ → [wiikale]   (cf. ikal-a 'sit!')
2sg. sit SUBJ
'that you sit'

In each case the initial /u/ glides, after which the following vowel undergoes CL. While this seems to exactly parallel the cases discussed above, consider the derivation of (37a) in the moraic and CV frameworks below.

(38)

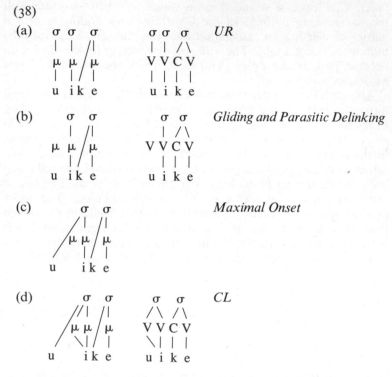

(a)   σ σ σ   σ σ σ   *UR*

(b)   σ σ   σ σ   *Gliding and Parasitic Delinking*

(c)   σ σ   *Maximal Onset*

(d)   σ σ   σ σ   *CL*

The derivation in the moraic framework works the same as it did in the other gliding example (34) above. Now consider the CV framework. After Gliding removes the association line from the /u/, the V slot is now free to associate with the /i/. The problem lies in what to do with the initial /u/. Whereas in example (34) it could associate to a previous C, in (38) there is no such timing slot available. What seems to be a prediction of CV theory – that CL should not occur when the initial segment glides before another vowel – finds counter examples such as those above. One can, of course, add a rule to insert an initial C slot in these cases, but this seems to suggest that gliding in initial position is somehow different from gliding in all other positions, and there seems to be no evidence that it is, at least in Chilungu.[10]

Let us now examine a case in which one segment becomes compensatorily lengthened due to the deletion of a non-adjacent segment. To begin, we will consider a case taken from Greek, whereby /odwos/ → [o:dos] after w-Deletion. The beginning of the derivation is given below in both frameworks.

(39)

(a)

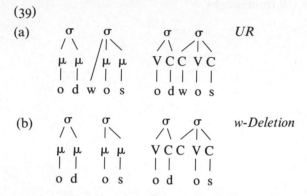

UR

(b)

w-Deletion

In both cases, the principle of maximal onset (cf. (15b)) is violated as the /d/ is represented as a coda rather than an onset. As mentioned above, after any alteration in the representation, the rules of syllabification will need to reapply. In both cases the /d/ must become the onset of the second syllable, after which the word-initial /o/ can lengthen.

(40)

(a)

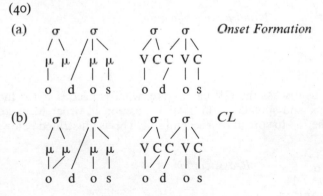

Onset Formation

(b)

CL

One question which arises in cases such as this is: why did the /d/ delink from the μ (or the first C slot)? In some cases this might be due to a language-specific prohibition on geminates, for unless there is some overriding theory, internal reason, or the delinking, both theories seem to predict the possibility of cases whereby /odwos/ → [oddos]. Let us move to a second case where the CL of one segment is triggered by the deletion of a non-adjacent one.

Consider the Middle English example /talə/ → [ta:l] as cited in Hayes (1989). Let us contrast the beginning of the derivations in the moraic and CV frameworks:

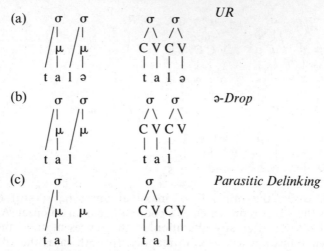

(a)   *UR*

(b)   *ə-Drop*

(c)   *Parasitic Delinking*

In the moraic case, once the syllable node deletes, resyllabification can reapply, as illustrated below.[11]

(42)

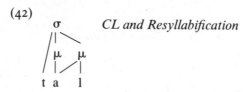

        CL and Resyllabification

Now let us discuss the CV case. Here, what is needed is for the /l/ to delink and spread to the final V position in order to make room for the /a/ to spread to a second slot. This is illustrated below.

(43)

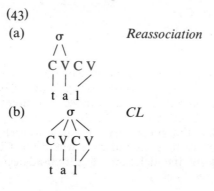

(a)   *Reassociation*

(b)   *CL*

Several comments are in order. First, it seems necessary to stipulate that the 'making room for CL' somehow stops as soon as a syllable nucleus can be lengthened. Otherwise, what is to prevent the /a/ from delinking and spreading to the C slot, enabling the /t/ to geminate yielding *[ttal]?

Second, and more importantly, the /l/ now occupies a V slot. The only other time we have seen a consonant link to a V slot was in example (28) in which a geminate /g/ was linked to both a V and a C slot. That case seemed to fall under the generalization that in the CV framework a long melodic unit is represented as a unit linked to (any) two skeletal slots. Since the linkage of consonant to a V slot in (43b) does not fall under this case, the theory must simply permit consonants which are normally linked to a C slot to become linked to a V slot, without any phonetic result.

We can now briefly return to our discussion above regarding the deletion of an onset. Example (31) is repeated as (44) below.

(44)

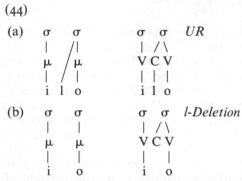

It should now be clear that CV theory cannot account for the lack of spreading of the /i/ by an outright stipulation on the spreading of a vowel to a C slot which was once an onset, as such an association is crucially necessary in (43). Some other, more complex constraint would be needed, such as: vowels cannot spread to a C slot which is tautosyllabic to a following V slot. Since Parasitic Delinking will remove the syllable node in (43) but not in (44), such a constraint could be maintained.

The examples in (39) and (41) above show that the deletion of a vowel can have the effect of lengthening a preceding V. We may now ask, does the deletion of a vowel ever affect the *following* vowel? It turns out that typologically, while there are attested cases of the CL process illustrated in (44) above, there are no cases of the type /VCV/ → [øCV:]. Let us consider such a derivation below.

(45)

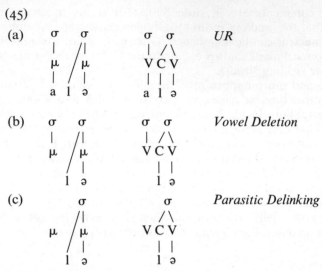

In the moraic account, after Vowel Deletion, Parasitic Delinking has the effect of deleting the first syllable node, but there is no reason to delete the second one, as it has not lost its nuclear melodic unit. Therefore, the stranded μ cannot associate to the schwa, and hence [lə:] is correctly predicted not to occur. In the CV framework, it is not immediately obvious what should happen next. We saw in example (43) that a consonant on the melodic tier can delink and reassociate to an adjacent V slot (as part of the process of making room for the CL of a vowel). Thus unless further stipulations are added, the theory makes the prediction that a vowel can be compensatorily lengthened after the deletion of a preceding vowel, and such seems never to occur.

It should be noted that both theories allow for the possibility of creating a geminate /l/. This is a possibility realized in several languages as cited in Hayes (1989: 281). If a language does not permit word-initial geminates or syllabic consonants of this kind, then the μ simply deletes by *Stray Erasure*, a process by which any element which cannot become a part of the syllable structure gets deleted (Itô 1986).

4 Summary

We have seen various manifestations of CL in different languages. In each case the deletion of one segment triggered the lengthening of another. Formally, this was accounted for by deleting a segmental element without deleting its corresponding timing unit. The stranded timing unit may then be associated to a segmental unit making it long. Importantly, however, in languages which exhibit CL it is not the case that deleting just any segment will induce the CL of another. In general it is the deletion of a rhyme element (and not an onset element) which induces CL (the only exception being the complex case discussed in (39)).

We described the moraic theory as presented in Hayes (1989) and contrasted it with other timing unit theories, specifically the CV and X theories. Moraic theory differs from these other two theories in several ways. First, it differs from CV theory (but not from X theory) in that all timing units are homogeneous. Next, it differs from both the CV and X theories in assuming that not all segments are linked to timing units – while some segments are linked to morae, others link directly to the syllable node. As far as determining which segments are moraic, the theory assumes that syllable weight units (used, e.g., in determining quantity sensitivity in stress systems) and timing units are isomorphic. (See also Zec, Katamba, this volume.) This makes the strong prediction, not made directly by the other theories, that no language will need some segmental unit to be linked to a weight unit for CL purposes, where that unit must not be linked to a weight unit for stress purposes). This is clearly an empirical issue which gives us some basis on which to evaluate the explanatory adequacy of the competing theories.

We saw that this assumption, in part, predicts that since onsets never contribute to syllable weight, their deletion should never induce CL of an adjacent vowel. In moraic theory this is accounted for by not assigning onsets to morae, but instead linking them directly to the syllable node. In the CV and X theories, however, every segment is assigned a timing unit, thus ensuring that the deletion of onsets does not induce CL requires additional stipulations not needed in moraic theory.

Notes

1. The rule in (6) is not the only way, of course, that a Vowel Deletion rule could be written. For example, if vowels are the only [-cons] sounds in the language, then a more SPE rule such as [-cons] → ∅ — [-cons] could be written as well.
2. The latter constraint certainly holds true for Chilungu, from which this example is taken.
3. While the example in (1a) also could be accounted for by a rule of total assimilation of the second vowel, other instances of CL do not lend themselves to an assimilation analysis, as will be shown below.
4. However, see Davis (1988) who examines several languages in which onsets seem to affect stress assignment.

5. The inverse of a → b, ~a → ~b does not hold true for the same reasoning, just because deletion of a consonantal coda does not induce CL of a previous vowel, it is not necessarily the case that VC rhymes are monomoraic.

6. In X theory this means it is dominated at some point by an R node; in CV theory, it is either dominated by a V or by a C which is tautosyllabic to a preceding V; in moraic theory, it is dominated by a mora.

7. It will be shown below, however, CV theory must, in fact, allow for such reassociations in order to account for certain attested instances of CL.

8. Assuming some notion of feature geometry, such a rule would merge the labio-velar features of the /u/ with the primary place features of the /m/ under a single root node. Such a process might be able to be built into the gliding rule itself, considerably complicating its structural change.

9. It should be noted that in the CV framework complex segments can be represented not only as two melodic units linked to the same C slot, but, like moraic theory, as a single melodic unit (i.e. one root node) having both a primary and secondary articulation.

10. Francis Katamba (personal communication) informs me that in Luganda no compensatory lengthening occurs precisely when there is no consonant onset. E.g. /i-a-gob-a/ (cl 9-past-chase-FV) → yagoba (*yaagoba). Thus, for Luganda the CV theory makes this prediction straightforward, while one would have to add a mora deletion rule for such cases within the moraic framework. The larger question then becomes which case (if either) is the unmarked one cross-linguistically, as the competing theories make different predictions in this regard; only further research will tell.

11. The question arises as to why the free mora reassociates to the /a/ (and not just the /l/). Hayes (1989) attributes this to Itô's (1986) principle that prosodic structure is created maximally.

Chapter 5

The role of moraic structure in the distribution of segments within syllables

Draga Zec

One of the central tenets of the moraic theory of syllable structure is that the mora serves as a primitive subsyllabic constituent and as a measure of syllable weight (Bickmore this volume, Katamba this volume, Hyman 1985, Itô 1989, Zec 1988, Hayes 1989, McCarthy and Prince 1986, 1990(a)). Syllables are parsed solely into moras, which in their turn function as weight units: a syllable with one mora is light, as in (1a), and with more than one mora, heavy, as in (1b).

(1)

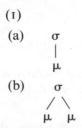

(a)   σ
       |
       μ

(b)   σ
      / \
     μ   μ

The goal of this chapter is to provide further support for the moraic theory of the syllable, by demonstrating that the patterning of segments is governed in crucial ways by organizational principles at the moraic level. This is in the spirit of Kahn's 1976 original argument for syllable structure, which made superfluous those morpheme-structure constraints that could be reduced to constraints on syllables. The claim advanced here, however, is that the relevant unit for capturing the patterns of sounds is the mora rather than the syllable. I argue that the projection of moraic structure from the segmental level is fully predictable and, as such, formally characterizable by phonological constraints.

My secondary goal is to account for complex interactions in Pali syllable structure. After introducing the general principles governing the projection of moraic structure, I turn to Pali, showing that this case becomes fully tractable under the assumption that this general mechanism is at work here, although in a less than obvious fashion.

While constraints on moraic structure are my primary focus, they will be studied through interactions with other principles responsible for the structure of syllables, also expressible in terms of constraints. The general view advocated here is that syllable structure results from a number of potentially complex interactions among constraints, and this is illustrated in detail in the intricacies of the Pali case. Moreover, I adopt a specific theory of constraints and constraint-interaction, Optimality Theory, recently proposed and developed in Prince and Smolensky 1991, 1992, 1993, McCarthy and Prince 1993, Itô and Mester 1992, etc. Within this approach, it is argued that, rather than imposing absolute requirements, constraints vary in degree of strength and are ranked accordingly. A further assumption is that output forms are evaluated directly with respect to a set of constraints, with no specific rules or repair strategies invoked as mediators. The basic principles of this framework are (based on McCarthy and Prince 1993):

(2)

  (a) *Violability*: Constraints are *violable* (but violation is minimal).
  (b) *Ranking*: Constraints are *ranked* on a language-particular basis, forming a constraint hierarchy.
  (c) *Parallelism*: Best-satisfaction of the constraint hierarchy is computed over the whole hierarchy and the whole candidate set.

The chapter is organized as follows: in Section 1, I present the general mechanism governing the alignment of moras and segments, which crucially draws upon the notion of sonority. In Sections 2–4 this approach is further justified by a detailed analysis of the complex facts of Pali syllable structure, in which the principles of moraic patterning are shown to play a crucial role. Concluding remarks are given in Section 5.

1   The alignment of segments and prosodic units

In earlier approaches to syllable structure it has been assumed that syllabification operates on segments linked to the skeletal, i.e. timing, tier – either the CV tier, as in Clements and Keyser 1983, Steriade 1982, or the X tier, as proposed in Levin 1985. Under the present approach, neither the CV nor the X tier is assumed. Rather, the sub-syllabic timing tier corresponds to the moraic level. The moraic framework is thus highly constrained: the weight units, that is, moras, are the only timing units posited in phonological representations. In the CV and X theories, every root node is projected onto the timing tier; in the moraic theory, only those root nodes are projected onto the timing tier which occupy 'weight-bearing' positions within the syllable.

The hypothetical forms in (3) illustrate the alignment of segments and prosodic constituents within the version of the moraic theory adopted in this chapter: (3a) represents the alignment within a light syllable, and (3b), within a heavy one. In (3c), it is shown that a non-moraic syllable-final consonant is attached directly to the syllable node.[1]

(3)

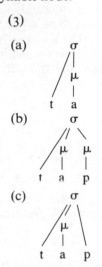

(a)

(b)

(c)

In brief, a mora may be linked to at most one segment. Thus, weight-bearing units are aligned with segments in a one-to-one fashion, and onset consonants, directly linked to the syllable node, are left out of this alignment. Note, however, that a segment may be linked to more than one mora, which is precisely the representation of a long vowel, as shown in (4):

(4)

Geminate consonants, on the other hand, are represented as linked to the mora and the syllable, following Hayes (1989):

(5)

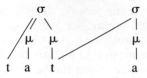

Both long vowels and geminate consonants will have to be underlyingly associated with prosodic structure, to indicate their special status. In all other respects, however, the alignment of segments and moras is predictable, and in order to show this we need to introduce the notion of sonority, which, as will be argued, serves as the governing principle of this alignment. The sonority of segments has commonly been represented by means of a scale, as in (6) (Hooper 1976, Steriade 1982, Selkirk 1984b, and the references therein):

(6)

Sonority Scale
vowels
sonorants
obstruents

From this scale we can derive the set of sonority classes listed in (7), which are characterizable in terms of the major class features, as shown in (8).[2]

(7)

(a) vowels
(b) vowels + sonorants
(c) all segments

(8)

Sonority classes
(a) [– cons]   vowels
(b) [+ son]   vowels + liquids + nasals
(c) ————   all segments

The alignment of segments and moras is governed by sonority, as proposed in Zec (1988). Specifically, the segment projecting a mora needs to satisfy a condition on relative sonority: its sonority has to be at least equal to, if not greater than, that of the following segment. In order to capture this formally, I posit the following constraint on moraic structure (following the proposal in Zec 1988: 100–105):

(9) *Constraint on Moraic Prominence*: Segment r_i projects a mora if it is not followed by a more sonorous segment r_j.

Condition: Son $(r_i) \geqslant$ Son (r_j)

Here r_i and r_j stand for adjacent root nodes; r_i forms a sonority peak and is therefore capable of being aligned with a mora if and only if its sonority is not lower than that of the following segment.

In English, for instance, the parse of the string *simply* in (10a) adheres to the constraint in (9), while those in (10b) and (10c) do not. In (10b) this is due to the failure of *m* to project a mora, although it is followed by a less sonorous segment; and in (10c) this is because the segment *p* projects a mora, yet it is followed by a more sonorous segment. In sum, such a segment also needs to satisfy constraint (9), which sets limitations on its relative sonority within a sequence, that is, in strictly paradigmatic terms.[3]

(10)

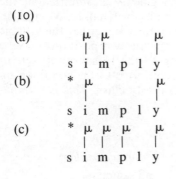

The parse of the string *simple* is given in (11): the projection of moras is in conformity with Moraic Prominence in (11a), but not in (11b) and (11c).

(11)

(a)   μ   μ   μ
           | | |
        s   i   m   p   l   (e)

(b)   * μ   μ
          | |
        s i m p l (e)

(c)   * μ μ μ μ
          | | | |
        s i m p l (e)

The constraint on moraic prominence is taken here to be universally valid, and as such operative in any system of syllable structure. However, this constraint is not sufficient for characterizing the alignment of segments and moras, and needs to be supplemented with an additional constraint, one that sets the minimal sonority of the segment aligned with a mora.

This latter constraint is subject to parametrization: in English we encounter an asymmetry between the minimal sonority of the first mora of a heavy syllable and the only mora of a light syllable on the one hand, and the second mora of a heavy syllable on the other. The former will be referred to as the syllabic position, and the latter as the moraic position. In the moraic position, any segment that adheres to Moraic Prominence can project a mora; in the syllabic position, this is the privilege of the set of [+ sonorant] segments, that is, of vowels, liquids, and nasals. To take another example, in Lithuanian only vowels may occupy the syllabic position, while the set of [+ sonorant] segments is admitted in the moraic position. And, as a final example, in Khalkha Mongolian only vowels, and no consonants, are admitted in either the syllabic or the moraic positions, while in Gonja the two positions may be occupied only by segments belonging to the [+ sonorant] set. In each case, the class of segments that conforms to the condition on minimal sonority corresponds to a sonority class. This is summarized in (12):[4]

(12)

	Syllabic position	Moraic position
English	[+ sonorant]	all segments
Khalkha	[− consonantal]	[− consonantal]
Mongolian		
Gonja	[+ sonorant]	[+ sonorant]
Lithuanian	[− consonantal]	[+ sonorant]

In sum, central in the characterization of moraic structure is the notion of sonority, which has a twofold impact on the distribution of segments within the syllable. First, sets of syllabic and moraic segments that languages select generally correspond to one of the universally posited sonority classes. Second, segments are assigned the moraic (or syllabic) status only if, in addition to belonging to the required sonority class, they also satisfy the condition on relative sonority, which is defined in purely paradigmatic terms. Segments left out of this alignment are linked directly to the syllable node, that is, to the 'onset'; crucial patterning is thus found at the moraic level.

2 The general properties of Pali syllable structure

The complex system of Pali syllable structure, partly manifested as an elaborate pattern of cluster simplification, has been the subject of a number of studies (Geiger 1968, Hankamer and Aissen 1974, Junghare 1979, Wetzels and Hermans 1985, Cho 1990, Murray 1982, Vaux 1992), yet no single analysis captures all the relevant aspects of this system.

The general properties of Pali syllables are stated in (13) below. Regarding syllable weight, Pali exhibits the bimoraic constraint: CV syllables are light, CVV and CVC syllables are heavy, and there are no super heavy (either CVVC or CVCC) syllables in the inventory. In addition, a syllable in Pali may include at most one consonant in the onset, and one in the coda.

(13)

    (a) light CV vs. heavy CVV, CVC
    (b) no super heavy syllables: *CVVC, *CVCC
    (c) at most one onset consonant: *CCV, *CCVV, etc.

Now we turn to the intricacies of the Pali system. Special restrictions hold of the coda consonant, which may be either a nasal (placeless, or homorganic with the following stop) or the first half of a geminate, as stated in (14):

(14) *Consonants permitted in the coda are*

    (a) nasal (placeless, or homorganic with the following stop)
    (b) first half of a geminate consonant

These properties are brought in relief by comparing Pali forms with those in Sanskrit, the 'parent' language of Pali. While Sanskrit permits a fairly free occurrence of word-final consonants, the corresponding forms in Pali do not possess word-final consonants, as shown in the following examples taken from Geiger (1968: 108).

(15)   *Loss of word-final consonants in Pali*

	Sanskrit	*Pali*	
(a)	tatas	tato	'therefrom'
(b)	punar	puno, puna	'again'
(c)	pra:patat	papata:	'hurled down'

As a result, the range of consonant clusters is highly limited in Pali. The comparison with Sanskrit further shows that the only type of Sanskrit cluster retained in Pali is a nasal + homorganic stop, as in (16a). Otherwise, Sanskrit consonant clusters were simplified in two fashions: in word internal contexts, the two consonants were reduced to one which geminates, as in (16b–e), while in word-initial position we encounter only cluster reduction, with no concomitant gemination, as shown in (17).[5]

(16)   *Simplification of intervocalic clusters*

		Sanskrit	*Pali*	
(a)	nasal +	danta	danta	'tamed'
	stop	sambuddha	sambuddha	'enlightened'
(b)	stop +	mudga	mugga	'bean'
	stop	sakthi	satthi	'thigh'
		bhakta	bhatta	'rice'
		śabda	sadda	'words'
		sapta	satta	'seven'
(c)	liquid +	karka	kakka	'a precious stone'
	stop	sarpa	sappa	'snake'
		valka	vakka	'the bark of a tree'
		kilbiṣa	kibbisa	'sin'
(d)	liquid +	karṣaka	kassaka	'farmer'
	fric	sparsa	phassa	'touch'
(e)	liquid +	dharma	dhamma	'righteousness'
	nasal	karṇa	kaṇṇa	'ear'
		kalmaṣa	kammasa	'spotted'

(17)   *Simplification of word-initial clusters:*

	Sanskrit	*Pali*	
	traana	taana	'protection'
	kramati	kamati	'walks'
	prati	paṭi	'against'
	śvaśru	sassu	'mother-in-l aw'

To foreshadow some of the conclusions regarding Pali syllable structure, the asymmetry between the intervocalic clusters, whose simplification results in a geminate, and word-initial clusters, which are reduced to a simplex segment, strongly suggests that weight relations are playing an important role in the Pali system, that is, that the pattern of cluster simplification is governed to a great extent by constraints on moraic structure.

Cluster simplification, as attested in the historical data, is also part of synchronic cluster simplifications across morpheme boundaries. As evidenced by the forms in (18), a consonant cluster created by virtue of morpheme concatenation is simplified in exactly the same fashion as in the historical data. Again, only clusters consisting of a nasal followed by a homorganic stop, as in (18d, k, l) and geminate consonants, as in all the other cases listed in (18), are permitted in intervocalic position.

(18) *Synchronic cluster simplification* (across morpheme boundaries):

-*tu*N (infinitival marker)

(a)	vas + tuN	vatthuN	cf. vasati	'to dwell'
(b)	kar + tuN	kattuN	cf. karoti	'to make'
(c)	labh + tuN	laddhuN	cf. labhati	'to take'
(d)	khan + tuN	khantuN	cf. khaṇati	'to dig'

-*ta* (past. part)

(e)	sup + ta	sutta	cf. supati	'to sleep'
(f)	tap + ta	tatta	cf. tapati	'to shine'
(g)	caj + ta	catta	cf. cajati	'give out'
(h)	kas + ta	kattha	cf. kasati	'to farm'
(i)	aarabh + ta	aaraddha	cf. aarabhati	'to begin'
(k)	dam + ta	danta	cf. dameti	'to tame'
(l)	vam + ta	vanta	cf. vamati	'to investigate'

-*na* (past.part.)

(m)	nud + na	nunna	cf. nudati	'to remove'
(n)	lag + na	lagga	cf. lagati	'to attach'
(o)	han + na	hanna	cf. hanati	'to empty'
(p)	kir + na	kiṇṇa	cf. kirasi	'to strew'

-*ya* (passive)

(r)	kar + ya	kayya	cf. karoti	'to make'
(s)	mas + ya	massa	cf. masati	'to touch'
(t)	kas + ya	kassa	cf. kasati	'to farm'
(u)	pac + ya	pacca	cf. pacati	'to cook'
(w)	khan + ya	khaṇṇa	cf. khaṇati	'to dig'
(y)	dam + ya	damma	cf. dameti	'to tame'

My goal is to account for the patterns of cluster simplification, that is, for consonant loss and gemination, by positing a set of interacting, ranked, constraints, in the spirit of Optimality Theory (Prince and Smolensky 1991, 1992, 1993, McCarthy and Prince 1993, Itô and Mester 1992). The types of constraints to be proposed are: (a) constraints on syllable margins, to account for the pattern of consonant loss and consonant retention, and (b) a constraint on moraic structure, to account for consonant gemination. It will be seen that consonant gemination forms a pattern of its own, independent of the patterns associated with syllable margins, and is best accounted for in terms of Moraic Prominence, the constraint on the alignment of moras and segments posited in its general form in Section 1. This constraint presents an important governing principle in the characterization of Pali prosodic structure, although its role is somewhat obliterated due to interactions with other principles at work. What contributes to the complexity of this system, I believe, is that different aspects of the phonological structure impose conflicting requirements, which is made fully explicit under the approach developed in Prince and Smolensky.

3   Constraints on syllable margins: pattern of consonant loss and retention

3.1   Constraints on codas

We start with the restrictions on the occurrence of segments in syllable-final position. As already noted, a Pali syllable may be closed either by the first half of a geminate or by a nasal, placeless or homorganic with the following stop. This pattern strongly suggests that consonantal place features are prohibited in the coda (cf. Itô 1986, Goldsmith 1990).[6] This is implemented here by positing a constraint which disallows the consonantal place node in syllable-final position, as stated in (19):[7]

(19)   *NoPlaceInCoda*: Consonantal place is prohibited syllable-finally (following Itô, 1989)

A consonant in syllable final position may satisfy this constraint by being linked to both the onset and the coda, since consonantal place occurs freely in the onset. The linking may be either partial, as in the forms listed in (18d, k, l), or total, giving rise to geminate consonants, as in all the other forms listed in (18).

However, nasal consonants may satisfy this constraint in yet another fashion. In addition to being homorganic with the following stop, a nasal may also be placeless, that is, an *anusvara* (cf. Trigo 1988). A nasal is realized as an anusvara (marked as N) if it is word-final or followed by a [+ continuant] consonant. Examples of *anusvaras* in word-final position and before *s* are given in (20):

(20) The distribution of placeless nasals (anusvaras) (Trigo 1988):

(a) janãN   'knowing (nom.sg.ppr.)'

(b) vicarãN   'wondering (nom.sg.ppr.)'

(c) hãNsati   'bristles'

(d) kãNsa   'vessel made of metal'

(e) pãNsu   'dust'

Forms derived with the prefix *saN-* provide further examples of *anusvaras*, as in (21). Note that the coda nasal adopts the place features of the following [– continuant] consonant, as in (21a–e), or remains placeless if the following consonant is [+ continuant], as in (22f–i) (Junghare 1979: 52, 99).

(21)

(a)	sampamodita	cf. pamodita	'delighted'
(b)	sambuddha	cf. buddha	'enlightened'
(c)	sandhamati	cf. dhamati	'blows'
(d)	sandhuupeti	cf. dhuupeti	'fumigates'
(e)	sannidhaana	cf. nidhaana	'putting down'
(f)	sãNyamati	cf. yamati	'draws together'
(g)	sãNrakkhati	cf. rakkhati	'guards'
(h)	sãNvasati	cf. vasati	'cohabits'
(i)	sãNyuñjati	cf. yuñjati	'joins with'

Note that the vowel preceding an anusvara is nasalized. It has also been noted that nasalized vowels are regularly short, the issue to be addressed in a moment.

The nasal may possess place features only if it shares them with a following consonant, which appears in the onset where place features are fully licensed. Word-finally, as in (20a, b), no place features can be provided by an onset-linked consonant, and in this position, the nasal is placeless. This analysis is supported by the fact that the preceding vowel is nasalized, which according to Trigo (1988) typically occurs in the environment of a placeless nasal.[8]

A placeless nasal, or anusvara, also appears before a [+continuant] consonant, as in (20c, d, e) and (21f–i). This is accounted for by invoking the constraint on segment structure in (21), which prohibits nasals marked as [+continuant] (following Padgett 1991).

(22) *No[+cont]Nasal*: A nasal may not be [+cont] (Padgett 1991)

$$* \quad \begin{array}{c} \text{[Nasal]} \\ | \\ \text{[+cont]} \end{array}$$

Under the further assumption that the feature [continuant] is a dependent of *place*, due to Padgett (1991), segments sharing their place features also share the specification for continuancy. Thus, a nasal sharing its place features with a [+continuant] consonant would have to be marked as [+continuant], in violation of the constraint in (22), which prohibits [+continuant] nasals (*No[+cont]Nasal*). As a result, the nasal remains placeless in this context, as evidenced by the nasalization of the preceding vowel.

Note also that the nasalized vowel which precedes the anusvara is regularly short, as in (20), or shortened if the anusvara belongs to a suffix added to a stem that ends in a long vowel, as in (23) (see Junghare 1979: 85). Here, the accusative ending is a nasal, which is realized as an anusvara; the preceding vowel is shortened and nasalized.

(23) The vowel preceding the anusvara is short and nasalized:

(a) sasu: (nom.sg.)   sasũN (acc.sg.)   'mother-in-law'
(b) nadi: (nom.sg.)   nadĩN (acc.sg.)   'river'
(c) kaṇṇa: (nom.sg.)   kaṇṇãN (acc.sg.)   'girl'

This I take as further evidence that the anusvara is indeed present in the structure. Although it is claimed in Junghare (1979: 52) that the nasal is dropped in this context, I argue that vowel shortening can be accounted for only under the assumption that the nasal segment remains in syllable-final position. The presence of an additional segment in syllable-final position contributes a third mora, which leads to vowel shortening, since a syllable in Pali is maximally bimoraic, as noted in Section 2.[9]

However, given that a placeless nasal, that is, the anusvara, does appear word-finally and before *s*, the question arises why a coda nasal is not always realized as an anusvara. This is explained by invoking another constraint on segment structure, which states that a consonant has to possess a place node.

(24) *NoPlacelessCons*: A consonant has to be linked to [*place*].

Note that, regarding nasals, this constraint is satisfied only if there is a source of place features in the immediate environment, as in *danta* (18k), but is violated if the nasal is word final, as in the accusative forms in (23), or adjacent to a [+ continuant] consonant (due to *No[+ cont]Nasal*), as in (20c, d, e) and (21f–i):

(25) *NoPlacelessCons* is

(a) observed in *danta* (18k)
(b) violated in *nadĩn* (23b) and *hãnsati* (20c)

The paradoxical behaviour stated in (25) is accounted for under the assumption that constraints vary in strength (Prince and Smolensky 1993), in particular, that the constraint prohibiting place in the coda (*NoPlaceInCoda*) and the constraint against [+ continuant] nasals (*No[+ cont]Nasal*) are stronger than the constraint against placeless consonants (*NoPlacelessCons*); while the latter may be violated, the former two never are. This is shown in (26), where the relevant output forms are inspected. Note that only the constraint *NoPlacelessCons* is violated in these cases, while the other two constraints are properly observed.

(26) *Constraint satisfaction*

	danta	nadĩn	hãnsati
NoPlaceInCoda:	ok	ok	ok
No[+ cont]Nasal:	ok	ok	ok
NoPlacelessCons:	ok	–	–

Note also that *NoPlacelessCons* is satisfied whenever the context provides a source of place features, and is violated only if no such source is available.

A further question may be asked at this point: Why is it that the placeless nasal is retained in the structure, in violation of the *NoPlacelessCons*? One way of satisfying all the constraints posited thus far would be simply not to include the placeless nasal into the structure. That this option is not taken is due to the general requirement that segments should be incorporated into prosodic structure. This is the constraint on Prosodic Licensing proposed in Itô (1986, 1989), and generalized in Optimality Theory to a set of constraints which govern not only the inclusion of segments into prosodic structure, but also the inclusion of moras into syllables, syllables into feet, and so forth (Prince and Smolensky 1993: 24, McCarthy and Prince 1993: 14). Relevant here is the role of this constraint, known as *Parse*, at the segmental level.

(27)   *Parse* A segment has to belong to syllabic or moraic structure
        (Prince and Smolensky 1993, McCarthy and Prince
        1993)

This constraint ranks higher than the constraint prohibiting placeless nasals, (*NoPlacelessCons*), which accounts for the retention of a placeless nasal in the structure, as shown in (28):

(28)   *Constraint satisfaction*

	danta	*nadĩɴ*	*hãɴsati*
NoPlaceInCoda:	ok	ok	ok
No[+ cont]Nasal:	ok	ok	ok
Parse	ok	ok	ok
NoPlacelessCons:	ok	–	–

The relative ranking of the constraints governing the distribution of segments at the right margin of the syllable is given in (29):

(29)   *Ranking*

NoPlaceInCoda ≫ *NoPlacelessCons*
No[+ cont]Nasal ≫ *NoPlacelessCons*
No[+ cont]Nasal ≫ *Parse*
NoPlaceInCoda ≫ *Parse*
Parse ≫ *NoPlacelessCons*
Note: *NoPlaceInCoda* and *No[+ cont]Nasal* do not interact

Both *NoPlaceInCoda* and *No[+ cont]Nasal* rank higher than *Parse* and *NoPlacelessCon*. Moreover, *Parse* ranks higher than

NoPlaceInCoda, while the two higher ranking constraints do not seem to interact, so that their mutual ranking remains undetermined.

3.2 Constraints on onsets

As noted earlier, Pali permits at most one consonant in syllable-initial position, as stated in the following constraint on Pali onsets:

(30) *OneOnsetCons*

At most one consonant may occur in syllable-initial position

Thus, only one consonant is selected among the candidates for the onset position. The pattern of which consonant is lost and which survives has been the major focus of the studies on Pali phonology. As observed in Geiger (1968), Hankamer and Aissen (1974), Murray (1982), Wetzels and Hermans (1985), Cho (1990) and Vaux (1992), several subpatterns emerge, as stated in (31):

(31) *Selection of the onset consonant*

(a) if the candidate consonants differ in sonority, the less sonorous one survives
(b) if the candidate consonants are equally sonorous, the second one survives
(c) in the sequence stop + homorganic nasal, the second one survives

This pattern was attributed in Geiger (1968) and Hankamer and Aissen (1974) to consonantal assimilation, partly driven by the sonority of segments. In Murray (1982), Wetzels and Hermans (1985), Cho (1990), and Vaux (1992), however, it is assumed that this pattern is directly related to the restrictions on onsets in Pali, and I adopt here the spirit of this proposal.[10]

More needs to be said about the pattern in (31): the survivor consonant is invariably geminated, which follows straightforwardly under the assimilation view (according to which the 'lost' consonant assimilates totally to the 'survivor'), but not under the view espoused here that the pattern in (31) follows from the restrictions on Pali onsets. In Section 3.3 I argue that the gemination facts should be treated as independent of the pattern of consonant loss and retention.

The cases in (32) and (33) exemplify the pattern described in (31a), according to which the less sonorous of the consonants survives. While in (32) it is the first consonant in the sequence that survives, in (33) it is the second one. In both cases, the survivor is the less sonorous consonant.

(32)

   (a) lag + na   lagga   cf. lagati   'to attach'
   (b) dam + ya   damma   cf. dameti   'to tame'

(33)

   (a) kir + na   kiṇṇa   cf. kirasi   'to strew'
   (b) kar + tuɴ   kattuɴ   cf. karoti   'to make'

In (34), the same root exhibits different patterns with different suffixes: the first consonant in the sequence survives in (33a), but the second one survives in (33b). Again, in each case, the survivor is the less sonorous consonant.

(34)

   (a) kas + ya   kassa   cf. kasati   'to farm'
   (b) kas + ta   kattha   cf. kasati   'to farm'

It has been claimed in Clements (1990) and Prince and Smolensky (1993) that there is a ranking of preferred onsets, which basically follows the sonority hierarchy: in a CV syllable, a less sonorous onset consonant is preferred to a more sonorous one. This is precisely the ranking that determines the retention pattern in the cases that we just examined.[11] The relative ranking is determined by the language specific sonority scale in (35) Proposed in Cho (1990) to account for Pali onsets:[12]

(35)   Stop < Fricative < Nasal < Liquid < v < y

Given the scale in (35), the inclusion of consonants into onsets is governed by the constraint in (36):

(36)   *OnsetSon*: A less sonorous onset consonant is preferred to a more sonorous one.
           (Clements 1990 and Prince and Smolensky 1993)

Next, we turn to the pattern in (31b): if two consonants are of equal sonority, then it is the second one that is included in the onset. In (37), where the two candidate consonants are both stops, the second one survives:

(37) sup + ta   sutta   cf. supati   'to sleep'

Note that the first available segment, so to speak, is incorporated into the syllable onset. This can be viewed as a case of the general requirement for exhaustive parsing (see Inkelas 1989, McCarthy and Prince 1990, 1993), which prohibits unparsed segments within the bounds of a prosodic constituent, in this case, within the syllable:

(38) *Exhaustiveness*: No stray segments are permitted within the bounds of a syllable.
       (Inkelas 1989, McCarthy and Prince 1990)

The *Exhaustiveness* constraint ranks lower than the *OnsetSonority* constraint and the constraint which prohibits more than one consonant in the onset – *OneOnsetCons*. This is shown by inspecting the output forms in (39). The form *lagga*, the first one listed, violates the constraint on *Exhaustiveness*, but conforms to the higher ranking constraint on *Onset Sonority*.

(39)

	lagga (lag + na)	sutta (sup + ta)	kattuɴ (kar + tuɴ)
OneOnsetCons	ok	ok	ok
OnsetSon	ok	ok	ok
Exhaustiveness	–	ok	ok

In (40) it is shown that, by conforming to *Exhaustiveness*, this form would violate the constraint on *OnsetSonority*. Because the latter constraint ranks higher, this output form is less acceptable than that in (39), and therefore unacceptable.

(40)

	*lanna (lag + na)
OneOnsetCons	ok
OnsetSon	–
Exhaustiveness	ok

And finally, the requirement in (31c) is illustrated in (41): if the members of the consonant cluster share their place features, then it

is the second member that is retained, regardless of the relative
sonority of the two members.

(41)

(a) nud + na   nunna   cf. nudati   'to remove'
(b) raj + na   raṇṇa   cf. raja   'king'

I attribute this pattern to a more specific version of the exhaustiveness requirement which, as stated in (42), prohibits an unparsed
segment which shares some of its features, in this case, the place
node, with an adjacent segment:

(42)   *LinkedStraySegment*: No linked stray segments are permit-
       ted within the bounds of a syllable.

Note that both the *OnsetSon* and the *Exhaustiveness* constraints
rank lower than the *LinkedStraySegment* constraint, as shown in
(43), where the output form of *nunna* is inspected:

(43)

	nunna (nud + na)
OneOnsetCons	ok
LinkedStraySegment	ok
OnsetSon	–
Exhaustiveness	–

In sum, I have posited the following set of constraints to account
for the occurrence of segments in the onset:

(44)   *OneOnsetCons*
       LinkedStraySegment
       OnsetSon
       Exhaustiveness

While *OnsetSon* and *Exhaustiveness* are violated, the remaining
two are not. Moreover, *OnsetSon* ranks higher than *Exhaustiveness*.
   How do the constraints proposed thus far interact? Those listed
in (45a) are not violated in any of the forms, while those in (45b)
are. Moreover, the ranking of the violated constraints is as given in

(45b). While all onset related constraints rank higher than *Parse*, the constraint on placeless consonants ranks lower, and is thus the lowest ranking constraint.

(45)

  (a) unviolated
     NoPlaceInCoda
     No[+ cont]Nasal
     OneOnsetCons
     LinkedStraySegment

  (b) violated
     OnsetSon
     Exhaustiveness
     Parse
     NoPlacelessCons

4 Constraint on moraic structure: pattern of consonant gemination

The set of constraints proposed thus far is not sufficient to account for the complex pattern of consonant gemination. Crucial here is the pattern resulting from morpheme concatenation in (18) above. Most of the forms listed contain sequences of unsyllabifiable consonants which are 'resolved' in the following fashion: one of the consonants is lost and the other geminates. We have already addressed the issue of which of the consonants remains and which 'disappears'. What remains to be accounted for is that the lost consonant leaves a trace, so to speak, as indicated by the gemination of the survivor. But, while the constraints posited thus far account for consonant loss, they do not account for gemination, since both the well-formed *sutta* in (46b) and the ill-formed **suta* in (46c) conform to this set of constraints. The same is true of the forms in (47): both (47b) and (47c) conform to the constraints posited so far, yet only the former is well-formed.

(46)

  (a) sup + ta   p.p. sup   'to sleep'
  (b) sutta
  (c) *suta

(47)

  (a) kar + tuN   inf. kar   'to make'
  (b) kattuN
  (c) *katuN

In sum, the constraints proposed so far are neutral as to whether the survivor consonant is geminated or not. It is at this point that the constraint on Moraic Prominence needs to be recognized as an important player, since it carries the full burden of accounting for the gemination pattern.

The constraint on Moraic Prominence, first introduced in (9), is repeated in (48):

(48)   *Constraint on Moraic Prominence*: Segment r_i projects a mora if it is not followed by a more sonorous segment r_j.

$$\mu_i$$
$$|$$
$$r_i \qquad r_j$$

Condition: Son $(r_i) \geqslant$ Son (r_j)

Note, however, that in the form given in (48), this constraint is too strong for Pali, in one respect: it requires that a segment that projects a mora necessarily links to this mora – that is, it puts Pali on a par with English in which this indeed is the case, as we saw in Section 1. However, English illustrates the relatively simple case of a language in which the segment that projects a mora also links to the projected mora. As we will see in a moment, this is not necessarily the case in Pali. The intuition that is valid for Pali is that a segment projects a mora in accordance with the constraint in (48), regardless of whether it links to this mora or not.

In order to capture this intuition, I propose to factor out two independent aspects of the constraint in (48), as shown in (49):

(49)   *Constraint on moraic structure*: Segment r_i projects a mora iff it is not followed by a more sonorous segment r_j.

(a) μ_i

$$r_i \qquad r_j$$

Condition: Son $(r_i) \geqslant$ Son (r_j)

(b) μ_i
$$|$$
$$r_i$$

The principle of mora projection is captured by (49a): a segment will project a mora if required by the constraint on moraic structure – and coindexation makes explicit the mapping between segments and the moras that they project. However, (49a) does not require that a segment projecting a mora should also link to the projected mora. This latter requirement is stated in (49b). My proposal therefore is that, in Pali, the constraint on moraic prominence should correspond to (49a). The subpart in (49b) can be subsumed under the general constraint *Parse*, repeated in (50), which we already saw in action in Section 3.1.

(50) *Parse*: A segment has to belong to syllabic or moraic structure.

For the sake of explicitness, I repeat here the final version of the constraint on moraic structure for Pali: [13]

(51) *Moraic Prominence* (Pali): Segment r_i projects a mora iff it is not followed by a more sonorous segment r_j.

$$\mu_i$$

$$r_i \qquad r_j$$

Condition: Son $(r_i) \geqslant$ Son (r_j)

Recall that this constraint was introduced to salvage a placeless nasal by allowing it to be included in the prosodic structure, in violation of the constraint against placeless consonants. We have thus seen that *Parse* is not the lowest ranking constraint. However, in Pali, in which stray erasure is quite prevalent, as has been documented by the resolution of consonant strings in the forms listed in (18), this constraint ranks fairly low. Although respected in some cases, it is violated in others, depending on its interaction with other, higher-ranking constraints.

In addition to the constraint on Moraic Prominence in (51), we also need to state the restrictions on the minimal sonority of moras, as discussed in Section 1. The syllabic position has to be minimally [−consonantal] in Pali, that is, only vowels may act as syllable peaks. The moraic position, however, is not restricted in terms of minimal sonority. It may be filled by any segment and, in this respect, Pali closely resembles English. In other words, if it were not for the coda constraints introduced in Section 3.1, the occurrence of segments in the moraic position would have been as free as in a language like English.

Let us start with a simple form which satisfies all the constraints proposed so far. This is the case with the form listed in (18k) above, the past participal form of 'to tame', *danta* (*dam* + *ta*). In the output form given in (52), the vowels and the nasal project moras, while the onset consonants do not; and crucially, in this case, the segment that projects a mora also links to the projected mora, which is in accordance with *Parse*. The nasal in this form does not violate any of the constraints on segment structure: it possesses the place node, which it shares with the following consonant, and is marked as [– cont]. Any other competing output form would violate at least some of the constraints, and as such, would necessarily be worse than the one we inspected here.

(52)   All constraints satisfied in *danta* (*dam* + *ta*), cf. (18k)

MoraicProminence	ok
NoPlaceInCoda	ok
No[+ cont]Nasal	ok
Parse	ok
NoPlacelessCons	ok

Next, we inspect a form whose best-formed output violates the constraint against placeless consonants (*NoPlacelessCons*), which requires that a consonant ought to possess place features. Here we see that *Parse* ranks higher than the constraint against placeless consonants (*NoPlacelessCons*). If *Parse* were ranked lower than *NoPlacelessCons*, the placeless nasal would simply be left out of prosodic structure, which is obviously not here the case. Note also that *NoPlacelessCons* could be satisfied by supplying the nasal with place features, which would result in violating the constraint against [+ continuant] nasals (*No[+ cont]Nasal*) if the place features were shared with a [+ continuant] consonant; alternatively, if the nasal possessed its own specification for place, not shared with any of the surrounding segments, this would result in violating the *NoPlaceInCoda* constraint, which prohibits place features in the coda.

(53) *NoPlacelessCons* violated: best-formed output of *hãɴsati*, cf. (20c)

h ã Nᵢ s a t i

MoraicProminence   ok
NoPlaceInCoda   ok
No[+ cont]Nasal   ok
Parse   ok
NoPlacelessCons   –

We now turn to the most interesting type of case, in which the segment projecting a mora does not link to the projected mora. Before presenting this case in some detail, I need to introduce another constraint, which is referred to as *Fill* in the framework of Prince and Smolensky. It is a counterpart of *Parse*, and requires that all nodes within prosodic structure should dominate the appropriate prosodic or segmental material. In our case, the requirement is that a mora necessarily dominate a segment.

(54) *Fill* A mora must be filled with (i.e., must dominate) a segment.
      (Prince and Smolensky 1993, McCarthy and Prince 1993)

As an example, we take the past participial forms of 'to sleep' and 'to make', listed in (18e) and (18b) respectively. The best-formed outputs of these forms are given in (55). Note that, in this case, the constraint *Parse* is violated.

(55) Best-formed outputs of *sutta* (*sup* + *ta*), cf. (18e) and *kattuɴ* (*kar* + *tuɴ*), cf. (18b)

s u pᵢ + t a   k a rᵢ + t u N

MoraicProminence	ok	ok
NoPlaceInCoda	ok	ok
No[+ cont]Nasal	ok	ok
Fill	ok	ok
Parse	–	–
NoPlacelessCons	ok	ok

As we will see, *Parse* ranks lower than any constraint other than the *NoPlacelessCons*. The violation of *Fill* results in unacceptable output, as shown in (28). Note that it is the violation of *Fill*, rather than that of *Parse* that is crucial in ruling out the output forms in (56), since we have seen acceptable outputs in which *Parse* is violated, as in (55).

(56)   *Fill* violated: outputs **suta* and **katuɴ*

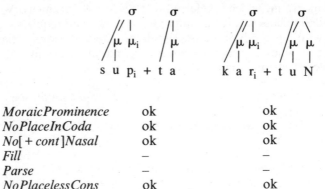

MoraicProminence	ok	ok
NoPlaceInCoda	ok	ok
No[+ cont]Nasal	ok	ok
Fill	–	–
Parse	–	–
NoPlacelessCons	ok	ok

The constraint on moraic structure, *MoraicProminence*, may not be violated either, since this violation also results in an unacceptable output, as shown in (57).

(57)   *MoraicProminence* violated: outputs **suta* and **katuɴ*

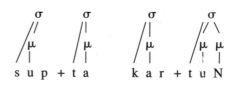

MoraicProminence	–	–
NoPlaceInCoda	ok	ok
No[+ cont]Nasal	ok	ok
Fill	ok	ok
Parse	–	–
NoPlacelessCons	ok	ok

And finally, *NoPlaceInCoda* which prohibits place features in the coda also ranks higher than *Parse*, since its violation results in an unacceptable output form.

(58) *NoPlaceInCoda* violated: outputs *supta and **kartu*N

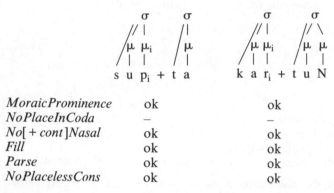

MoraicProminence	ok	ok
NoPlaceInCoda	–	–
No[+ cont]Nasal	ok	ok
Fill	ok	ok
Parse	ok	ok
NoPlacelessCons	ok	ok

In sum, we have invoked *MoraicProminence*, that is, the constraint on moraic structure, to account for the gemination pattern so prevalent in Pali. The guiding intuition has been that this constraint is independent of *NoPlaceInCoda* (prohibiting consonantal place in the coda), *Parse* and *Fill*, which jointly govern the inclusion of segments into prosodic structure. (Of course, *MoraicProminence* is also independent of *No[+ cont]Nasal* and *NoPlacelessCons*, both governing segment internal structure, but these constraints are not relevant for the point I am making here.) Several predictions are made under the assumption that *MoraicProminence* is responsible for the gemination pattern. Note that thus far we have only inspected roots of the CVC form, and that the root-final consonant projects a mora if combined with a consonant-initial suffix, as shown, for example, in (55), and repeated in (59):

(59)   Forms satisfying *MoraicProminence*:

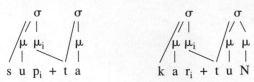

First, we predict that a single intervocalic consonant will not geminate, and consequently, that no gemination will be evidenced in the case of CV and CVV roots.[14] This is supported by the CV root listed in (60) and by the CVV root given in (61). In neither case does the intervocalic consonant, which belongs to the suffix, geminate in the past participial or infinitival forms.

(60)   CV root: *hi* 'send'

− *ta* (past.part)
   hi + ta   hita   cf. hi(n)ati

(61)   CVV root: *ghaa* 'smell'

− *ta* (past.part)
   ghaa + ta   ghaata   cf. ghaayati
− *tu*N (infinitival marker)
   ghaa + tuN   ghaatuN   cf. ghaayati

Obviously, this pattern departs from that illustrated by the forms in (32), which are derived from CVC roots.

We also predict that the final consonant in CVVC roots projects a mora in order to comply with *MoraicProminence*. That this is indeed the case is shown in (62), where the root vowel is shortened before a consonant-initial suffix, in compliance with the bimoraicity requirement.

(62)   CVVC root: *bhaas* 'to speak'

− *ta* (past.part)
   bhaas + ta   bhaṭṭha   cf. bhaasati

This is represented explicitly in (63), where the first syllable includes only two of the three candidate moras. One of the moras − the second half of the long vowel − is unparsed, that is, unlinked to the syllable node, due to the bimoraicity requirement; in other words, the root vowel is 'shortened'. The excess of moras results from the compliance of the output form in (63) with *MoraicProminence*, which requires that the consonant *s* project a mora.

(63)   Partial output of *bhaṭṭha*: *MoraicProminence* satisfied

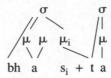

This case, I believe, presents a particularly convincing argument for associating the gemination pattern with the weight system of the language, and attributing it to the *MoraicProminence* constraint.

To summarize, I have proposed the constraints listed in (64), to account for the pattern of consonant loss and gemination in Pali which, as has been argued here, results from intricate interactions among the proposed constraints, with constraint ranking playing a most significant role. Thus, we have seen that the constraints in (64a) are not violated in any of the forms we have inspected, while those in (64b) are. Moreover, *Parse* ranks higher than *NoPlaceless-Cons*, as shown by the behaviour of *anusvaras*, which get included in prosodic structure although, as placeless consonants, they violate *NoPlacelessCons*.

(64)   Summary of the proposed constraints:

(a) unviolated
      MoraicProminence
      NoPlaceInCoda
      No[+ cont]Nasal
      Fill
      OneOnsetCons
      LinkedStraySegment

(b) violated
      OnsetSon
      Exhaustiveness
      Parse
      NoPlacelessCons

The best-formed outputs of the relevant forms discussed here are inspected in (65). Note that *danta* is the only output form that satisfies all the proposed constraints:

(65)

	nunna (nud + na)	lagga (lag + na)	sutta (sup + ta)	kiṇṇa (kir + na)	hāɴsati	danta (dam + ta)
Moraic Prominence	ok	ok	ok	ok	ok	ok
NoPlaceInCoda	ok	ok	ok	ok	ok	ok
No[+cont]Nasal	ok	ok	ok	ok	ok	ok
Fill	ok	ok	ok	ok	ok	ok
OneOnsetCons	ok	ok	ok	ok	ok	ok
LinkedStraySegment	ok	ok	ok	ok	ok	ok
OnsetSon	–	ok	ok	ok	ok	ok
Exhaustiveness	–	–	ok	ok	ok	ok
Parse	–	–	–	–	ok	ok
NoPlacelessCons	ok	ok	ok	ok	–	ok

In sum, the fact that certain configurations are well-formed in some environments but not in others is viewed as a consequence of constraint ranking, that is, the systematic way in which constraints override each other. *MoraicProminence* is one of the constraints accounting for prosodic structure, and as such interacts with other relevant constraints. However, as we have seen, it is crucial in explaining the gemination pattern exhibited by most of the intervocalic consonantal 'clusters'.

5 Concluding remarks

The central aspects of Pali syllable structure are not uncommon in world languages. A similar pattern is encountered, for example, in Japanese or Ponapean (Itô 1986). Just like Pali, these languages permit only a (placeless) nasal or the first half of a geminate in the coda. Itô's is a notable attempt to account for this type of pattern. The account consists in positing a constraint which prohibits place features in the coda, as in (66), and is overridden by doubly linked structures (in accordance with Hayes' 1986 linking constraint):

(66)   *[Place]σ

By being able to override this constraint due to double linking, geminates may freely occupy syllable-final position.

However, while Itô's constraint accounts nicely for the occurrence of geminates in underived forms, it does not exclude the nongeminated form in (46c) above, repeated below as (67c).

(67)

(a) sup + ta   p.p.sup   'to sleep'
(b) sutta
(c) *suta

Recall, moreover, that the pattern in (67) has served as the prime motive for invoking the constraint *MoraicProminence* to account for the gemination facts. Thus, although necessary, the constraints on codas are not sufficient to capture the gemination pattern observed in Pali derived forms, nor would they be sufficient to account for the gemination patterns under similar circumstances in any of the other languages that belong to the same class as Pali.

This has constituted the empirical argument for the presence of the constraint on *MoraicProminence* in Pali. By giving *MoraicProminence* a central role in accounting for Pali syllable structure, the gemination pattern is properly motivated, as well as appropriately constrained, since it is correctly predicted under what circumstances gemination will be manifested (in CVC and CVVC forms), and when it will be absent (in CV and CVV forms).

Moreover, the gemination pattern is attributed to a constraint which is independently needed, and which, I believe, is universally valid. But the specific case of Pali further shows that this constraint can be manifested in less than obvious ways in those languages which place special restriction on the inclusion of consonants into syllable margins. While often obliterated by the other constraints that participate in characterizing the Pali syllable structure, *MoraicProminence* still leaves a trace, so to speak, in the weight structure of the syllable, which is precisely the kind of effect expected from a constraint of this nature.

Notes and Acknowledgements

I am grateful to Abby Cohn, John McCarthy and Lisa Selkirk for most helpful comments and discussions of the work presented here. An earlier version of this chapter was presented at CLS 29, the 29th meeting of the Chicago Linguistic Society, held April 1993.

1. This version of the moraic representation is proposed in McCarthy and Prince (1986). Several other versions are also encountered in the literature. In Hyman (1985), Zec (1988) and Itô (1989) all segments are linked to moras, and the syllable node dominates directly only moras and no segments. In Hayes (1989), on the other hand, onset consonants are linked directly to the syllable, while all other segments are dominated by moras, in an attempt to recapture the onset/rhyme division assumed in the arboreal representation of the syllable.
2. Sonority is taken here to be a derivative notion dependent on the structural properties of segments, a view espoused in Basbøll (1977), Lekach (1979), Steriade (1982), Levin (1985), Clements (1990), Zec (1988) and, most recently, Rice (1992).
3. English is used here simply to illustrate the relevant point. For a

detailed analysis of English within the moraic framework, see Lamontagne (1993).

4. These cases are studied in detail in Zec (1993), based on the following sources: Mohanan (1986) for English, Street (1963) and Hayes (1981) for Khalkha Mongolian, Painter (1970) for Gonja, and Senn (1966) for Lithuanian. The asymmetry in minimal sonority between the two moras of a heavy syllable is given a formal account in Zec (1988 and 1993).

5. The data in this chapter are taken from Fahs (1985), Geiger (1968), Hankamer and Aissen (1974), and Junghare (1979).

6. Cho recognizes the need for a coda constraint in Pali. The constraint she proposes (on p. 226), however, prohibits all features in the coda; the facts discussed in this section make it clear that the prohibition should be restricted to the place features.

7. An alternative formulation of this constraint would be to allow the place features only in the onset, following the proposal of Lombardi (1991). The two formulations yield identical results in the case under discussion, although they may be empirically different in more complex cases.

8. Trigo (1988) refers to placeless, or debuccalized, nasals as nasal glides, and notes the process of nasal 'absorption' whereby a nasal glide causes the nasalization of the preceding vowel.

9. According to Geiger (1968: 63) the fact that a nasalized vowel is regularly short suggests that 'every syllable with a nasal vowel is considered as closed', which is consistent with the claim advanced here that a nasalized vowel corresponds to a vowel + nasal sequence.

10. The general proposal advanced in Wetzels and Hermans (1985), Cho (1990) and Vaux (1992) is that the pattern of cluster simplification is due to the constraints on Pali onsets, largely inherited from Sanskrit. However, they also assume that Pali is similar to Sanskrit in allowing complex onsets, but differs from it in reducing a complex onset to a single consonant at some level of representation. Although this insight most likely mirrors the historical development from Sanskrit to Pali, I am not assuming here that Pali possesses ghost complex onsets.

11. See Gnanadesikan (1991), where a proposal of this sort is made specifically for Pali.

12. In the scale proposed by Hankamer and Aissen (1974), r is treated as more sonorous than the glides, in order to account for the cases such as (18r), in which kar + ya yields kayya rather than *karra. According to Wetzels and Hermans (1985: 216) and Cho (1990: 225), r cannot be the first element of a complex onset in Sanskrit, which extends to Pali, accounting for the gemination pattern. Under this view, r patterns together with (1) with respect to sonority, and its aberrant behaviour is treated as an idiosyncrasy. This would be implemented within the analysis proposed here by positing an additional constraint which prohibits r in the onset if it is followed by a stray segment, a more specific version of Exhaustiveness in (38).

NOTES AND ACKNOWLEGEMENTS

NOTES AND ACKNOWLEGEMENTS

13. In the set of forms in (18r–y), a consonant projects a mora although it is followed by a more sonorous segment, i.e. a glide. If we assume that glides in Pali are [+ consonantal], then this can be attributed to a language-specific constraint in Pali which requires that a consonant should project a mora when followed by another consonant, regardless of the relative sonority of the two. This constraint should rank higher than that in (51), in order to be able to override it. An alternative would be to incorporate this special restriction by adapting the constraint in (51). This, however, seems to be the less desirable alternative, since (51) is, I believe, a highly general constraint, and therefore present in Pali as well.

14. It is worth noting that Cho's (1990) account of Pali, in which both the restrictions on onsets and on codas (of the type proposed by Itô) are brought into play, a separate mechanism is posited to account for consonant doubling. Consonant gemination is stated as an independent rule, affecting only intervocalic *clusters*, and an additional statement needed to be made to prevent single intervocalic consonants from geminating.

Chapter 6

Skeletal and suprasegmental structure within Government Phonology

Wiebke Brockhaus

1 Introduction

The purpose of this chapter is to give an overview of the skeleton and constituent structure in Government Phonology (GP),[1] along with licensing and governing relations, as provided for in the theory. It is intended as a critical overview (drawing heavily on work by other researchers in the field, as indicated by the references) which both extols the virtues of GP and points out possible shortcomings, in the hope that these will be addressed in future work.

The reader should be warned that my discussion may not always be completely impartial, as my own commitment is to GP, which (*pace* Coleman this volume and, perhaps, pending further developments in Declarative Lexical Phonology) I consider to be, at least potentially, the most highly restricted phonological theory currently available.

The discussion proceeds as follows. I begin with a comparison of different approaches to the skeleton itself (CV Phonology (Clements and Keyser 1983), X theory (Levin 1985, Lowenstamm and Kaye 1986) and Moraic Phonology (e.g. Hyman 1985, Hayes 1989, Bickmore, this volume, Zec, this volume)). This will lead on to the presentation of central aspects of GP in Sections 3 and 4, with Section 3 dealing with governing relations and constituent structure and Section 4 with the GP notion of licensing. The next section (Section 5) is wholly devoted to a comparison of GP and moraic approaches to specific phonological issues. Section 6 concludes the chapter.

2 The skeleton

2.1 Introduction: standard function and common ground

The skeleton provides a kind of hub which mediates between the melody, or segmental, tier (where feature bundles, autosegments, elements, or whatever other atoms of phonological representations are used in a particular theory, are located) and higher-level prosodic tiers (e.g. the syllable tier in the framework of Clements and Keyser 1983. See, too, Bickmore, this volume). What exactly are the units which are represented on the skeletal tier? The answer with probably the longest tradition in modern phonology is that these units represent time slots which correspond roughly to the duration of an individual segment. So, a short vowel (or light diphthong) or a single consonant would take up one of these units, while a long vowel (or heavy diphthong) or a geminate consonant would be associated with two. Conversely, a contour segment with linearly ordered internal structure (as described e.g. in Steriade 1982 and McCarthy and Prince 1986), such as an affricate or a prenasalized stop, for example, would be represented by two feature bundles (or sets of whatever phonological atoms are in use) being associated with a single unit on the skeletal tier. Theories based on this kind of skeleton generally consider what I have just described to be common ground. The picture becomes rather less harmonious, though, when the actual identity of the units of the skeletal tier is at issue. Essentially two approaches can be distinguished here.

2.2 The CV tier approach

One of the two approaches to the skeletal tier is that adopted by, among others, Clements and Keyser (1983). This is often referred to as the CV approach and was first proposed by McCarthy (1979). It makes the claim that the units on the skeletal tier are of two distinct types and that the distinction between them plays a vital role in phonological representations. Cs and Vs are employed, together with an essentially flat syllable structure, which exhibits no internal hierarchy. The English word *bit* would be represented

(1) Syllable tier

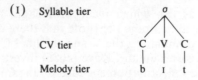

as shown in (1) in Clements and Keyser's CV approach. The representation in (1) indicates that *bit* is interpreted as consisting of a single closed syllable, with the vowel (marked as V on the CV tier) constituting the nucleus or peak of that syllable and the two consonants (marked as C) occupying non-peak positions within the syllable.

The advantage of the CV tier, according to Clements and Keyser (1983: 10), is that 'the units of the CV tier themselves define functional positions (peak versus non-peak) within the syllable'. Therefore, no hierarchical syllable structure is required. In other words, Cs and Vs can be daughters of the syllable node. There is no need for other nodes (such as an onset or rhyme node, see e.g. (5) on p. 184) to intervene and group them into constituents dominated by the syllable node. Whether a segment constitutes a syllable peak or whether it belongs to the syllable margin can be read off the CV tier itself. Hierarchical structure above the CV tier (but within the syllable itself) would only introduce redundancy.[2]

Assuming a framework which employs binary features, the CV tier further has the effect of 'subsuming' (1983: 10) the feature [±syllabic]. This is the case because Clements and Keyser equate a V on the CV tier with a [+syllabic] segment on the melody tier and a C with a [−syllabic] segment. Clements and Keyser's approach here is by no means uncontroversial. Marantz (1982), for example, makes a case for both a CV tier *and* the feature [±syllabic] to prevent vocalic segments from being linked to a C-slot and consonantal segments to a V-slot. This issue will be discussed in more detail in Section 2.3.

2.3 The X theory approach

An alternative to the CV tier is a skeletal tier where all units are of the same type. The most common representation of these units in recent work is as a series of xs (or Xs), so that theories employing this particular kind of skeletal tier are sometimes referred to as X theories (e.g. in Hayes 1989). The X theory approach to the skeletal tier was first argued for in Levin (1985) and in Lowenstamm and Kaye (1986).

Taking representations such as (2), which incorporate both a standard CV tier and a hierarchical prosodic tier (note that there is an additional node immediately dominating the V and the final C) as their point of departure, Lowenstamm and Kaye (1986) investigate whether there is any necessary information encoded on the CV tier which is not completely derivable from the shape of the prosodic tier (that is, Clements and Keyser's syllable tier and the

(2) Prosodic tier   σ

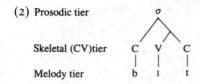

Skeletal (CV)tier   C   V   C

Melody tier   b   I   t

constituents dominated by the syllable node). They come to the
conclusion that, given this comparatively rich hierarchical structure
on the prosodic tier (as opposed to the flat structure illustrated in
(1)), the CV tier contains redundancies, since the functional positions within the syllable assumed by individual segments can be
read off the prosodic tier anyway. So, in (2), for example, the onset
is immediately dominated by the syllable node. It is followed by a
branching constituent which dominates the nucleus of the syllable
(left branch) and its coda (right branch). The Cs and the V on the
skeletal tier have nothing to add to this information.

All this stands to reason, but it is not immediately obvious why
we should dispense with the CV tier rather than the hierarchical
structure of the prosodic tier. Or, to put it differently, does encoding
this kind of information on the prosodic tier have advantages over
encoding it on the skeletal tier? If it can be shown that there are
phonological processes which make reference to information enco-
dable only on the prosodic tier and not the CV tier, then we would
have an argument in favour of abandoning the CV tier, and not
the rich structure on the prosodic tier.

Such evidence is provided by Lowenstamm and Kaye (1986) in
their study of gemination and compensatory lengthening (defined
by Hayes (1989: 260) as 'the lengthening of a segment triggered by
the deletion or shortening of a nearby segment'; see also the
discussion in Bickmore, this volume) in Tiberian Hebrew. They
begin by showing that all properties ascribed to the skeletal tier are
in fact predictable from information encoded on the prosodic tier,
which leads them to propose the syllable structure illustrated in
(3a), the geometry of which is partially ambiguous. It is clear that
the left branch of the syllable constitutes the onset (and would be
represented by a C in a CV tier framework). As such, it dominates
a [− vocalic] segment. The right branch of the syllable, by contrast,
may constitute either a (branching) rhyme, dominating a non-
branching nucleus and a coda (as shown in (3b)) or a branching
nucleus (as shown in (3c)). In the former case, we are dealing with
a closed syllable (containing a short vowel. defined as [+ vocalic],
followed by a consonant, defined as [− vocalic]) and in the latter,

(3)

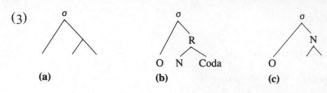

(a)   (b)   (c)

with a long vowel or heavy diphthong ([+ vocalic] followed by [+ vocalic]). They also introduce the universal principle in (4).

(4)   Null elements may not appear in branching constituents, where constituent refers to the prosodic constituent immediately dominating the null element.

This principle essentially states that the only licit null elements are null onset (5a), null rhyme (5b), null nucleus (5c) and null coda (5d). For greater clarity, I have inserted constituent labels (O for

(5)

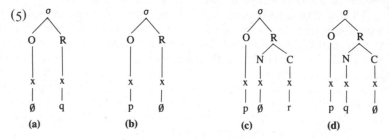

(a)   (b)   (c)   (d)

onset, R for rhyme, N for nucleus and C for coda) and a skeletal tier with xs. The constituent labels do, however, have the undesirable effect of implying that R dominates N and C. This in itself is perfectly reasonable, but I must point out that Lowenstamm and Kaye (1986) make no such claim. On the contrary, the partial ambiguity of their syllable structure (as illustrated in (3)) plays an important role in their argumentation. The variables p, q and r in (5) represent suitable segments. Given the restrictions on null elements illustrated in (5), certain structures can be excluded. For example, in (3c), the nucleus could not dominate a skeletal position without phonetic content, since the nucleus is branching (Lowenstamm and Kaye 1986: 103). The nucleus in (3b), by contrast, could dominate an empty position, as it itself is non-branching.

Now consider the Tiberian Hebrew word *seefer* 'book', which undergoes gemination of the initial consonant when the clitic definite article *ha* is added, yielding *hasseefer* 'the book'. In my interpretation of Lowenstamm and Kaye (1986), *hasseefer* would

(6)

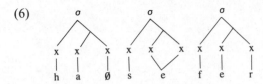

have the underlying representation shown in (6). The question is now whether the null element at the end of the initial syllable is part of a branching nucleus or whether it is within a non-branching coda. The prediction made by (4) is unequivocal. The null element cannot be dominated by a branching nucleus. Therefore, it must be dominated by a coda. A coda position can be filled by a [– vocalic] segment, so that the *s* should spread into it, resulting in gemination. This is indeed what happens, as witnessed by the form *hasseefer*. The same effect could have been achieved in a CV-tier framework by specifying the empty position as a C. However, this specification would have raised the issue of how to deal with related forms, where gemination is blocked and compensatory vowel lengthening takes place instead. To derive the correct forms one would probably have to posit a CVV... rather than a CVC... template for these cases, missing the generalization that compensatory lengthening is a direct consequence of the blocking of gemination. The flexibility of the skeletal tier employed by Lowenstamm and Kaye (1986), the authors argue, makes it possible for this generalization to be captured through a universal principle (but see Hayes 1988 for some critical comments on their argumentation).

Lowenstamm and Kaye (1986) also point out a problem with the interpretation of vowels which are attached to a C slot.[3] They observe that analyses within a CV-tier framework sometimes require vowel segments to be attached to a position which is specified as a C. This raises the question of how such a segment should be interpreted. Given Clements and Keyser's (1983: 10f.) definitions of C and V, as presented in Section 2.2, we should be dealing with a non-syllabic vowel which occupies a non-peak position within a syllable. To see whether this is the desired interpretation, consider the example of certain types of word-final long vowels in Turkish, for which Clements and Keyser (1983: 70) posit representations such as the one shown in (7). This representation is derived by a rule spreading /a/ to the final C, which has no segmental content in the underlying representation. It captures the fact that, with regard to suffixation, words ending in these particular vowels behave as if they ended in a consonant. Such words contrast with others which also end in a long vowel, but where a suffix allomorphy rule

(7)

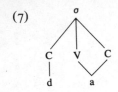

triggered by final consonants (and also by vowels of the type illustrated in (7)) fails to apply. The latter type would then be represented as in (8). This is an elegant solution. However, we have

(8)

to bear in mind that the second half of the [aː] vowel as represented in (7) is claimed to be [−syllabic] and non-peak by its association with the C on the CV tier. Therefore, we would expect it to have some special phonetic properties, perhaps a sudden drop in amplitude in the signal. Clements and Keyser discuss some of the phonetic implications of their analysis, but they have nothing unusual to report about the realization of structures such as the one illustrated in (7).

Let us now turn to a possible X theory approach to the same phonological phenomenon of Turkish and see whether it fares better. Dealing with the purely phonological aspects of this phenomenon is as straightforward in X theory as it is in CV Phonology. All that has to be done is to syllabify the final portion of the long vowel in (7) into, say, a syllable coda and the corresponding part of the long vowel in (8) into a nucleus, as illustrated in (9a) and (9b) respectively. (See Levin 1985: 188–96 for a very thoroughly argued analysis of the same data, which comes essentially to the same

(9)

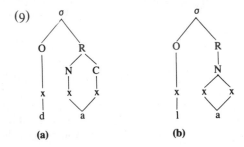

(a)   (b)

conclusion.) As we have seen, Clements and Keyser's proposals predict that the vowel in [da:] should differ from the vowel in [la:] phonetically, if their claims about syllable peaks vs. non-peaks are to be meaningful. The same prediction is made by the X theory alternative, as shown in (9). As far as we can ascertain, this prediction is incorrect.

It seems that, although Lowenstamm and Kaye (1986) may well have a point in arguing that structures where a vowel is associated with a C slot should be ruled out, this is not necessarily a valid argument against the CV tier and in favour of X theory. On the contrary, the problems identified for the CV tier can equally well arise in frameworks employing an x skeleton with hierarchical prosodic structure.

Evidence which, in my view, does provide reasonably good arguments against the CV tier and in favour of X theory is contained in Levin (1985: 29ff.). Applying a CV-tier-based analysis to reduplication in Mokilese, a Micronesian language, Levin finds that 'encoding on the CV tier is vacuous, since whether a slot is C or V does not play a role in association' (p. 39). In fact, the CV tier analysis turns out not just to contain redundancy but to make incorrect predictions as well. Levin, therefore, concludes that 'the CV analysis is untenable' (p. 40), at least for Mokilese reduplication.

Her investigation of reduplication in Ponapean, another Micronesian language, provides further evidence that CV analyses only introduce redundancy. She observes that 'there is no sense to marking slots as C's or V's since . . . association will proceed one-to-one left-to-right regardless of the skeletal specifications' (p. 47).

Levin (1985: 187–256) also tackles data from Turkish, Klamath (both dealt with in Clements and Keyser 1983), Hungarian (Vago 1987) and Ancient Greek (Steriade 1982), for all of which CV-based analyses have been proposed in the works cited. She argues, in my view convincingly, in favour of alternative analyses which make reference only to x slots, not Cs and Vs.

It seems, then, that X theories have a slight advantage in that they incorporate less redundancy (as shown by Levin 1985) and provide greater flexibility through the combination of unspecified timing slots and rich hierarchical syllable structure. Choosing a skeletal tier consisting solely of xs, together with such hierarchical syllable structure may then be the best course to follow. As observed by Durand (1990a: 265), 'this type of representation has now become extremely common in phonology and is accepted by most phonologists working within a multidimensional framework'. It is also the approach chosen in GP.

2.4 Dispensing with a segment-based skeleton: Moraic Phonology

Before moving on to structures above the skeletal tier, I would like
to address a question posed by a phonological theory which dispenses with a skeleton representing segmental timing units altogether: Moraic Phonology (also referred to as Moraic Theory, e.g.
in Tranel 1991). The question asked by this theory is this: is there
any point in representing segmental timing units? After all, as
McCarthy and Prince (1986: 2) put it, 'it is a commonplace of
phonology that rules count moras, syllables or feet but never
segments'. If that is indeed the case, then it would make sense to
abandon the units represented by xs (or Cs and Vs) and to replace
them with weight units, which essentially correspond to moras.
Such an approach was first developed in Hyman (1985) and has
received interesting modifications in Hayes (1989) (see also Bickmore this volume and Katamba this volume) for discussion as well
as Itô 1989 and McCarthy and Prince 1986, 1990 for related work).

According to Hayes (1989), the syllable node immediately dominates moras, to which those units on the melody tier which carry
phonological weight are linked. In other words, the mora has two
functions. First, it encodes phonological weight inasmuch as a
phonologically light syllable has only a single mora, while a heavy
syllable has two. Second, it represents a phonological position. In
this role it can be used to indicate length, just as xs or Cs and Vs
can. For example, a single vocalic feature matrix linked to two
moras would be interpreted as both long and phonologically heavy.
An interesting prediction made by this interpretation of the mora is
that no long vowel can ever be phonologically light, which, to my
knowledge, is correct. Melodic units which are phonologically
weightless (such as onsets, which play no role in the determination
of syllable weight, e.g. for stress assignment) are directly linked to
the syllable node, as illustrated in (10) (adapted from Hayes 1989:
254).

(10)

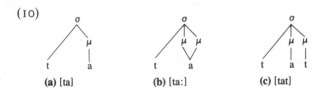

(a) [ta]   (b) [ta:]   (c) [tat]

Let me return, for the moment, to McCarthy and Prince's (1986)
claim about the absence of segment-counting rules (and thus processes), which sums up the motivation of Moraic Phonology. If this
claim is correct, why have so many phonologists in the past wasted
time and ink on CV tiers and x tiers, and still continue to do so?

My answer to this question is that McCarthy and Prince are only partially right. It does indeed seem unlikely that actual segment-*counting* processes exist. It may, however, be the case that there are processes which make reference to skeletal positions in some way other than counting. They may, for example, be sensitive to the presence vs. the absence of a skeletal position (as in the case of the distinction between words beginning in *h-aspiré* or a vowel in French; see Section 5.1). Similarly, there may be constituents derived from relations between skeletal positions (including onset positions) which have to be referred to in the context of processes such as reduplication (see discussion in Section 5.2).

Another aspect of McCarthy and Prince's claim about 'rules count[ing] moras, syllables or feet but never segments' which I would like to challenge here is that phonological processes count syllables. As far as I know, no evidence has been put forward in the literature to show conclusively that it is indeed entire syllables which are being counted, rather than rhymes. Still, the fact that, in their treatment of reduplication in a variety of languages, McCarthy and Prince (1986) make extensive reference to the syllable seems to suggest that the syllable plays an important role, at least for accounts of this particular phonological event. As has been shown by Kaye (1991), it is, however, possible to capture the same generalizations reasonably elegantly without invoking a syllable node. How this can be done will be illustrated in Section 5.2.

Whether moras are indispensable in phonological theory is a question which I will not address in this chapter. The reader is referred to Yoshida (1990, 1991) for a GP analysis of aspects of Japanese phonology which calls into question the claim that moras have to be invoked. Yoshida (1991: 70ff.) also provides some discussion of problematic aspects of Moraic Phonology.

Clearly, no further arguments in favour of the GP approach to the issues raised by Moraic Phonology can be put forward until a more complete picture of GP has been presented. So, let me move on from the discussion of the skeleton *per se* to prosodic levels above the skeleton and their specific properties in GP. This discussion will establish the background to the comparative section (Section 5) towards the end of this chapter.

3   Governing relations and constituent structure in GP

3.1   Governing relations define constituents

In this Section I provide a brief overview of the governing relations which apply in GP and of the constituents which they define. More detailed discussion of their implications follows in Sections 4 and 5 below.

We have seen that GP employs a maximally simple skeletal tier containing only xs. These xs are not just arranged next to one another. Instead, they enter into asymmetric binary relations with one another which are known as governing relations. Governing relations define the prosodic constituents into which the skeletal positions are grouped.

The 'area' over which a governing relation extends defines a governing domain. In other words, two skeletal positions in a governing relation constitute a governing domain. A governing domain is sometimes called a phonological domain. The term 'domain', however, is used in GP not just to refer to governing (or phonological) domains, as just defined, but also to morphological domains.

A detailed discussion of morphological domains in GP would be beyond the scope of this chapter and what follows should be taken as a very brief sketch intended to provide some background for the discussion of licensing in Section 4 (see also Kaye, this volume, section 2.2).

Morphological domains (also known as analytic domains) would typically be delimited by #(word-)boundaries in an orthodox SPE-type framework. A morphological domain may contain a + (morpheme- or formative-)boundary, but the phonology is not sensitive to + -boundaries. In other words, + -boundaries are treated by the phonology as if they did not exist. For example, a denominal adjective such as #parent + al# is interpreted as a single morphological domain by the phonology. Morphology involving nothing stronger than a + -boundary is, therefore, known as non-analytic morphology.

There are essentially the following three morphological configurations which play a role in GP, most of which can, of course, be further expanded by concatenation.

The first configuration consists of a single analytic domain, e.g. [A] or [A + B]. (Analytic boundaries appear as single brackets [ ] and non-analytic boundaries as + .) An example of [A] would be a morphologically simple word such as [boy] or [go]. [A + B], by contrast, shows the morphological structure of a word such as the above-mentioned [parent + al]. Non-analytic affixation in GP corresponds very roughly to Level 1 morphology in the framework of Lexical Phonology (see Kaisse and Shaw 1985 for an overview). A suffix such as adjectival -al, for example, would be treated as non-analytic in GP because its presence affects the location of primary stress, with primary stress falling on the initial syllable in parent but on the penultimate syllable in parental. Apart from affecting stress assignment, non-analytic affixes are typically unproductive and exhibit a good deal of lexical selectivity. They may also be associated with phenomena such as so-called closed-syllable shortening (e.g. *keep* vs. *kept* in English; see Section 4.1 for discussion). Analytic affixes, on the other hand, are usually stress-neutral, clearly productive and exhibit no lexical selectivity. No closed-syllable shortening effects are observed in the context of analytic affixation.

Analytic affixation characterizes both the second and third morphological configurations provided for in GP. The second involves cases such as [[A]B], which contains two analytic domains. This can be exemplified by words such as the regular past tense form [[*peep*]*ed*]. The root (*peep*) occupies a domain of its own, while the analytic suffix does not, which, among other things, makes the prediction that the suffix is unstressed.

Third, there is the three-domain [[A][B]]-type configuration, which is best illustrated by compounds, e.g. [[*black*][*board*]] or [[*tea*][*spoon*]]. Each term of the compound occupies its own domain, so that a full vowel and some degree of stress would be expected for each one.

In what follows I will not always distinguish phonological and morphological domains from one another explicitly. This is because it is either clear from the context what is meant or because the distinction is unimportant.

The fact that governing relations are asymmetric means that one position within a governing domain governs, while the other is governed. The former is usually referred to as the governor (or sometimes as the head), while the latter, i.e. the governed position, is known as the governee (or complement).

According to Kaye et al. (henceforth KLV) (1990: 221), governing relations are established at the level of lexical representation, where the level of lexical representation is defined as 'the level at which the stem is attached to accompanying affixes, if any' (KLV 1990, note 34). A principle of grammar, the Projection Principle (KLV 1990: 221), ensures that there is no change in governing relations (and thus constituent structure) from underlying representation to the final output of a derivation. So, according to the Projection Principle (11), the phonology cannot manipulate governing relations.

(11)   *Projection Principle*

   Governing relations are defined at the level of lexical representation and remain constant throughout a phonological derivation.

The Projection Principle precludes any changes in governing relations during the course of derivation, which means that resyllabification is impossible. This is desirable, because it makes the framework more constrained than any theory which countenances resyllabification. Note that the Projection Principle allows for governing relations to be *added* in the course of derivation, while *changing* or *deleting* existing governing relations is prohibited.[4] This interpretation of (11) is required for handling analytic morphology, i.e. analytic affixation and compounding. As far as analytic morphology is concerned, on the first cycle, governing relations hold within an analytic domain only. On the second cycle, however, additional skeletal points become available, and there is evidence to suggest that new governing relations are established which involve skeletal positions formerly separated by an analytic domain boundary (see e.g. Brockhaus 1992: 224 for a relevant representation). One piece of evidence to support this reading of (11) comes from stress assignment, which entails building governing relations at various levels of nuclear projection. These governing relations are first established within analytic domains and preserved on successive cycles, but, as further domains become available (until word formation has been completed) additional governing (= stress) relations are added.

To return to the discussion of government in GP, the theory recognizes government at three levels, viz. constituent government (holding between skeletal positions within a constituent and perhaps more aptly named intra-constituent government), inter-constituent government (holding between skeletal positions in two contiguous constituents) and government at a level of nuclear projection, which holds between heads of nuclear constituents. Government at the first two levels is strictly local[5] and strictly directional. In other words, positions which are in a governing relation must be adjacent (strict locality). Government is universally defined as being left-headed for constituent government and right-headed for inter-constituent government (strict directionality).

A direct result of these two principles (strict locality and strict directionality) is that constituents are maximally binary, as it is logically impossible for *both* strict directionality *and* strict locality to be respected in a branching constituent which is anything other than binary (see also Kaye 1987: 132, Kaye 1990a: 306f., or Charette 1991: 16f. for the proof). In a ternary constituent, for example, the governor is either the skeletal position in the centre, which means that it has to govern in more than one direction, or it is a position at one of the two edges of the constituent, with the result that it is not adjacent to one of its governees. At first sight, restricting constituents to maximally two positions may appear to be an approach which is faced with numerous counterexamples, e.g. initial *s* + consonant sequences such as, say, *str* in Italian. As shown in KLV (1990), however, the members of this sequence are not syllabified into a single constituent, but *two* adjacent constituents. Further evidence regarding the syllabification of *s* + C clusters into two separate constituents is adduced in Kaye (1992b) for (European) Portuguese, (Ancient) Greek and English. To the extent that this analysis can be applied to other languages (and there is no particular reason why this should be impossible), such *s* + consonant sequences do not constitute counterexamples to the GP claim that constituents are maximally binary.

There are three prosodic constituents, viz. onset (O), nucleus (N) and rhyme (R). The nucleus is the head of the rhyme (left branch). In other words, the rhyme is the first projection of the nucleus, so that R can be understood as N'. Where the rhyme node dominates only a nucleus (as in (12b) below), the rhyme node is, therefore, frequently omitted, a practice which I shall adopt throughout this chapter. The three GP constituents take the forms shown in (12a–c) below. All three may or may not be branching, but the only constituent which may lack a skeletal point is the onset (as shown in (12a)). Note that the syllable and the coda are not among the GP constituents, a claim which I discuss in more detail in Section 3.4. All references to 'syllable structure', 'syllabification' and so on should, therefore, be interpreted as concessions to readers more familiar with syllable-based frameworks. Similarly, the terms 'onset', 'nucleus' and 'rhyme' should not be taken to indicate that the constituents to which they refer are parts of some larger unit, such as the syllable. Instead, to paraphrase Rennison's (1992) view of this issue, the constituents labelled by these three terms are primitives of the theory of GP, and the terms used are suggestive only of the historical derivation of these primitives from earlier work on the syllable.

(12)

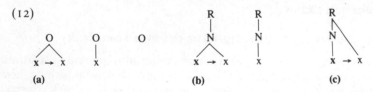

(a)   (b)   (c)

The arrows in (12) indicate the direction of government. Heads are emboldened. GP allows for the inter-constituent governing relations illustrated in (13a–c). In (13a), a nucleus governs a preceding onset, and an onset position governs a preceding post-nuclear rhymal position (or 'coda' for short) in (13b). The configuration in (13c) involves a governing relation between nuclear positions at the skeletal level. Such a governing relation can be established only where the intervening onset position has no skeletal point. Otherwise, a conflict with the principle of strict locality would arise. Like

(13)

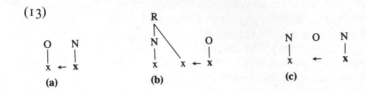

(a)   (b)   (c)

constituent government and inter-constituent government, government at a level of nuclear projection is also local (but not strictly so), in the sense that, at the relevant level of projection, the two nuclear constituents concerned are adjacent, although other material may intervene at lower levels. Unlike constituent and inter-constituent government, government by nuclear projection is language-specific in its directionality. Directionality at this level of government is parametrically variable and is reflected in prosodic phenomena such as tone, stress and harmony. Both right-headed and left-headed government at this level are shown in (14) below.

(14)

For governing relations to hold, the segments associated with the skeletal positions which enter into a governing relation have to fulfil certain charm or complexity requirements. These are discussed in the next section.

3.2   Governing relations depend on charm and complexity

We have seen that skeletal positions enter into governing relations which define constituents. Given a string of skeletal positions, how do we know exactly what sort of governing relations they contract with each other? Take the English verb *foster* (RP pronunciation [fɒstə]) as an example. As suggested by Charette (1991: 11f.), its underlying representation would take a form something like that shown in (15).

(15)

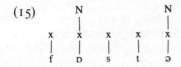

The two nuclear positions are lexically associated with a constituent nucleus, while the remaining positions still have to be projected to be incorporated in constituents. Clearly, some of them will be part of onsets, but which ones? The initial fricative is a clear-cut case. It simply has to be projected to a non-branching onset. What about the $s + t$ cluster, though? Should this be treated as a branching onset? In spite of the fact that word-initial $s + t$ sequences are attested, GP does not allow us to simply assume that such clusters are onsets. Recall that (initial) $s + C$ clusters in languages such as Italian, Ancient Greek, European Portuguese and English have been shown not to form branching onsets (see KLV 1990 and Kaye 1992). For the sake of argument, let us assume, for the moment, that we are unaware of this evidence. The decision which has to be made at this point then boils down to the following question. Which of the two segments concerned (s and t) can govern the other? If it turns out that s can govern t, then left-to-right government applies, which means that the two positions are members of a branching constituent – a branching onset, to be precise. If, however, t can govern s, but not vice versa, then a right-to-left governing relation holds. Right-to-left government is inter-constituent government, so that the s would occupy a post-nuclear rhymal position, while the t must be in the governing onset. To determine this, we need to consider the segmental representations involved.

Let me begin with a general discussion of segmental composition and charm. As discussed in Harris and Lindsey (as well as Coleman, this volume), all segments are either elements themselves or consist of a combination of elements (see especially KLV 1985, KLV 1990, Harris 1990b and Kaye 1990c for further details). Each element is fully specified, which means that elements are pronounceable at all levels of derivation, by themselves or in combination with others. There is no underspecification in GP. One of the inalienable properties of each element is its charm value. Elements, by definition, are either charmed (positively or negatively) or charmless (also, somewhat misleadingly, referred to as 'neutrally charmed' or simply 'neutral'). Charm values are indicated by superscript $^+$ (for positive charm), $^-$ (for negative charm) and $^\circ$ (for charmlessness or neutral charm).

The combination of elements is carried out through fusion

operations, each of which involves a pair of elements, with one being defined as the head and the other as the operator. When elements fuse with one another to form complex segments, charm values impose certain restrictions on which elements can fuse with which. Elements with like charm typically repel one another, whereas elements with opposite charm values (+ and −) attract one another. Charmless elements, however, can freely fuse with one another, as well as with charmed elements.

Each element has a single salient, or marked, property. It is this property which is contributed by the operator in the process of fusion, while everything else (including the charm value) is normally taken from the head. The only element which does not have a salient property is the so-called 'cold vowel' v°. The implication of this is that fusion with the cold vowel in the operator role results in no change to the head at all. The presence of the cold vowel only manifests itself when the cold vowel itself is the head.

All GP elements, together with their charm values and their phonetic realizations, as well as their salient and unmarked properties, are listed in (16) below. The unmarked properties are background properties which make it possible for elements to be realized even in isolation. Note that salient and unmarked properties are expressed in articulatory terms for the sole reason that full acoustic definitions of all elements are not yet available. See Lindsey and Harris (1990), Harris and Lindsey (1991), Harris and Lindsey, this volume, Williams (1992) or Williams and Brockhaus (1992) for some of the sort of definitions I would have liked to use here. (But see Harris and Lindsey, this volume for a less traditional account of GP elements.)

(16)

		Salient property	Unmarked properties
Uᶜ	[ʊ]	labial	back, high, lax . . .
R°	[ɾ]	coronal	tap, . . .
I°	[ɪ]	palatal	non-labial, high, lax . . .
A⁺	[a]	non-high	non-labial, lax . . .
Ɨ⁺	[ɨ]	ATR-ness	non-labial, back, high . . .
v°	[ɨ]	*none*	non-labial, back, high, lax . . .
h°	[h]	narrowed	glottal, . . .
ʔ°	[ʔ]	occluded	glottal, . . .
N⁺	[ŋ]	nasal	nonlabial, back . . .
L⁻	L	slack vocal folds	
H⁻	H	stiff vocal folds	

Elements are arranged on autosegmental lines in such a way that each element occupies its own line (labelled according to the salient property of the element).[6] Phonological representations consist of a two-dimensional grid where autosegmental lines and segmental positions intersect. According to KLV (1985: 308), 'the absence of a real element [i.e. an element with a salient property] at intersections has a specific interpretation: these "empty" intersections are in fact filled by the cold vowel'.

In the GP framework, charmed as well as charmless segments can govern, while only charmless segments are potential governees. Positively charmed segments may only occupy nuclear head positions, while negatively charmed segments are restricted to non-nuclear (head) positions (KLV 1990: 204). This is illustrated in (17), where the variable α stands for any suitable segment.

(17)

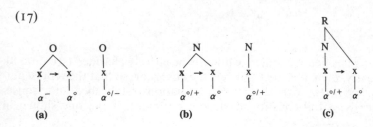

(a)   (b)   (c)

Charmed segments are 'strong' governors in the sense that they can govern simply by virtue of their charm, while charmless segments are 'weak' governors which, according to the Complexity Condition (18) (closely following Harris 1990b and KLV 1990), can govern only if they are no less complex than their governees.[7]

(18)   *Complexity Condition*

Let α and β be charmless segments occupying the positions A and B respectively. Then, if A governs B, β must be no more complex than α.

Complexity is calculated on the basis of the number of elements (excluding the cold vowel in the operator role) of which a segmental representation is composed. The more elements it contains, the more complex it is deemed to be.

We are now in a position to take a closer look at the segmental representations of *s* and *t*, as they occur in *foster* (see (19) below). The remaining segments are still in broad transcription. Also, the autosegmental element lines and the cold vowels at empty intersections have been omitted to keep representations as simple as possible. The arrangement of elements on the representational grid has the additional effect of obscuring the fact that segmental composition involves pairwise fusion of elements. This property of segmental composition in GP is only visible when the matrix calculus introduced in KLV (1985) (and updated in Kaye 1990c) is employed, which would assign the expression (H⁻.(h°.(ʔ°.R°)°)°)⁻ to the t^8 in *foster*. The segmental representations in (19) indicate

(19)

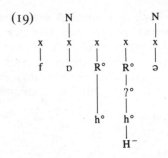

that *s* has neutral charm, while *t* is negatively charmed (see note 8). Clearly, then, it is the *t* which is the governor, so that the representation of *foster* with all governing relations established and, consequently, a full constituent structure present, is the one shown in (20).

(20)

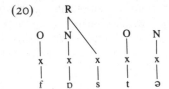

3.3   A special form of government: proper government

Before leaving this discussion of governing relations, let me introduce a special type of governing relation, that of proper government. This plays an important role in GP and will feature in part of the discussion of specific phonological events in Section 5. Proper government is defined by Kaye (1990a: 313) as follows.

(21)   *Proper government*

A nuclear position α properly governs a nuclear position β if

(a) α is adjacent to β on its projection,
(b) α is not itself licensed, and
(c) no governing domain separates α from β.

According to (21), proper governing relations hold between nuclear positions at some level of nuclear projection. Charette (1990) proposes that proper government applies at the level of licenser projection. To keep things as simple as possible for the purposes of the present discussion, I will, however, not introduce this level. Like all governing relations at a level of nuclear projection, proper governing relations should then be parametrically variable in their directionality. More research is required on this, but it seems that, until now, no clear-cut cases of left-to-right proper government have been discovered (see Kaye 1990a, note 21). It is possible that this is a universal property of proper government.

Proper government plays a vital role in the phonological version of the Empty Category Principle (ECP), which was first proposed in KLV (1990: 219). My version of this principle, which closely follows the spirit of Kaye (1990a: 314), is set out in (22).

(22) *Empty Category Principle*

    (a) A licensed empty nucleus has no phonetic realization
    (b) An empty nucleus is licensed if (i) it is properly governed or (ii) it is domain-final in languages which parametrically license domain-final empty nuclei.

The details of licensing will be discussed in Section 4. What matters at this stage is that GP recognizes so-called empty skeletal positions. Strictly speaking, these positions are not empty, since they contain the cold vowel v°, which, as mentioned in Section 3.2, is present at empty intersections between autosegmental lines and segmental positions. The distribution of such empty skeletal positions is very tightly constrained by the ECP. Apart from parametrically licensed domain-final positions, only properly governed positions may remain empty. As shown in a good deal of work in GP, especially Kaye (1987) and Kaye (1988), a range of vowel/zero alternation events can be accounted for quite elegantly if the ECP and proper government are invoked.

Consider the Moroccan Arabic radical |KTB| 'to write' (as discussed in Kaye 1987), for example. Its causative forms are [kɪttɪb] (singular) and [kɪttbuː] (plural) respectively. The structures Kaye proposes for the causative singular and plural forms are shown, with |KTB| applied to them and all governing relations established, in (23a) and (23b) respectively. Note that Moroccan Arabic parametrically licenses domain-final empty nuclear positions (see section 4.2 for discussion). Recall that the way empty nuclear positions are represented in (23) and elsewhere in this chapter is shorthand

(23)

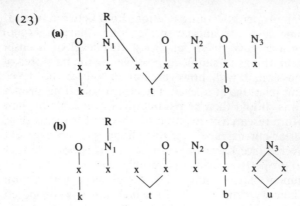

for a representation containing the cold vowel v°. In Moroccan Arabic, this vowel (realized as [ɨ]) is audible whenever an empty nuclear position is unlicensed. So, according to the ECP, we should expect to hear it, unless the relevant position is parametrically licensed (as in the case of the final position in (23a)) or properly governed. Which of the positions in (23) are properly governed? To answer this question, we first of all need to note that proper government applies from right to left in Moroccan Arabic. Now we can work our way through a morphological domain.

Let me begin with (23a). N_3 is parametrically licensed, so it can remain inaudible. Being itself licensed, N_3 is unable to properly govern (see (21b)), so N_2 is predicted to be unlicensed and hence audible. Being unlicensed, N_2 could properly govern N_1. However, there is a governing domain (consisting of an empty coda position governed by a following onset and deriving its segmental content through spreading from this onset) intervening between the two nuclear positions. Therefore, no proper governing relation can be established (see (21c)) and N_1 remains unlicensed, which means that it has to be audible. The predicted realization is [kɨttɨb], which is correct.

The plural form in (23b) ends in an unlicensed nucleus (realized as [uː]), which is a potential proper governor. Indeed, all requirements for proper government to be able to apply are met, so that N_3 properly governs N_2, which now remains inaudible. Being licensed itself, N_2, however, cannot properly govern N_1 (see (21b)). (The governing domain intervening between N_1 and N_2 would have blocked proper government anyway, even if N_2 had not been licensed itself.) So, we predict that N_1 and N_3, but not N_2, are realized, which, again, is correct: we hear [kɨttbuː].

This example illustrates the operation of proper government, involving nuclear positions only. In recent work (e.g. Charette 1991: 91ff. and Cyran 1992), however, proper governing relations have been shown also to play a role in the licensing of non-nuclear empty positions. An example of this (from Charette 1991) will be discussed in Section 5.1.

Having seen how governing relations define constituent structure and how the establishment of governing relations (with proper government being a special case), in turn, depends on segmental structure, we can now consider one of the more striking implications of the discussion in this section, namely the absence of the syllable as a constituent.

3.4   There is no syllable in GP

As already observed, there is no such thing as a syllable (node) in GP. This may seem a surprising state of affairs. Dispensing with the syllable could even be interpreted as a retrograde step. After all, as Haugen pointed out in 1956, 'sooner or later everyone finds it [the syllable] convenient to use' (p. 213). To what considerable extent phonologists appear to have, at least tacitly, agreed with this statement can perhaps be gauged by the scale of protest resulting from Kohler's (1966) paper in which he rejects the syllable as being an 'unnecessary', 'impossible' or even 'harmful' concept in phonology (p. 207). His claims were countered by, among others, Anderson (1969) and Fudge (1969), with the latter providing very detailed arguments in favour of the syllable as a phonological universal. Chomsky and Halle (1968) excluded the syllable from the formalism of the SPE-theory (in spite of making frequent informal reference to it both in the text and in some rules, as pointed out by Fudge (1969: 216ff.)). When applying the SPE-formalism to a range of phonological events (final devoicing in languages such as German[9] or Russian being one of the most well-known), researchers were again and again forced to employ the conjunction {C, # (consonant or word boundary). Its recurrence suggested that a generalization was being missed in non-syllable-based analyses of such phonological phenomena. When, however, the syllable was adopted as part of the formalism of generative phonology (e.g. in Vennemann 1972 for final devoicing and other phenomena; and Hooper 1976, Kahn 1976 and Selkirk 1982b; see also the references in the latter), this conjunction appeared much less frequently in phonological work, and many of the hitherto recalcitrant events became amenable to comparatively simple and elegant analyses.

Over the years, more and more evidence in favour of the syllable as a crucial concept in phonological theory has been adduced, so that authors of recent textbooks can feel confident in stating that 'the syllable is at the heart of phonological representations' (Katamba 1989: 153) and that 'today the place of the syllable [in mainstream phonology] is secure' (p. 164). However, the picture is actually not quite as harmonious as these quotes suggest: Kohler was by no means the only author who had doubts about the status of the syllable in phonology. In 1980 Halle and Vergnaud (1980a: 93), for example, reported that they had uncovered 'many phonological processes where the constituents of the syllable – in particular, the onset and rime – function independently of one another'. This led them to the conclusion that 'the superordinate unit, the syllable, plays a much more marginal role in phonology than do its constituents' (p. 93). To some extent, this view appears to be shared by at least one proponent of Moraic Phonology as well, since Hyman (1985) argues that certain languages (e.g. Gokana) do not have syllables, while others may do. His syllable formation rules are language-specific and do not apply in languages such as Gokana.

GP takes this approach one step further and dispenses with the syllable universally, which has the advantage of simplifying phonological representations. The claim being made is that alleged arguments in favour of the syllable can be reduced to arguments in favour of a potentially branching rhyme, with the potential for nuclear projection.

An argument against the syllable which is theory-internal to GP is that the syllable would be anomalous in being the only right-headed constituent, given that each N governs the immediately preceding O. Moreover, the principle of strict locality would have to be relaxed, since a maximally binary syllable would be too restrictive. If, however, the syllable node were to dominate three or more skeletal positions, the governor would not be immediately adjacent to one or more of its governees (but see note 5 for a problem with strict locality which exists in GP even in the absence of a syllable node). For a more detailed discussion of this and other arguments and for further evidence the reader is referred to, e.g. Charette (1991) or KLV (1990), where arguments against a coda constituent can also be found.

In the context of non-constituents in GP, recall that there is no coda constituent either. Detailed arguments against such a constituent can be found in KLV (1990), and Charette (1989 and 1991) as well as in Hogg and McCully (1987: 45ff.), so suffice it to say here that the presence of a maximally binary coda constituent could lead to the rhyme dominating no fewer than four skeletal positions (two in the nucleus and two in the coda). Since the rhyme is also a constituent and the positions it dominates are subject to strictly local and strictly directional constituent government, the requirement of strict locality would, again, have to be relaxed, since adjacency of governor and governee would be limited to two out of the four positions. Therefore, a post-nuclear rhymal position is directly linked to the rhyme node, without an intervening coda node. The term 'coda', however, is considerably shorter and more convenient than 'post-nuclear rhymal position', which is why it features frequently in the GP literature. It should be noted, though, that this is simply shorthand and does not imply the existence of a coda constituent.

4   Licensing as the motor driving phonology

4.1   Licensing domains and government as a form of licensing

After this excursus on the absence of the syllable, let me now return to the existing constituents in GP. As already mentioned, these are defined by governing relations, and governing relations are an instantiation of a more general principle of phonology, the principle of licensing. It is particularly in relatively recent work in GP (e.g. Kaye 1990a, Charette 1991 and, especially, Harris 1992, where the rather vague notion of licensing to be presented here is made much more precise) that the importance of licensing in phonology is being more fully recognized.[10]

Licensing is the motor which drives phonology, and every skeletal position within a domain, except for the head, has to be licensed, as stated in the Licensing Principle (24) (Kaye 1990a: 306).

(24)   *Licensing Principle*

All phonological positions save one must be licensed within a domain. The unlicensed position is the head of this domain.

Consider the following representation (adapted from Harris 1992: 384), which illustrates how the head of the morphological domain licenses other positions within that domain. (25) is the representation of the English word *tawdry*, as pronounced in RP. As mentioned in Section 3.1, GP distinguishes between morphological

(25)

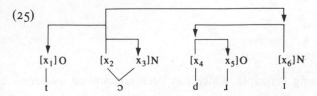

(analytic) and phonological (governing) domains. This distinction receives clear illustration in (25). Within the single morphological domain, there are five phonological domains, involving the following pairs of positions (governor first): x_2 and x_1, x_2 and x_3, x_2 and x_6, x_6 and x_4, and x_4 and x_5. Two of the five represent cases of constituent governing relations between adjacent positions, viz. x_2 and x_3 (branching nucleus), and x_4 and x_5 (branching onset). The governing relation between x_2 and x_1, by contrast, is an inter-constituent governing relation (nucleus governing preceding onset). The heads of these three domains are unlicensed within each domain, but, with one exception, receive their own licensing from positions outside these domains. So, x_4 is licensed by x_6 (through the problematic inter-constituent governing relation discussed in note 5) and x_6, in turn, is licensed by x_2 at a level of nuclear projection, to be precise, at the level of the foot. The only unlicensed position within the morphological domain is x_2, the head of this domain. The head of a domain bears primary stress in languages which exhibit stress.

So far I have merely implied that government is a form of licensing. Let me now make this view more explicit and discuss some particular cases of licensing which have far-reaching implications. It is worth recalling from the discussion of the ECP (22) in Section 3.3 that government is not the only form of licensing. Licensing by parameter setting is also counternanced in GP. This form of licensing, however, is available only for empty domain-final nuclear positions (to be discussed in detail in Section 4.2), while licensing through government accounts for the remainder of the licensing work within a domain.

Licensing within a branching constituent is effected by (intra-) constituent government, as shown in (26) below. Each onset is

(26)

licensed by an immediately following nucleus through inter-constituent government, as illustrated in (27). This is stipulated in the

(27)   O   N

     | |

    x ← x

Onset Licensing Principle, which has been an implicit assumption in GP work for some time but was first formally stated as a separate principle by Harris (1992: 380).

(28)   *Onset Licensing Principle*

An onset head position must be licensed by a nuclear position.

As observed by Charette (1991), a governor has to have a skeletal position. Consequently, nuclei, which always govern a preceding onset, can never lack an x on the skeletal tier. Onsets, on the other hand, which have no governing work to do may well lack a skeletal point, as illustrated in (12a). In her discussion of *h-aspiré* in French (see Section 5.2) she motivates onsets both with and without a skeletal point.

The Onset Licensing Principle (28) in itself has relatively little impact, as all it requires is for an onset to be followed by a nucleus (even an empty nucleus), which, on the face of it, is nothing unusual in phonology anyway. However, when combined with another principle of GP, the Coda Licensing Principle (quoted from Kaye 1990a: 311 in (29)), the Onset Licensing Principle has far-reaching implications both for the handling of the special properties of word-final consonants as well as for language typology. As mentioned in 3.4, the term 'coda' is used as shorthand for 'post-nuclear rhymal position'.

(29)   *Coda Licensing Principle*

Post-nuclear rhymal positions must be licensed by a following onset.

A well-formed representation involving a rhymal consonant must then take the form in (30). The governing onset head, which provides the licensing for this rhymal position, is emboldened, as before.

(30)

As observed by Harris (1992), the unusual behaviour of apparently word-final consonants has not escaped the notice of many phonologists. Their extrametrical status in stress assignment has been observed by, among others, Hayes (1982) and Segundo (1990), their failure to undergo closed-syllable shortening by Myers (1987)[11] and their tendency to contravene otherwise general sonority sequencing generalizations by Levin (1985). To see how this aberrant behaviour can be accounted for in GP, first consider the representation of the English noun *bus* in (31), which conforms to the widespread assumption that a word-final consonant is part of the rhyme. This representation is in accordance with the Onset

(31) *

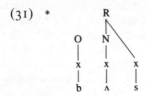

Licensing Principle, but it is in conflict with the Coda Licensing Principle, It is ill-formed, since there is no following onset position to enter into an inter-constituent governing relation with the coda position and thus license it. The well-formed alternative to (31) is shown in (32). Here the apparently word-final consonant occupies

(32)

an onset position, which, according to the Onset Licensing Principle, has to be licensed by a following nucleus. (The empty nucleus which licenses the onset will be discussed in Section 4.2.) The *s* is not a member of the rhyme, which means that, for the purposes of stress assignment, the rhyme is non-branching. Coda Licensing achieves the same effect as extrametricality here. Second, the failure of closed-syllable shortening to apply also finds an explanation in Coda Licensing. Consider the representation of the verb *keep* in (33). The GP representation does not predict closed-syllable shorten-

(33)

ing, as there is no consonant to close the syllable. The non-analytic past tense form of the same verb, by contrast, can only accommodate a short vowel, as the *p* is part of the rhyme. This is shown in

(34).[12] Incidentally, *keep* and *kept* have separate lexical entries, that is, *kept* is not derived from *keep*. Such a derivation would be in conflict with the Projection Principle, since it would involve a change in governing relations. Third, the tendency of word-final

(34)

consonants to contravene sonority sequencing generalizations in words such as French *quatre* [katr] or *table* [tabl] could be dealt with by interpreting the final consonant as extraprosodic. Quite apart from the inherent weaknesses of this approach, which receive detailed discussion in Harris (1992), extraprosodicity would be an unnecessary complication of the grammar from the point of view of GP, since an alternative is available. All that is needed is to interpret these consonant sequences as branching onsets rather than codas, which is what one would do word-internally anyway. *Quatre*, for example, would then have the structure in (35).

(35)

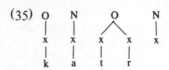

Continuing the survey of licensing relations, let me now turn to the licensing of nuclear heads. Every nucleus (bar the head of the analytic domain) is licensed either through being governed by another nucleus at a level of nuclear projection (see (36), which illustrates left- and right-headed government by nuclear projection) or, as already mentioned in the ECP (22), by parameter setting (if domain-final, see Section 4.2).

(36)

A post-nuclear rhymal position (e.g. the position occupied by *p* in (34)) appears to have a special status in the context of licensing in that, on the one hand, it is licensed (through constituent government) by the nucleus which c-commands it and, on the other hand, it has to be further licensed by a following onset. It is the only skeletal position which requires this kind of 'double licensing'. This may be a function of the fact that, although the governing relation between a nuclear head and the post-nuclear rhymal position is a constituent governing relation inasmuch as both positions are sisters within the rhyme, it differs from the two remaining constituent government configurations. This difference lies in the fact that the two positions are not immediately dominated by the same node. The nuclear head position is immediately dominated by N, whereas the coda is immediately dominated by R. This suggests that the governing relation is less 'close' (for want of a better word) than it is in the cases of branching onsets and branching nuclei. The prediction derivable from this interpretation is that greater variation in terms of charm and complexity should be tolerated in both governor and governee. This prediction appears to be borne out by the facts, as charmless vowels are associated with the nuclear-head position with remarkable frequency (whereas positive charm typically seems to be required for branching nuclei; see KLV 1990: 207), and comparatively complex segments, such as nasals, frequently occupy the 'coda', whereas segments of such a high degree of complexity are excluded from the governed position in a branching onset or nucleus.

4.2 Parametrically licensed domain-final empty nuclear positions

Let me now return to the Coda Licensing Principle (29) for a moment. We have seen that it can help provide solutions to traditional problems posed by apparently word-final consonants. Apart from this, the Coda Licensing Principle also has clear typological implications. These partly depend on the status of the domain-final nuclear position, which was simply taken for granted in representations such as (32), (33), (34) and (35). Clearly, the presence of this position is a necessary consequence of the existence of the Onset Licensing Principle and the Coda Licensing Principle. But how is it licensed and what are the predictions its presence makes? Under the ECP (22), an empty skeletal position can be licensed (that is, permitted to be present and remain inaudible) either by proper government (as discussed in Section 3.3) or by parameter setting, if it is domain-final. The relevant parameter is expressed in (37).

(37)   A domain-final empty nuclear position is licensed:
       YES/NO

We saw in Section 3.3 that empty nuclei manifest themselves phonetically when, for some reason, they are unlicensed. In Moroccan Arabic, for example, an [ɪ] surfaces. What about para-metrically licensed domain-final empty nuclear positions? In principle, such positions should never be audible (but see Kaye 1990a for discussion of an apparent exception to this in Turkish). There may, however, be other indications of the presence of such a position.

Segundo (1990) argues that domain-final empty nuclear positions affect stress assignment in Brazilian Portuguese (BP). BP has words with antepenultimate, penultimate and final stress, e.g. ['sintɛzi] 'synthesis', [batu'kada] 'noise of drums' and [ʒaka'rɛ] 'alligator', respectively. One could generalize that BP stress is restricted to one of the last three syllables of a word. Now consider the hypothetical words from Segundo (1990:45) in (38).

(38)

```
* 'patanal    * 'nitiron
* 'satidor    * 'natalis
```

These items are judged impossible words by native speakers of BP, in spite of the fact that primary stress apparently falls on one of the last three syllables of the word. According to Segundo, this native-speaker judgement can only be squared with the generalization that BP stress falls on one of these syllables if the final consonant in each word is actually followed by a nuclear position, which, although inaudible, is taken into account for stress assignment. This is precisely what Coda Licensing and Onset Licensing would predict. The left-most [a] in [patanal], for example, would then be the fourth nucleus from the right (as shown in (39)) – a position which cannot bear primary stress in BP.

(39)
```
     O   N   O   N   O   N   O   N
     |   |   |   |   |   |   |   |
     x   x   x   x   x   x   x   x
     |   |   |   |   |   |   |
     p   a   t   a   n   a   l
```

Having seen that there is at least some evidence from stress assignment in favour of the final empty nuclear position posited for apparently consonant-final words in GP, we now turn to the typological implications of the existence of this position. What has been said so far makes the prediction that there should be a four-way typological distinction, which cuts across the parameter in (37) and another parameter which controls whether rhymes are branching. A widespread assumption is that the absence of final consonants in so-called CV or open-syllable languages is due to the absence of branching rhymes, since the final consonant is usually interpreted as part of the final rhyme.

Even a superficial glance at a language such as Italian, which exhibits both word-internal geminates and nasal + stop clusters but no word-final consonants, suggests, however, that this is too simplistic a view.[13] What appears to be required is the four-way distinction provided by GP. All that needs to be said about Italian is, then, that domain-final empty nuclear positions are not licensed, while branching rhymes are. In languages where words can end in consonant clusters, such as English, German and French, for example, both parameters are set to YES. Strict CV languages, such as Desano (Eastern Tucanoan; Colombia, Brazil), by contrast, have both parameters set to NO. Finally, if domain-final empty nuclear positions really are motivated, then we should also find a group of languages where the relevant parameter is set to YES, but where branching rhymes are prohibited. Luo (Nilo-Saharan; Kenya, Tanzania; see Harris 1992: 367) and, according to Kaye (1990a), some Gur languages of Burkina Faso belong to this group.

5   GP approaches to some phonological issues

In this Section I discuss GP approaches to two issues in phonology and compare them with weight-unit/mora-based alternatives. For this purpose I have chosen *h-aspiré* in French and reduplication in languages such as Sanskrit, Ancient Greek, Tagalog and others. The reasoning behind this choice is the following. In my view, *h-aspiré* provides quite strong evidence in favour of the skeletal tier, the existence of which is denied in Moraic Theory (see e.g. Hayes 1989, Bickmore this volume). Certain aspects of reduplication, on the other hand, point towards the need for constituent governing relations, as provided for in GP and, more generally, 'reduplication has now arrived centre stage as a testing ground for alternative theories of multitiered morphology and phonology' (Mutaka and Hyman 1990: 73; see also references there), so it is particularly relevant in the present context. For reasons of space it is not possible to give a comprehensive account of the treatment of *h-aspiré* or of the GP approach to reduplication. The aim is to provide an insight into the particular benefits which GP can bring to these issues. I will begin with Charette's analysis of *h-aspiré* in French.

5.1 Charette's treatment of h-aspiré in French

In Section 3.1 I observed that an onset may or may not dominate a skeletal position (see 12a). Following Vergnaud (1982), Charette (1988, 1991) motivates both configurations in her discussion of the behaviour of the definite article (singular) in French preceding a vowel-initial noun and preceding a noun beginning with *h-aspiré*. In the former case, the vowel of the definite article is lost, so that *la amie* 'the (female) friend', for example, is realized as [lami]. Words beginning with *h-aspiré* (which is completely inaudible), by contrast, pattern with consonant-initial words, where the final vowel of the definite article is preserved. So, *le génie* 'the genius' is realized as [ləʒeni] and *le havre* 'the haven' as [ləɑvr]. This, of course, is a very simplistic account of the phenomenon, ignoring all the complexities which are mentioned, e.g. in Durand (1986) and which find detailed discussion in Tranel (forthcoming). Still, for the purposes of this section, it seems reasonable to put them to one side.

The underlying representation Charette (1991: 90) proposes for forms such as *la amie* is essentially that given in (40) (with governing relations estalished and morphological bracketing omitted).

(40)

```
    O   N   O   N   O   N
    |   |   |   |   |   |
    x   x   x   x   x
    |   |   |   |   |
    l   a   a   m   i
```

The first two nuclear positions (both occupied by /a/) are treated as adjacent, since there is no skeletal position to separate them. Charette proposes that the Obligatory Contour Principle (OCP; see e.g. Goldsmith 1990: 307ff, McCarthy 1986, Odden 1986 and Yip 1988a for discussion), which prohibits two identical melody units from occurring adjacently, applies to eliminate the left-most nucleus (along with the empty onset to its right). The resulting representation is shown in (41).

(41)

```
    O   N   O   N
    |   |   |   |
    x   x   x   x
    |   |   |   |
    l   a   m   i
```

This proposal is not without its problems. First, invoking the OCP in this way may seem a surprising move. Under a relatively standard interpretation of the OCP, one might have expected the

loss of one of the two adjacent identical expressions on the melody
tier (both realized as [a]), resulting in a long vowel (attached to two
nuclear positions), as shown in (42). Structures of precisely this
type are in fact proposed in two recent GP papers, viz. Pagoni
(1993) for Ancient Greek verbs displaying Attic reduplication) and Yoshida (1992) (for long vowels in Palestinian Arabic).

(42)
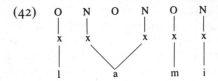

However, it has also been fairly general practice among GP phonologists to interpret the OCP in the way Charette does, that is, as a
mechanism to eliminate certain nuclear positions. To my knowledge, this usage has never been justified in the literature. (Brockhaus
(1992: 124ff.) does no more than to mention the uniqueness of the
GP interpretation of the OCP.) In fact, it appears that the use of
the term OCP is coming to be seen as inappropriate for this
operation. (Gussmann and Kaye (1992) refer to it as 'reduction'.)
It may even be the case that the operation itself is in conflict with
the Projection Principle.

This is the second reason why (40) and (41) are problematic. It is
likely that the deletion of a skeletal position does not comply with
the Projection Principle. After all, as Coleman (this volume) points
out in a different context, if one or more of 'the governor-governee
relations that make up the set of government relations pertinent to
the Projection Principle' are removed, we are faced with a violation
of the Projection Principle. Things may not be this clear-cut, but
there can be little doubt that there is something amiss here in the
GP approach, and further research into the Projection Principle
and the so-called OCP is urgently required. My hunch is that the
Projection Principle with its restrictive force is a step in the right
direction and that it is the question of whether it is really necessary
to delete skeletal positions in the course of derivation which should
be re-examined.

These observations may cast some doubts on Charette's approach to *h-aspiré*, but I do not believe that they invalidate every
aspect of it. It seems reasonable to assume that the interaction
between the two nuclei (resulting in the loss of one of them) is a
direct consequence of the fact that they are not separated by a
skeletal position. This makes the prediction that no such interaction
should occur where there is an intervening onset position present.

This, of course, is the case where a noun begins with a consonant, as shown in (43a). Charette proposes the presence of an onset

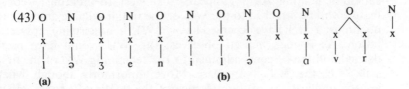

position also for words beginning with *h-aspiré*, thus capturing the parallel behaviour of consonant-initial words and of words beginning with *h-aspiré*, as illustrated in (43b). Note that the onset position representing *h-aspiré* is empty, accounting for the fact that *h-aspiré* is inaudible. Hyman (1985: 58) also addresses the question of how *h-aspiré* should be represented within his framework of weight-unit phonology. His approach is similar to Charette's in that it involves the presence of what could almost be interpreted as a kind of skeletal position, without phonetically interpretable features. He uses a floating [+ cons] feature, as shown in the underlying representation of *le héros* 'the hero' [ləero] in (44). His floating consonant (with an incomplete segmental representation) prevents the definite article from syllabifying onto the initial vowel, which would yield *[lero]. It is important to recognize the difference

(44)

between Hyman's xs and the xs used in GP. The latter represent segment-sized timing units, while the former represent weight units (WUs). In the WU-framework, each segmental matrix is associated with one or two xs (with two feature matrices sharing an x in the case of contour segments) in underlying representation. During the course of derivation a number of phonological rules apply to this string, including the universal onset creation rule (OCR), which attaches a [+ cons] matrix to the x of a following [– cons] feature matrix and subsequently deletes the x which originally accommodated the [+ cons] matrix. This results in syllables such as *ta* having only a single WU. At this point, Hyman's WUs are practically identical with the moras of Moraic Phonology, while in underlying representation Hyman's xs are indistinguishable from the xs of any kind of X theory. It seems that Hyman is operating both with segment-sized units *and* with moras, then.

Leaving this potentially problematic property of his framework

aside, there is a certain amount of indeterminacy in his analysis of
h-aspiré. For example, it is not entirely obvious why the [+cons]
should be floating. As (44) appears to suggest, the floating [+cons]
feature will be attached to the WU of the initial syllable anyway. It
might just as well have occupied its own WU in underlying representation. As Hyman himself observes, this WU would have been
deleted and the [+cons] adjoined to the remaining WU of the first
syllable by the OCR in any case. More importantly, though, what
are the implications of the presence of the floating [+cons], other
than the one it was introduced to capture in the first place?
Besides, can such floating consonants with incomplete segmental
representations be employed anywhere? As far as I can see,
Hyman's approach has no clearly defined implications, and there
are no restrictions on the use of this type of floating consonant.

The GP analysis put forward by Charette, by contrast, is more
tightly constrained. Recall that she proposes the presence of an
empty skeletal position. Like all other skeletal positions, empty
skeletal positions may only be present if they are licensed. In
addition to this standard licensing, as it were, empty skeletal
positions have to be licensed in a special way in order to remain
inaudible. This special licensing was introduced in the ECP (22) in
Section 3.3, in the context of empty nuclear positions. The version
of the ECP given in (22), however, is just one possible formulation
of it. There is a more general alternative, which can be applied to
non-nuclear positions as well. This is quoted from KLV (1990:219)
in (45).

(45)   *Empty Category Principle (general version)*

A position may be uninterpreted phonetically if it is properly governed.

Given (45), an empty onset position, as posited by Charette for *h-
aspiré*, has to be properly governed. The only proper governor
available is the following nuclear position. The definition of proper
government in (21) requires a proper governor to be itself unlicensed. One of the hallmarks of an unlicensed position is that it
receives phonetic interpretation, i.e. that it is audible. If the following nucleus properly governs the empty onset position, the prediction is made that this nucleus must have phonetic content. As
Charette (1991: 95) points out, this is precisely what we find. In
fact, not even schwa can occupy this particular nuclear position,
since, in French, schwa is the manifestation of an empty nucleus,[14]
so that no proper governing relation could hold between it and the
preceding onset. She identifies further consequences of the presence

of the empty onset position (see pp. 91ff.), a detailed discussion of which would be beyond the scope of this chapter.

As we have seen, the use of empty positions is quite tightly constrained in GP, whereas Hyman appears to be able to invoke floating [+cons] features with incomplete segmental representations wherever they are needed. Furthermore, the presence of a licensed empty position has clearly predictable effects in GP, while the implications of Hyman's approach to *h-aspiré*, are not easily identifiable.

5.2 The GP approach to reduplication

In this subsection I will briefly outline some of the basic principles of the GP approach to reduplication, using Ancient Greek (AG) reduplication of the verbal paradigm to illustrate some of the predictions. For this purpose I will draw heavily on Pagoni (1993).

Following the spirit of Kaye (1991), Pagoni outlines the following assumptions (among others), which define the GP view of reduplication. (Some of these assumptions, of course, go back further than Kaye (1991) and are due to Marantz (1982), McCarthy and Prince (1986), Steriade (1982, 1988) and others.) First, reduplicative affixes resemble other types of affixes, the only difference being that the former generally lack segmental content. Second, the structure of a reduplicative affix is fixed and association takes place by aligning indexes from the base and the reduplicative affix. The algorithm for assigning indexes is simple. The count starts at the left-most onset, with an increment of 1 at each subsequent onset. Third, association is local, that is, there is no skipping over vowels or consonants. The implication of this assumption is the following. Where prespecified and invariant nuclear melodic material (i.e. a fixed vowel) is present, association cannot proceed beyond it. The first person singular present perfect form of the verb [teleo:] 'I execute' would then take the form in (46). The [e] of the reduplica-

(46) pref. O_1 N_1 base O_1 N_1 O_2 N_2 O_3 N_3

x   x   x   x   x   x   x   x

t   e   t   e   l   e   k   a

tive prefix is prespecified, as witnessed by forms such as [memakʰeːmai] 'I have fought'.

Clearly, relatively straightforward cases such as (46) can also be handled quite easily by other approaches to reduplication (e.g. Steriade 1982, 1988), including those based on the principles of

Moraic Phonology (e.g. McCarthy and Prince 1986). It is where so-called simplification comes into play that GP can account for data posing problems for other frameworks. In a very detailed study of reduplication, Steriade (1988) discusses such simplification cases from a variety of languages, including Sanskrit, Tagalog, French, Klamath and Ancient Greek. The French hypocoristic forms from her study (p. 132) in (47a) are supplemented by further relevant data from Tagalog (McCarthy and Prince 1986: 16) and Ancient Greek (Pagoni 1993) in (47b) and (47c) respectively. The hyphen indicates a morpheme boundary.

(47)

   (a) Claire   keker, keke
       (Al)fred   fefed
       Bri(gitte)   bibi

   (b) ka-ta-trabaho   'just finished working'
       ka-bo-bloaut   'just gave a special treat'

   (c) ke-klika   'I have reclined'
       ke-kriːka   'I have judged'
       pe-pleuka   'I have sailed'

In all cases in (47), onset clusters are simplified in the reduplicated forms. The question is how to formalize this simplification. McCarthy and Prince (1986: 16) merely observe that the least sonorous member of the cluster is preserved. They point out that Steriade (1982) can achieve this with left-to-right mapping on the assumption that onsets are of stictly rising sonority. So, if only a single position is available for the onset of the reduplicative prefix, then only the left-hand member of the onset, i.e. the least sonorous position, will be associated with a skeletal position and thus be phonetically interpretable. To some extent this approach appeals to sonority scales, which, as Harris (1985) points out, are little more than taxonomic statements which can serve as look-up tables, but which cannot be directly encoded in phonological representations (at least not with binary features).

This view may even be shared by Steriade herself, since in her 1988 paper on reduplication, sonority considerations play a much less central role. Instead, she describes onset simplification as elimination of non-initial consonants. To my knowledge, there are no phonological events other than the onset simplification illustrated in (47) which make reference to non-initial consonants, so this seems to be very much an *ad hoc* description.

McCarthy and Prince (1986: 17), by contrast, entertain a third possibility (albeit in a footnote), namely that 'mapping is not really

LR but rather head-to-head on prosodic constituents. Then the head – least sonorous member – of the onset cluster would be chosen'. This suggestion would indeed capture the facts. What is surprising and problematic about it is the fact that it presupposes the existence of an onset constituent, which, if I understand the principles of Moraic Phonology, on which McCarthy and Prince (1986) is based, correctly, is non-existent. Onsets (let alone onset constituents) have no role to play in Moraic Phonology, so that head-to-head mapping is not an option here.

As shown in Section 3, GP, by contrast, operates with binary onset constituents, where the head is defined as the governing, and hence the left-most, position (recall that constituent governing relations are universally left-headed). Kaye (1991), in fact, proposes that only head projections of the stem melody can be reduplicated. This makes the prediction that governed members of a prosodic constituent can never be reduplicated. In other words, onset simplification is a universal property of reduplicative affixation (with the exception of 'echo cases', that is). To my knowledge, this prediction is correct.

A second problem for most accounts of reduplication is the behaviour of s + consonant clusters. As observed by Pagoni (1993), Kaye (1991) and Steriade (1988), these clusters are not subject to Steriade's (1988) rule that non-initial consonants are eliminated. On the contrary, it is the initial s and not the following consonant which disappears, as illustrated in (48a) for Ancient Greek (nominal reduplication) and in (48b) for Sanskrit (data from Steriade 1988).

(48)

(a) ka-skandiks   'wild chervil'   skandiks 'spring onion'
     ko-skulmat-i a 'leather cuttings' skulmat- 'hair plucked out'

(b) **Root**   **Intensive**   **Gloss**
    stan   tan-stan-   'thunder'
    skan   kan-i-skand-   'leap'

Steriade attributes this loss of an *initial* consonant to the fact that s + consonant clusters do not form onsets, a claim which is substantiated in Steriade (1982). KLV (1990) and Kaye (1992b) show that the principles of GP lead to the same conclusion and adduce empirical evidence to support it. The syllable structure proposed for an initial s + consonant cluster (*sk* in this case) is that shown in (49). This structure, of course, raises the issue of how the initial empty nuclear position is licensed. Kaye (1992b) provides detailed discussion of this point. The apparently word-initial *s* actually

(49)

```
        R
        |\
   O    N \       O
   |      \       |
   x     x  ←  x
   |          |
   s          k
```

occupies a post-nuclear rhymal position which is governed by a following onset. The head of this particular governing domain is this onset, occupied by k. On the assumption that only heads are reduplicated, the initial position of the reduplicated prefix necessarily has to be k.

I have left a considerable number of important aspects of reduplication out of this discussion (see also Katamba, this volume for an investigation of further interesting properties of reduplication), but I hope to have shown that some basic principles of GP can make a substantial contribution to the solution of some of the more intractable problems of reduplication, without making reference to the syllable (or the mora).

6 Conclusion

In this chapter I have presented an overview of the skeleton and suprasegmental (i.e. constituent) structure in GP. I have discussed some arguments in favour of the x-skeleton employed in GP and, moving beyond the skeleton, I have introduced the reader to the GP notions of government and licensing. I have explored some of the striking predictions made by GP and shown them to be borne out by the facts of a variety of languages.

Considerations of space have forced me to omit some important theoretical constructs (such as government-licensing, as developed in Charette 1988, 1990, 1991) and to keep comparisons with other theories to a minimum in Sections 3 and 4. In Section 5, however, I have briefly discussed different approaches to phonological issues such as the representation of *h-aspiré* in French and reduplication in a range of languages. I hope to have shown that GP, in spite of having relatively restricted machinery at its disposal, can account for data which have proved problematic in other frameworks, by referring to independently motivated skeletal and constituent structures.

Notes and Acknowledgements

I would like to thank John Harris, Monik Charette and Jacques Durand for their immensely helpful comments on earlier drafts of this chapter. Any remaining errors, inaccuracies and superficialities are, of course, my responsibility alone. Many thanks also to Stamatoula Pagoni for much-valued practical help.

1. See Kaye et al. (1985) and Kaye et al. (1990) for basic GP policy statements. Further important work in this framework is contained in Charette (1988, 1989, 1990, 1991, 1992), Harris (1990b, 1992), Harris and Kaye (1990), Kaye (1988, 1990a,c, 1992b, this volume), Lindsey and Harris (1990) and in Yoshida (1991). ˙
2. The existence of the nucleus display (see Clements and Keyser 1983: 16f.) in this framework seems to partially contradict this claim, as it could be interpreted as introducing an additional division of the syllable. However, Clements and Keyser adopt the view that this display is located on a different plane from the syllable display (as illustrated in (1)), so that the syllable node as such still has no subordinate nodes above the CV tier. In any case, the nucleus display is hardly ever invoked.
3. The basic point is theirs, but my argumentation is different. See also Durand (1990a: 264ff.) for yet another way of making the same point.
4. Coleman (this volume) provides examples of GP derivations where a conflict with the Projection Principle appears to exist. I share his concerns about the deletion of a skeletal position in the Yawelmani derivations discussed in Kaye (1990a: 309ff.). Regarding the derivations from KLV (1985), his criticism is less well founded, as the Projection Principle in its present form had not seen the light of day in 1985. After all, even phonological theories take time to hatch.
5. There is a reasonably common configuration which is actually in conflict with the strict locality requirement for inter-constituent government. This configuration involves a branching onset followed by a nuclear head. As we will see in Section 4.1, every skeletal position (bar the head of a morphological domain) has to be licensed, normally by being governed. Onsets are governed by a following nucleus (as shown in (13a)). If inter-constituent government is strictly local, how can the left-most position in a branching onset be governed by the following nucleus? After all, the two positions are not adjacent at the skeletal level. Government phonologists are well aware of this problem, but, to my knowledge, no definite solution to it has as yet been proposed.
6. Lines may be fused (parametrically variable) to prevent the elements occupying these lines from combining with one another and thus to account for the absence of certain segment types from particular languages, e.g. of front-rounded vowels from (conservative) RP (fusion of U°- and I°-lines). It is physically impossible for the vocal folds to be stiff and lax at the same time, which is why the L⁻- and H⁻-lines must be fused universally. Contour tones may involve either a sequence of separate nuclei, each with its own laryngeal element, or a contour segment, where two laryngeal elements are attached to a single skeletal point by separate association lines. In neither case would fusion of the L⁻- and H⁻-lines be a problem.
7. Harris (1990b: 273f.) actually argues that 'any segment, be it charmless

or charmed, must satisfy certain complexity requirements before it can occupy a governing position'. It seems that this claim is too strong. The most spectacular counterexamples can be found in the context of branching rhymes, where it is quite possible for a simplex segment such as [a] (consisting only of the element A^+) to govern a segment which is more complex, e.g. a lateral (composed of two elements) or a nasal (composed of three or four elements). Examples such as *Wald* ([valt], 'forest') or *Hand* ([hant], 'hand') are easy to come by, not just in German.

8. I assume that $R°$ is the head of the expression. As a result, H^- can only be an operator, and yet, I claim that the entire expression is negatively charmed. This, of course, conflicts with my earlier claim that the charm value is taken from the head. Two points have to be made here. First, the assignment of headship to expressions is an area which requires a great deal of further investigation. Second, the laryngeal elements H^- and L^- appear to differ from other elements in contributing their charm value to an expression even when they are not the head of the expression. Their special status is discussed in Brockhaus (1992: 133–7). In any case, charm considerations are not crucial for the present example, as the t is more complex than the s and would, therefore, be able to govern it on complexity alone.

9. See Brockhaus (1992: 53–72) for a detailed discussion of the drawbacks of the non-syllabic account of final devoicing proposed in Vennemann (1968).

10. This is not to say that GP is the only phonological theory to employ the notion of licensing. For other approaches to licensing see, for example, Selkirk (1978), McCarthy and Prince (1986), Nespor and Vogel (1986), Itô (1986) and Goldsmith (1989, 1990).

11. McCarthy and Prince's (1986: e.g. 21, 106) observations about word-finally well-formed CVVC syllables not being available word-internally in Mokilese refer to essentially the same phenomenon, and Borowsky (1989) discusses similar facts with regard to English.

12. The reader may wonder how words such as *child, wild, Christ, point, wield, mind,* etc. can be represented, as they appear to require a branching nucleus followed by a filled coda position and could, therefore, not be accommodated by a binary rhyme. This is another problem of which Government phonologists are well aware (see e.g. KLV 1990, note 5 and Kaye 1990a, note 20) and to which no solution has as yet been found. It may, however, be worth noting two things. First, as has been observed by a number of phonologists, including Fudge (1969) and Selkirk (1982b), the problematic forms invariably involve coronal clusters. Second, related forms with a short vowel exist for some of these words, e.g. *children, Christian* and *wilderness*.

13. Vennemann (1988: 33) is forced to interpret these facts about Italian as an exception to his Law of Finals, which expresses the insight that 'word-medial syllable codas are the more preferred, the less they differ from possible word-final syllable codas of the language system'. GP makes the much stronger claim that there is no difference between

word-medial codas and word-final codas (in Vennemann's sense of the term) *and* it can accommodate the Italian facts.
14. In some languages (e.g. in Moroccan Arabic, see Kaye 1987 and discussion in Section 3.3 above), the manifestation of an unlicensed empty nucleus is the cold vowel itself. In others, e.g. in French and German, an 'ambient' element A^+ is attached, yielding schwa. The apparent existence of ambient elements, for which no local source can be identified, is problematic for GP, since it is in conflict with the metatheoretical principle of non-arbitrariness (see KLV 1990: 194). See Brockhaus (1992: 122ff.) for discussion.

Chapter 7

Skeleta and the prosodic circumscription of morphological domains

Francis Katamba

1 Introduction

The nature of the interaction between units of the prosodic hierarchy and other modules of the grammar has been one of the major areas of linguistic research in recent years. The part played by prosodic domains, in conjunction with syntactic domains, in delimiting the context in which postlexical (i.e. phrasal) phonological rules apply has received a considerable amount of attention (cf. Selkirk 1984a, Kaisse 1985, Nespor and Vogel 1986, Hyman et al. 1987 among others).

However, what this chapter presents is a related concern, namely the role of units of the prosodic hierarchy such as the mora, the syllable, the foot and the prosodic word in specifying the phonological domains required by morphological operations. The discussion will focus especially on those prosodic domains that play a key role in morphology which are defined in terms of the skeletal tier. But while emphasizing the prosodic conditioning of morphological processes, we will not go so far as to suggest that all morphological domains are prosodically conditioned. Clearly, many morphological processes can be specified in purely morphological terms, e.g. in English to derive an agentive or instrumental noun from a verb, the suffix *-er* is attached to a verbal base without taking into account the prosodic properties of the base, such as its syllable structure (cf. *do-er, review-er, schoolteach-er*). Similarly, many reduplicative processes affix to some morphologically defined base a morpheme that is simply a copy of a portion of that base which is made with no regard to the phonological characteristics of the base. For instance, in Luganda a verb stem (i.e. the root and any suffixes following it) is reduplicated to convey the meaning of 'do something frequently, do something half-heartedly, hurriedly, etc.'

(1)

ba-soma	ba-soma**soma**
'they read'	'they read frequently'
ba-somera	ba-somera**somera**
'they read for'	'they read for (someone) frequently'
ba-someragana	ba-someragana**someragana**
'they read for each other'	'they read for each other frequently'

Obviously, many morphological processes only take into account the morphological characteristics of a base. But there are cases where the application of morphological rules is dependent not only on the input being morphologically appropriate, but also on its having certain phonological properties. It is these latter cases that interest us here.

The theoretical framework in which the issues will be discussed is the theory of Prosodic Domain Circumscription proposed by McCarthy and Prince, and others. The theory has been developed in the course of recent investigations into the relationship between phonology and morphology. These investigations have taken the form of a two-pronged attack on the problem. Some linguists have been primarily concerned with the interaction between phonological rules and the rules of inflectional and derivational morphology. These scholars have proposed the theory of Lexical Phonology to explain the symbiotic nature of the relationship between phonological and morphological rules (cf. Kiparsky 1982a, 1982b, 1985, Mohanan 1986, Rubach 1984a, Pulleyblank 1986a, Yip 1988b).

The other line of attack has concentrated on the job performed by phonological structure in providing the mould in which morphological generalizations are captured. This research crystallized into the theory of Template Morphology (cf. McCarthy 1979, 1981, 1982, 1983, 1984b, Marantz 1982, Archangeli 1983, Broselow and McCarthy 1983, Yip 1982), the precursor to the current theory of Prosodic Morphology put forward recently by McCarthy and Prince (1988, 1990a, 1990b, 1993), Poser (1990), Mester (1990), Archangeli (1991), Itô (1991) and a number of other scholars.

Template Morphology received its original impetus from two main types of phenomena: the analysis of *non-concatenative morphological systems* such as those found in Semitic languages on the one hand, and *reduplication* on the other. I will briefly outline these phenomena below and show the challenges that they pose for a theory of the interplay between morphology and phonology. Let us take non-concatenative morphology first. Arabic morphology, which is typical of Semitic morphology, very often involves internal changes in roots and stems instead of, or in addition to, the concatenation of prefixes or suffixes with bases. This can be seen in the following *binyanim* or morphological classes of verbs (singular *binyan*) in Standard Arabic:

(2) *Binyan*

I	katab	'he wrote'	fahim	'he understood'
II	kattab	'cause to write'	fahham	'cause to understand'
III	kaatab	'correspond'	faahim	'understanding' (adj.)
IV	ʔaktab	'write'	ʔafham	'understand'
VI	takaatab	'write to each other'	tafaaham	'understand someone'
VIII	ʔiktatab	'write, be registered'	ʔiftaham	'understand'

Morphology in modern linguistics was developed in order to provide a model for the description of languages in which the norm is the attachment of prefixes and suffixes to roots and stems. So, it is not surprising that for a long time morphological theory was left non-plussed by the challenge of systems like that of Arabic where word-building typically takes the form of some root-internal change. Template morphology offers a means of confronting this challenge.

The other obstinate morphological problems that lend themselves to a templatic approach also involve stem-internal changes. Chief among these is reduplication. There are two types of reduplication: *total reduplication* and *modified reduplication*. Total reduplication merely makes a copy of the base in its entirety, without altering it in any way, and attaches it as an affix to the original base. By contrast, modified reduplication takes a copy of the base and attaches it as an affix after altering it in some way.

Total reduplication is both widespread and straightforward. A typical example is provided by Blake (1979) who reports that in the Australian language Pitta-Pitta verbs are reduplicated in full to indicate repeated action:

(3)

tarri	'crawl'	tarritarri	'keep crawling'
k̲uri	'cut (the surface)'	k̲urik̲uri	'scratch (repeatedly)'
ŋunʸtʸi	'give'	ŋunʸtʸiŋunʸtʸi	'teach'

According to Bender (1969), reduplication in Marshallese may be total as in (4a) or modified as in (4b),

(4)

(a)	wit	'flower'	witwit	'wear a flower'
	hat	'hat'	hathat	'wear a hat'
	waj	'watch'	wajwaj	'wear a watch'
(b)	riyig	'ring'	riyigyig	'wear a ring'
	jehet	'shirt'	jehethet	'wear shirt'
	kagir	'belt'	kagirgir	'wear a belt'

As seen, a verb meaning 'to wear an item of apparel' is formed by reduplication, with the choice of the reduplicative pattern being determined by the syllable structure of the word. There is total reduplication if the base is monosyllabic as in (4a). But modified reduplication takes place if the base is disyllabic. In that case only the second syllable is reduplicated. This pattern is exemplified by (4b).

Let us now examine modified reduplication more closely because it raises interesting questions concerning the interplay between phonological structure and morphological processes. We will begin by observing that modified reduplication comes in several varieties. Steriade (1988) distinguishes three types of modified reduplication:

1. *Partial reduplication*: copies a portion of the base

2. *Prespecified reduplication*: introduces segmental changes in the copied base

3. *Partial + prespecified reduplication*: copies a portion of the base and introduces in it segmental changes.

Partial reduplication is exemplified by the Marshallese examples in (4b) above and prespecified reduplication by the English examples below:

(5)

hoity-toity	shilly-shally
hocus-pocus	dilly-dally
hanky-panky	wishy-washy

The combination of partial and prespecified reduplication can be seen in the following Squamish data from Kuipers (1967).

(6)

	Singular		*Plural*
(a)	q°λa'i̯ʔ	'driftwood'	q°əλ-q°λa'i̯ʔ
	mi'x̌aλ	'black bear'	mə'x̌-mi'x̌aλ
	k°u'pic	'elder sibling'	k°əp-k°u'pic

(b) ʔiˈmac   'grandchild'   ʔm-ʔiˈmac
    lamʔ   'house'   lm-laˈmʔ
Note: "'" occurs after a stressed vowel.

The first two consonants of the singular noun stem are copied as a plural suffix in (6b). The same is done in (6a) but, in this case, in addition the vowel [ə] is inserted between the consonants. As we shall see below in Sections 2 and 3, the challenge is to find satisfactory formal tools to express the intuition that some phonological aspects of the base are 'transferred', as it were, to the affix when prespecified reduplication occurs.

As mentioned earlier, various proposals intended to deal with the problems which we have outlined of mapping morphemes onto phonological representations have been made by linguists working in the post-SPE (*The Sound Pattern of English*) framework. We shall now examine the main ones in turn.

2 Template morphology

The first proposal was made by McCarthy (1979, 1981) who demonstrated that Goldsmith's (1976) model of Autosegmental Phonology, with its simultaneous levels or tiers of representation, association lines and mapping principles, offered an insightful way of analysing nonconcatenative morphology (cf. also Goldsmith 1990). In his analysis of the morphology of verbs in Classical Arabic, McCarthy proposed a three-tiered representation. He argued for an analysis where the canonical pattern of segments representing a given *binyan* is shown at a level referred to as the *CV-skeleton* (or *skeletal tier* or *prosodic tier*). Essentially, the skeletal tier represents the canonical morphological form of the *binyan* (e.g. CVCCVC represents 'causative', CVVCVC represents 'reciprocal', etc.).

By contrast, information about the actual segments that occur in a particular word is represented separately on the vocalic and consonantal tiers. The consonantal tier represents the root which represents the lexeme (e.g. *ktb* 'write', *fhm* 'understand', *drs* 'study', *ksr* 'break') while the vocalic tier represents verbal categories such as aspect and voice. Elements on the vocalic and consonantal tiers are referred to as *melodies*. (The term reflects the origins of the Template Morphology in autosegmental phonology – a theory initially developed to account for tonal phenomena.) The active/passive distinction in the causatives *kattab* and *kuttib*, illustrates well the need to separate the vowel tier from consonant tier. While the CVCCVC template is used for the causative *binyan* in each case, the vocalic melody employed is *a* in the active and *u/i* in the passive. Vocalic and consonantal melodies are mapped onto C and V positions of the Prosodic or CV-skeletal tier by the standard autosegmental *well-formedness condition* or *mapping principle* (cf. Goldsmith 1976, 1990; Clements and Ford, 1979; Pulleyblank 1986a). Melodies or autosegments (in this case vowels or consonants) are mapped, going from left to right, onto the appropriate elements of the CV skeleton capable of bearing those units. So, consonants are mapped onto C positions and vowels onto V positions. All autosegments are associated with at least one skeletal position and every skeletal position is associated with at least one autosegment. If there are more skeletal positions than there are segments to be linked with them, *spreading* may take place: one segment may be multiply linked with several skeletal positions so that every segment ends up being associated with a skeletal position and, conversely, every skeletal position ends up being linked with some segment. But spreading is not automatic. So, multiple linking of a vowel or consonant to several skeletal positions needs to be expressly permitted by the grammar of the language. Finally, association lines are not allowed to cross.

Using these principles, McCarthy (1979, 1981) shows that Arabic infixing morphology can be represented as shown in (7).

(7)

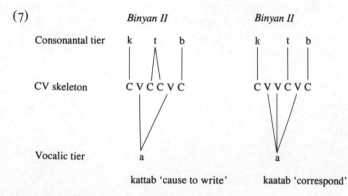

The role of the skeletal tier is vital. The C and V slots of the skeleton are the melody bearing units to which elements of other tiers are hooked. They hold phonological representations together.

Further, as mentioned above, various morphological categories are manifested by CV skeleta. For instance, CVCCVC, with the vocalic melody *a*, represents the causative, CVCVC, with the vocalic melody *a* represents the perfective, and so on. The particular lexical content is contributed by the root consonant melody, e.g., *ktb* 'read', (> *kattab* 'cause to read'), *fhm* 'understand' (*fahham* > -'cause to understand'), *qtl* 'kill' (> *qattal* 'cause to kill'), *ksr* 'break' (> *kassar* 'cause to break').

Marantz (1982) has extended McCarthy's Template Morphology to cover reduplication. The essence of Marantz's proposal is that the reduplicative process makes a *copy* of the melody of the base and attaches it to an *underspecified affix morpheme*. The affix is said to be underspecified because it has a CV-skeletal representation but is segmentally defective in that it lacks consonant or vowel segments. The process of fleshing out such an underspecified affix with a melody is formally similar to the mapping of consonantal and vowel melodies onto the skeleta representing binyanim of the Arabic verb system.

Marantz (1982) illustrates this with examples of various types of plural formed by CVC-prefixing reduplication in Agta, a language of the Phillipines:

(8)

bari	'body'	**bar**bari-k kid-in	'my whole body'
mag-saddu	'leak' (verb)	mag-**sad**saddu	'leaking in many places'
na-wakay	'lost'	na-**wak**wakay	'many things lost'
takki	'leg'	**tak**takki	'legs'

As seen, the consonant-vowel-consonant melody at the beginning of the base is copied and mapped on to the empty slots that are then associated with the CVC positions. Thus the formation of the plural form *taktakki* 'legs' would proceed as shown in (9):

(9)

$$
\begin{array}{c}
\text{t a k i} \\
\text{| | } \wedge \text{ |} \\
\text{C V C C V}
\end{array}
\;\rightarrow\;
\begin{array}{c}
\text{t a k i} \\
\text{| | } \wedge \text{ |} \\
\text{C V C + C V C C V}
\end{array}
\;\rightarrow\;
\begin{array}{c}
\text{t a k i} \\
\text{| | } \wedge \text{ |} \\
\text{C V C + C V C C V}
\end{array}
\;\rightarrow
$$

$$
\begin{array}{c}
\text{t a k i} \\
\text{t a k i} \\
\text{| | } \wedge \text{ |} \\
\rightarrow \text{C V C + C V C C V} \\
\text{| | |} \\
\text{t a k i}
\end{array}
\qquad \text{(Output: taktakki)}
$$

After the appropriate part of the base melody has been copied and then mapped onto the underspecified CVC template of the reduplicative morpheme, any surplus segments that remain unassociated with the CV-skeleton (in this case the vowel *i*) are deleted by the standard Stray Erasure Convention of autosegmental phonology.

3 Transfer

Clements (1985b) has proposed a solution to the problem of representing reduplication which is based on *melodic transfer*. According to Clements, instead of the underspecified reduplicative affix getting its segmental representation by mapping directly the melody of the stem, it obtains its melody from the stem skeleton by transfer.

First, the skeleton of the affix is *parafixed* to the skeleton of the stem as in (10). Contrast the representation in (10) with the Marantzian representation in (9) where the affix is regarded as a prefix.

(10)
```
 t  a  k  i
 |  |  /\ |
 C  V  C C  V
```

        C V C

Next the vocalic and consonantal melodies of the skeleton are *transferred* to the parafix. What this means is that all the phonological properties associated with the skeleton, and indirectly with its melodic tiers, drip directly onto the skeleton of the parafix and its associated melodic tiers.

The final step is *linearization*: instead of being super-imposed on the skeleton, the parafix is converted into an affix, which in this case is a prefix as seen in (11).

(11)

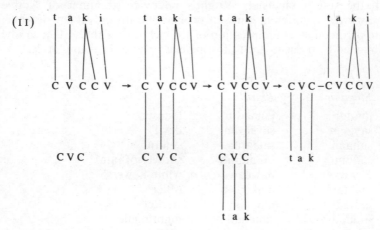

Hammond (1988) has used Clements's theory of templatic transfer to tackle some problems in Arabic morphology which remain unresolved in McCarthy's original mapping approach. Many of these problems are raised acutely by noun pluralization and diminutives which are formed in a similar way. The focus here will be on pluralization.

Before we are in a position to outline a templatic transfer approach to problems of Arabic morphology, we need to sketch the process of plural formation. In Arabic there are two ways of forming the plurals of nouns. A small minority of nouns have *sound plurals*, i.e. plurals which are formed by the suffixation of *-uun* (if the noun is masculine) or *-aat* (if the noun is feminine). The stems to which these suffixes are attached are themselves normally unmodified:

(12)

		Singular		Plural
(a)	Masculine	mudarris	'teacher'	mudarrisuun
		rassaam	'painter'	rassaamuun
		muhandis	'engineer'	muhandisuun
(b)	Feminine	mudarrisa	'teacher'	mudarrisaat
		rassaama	'painter'	rassaamaat
		muhandisa	'engineer'	muhandisaat

However, the vast majority of Arabic nouns have *broken plurals*. This term refers to plurals which involve drastic internal change. The same root consonants are kept as in the singular but virtually all the rest is changed. Wright's reference grammar of Arabic recognizes 31 different kinds of broken plurals, only a few of which are predictable. An impression of the richness of the system can be obtained by perusing the following examples of broken plurals:

(13)

Singular	Plural	
ǰundub	ǰanaadib	'locust'
šayṭaan	šayaaṭiin	'devil'
sulṭaan	salaaṭiin	'sultan'
šuʔbuub	šaʔaabiib	'shower of rain'
nuwwaar	nawaawiir	'white flowers'
maktab	makaatib	'office'
ǰudǰud	ǰadaaǰid	'cricket'
ʕandaliib	ʕanaadil	'nightingale'
ǰaamuus	ǰawaamiis	'buffalo'
xaatam	xawaatim	'signet ring'
ʕankabuut	ʕanaakib	'spider'
ʕajuuz	ʕajaaʕiz	'old woman'
saḥaab(at)	saḥaaʔib	'cloud'

jaziir(at)   jazaaʔir   'island'
fuqqaaʕ(at)   faqaaqiiʕ   'bubble'
(Data selected from Halle and Clements 1983: 175, which is
based on McCarthy 1983)

As various writers, including McCarthy himself and Hammond
(1988), have pointed out, the template mapping approach of
McCarthy (1979, 1981) which was generally successful in dealing
with the *binyanim* of verbal morphology, has encountered serious
difficulties in providing an adequate framework for analysing
broken plurals.

First, the spreading of consonants in the plural is clearly based
on the spreading of consonants in the singular. If a consonant is
multiply linked in the singular, it is also multiply linked in the
plural. Thus *nuwwaar* ~ *nawaawiir* and *fuqqaaʕat* ~ *fuqaaqiiʕ*, with
the consonant melodies *nwr* and *fqʕ*, both spread the second
consonant not only in the singular but also in the plural. Similarly,
šuʔbuub ~ *ʔaʔaabiib*, with the consonant melody *šʔb*, spreads the
third consonant in both the singular and plural. Clearly, despite
the changes wrought by broken plural formation, the mapping of
the consonant melody remains constant.

Second, the existence of a rule inserting *w* after the first mora if
the first syllable contains a long vowel in the singular (cf. *xaatam*
~ *xawaatim*) is problematic from a theoretical perspective because
the length of the vowels in the singular stem templates cannot be
directly accessed by the rule that maps the plural template.

Working in the template mapping framework, McCarthy (1979,
1983) proposes a solution in terms of *infixing*. His proposal is
implemented by the three rules below.

(14)

ø → VV/[σ_/plural
This rule inserts VV after the first syllable of the world.

(15)

[a i]
This rule introduces the plural vocalic melody.

(16)

Plural template filter: [C V C **VV** CV (V) C] [plural]
The plural template filter rejects any putative plural whose CV
skeleton does not conform to this template. (Note that here **VV**
is an infix.)

When the two rules in [15] and [16] are applied and the template in [17] is used, a plural like *salaaṭiin* which meets the requirements of the template goes through in a straightforward manner. Likewise, *jawaamiis* is not a problem since it has all the slots in the template appropriately filled, once epenthetic *w* has been inserted after the first V of the initial CVV syllable. In the case of forms like *junaadib* and *makaatib*, with the exception of the last V slot, all the positions in the plural template are filled. The single V slot and consequently the short vowel in the final syllable is allowed by the template in [16] since one of the V positions is optional (cf. McCarthy 1983, Hammond 1988 for the details of the derivations).

Hammond (1988) argues that McCarthy's mapping solution is unsatisfactory. First, it fails to capture the generalization that truncation and infixation are related operations in a form like *jahmariš* 'lazy old woman' which undergoes both infixation and truncation to form *jahaamir*. So, ideally, the same operation should handle both of them.

Second, the interaction between the plural template and infixation seems to be haphazard or ill-defined. In *jahmariš* the template both allows infixation of *a* in the second syllable and also requires the elimination of the surplus final *š*. But in *namuuðaj* 'type' the template blocks infixation and consequently no truncation is required to give *naumaaðij* (plural). Note also that while the template motivates *w* insertion in triconsonantal roots like *xtm* and *jzr* (see next paragraph) in order to fill all skeletal positions in the template, it does not have any effect in some other triconsonantal roots. Arabic allows forms like *nafs* ~ *nufuus* (pl) 'soul' and *bahr* ~ *bihaar* 'sea' that only exploit the initial CVCVVC portion of the broken plural template, leaving the last VVC to whither away.

Lastly, although the mechanics of *w* epenthesis are handled adequately by McCarthy (1983), there is a problem in this analysis with regard to specifying the *locus* of the epenthetic consonant. McCarthy correctly shows that consonant epenthesis is motivated by the need to have all available skeletal C positions in a template filled. Epenthesis fills the empty C slot thereby satisfying the broken plural template. But, unfortunately, there is some indeterminacy. Does the epenthetic consonant attach to the second or third C slot? The analysis leaves this unclear. Forms like *xaatam* undergo [w] insertion in the *second* C slot to yield *xawaatim*, thereby filling all four C positions of the broken plural CvCvvCvC template. But forms like *jazaaʔir* satisfy the broken plural template by having [ʔ] inserted, this time in the *third* C position. (It is assumed that /w/ is always the underlying epenthetic consonant but it surfaces as [ʔ] in some contexts.)

Hammond's proposal is that these problems can be overcome by pressing into service Clements's transfer theory. As already mentioned, Clements developed his theory in order to deal with problems of reduplication. Hammond assumes that there are close enough formal parallels between reduplication and broken plurals for the transfer theory to be extended to broken plurals. He assumes, like McCarthy, the plural template and the [a i] broken plural vowel melody in (17):

(17) C V C V V C V V C

           a   i

The crucial difference is that unlike McCarthy (1983), Hammond (1988: 258) assumes that the plural template acquires its melody via transfer, as opposed to direct mapping. He proposes that the plural template is introduced as a *suprafix* superimposed on the singular template as shown in (18):

(18)

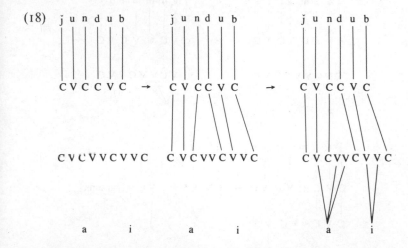

Standard mapping principles apply. The mapping of the plural template and the singular template takes place, driven by the singular template. The linking of the plural template with the plural vowel melody is driven by the melody. It is assumed that elements directly associated to the new template replace original melodic properties.

Furthermore, Hammond stipulates that (i) the vowel *i* of the vocalic melody is mapped onto the last V or VV position(s) of the template, and (ii) before transfer takes place, the representation is subject to a rule peculiar to Arabic which deletes the surplus final vowel of a plural melody that remains unassociated to the singular template. These stipulations are executed by rules (19) and (20).

(19)   V (V) C]   (20)   Vowel shortening

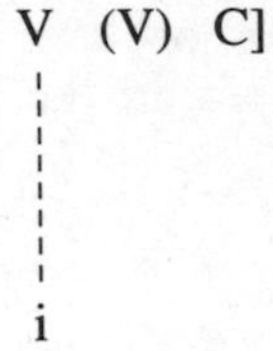

          ┊
          ┊
          ┊
          ┊
          i   V → Ø / V__C]

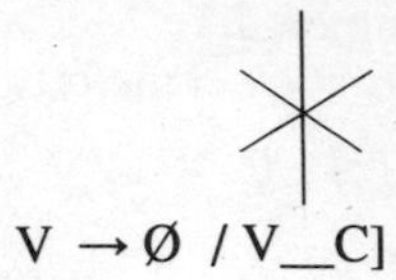

Observe that unlike template transfer in reduplication, which involves linearization (cf.11), template transfer in this case is not accompanied by linearization.

If the same procedure is followed, the following representations are obtained for *jaḥaamir*:

(21)

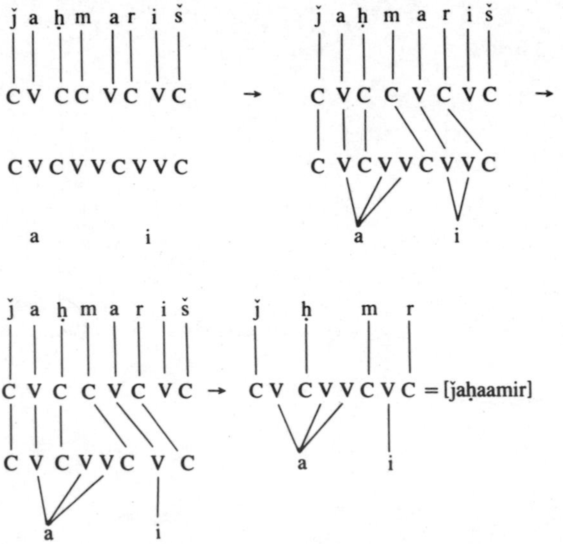

Once the two templates are associated, transfer takes place, followed by Stray Erasure (cf. Marantz 1982). Given that there are only four C positions in the plural template, Stray Erasure removes š, the surplus fifth consonant.

The insertion of [w] as in *xawaatim* in (22) seems to pose no problems either. First, the plural template is aligned with the singular template. Next rule (20) truncates the last V slot and finally rule (23) inserts *w* in the available, unfilled C slot of the plural template prior to the transfer of the plural vocalic melody.

(22)

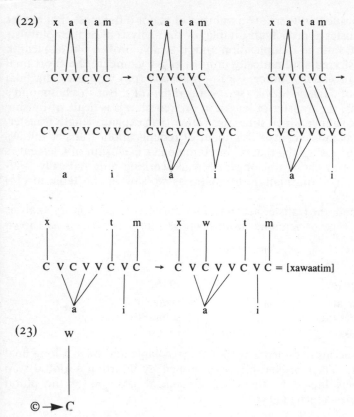

(23)   w
            │
            │
         ©──▶ C

(As already mentioned above, the default consonant /w/ that is inserted surfaces as [ʔ] in certain phonological contexts.)

Hammond's transfer solution has its merits: (i) it accounts successfully for *w* insertion as we have just seen; (ii) it accounts for consonant spreading as in *nuwwar* ~ *nuwawir* (pl.) 'white flowers' and *tinniin* ~ *tanaaniin* (pl.) 'sea monster' and (iii) it accounts for quadrilateral, trisyllabic singulars like *ǰaḥmariš* ~ *ǰaḥaamir* (pl.) 'lazy old woman' where the fifth consonant of the singular form (*š*) is lost in the plural because there is no place for it to squeeze in since the plural skeletal template has only four C positions. In general, it offers a very plausible account of the stable and predictable behaviour of consonants. But despite these virtues, McCarthy and Prince (1990a) are critical of the transfer analysis. In essence, their charge is that Hammond assumes far greater similarity between reduplication and Arabic broken plurals than is warranted by the evidence.

They argue that there are a number of major differences that render the transfer approach unsuitable for the analysis of broken plurals.

First, both in reduplication and in Arabic broken plurals, length is transferred automatically in most cases. Compare the short final vowel of *maktab* 'office' (sg.) ~ *makaatib* (pl.) with the long final vowel of *šayṭaan* 'devil' (sg.) ~ *šayaaṭiin* (pl.). But in Hammond's analysis, the transfer of length in broken plurals is dealt with using rule (20) above which stipulates rather than explains length transfer. Whereas in Clements's treatment of reduplication, transfer follows from the rest of the theory, in Hammond's extension of Clements's theory transfer is no longer seen as working automatically – although it is (normally) automatic as we saw in the table in (13) above.

Second, the transfer account does not offer a satisfactory analysis of the type of feminine nouns whose plural is formed as shown below:

(24)

Singular		Plural
ǰaziir(at)	'island'	ǰazaaʔir
saḥaab(at)	'cloud'	saḥaaʔib
ʕajuuz	'old woman'	ʕajaaʔiz

These nouns commence with a short syllable and have a long final syllable. Their broken plural is formed by inserting a glottal stop that gets linked to the third C skeletal position of the plural template as seen in (25):

(25)

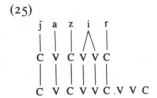

The problem is that transfer of the plural template onto the singular template in (25) would wipe out the third C position of the singular template and the consonant associated with it. Then, when standard mapping rules applied, the glottal stop associated with the third C of the plural would spread to the final C position. The result would be an incorrect plural like *ǰazaaʔiʔ.

To ensure that this is avoided, a special rule is provided by Hammond to reassociate the final C (and associated melody) of the singular template with the final C of the plural template. This

(26)   *Consonant reassociation*

special rule is not only *ad hoc*, serving no other purpose in the
language, it is also formally unorthodox for it erases one association
line and at the same time creates a new association line linking the
unassociated consonant with a C slot. For these reasons, we should
be reluctant to accept the transfer solution.

Hammond (1988: 267) is careful to emphasize that he is not
claiming that all broken plurals can be dealt with using his approach. Direct melody mapping as proposed in McCarthy (1979,
1983) still has a place. On his own admission, no transfer analysis
is available for a number of non-marginal broken plural types. For
instance, he acknowledges that the transfer model cannot derive
the hundreds of nouns with the CVC(V)C plural template exemplified by *nafs* ~ *nufuus* (pl.) 'soul'. But he argues that this does not
invalidate his analysis for two reasons. First, the pattern that such
nouns take in the plural is unpredictable. Second, they exhibit
different vocalism and their templates have a different number of
consonants from those discussed in his paper.

(27)

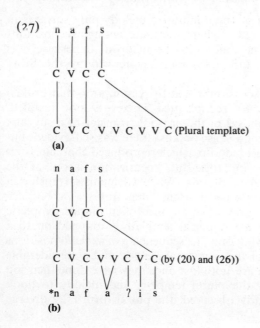

In (27) we can see that the result of applying Hammond's analysis would be an incorrect output. As can be seen, if the vowel shortening rule in (20) and the consonant reassociation rule in (26) apply here, the result is the incorrect form *nafaaʔis. This is a serious shortcoming. Any analysis must cover such 'iambic plurals' like nufuus and rajul because they represent a general pattern which is also found in diminutives (cf. section 4 below). Diminutives are identical in all respects, except for their vocalic melody, to the iambic plurals. As can be seen, the diminutive vocalism u + ay + i contrasts with the plural vocalism which is (usually) i + a, with everything else being the same:

(28)

Noun	Plural	Diminutive	
(a) CvCC			
nafs	nufuus	nufays + at	'soul'
qidħ	qidaaħ	qudayħ	'arrow'
(b) CvCvC			
rajul	rijaal	rujayl	'man'
ʔasad	ʔusuud	ʔusayd	'lion'
(c) CvvCv(v)C			
xaatam	xawaatim	xuwaytim	'signet-ring'
ǰaamuus	ǰawaamiis	ǰuwaymiis	'buffalo'

Observe that the final i of the diminutive melody only surfaces in trisyllabic words as in (28c) where there are enough V positions for all the vowels of the melody to be mapped. Otherwise it is unrealized as in (28a) and (28b) and is removed by the Stray Erasure Convention.

The upshot of our discussion is that the assumption that broken plurals are analogous to reduplicated affixes is not justified. Clements's original proposal of the prosodic transfer of a suprafix in reduplication made good sense because there was self-evident linearization of the reduplicated affix which reproduced characteristics of the base (as we saw in (10)). But, linearization is out of the question in Arabic broken plurals. While Clements's transfer in reduplication is directional (in the sense that transfer takes place going from left-to-right or vice versa), in broken plurals templatic transfer is not directional. A plural template is mapped on to a singular template following only the sequencing of skeletal positions in the singular. Much of the segmental melody and a considerable part of the CV skeleton are both lost once they have done their job of offering a place for the plural template and melody to hook onto. As we have already observed, the plural form may diverge very considerably from the singular form (cf. *nafs* ~ *nufuuus* (pl.) 'soul', *ħukm* ~ *ħakaam* (pl.) 'judgement', *jaamuus* ~ *jawaamiis* (pl.) 'buffalo', etc.). Hence, the claim that 'transfer' takes place in broken plurals is not sustainable.

The failure of the CV-template approach, both in its original mapping guise (McCarthy 1979) and in its later transfer manifestation in Hammond's proposal, is due to conceptual flaws in its characterization of the relationship between the singular and plural templates. It fails to distinguish between obligatory and optional elements in a template. Furthermore, the templates that it envisages are not sufficiently rich phonologically. Below we shall consider Prosodic Morphology, an alternative model that addresses these problems and characterizes broken plural formation with a greater degree of success.

4 Prosodic Morphology

In this Section I present the theory of Prosodic Morphology proposed by McCarthy and Prince. At the heart of Prosodic Morphology there are three basic propositions concerning the nature of phonological representations and its implications for morphology. McCarthy and Prince (1990a: 209–10) state them as follows:

(29)

(a) *Prosodic Morphology hypothesis.* Templates are defined in terms of authentic units of prosody: mora (μ), syllable (σ), foot (F), prosodic word (W), and so on.

(b) *Template satisfaction condition.* Satisfaction of templatic conditions is obligatory and is determined by the principles of prosody, both universal and language specific.

(c) *Prosodic circumscription of domains.* The domain to which morphological operations apply may be circumscribed by prosodic criteria as well as by more familiar morphological ones. In particular, the *minimal word* within a domain may be selected as the locus of morphological transformation in lieu of the whole domain.

McCarthy and Prince apply their theory to the complex problems of Arabic broken plurals as well as to a number of comparable phenomena in several other languages. With regard to Arabic, the essence of their claim is that there is a strong tendency for prosody to impose constraints on the structure of the noun stem in the plural. Normally, noun plurals are formed by (i) parsing out a

prosodically circumscribed portion of the base which they refer to as the *minimal word* and (ii) mapping the minimal word onto an *iambic foot*. An iambic foot consists of a metrically light syllable followed by a heavy syllable (CvCvv), e.g. *rajul* (sg.) 'man' *rijuul* (pl.). A Cv syllable counts as light while a Cvv or CvC syllable counts as heavy. However, because a consonant appearing in word-final position is not taken into account in determining syllable weight, a CvC syllable at the end of the word is deemed to be light. (See the discussion of *extrametricality* in Section 4.2 below.)

Let us now examine closely the three propositions in (29). We will begin with the first proposition and then, for the sake of clarity of exposition, we will consider the other two in reverse order.

4.1 The Prosodic Morphology hypothesis

The first tenet of Prosodic Morphology is that morphological templates are defined in terms of authentic units of the phonological hierarchy such as the syllable, the foot and the prosodic word. We are now going to see this at work in the next two subsections.

4.1.1 The syllable and mora

We have established above that the basic assumptions of direct template transfer are fraught with difficulties. The relationship between the singular template and the broken plural template is not one of direct transfer although it is clear that the relationship between them is far from arbitrary. In addition to the individual consonants found in the singular turning up in the plural, the prosodic characteristics of the singular dictate those of the plural. The number of syllables in the plural is determined by the number of *moras* in the input base. If the singular form is bimoraic, then the plural form is disyllabic, as in (30).

(30)

Root	Singular	Plural	
/ʕnb/	ʕinab	ʕanaab	'grape' (phonetically [Paʕnaab])
/ʔsd/	ʔasad	ʔusuud	'lion'

Note: For a discussion of the apparently exceptional form Paʕnaab] see section 4.1.2 below.

If the prosodic base provided by the singular exceeds two moras, the plural form has three syllables as in *sulṭaan* > *salaaṭiin* (pl.) 'sultan'. (At this point in a derivation VV as well as VC sequences are bimoraic.)

4.1.2   The iambic foot and broken plurals in Arabic
Many morphological processes are best construed in terms of the
mora and foot rather than the syllable (cf. Poser (1990) for an
extensive study of this in Japanese (*pace* Brockhaus this volume)).
McCarthy and Prince (1988, 1990a) have shown that the complex
patterns of the Arabic broken plurals (as well as diminutives which
are formally similar to broken plurals (see (28) above)) are best
analysed in terms of prosodic feet. All the 31 broken plural patterns
identified by Wright (1971), can be reduced to a few prosodic
classes such as iambic, trochaic monosyllabic, and so on. Most
nouns fall into the first two categories, and of these the iambic
pattern is by far the more common. (Indeed, it is the only pattern
that is genuinely productive.) The *iambic foot* typically has the
shape CvCvv + (e.g., *rassaa(m)* 'painter' while the *trochaic foot* has
the form CvvCv(C) e.g., *Maalik* (proper name) or two syllables
with equal wait CvCv *raju(l)* 'man'. (The last consonant of the
word does not contribute to the weight of a syllable.) In the
discussion below we shall concentrate exclusively on the iambic
foot because it is the dominant type in the language.

The data in (31) exemplify broken plurals with the iambic foot
template:

(31)

	Singular	*Plural*	
(a)	CvCC		
	nafs	nufuus	'soul'
	qidħ	qidaaħ	'arrow'
	hukm	/ħakaam/ [ʔaħkaam]	'judgement'
(b)	CvCvC		
	ʔasad	ʔusuud	'lion'
	rajul	rijaal	'man'
	ʕinab	/ʕanaab/ [ʔaʕnaab]	'grape'
(c)	CvCvvC + at		
	saħaab + at	saħaaʔib	'cloud'
	jaziir + at	jazaaʔir	'island'
	kariim + at	karaaʔim	'noble'
	ħaluub + at	ħalaaʔib	'milk-camel'
(d)	CvvCvC + at		
	faakih + at	fawaakih	'fruit'
	ʔaanis + at	ʔawaanis	'cheerful'
(e)	CvvCv(v)C		
	xaatam	xawaatim	'signet-ring'
	jaamuus	jawaamiis	'buffalo'

(f)   CvCCv(v)C
    ǰundub   ǰanaadib   'locust'
    sulṭaan   salaaṭiin   'sultan'
(from McCarthy and Prince 1990a: 217)

Despite their obvious diversity, these forms all share the iambic CvCvv-foot. (Wright points out that the apparent counter-examples like [ʔaʕnaab] 'grapes' and [ʔaħkaam] 'judgements' are the product of a metathesis rule applying respectively to iambic /ʕanaab/ and /ħakaam/. The first consonant and the first vowel trade places then a glottal stop is inserted to function as a syllable onset because onsetless syllables are not allowed: $C_1v_1C_2vv \rightarrow v_1C_1C_2v_2v_3 \rightarrow ʔv_1C_1C_2v_2v_3$.)

By contrast, the broken plurals in (32) are totally unproblematic. The iambic foot introduced by the plural template is realized just as the theory predicts and the vowel *a* of the plural melody is associated with all the vowel positions in the initial iambic foot as in *ǰanaa*(*dib*), etc.:

(32)

Root	Singular	Plural		
/ǰndb/	ǰundub	ǰanaadib	'locust'	
/slṭn/	sulṭaan	salaaṭiin	'sultan'	
/krm/	kariim + at	karaaʔim	'noble'	

The discussion has only dealt with broken plurals. But, as we have already mentioned, it can be easily extended to diminutives which are formally very similar to broken plurals. The only significant difference between the two is that whereas the broken plural vocalic melody is (normally) [a_i], the diminutive vocalic melody is [u_ay_i] (see (28)). In the plural, all the V positions of the first foot take the melody *a* and the vowel(s) of the next foot take(s) *i*. In the diminutive, however, the V positions in the first foot take the vowels *u* and *ay* respectively in the first and second syllables. In the second foot, all available V positions are associated with *i*. Thus the diminutive of 'locust' is *ǰunaydib*, the diminutive of 'buffalo' is *ǰuwaymiis*.

4.2   Prosodic circumscription

Prosodic circumscription may take the form of the requirement that morphological processes only apply to prosodically minimal forms. The input to a process might be only a fragment of a word (e.g. a syllable or a bimoraic foot) if the whole word is bigger than the smallest permissible word in the language. For instance, in English the comparative -er and superlative -est suffixes are only attached to one-foot adjectives which may be either monosyllabic as in (33a), or disyllabic if they end in a weak [ɪ] vowel, a syllabic [l̩] or the diphthong [əʊ]. But as (33f) shows, the bases to which these suffixes are attached cannot be longer than one foot.

(33)

(a)	tall	taller	tallest
	big	bigger	biggest
	loud	louder	loudest
(b)	trendy	trendier	trendiest
	funny	funnier	funniest
	happy	happier	happiest
(c)	gentle	gentler	gentlest
	feeble	feebler	feeblest
(d)	shallow	shallower	shallowest
	narrow	narrower	narrowest
(e)	clever	cleverer	cleverest
	obscure	obscurer	obscurest
	mature	maturer	maturest
	severe	severer	severest
(f)	expensive	*expensiver	*expensivest
	intelligent	*intelligenter	*intelligentest
	beautiful	*beautifuler	*beautifulest
	enthusiastic	*enthusiasticer	*enthusiasticest

In addition to determining whether or not morphological pro-cesses (e.g. -er and -est suffixation) can apply, prosodic circumscrip-tion may operate more delicately. It may affect the choice of allomorph of a morpheme used with a particular type of stem. In a number of native Australian languages, for example, there are two allomorphs of the ergative case suffix which are in complemen-tary distribution. Choice of the allomorph used with a particular stem depends on the number of syllables in the noun or adjective stem to which they are attached. Thus in Walpiri -ŋgu cooccurs with disyllabic stems and -lu with stems exceeding two syllables. In Walmatjari, certain consonants condition the selection of the suffix (e.g. -u is selected if a stem ends in -r and -du after a stem ending in a bilabial or apico-alveolar nasal or stop). But where a stem ends in a vowel, the shape of the ergative allomorph de-pends on the syllable structure of the base. After a disyllabic stem ending in a vowel, -ŋu is used while after vowel-final stems of three or more syllables -*ḷu*. is the allomorph selected (Dixon 1972: 10).

An important plank of McCarthy and Prince's theory of the Prosodic Circumscription of morphological bases is the idea of *extrametricality*. Originally extrametricality was developed to account for situations where peripheral elements of a phonological constituent (e.g. segment, syllable, foot or word) are disregarded when establishing whether a given rule is applicable at (or within a certain distance from) the edges of a constituent (Hayes 1982, Inkelas 1989). For instance, in some languages the first or last syllable of a word is extrametrical, which means that it is *invisible* to the rules that assign stress. In Latin, for example, stress falls on the penultimate syllable if that syllable is heavy, or else on the ante-penultimate syllable if the penultimate syllable is light as you can see below. The extrametrical portion of the word is in parenthesis outside the square brackets.

(34)

['regi] (tur) 'he is being ruled'
[re'gē] (tur) 'he will be ruled'
[regē'bāmi] (nī) 'you were being ruled'
[rēk'seri] (mus) 'we shall have ruled'

Note: the diacritic '`' appears before a stressed syllable and a macron '¯' indicates a long vowel.

Using the idea of extrametricality, we can restate the Latin stress rule as shown below in order to bring out the fact that the presence of certain peripheral elements is ignored when stress is assigned:

1. Treating the last syllable as extrametrical (i.e. invisible), construct bimoraic feet, going from right-to-left.

2. Stress the first mora of the rightmost bimoraic foot.

We will now consider a comparable example from Luganda where peripheral elements are overlooked when establishing the domain in which a phonological rule applies. This time it is tone that is involved. Luganda has a tone assignment rule that places a high tone (´) on the second mora of a noun stem. To determine what counts as the second mora it is necessary to first bracket off and ignore the initial mora, for it is extrametrical. A further complication is an initial vowel or augment which is required in certain syntactic contexts but is absent in others. Depending on whether an augment (*o-* in the examples below) is present or absent, a different stem mora may receive a high tone after the

invisible initial mora has been bracketed off. Contrast (mù)
mànyífù 'famous (person)' vs. (ò)mùmànyifù; (mù)tàmíivù
'drunkard' vs. (ò)mùtámìivù.
  In McCarthy and Prince's work, extrametricality refers to *negative prosodic circumscription*, i.e. a situation where a particular
prosodic constituent is removed from the scope of a phonological
or morphological operation as in the case of Latin stress.
  It is not being suggested that in all cases where only a portion of
a base forms the domain of a phonological or morphological
process a circumscriptional analysis is appropriate. We will illustrate this with Diyari examples from Austin (1981):

(35)

	Root		Reduplicated root	
(a)	maḍa	'stone, rock'	maḍa maḍa	'little stone'
	piṭa	'tree'	piṭa piṭa	'small tree'
	kanku	'boy'	kanku kanku	'little boy'
(b)	kiṇṭala	'dog'	kiṇṭakiṇṭala	'doggy, puppy, little dog'
	wiḻapina	'old woman'	wiḻawiḻapina	'little old woman'
	ṭilparku	'bird type'	ṭilpaṭilparku	'little ṭilparku'
	ŋankaṇṭi	'cat fish'	ŋankaŋankaṇṭi	'little cat fish'

  According to Austin, the generalization that covers both sets of
data, is that nouns (and adjectives) are reduplicated by repeating
the first CVC(C)V of the root. In other words, Diyari exemplifies
simple *reduplicative affixation*. The reduplicative prefix is the minimal word, and it is satisfied by copying and mapping the segmental
melody CVC(C)V – and no more – borrowed from the first two
syllables. The fact that the prefix is always vowel-final (e.g. ṭilpa-
ṭilparku) corresponds to a general property of Diyari: all words,
including minimal words, must end in an open syllable. So, from
ṭilparku we do not obtain *ṭilpar-ṭilparku, which we would get if
consonant-final minimal words were allowed, and if whole syllables
were necessarily copied rather than strings that simply satisfy the
CVC(C)V diminutive prefix template. We will return to this point
below for further discussion.
  Compare Diyari with the Marshallese data in (4) above where
the reduplicative suffix is again the minimal word. Note that unlike
the Diyari minimal word, the Marshallese minimal word is monosyllabic. So, any monosyllabic base undergoes total reduplication in
Marshallese. But in a disyllabic base, the portion of the base that is
reduplicated consists only of the last syllable. The rest is overlooked
(cf. *hat* 'hat' > *hathat* 'wear a hat' vs *ka[gir]* 'belt' > *ka[gir]-[gir]*
'wear a belt').
  Our next example of a morphological process which is character-

ized in prosodic terms is provided by Kaingang pluralization (cf.
Wiesemann 1972, cited by Steriade 1988: 76):

(36)

   (a) *Final syllable reduplication*

Singular	Plural	
kry	kry-**kry**	'irritate'
jengag	jengag-**gag**	'roasted meat'

   (b) *Insertion of g into the penultimate rhyme*

kavi	ka**g**vi	'stretch'
jeten	je**g**ten	'strike with hammer'

   (c) *Penultimate V raising to* [+ *high*]

kagje	k**y**gje	'knot'

   (d) *Penultimate V raising and insertion of **g** into the penultimate rhyme*

jakajen	jak**yg**jen	'turn, twist'
pefam	p**ig**fam	'quiet'

   (e) *Reduplication and penultimate V raising*

gon	gun-**gon**	'swallow'
ʔog	ʔug-ʔ**og**	'drink'

In this language pluralization can be indicated using three distinct
methods:

   (a) a copy of the *final syllable* is attached as a reduplicative
suffix as in *jengag ~ jengaggag* (pl.) 'roasted meat'

   (b) insertion of /g/ *into the zero coda of the rhyme of the
penultimate CV syllable* as in *kavi ~ kagvi* (pl.) 'stretch'

   (c) raising the vowel of the *penultimate syllable* to [+ high] as in
kagje ~ kygje 'knot'.

These separate methods can also be combined in a single plural
form, e.g. *gon ~ **gungon*** (pl.) 'swallow' where reduplication as well
as penultimate vowel raising are used and *pefam ~ **pigfam** 'quiet'*
which combines /g/ insertion in the zero coda of the first syllable
with vowel raising. Clearly, it would make little sense if one
described pluralization in this language without recognizing the
role of the syllable in determining the domain in which pluralization
is manifested.

   Let us now turn to reduplication that defies a simple affixational
analysis of the kind which we have considered so far and requires
instead a circumscriptional analysis incorporating extrametricality.
A good example of such prosodic circumscription is to be found in
Ulwa, a language of Nicaragua described by Hale and Lacayo

Blanco (1988) which is cited by McCarthy and Prince (1990a). In this language, the first iambic foot of the base is the *minimal base*. And it is immediately after this minimal base that the third person singular possessive marker *-ka* must be placed. As far as the rule that forms the possessive is concerned, all that is visible is the first foot. The rest of the word is extrametrical:

(37)

	Base	Possessed	
(a)	al	al-**ka**	'man'
	bas	bas-**ka**	'hair'
	kii	kii-**ka**	'stone'
(b)	sana	sana-**ka**	'deer'
	amak	amak-**ka**	'bee'
	sapaa	sapaa-**ka**	'forehead'
(c)	suulu	suu-**ka**-lu	'dog'
	kuhbil	kuh-**ka**-bil	'knife'
	baskarna	bas-**ka**-karna	'comb'
(d)	siwanak	siwa-**ka**-nak	'root'
	anaalaaka	anaa-**ka**-laaka	'chin'
	karasmak	karas-**ka**-mak	'knee'

(From McCarthy and Prince 1990a)

As seen, *-ka* always immediately follows the first iambic foot of the base. So, it is a suffix where the base is monosyllabic as in (37a) or disyllabic in (37b) but an infix where the base is longer as in (37c) and (37d).

To summarize, Ulwa illustrates well the important notion of *minimality*. Where prosodic circumscription occurs, morphological rules may apply within the rump of a base which constitutes the minimal base, with the rest being treated as extrametrical and ignored.

Reduplication is by no means unusual in applying to a minimal base. There are several other morphological processes, probably the best studied of which are *hypocoristics* which also involves truncated, minimal stems.

The minimal word in many languages is a bimoraic foot (cf. Estonian (Prince: 1980), Luganda (Hyman and Katamba: 1990) and Japanese (Poser 1990). It is on Japanese that we will focus. Poser (1990) has shown in detail that the bimoraic foot plays a vital role in at least eight morphological properties in Japanese including, among others, the delimitation of the base to which the hypocoristic suffix /tyan/ ([šaN] where N represents a moraic nasal) is productively attached to given names.

248 SKELETA AND MORPHOLOGICAL DOMAINS

It is possible to attach the hypocoristic to a noun without modification:

(38)

Akiratyan	<	Akira
Emityan	<	Emi
Hanakotyan	<	Hanako
Hirotarootyan	<	Hirotaroo
Midorityan	<	Midori

But hypocoristic attachment to an unmodified base is stylistically stiff and unfriendly. Suffixation of -*tyan* to a clipped base is more intimate.

Poser shows that several hypocoristic forms can be derived from a truncated name so long as one absolute and inviolable requirement is met: the base must satisfy a bimoraic template. If initially this requirement is not fulfilled, the bimoraic base can be obtained in a variety of ways including:

(39)

(a) lengthening of a monosyllabic base, e.g. *Ti* > *Tii-tyan*
(b) by lengthening the first syllable of a longer name, e.g. *Midori* > *Mii-tyan*
(c) by truncation, e.g. *Akira* > *Aki-tyan*, *Taroo* > *Taro-tyan*
(d) by making non-moraic segments moraic, e.g. *Atuko* > *At-tyan*

(Here the /t/ that is at the onset of the second syllable in the name is re-analysed as the second mora of the hypocoristic.)

Mester (1990), discussing the role of the template in Japanese in the light of Poser's work, points out that the hypocoristics above exemplify the most common function of the template: it functions as a *mapping target*. The template consisting of a bimoraic foot is satisfied by mapping the base melody. Obviously, as (39) shows, what is going on is not simply copying the first bimoraic foot of the base.

Similarly, in Luganda the template functions as a mapping target for hypocoristics. Many long personal names with at least four syllables (CvCvCvCv, CvvCvCvCv or CvCvvCvCv, etc.) are truncated in order for them to fit in the minimal initial trochaic foot template of hypocoristics. (The trochaic foot consists of heavy-light syllables, i.e. CvvCv.)

(40)

Nàmúsóké	>	Náàmú
Nákíjóbáà	>	Náàkí
Sékásózì	>	Séèká
Gòdìfùlé (Godfrey)	>	Góòdí
Sàmwéélí (Samuel)	>	Sáàmú
Kàtéégáyáà	>	Káàté
Kyòòtónnályáà	>	Kyóòtó

Note: "'" marks high tone and "`" marks low tone.

If the first syllable contains a long vowel, simple truncation satisfies the trochaic foot template (as in *Kyòòtónnályáà > Kyóòtó*). If the first syllable contains a short vowel a heavy, bimoraic, first foot is obtained by lengthening the vowel (as in *Nakijoba > Naaki*). Finally, if the input contains an initial light syllable followed by a heavy syllable, the first syllable is made heavy and the second one light (as in *Kàtéégáyà > Káàté*).

Iambic feet are common as we have seen elsewhere in this chapter; the trochaic 'anti-iamb' foot, i.e. heavy-light foot is not. And it is not part of the universal foot typology assumed by McCarthy and Prince. We will assume that the length of the heavy first syllable is derived. The reason for the lengthening is the need to supply a bimoraic first foot to bear the falling (´` i.e. high-low) contour tone melody of hypocoristics since a single mora of a light syllable cannot bear a contour tone in this language (Hyman and Katamba 1993).

Our next set of data comes from French. In his study of French hypocoristics, Plénat (1984) reports that one common type of hypocoristic truncates the name and only preserves two syllables:

(41)

Isabelle	/i.za.bel/	→	iza, zabel, zabe
Dominique	/do.mi.nik/	→	domi, minik, mini
Marie-Claude	/ma.ri-klod/	→	mako
Marie-Alice	/ma.ri-a.lis/	→	mali, malis
Thierry	/tye.ri/	→	teri

The modification may take different forms. Syllables may be eliminated either from the beginning (e.g. *mini, minik, zabel*) or from the end as in (e.g. *iza, domi*). In other cases, syllables may be simplified by dropping consonants from clusters as in (*Marie-Claude > mako*). However, the diversity of the truncation strategies employed does not conceal the fact that hypocoristic truncation processes conspire to produce truncated forms with a CvCv syllable pattern – or something close to it.

Steriade (1988: 75) argues that these stem truncations and syllable simplifications are formally similar to the stem modifications found in truncated partial reduplications. For instance French hypocoristic *zabel* (< *Isabelle*) is like Madurese reduplicative *sap-lati* 'handkerchief' (<*usap* 'wipe'; *lati* 'lip') and the syllable simplification in French that yields *mako* from *Marie-Claude* (with *ko* < *klod*) is analogous to the Sanskrit syllable simplification that gives *di* from *dvis* in *di-dvis*, the perfect form of *dvis* 'hate'. From this Steriade concludes that the segmental changes which are often attested in modified partial reduplication are in principle independent of the core process of copying that is at the heart of reduplication. They are part of a wider phenomenon of creating a minimal base that is required by certain morphological rules.

The processes we have just described share the property of applying to a portion of the base. This is common not only in morphology but also in phonology. We have already seen examples of phonological processes applying to a portion of a word in our discussion of Latin stress and Luganda tone.

Having established the fact that many phonological and morphological processes operate on a prosodically circumscribed minimal base, we shall now turn our attention to the task of providing a more rigorous characterization of *prosodic circumscription* in the McCarthy and Prince model. It is proposed that there is a *parsing function* Φ which is responsible for factoring out of a base B that portion which is subject to phonological or morphological operations. The parsing function of Φ can be stated thus:

(42)

Φ (C, E) applied to some base B, returns the prosodic constituent C lying at the edge E of B. Thus, Φ factors B into two components:
(a) the kernel B:Φ, which is the constituent C at the edge of B, and
(b) the residue B/Φ, which is simply the rest of B.

If '*' stands for the relation between the residue and the kernel (usually one simply precedes the other), then the following identity holds:

(43)

$$B = B{:}\Phi * B/\Phi$$

There are two principal types of prosodic circumscription, depending on the use to which they put the kernel and the residue. In *positive prosodic circumscription*, of which Ulwa and the Arabic broken plural are important examples, the kernel returned by Φ is subject to a morphological operation. Let O stand for some arbitrary morphological operation (such as suffixation) and let O: Φ(B) stand for the result of applying O to the circumscribed kernel of B. Then positive prosodic circumscription is defined as follows:

(44)

$$o:\Phi(B) = o(B:\Phi) * B/\Phi$$

The operation applies to the B:Φ portion of B; the residue B/Φ is unaffected.

By contrast, in *negative prosodic circumscription* (or extrametricality), the residue, rather than the kernel, undergoes the morphological or phonological operation. Let O/Φ(B) stand for the result of applying O to the residue of circumscription in B. Then negative prosodic circumscription is defined as follows:

(45)

$$O/\Phi(B) = B:\Phi * O(B/\Phi)$$

For example, in Latin a final syllable is circumscribed by Φ (Syllable, Right), and the phonological operation of penultimate stress assignment applies to the residue, which is simply the rest of the word. Thus, to assign stress to *regē`hāminī* 'you were being ruled', the following operations would be required:

(46)

O/Φ (regēbāminī)	= regēbāminī: Φ	* O (regēbāminī/Φ)
	= nī	* O (regēbāmi)
	= nī	* [regē`bāmi]
	= [regē`**bā**mi) ni	

We are now ready to apply the same analysis in morphology. Let us take first cases of reduplicative affixes that apply in minimal prosodically constrained domains of the kind that we saw in Ulwa in (37). McCarthy and Prince (1990a: 229) propose that the parsing function Φ that factors the base is (F$_1$, Left), where F$_1$ is an iambic foot. The function Φ (F$_1$, L) singles out the initial iambic foot. So, for instance, it factors *siwanak* 'chin' as:

(47)

| siwanak | = siwanak:Φ | * siwanak/Φ |
| | = siwa | *nak |

As mentioned earlier, Ulwa is a good example of positive prosodic circumscription. The morphological operation applies to the prosodically circumscribed kernel and not to the residue. Finally, let me reiterate the basic observation made earlier about Ulwa that the Prosodic Criterion requires morphological rules that operate on a minimal base not to apply to an arbitrary string but rather to a minimal base that is prosodically characterizable as a syllable, a disyllabic foot, etc. With this we will leave prosodic circumscription and turn to the third principle of Prosodic Morphology, namely the Template Satisfaction Condition.

4.3 Template Satisfaction Condition
In this theory, it is obligatory for morphological rules to satisfy the requirements of a template. For instance, if a morphological operation introduces a reduplicative affix with a bimoraic foot, then the morphological and phonological rules must ensure that a bimoraic affix is delivered.

Let us exemplify the Template Satisfaction Condition with a case study of Kinande nominal reduplication based on Mutaka and Hyman (1990). Typically, a Kinande noun has the structure in (48).

(48)

Augment-	prefix-	stem	
o	ku	gulu	'leg'
a	ká	tì	'stick'
e	kí	témbekalị	'a kind of tree'

Note: The symbol ị represents a very high front vowel.

Most Kinande noun stems are bisyllabic, although there are some longer nouns as well as a small number of monosyllabic ones. This fact is important as we shall soon see.

Kinande is a tone language, with a three-way underlying phonological contrast between high (´), low (`) and toneless (unmarked) vowels. However, on the surface, there is only a two-way contrast between high and low tone. Any toneless vowel is assigned a tone post-lexically. For simplicity's sake, we will not refer to tone in what follows because it is not relevant.

We are now ready to discuss reduplication. A noun can be reduplicated to create a new noun with an intensified meaning that can be glossed as 'a really (good) x'. We will start by presenting reduplication in disyllabic nouns.

(49)

(a) *Nouns with bisyllabic stems*

o.ku-gulu	'leg'	o.ku-gulu.gulu	'a real leg'
o.mu-góngò	'back'	o.mu-góngo.góngò	'a real back'
a.káhúkà	'insect'	a.ká-huká.húkà	'a real insect'
o.mu-síkaa	'girl'	o.mu-síka.síkaa	'a real girl'

(b) *Nouns with monosyllabic stems*

o.mú-twe	'head'	o.mú-twe.mú-twe	'real head'
e.bi-laa	'bowels'	e.bi-laa.bi-laa	'real bowels'
a.ká-ti	'stick'	a.ká-tí.ká-tì	'real stick'

Note: The augment is separated from the prefix with a dot (.) for reasons that will become clear shortly.

If a noun has a monosyllabic stem, the stem syllable, together with the prefix, is reduplicated. However, if a noun has a disyllabic stem, both stem syllables are reduplicated but the augment is excluded from the domain of reduplication. In other words, the *minimal word* targeted by reduplication is that portion of the word that includes the prefix and the stem but not the augment. On the basis of this analysis, Hyman and Mutaka propose that Kinande reduplication should be accounted for by the statements in (50).

(50)

(a) The reduplicative template is a prosodic unit consisting of *two syllables*.
(b) The template is suffixed.
(c) Copy the entire melody of the noun (except for the augment).
(d) Map the melody to the template right-to-left.

Following these principles, they provide these derivations for *okugulugulu* and *a.ká-tí ká-tì*:

(51)

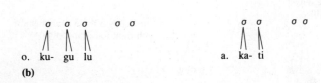

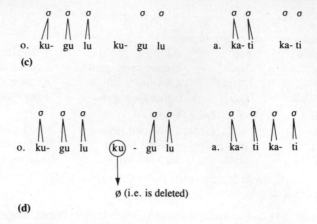

(c)

(d)

ø (i.e. is deleted)

In (52) we have even clearer evidence of the fact that the reduplicated suffix must be a bisyllabic foot. Here the base, including the nasal prefix, gives us just one syllable. The requirements of the Template Satisfaction Condition are not met. So, the reduplication process demands a double reduplication to provide enough syllables:

(52)

e.n-daa	'belly'	e.n-da.n-da.n-daa
e.n-dee	'cow'	e.n-de.n-de.n-dee
é.m.bwa	'dog'	é.m-bwá.m-bwá.m-bwa
e.n-dwa	'wedding'	e.n-dwa.n-dwa.n-dwa

The derivation of reduplicated *e.n-dwa.n-dwa.n-dwa* which exemplifies the bisyllabic foot template is given in (53):

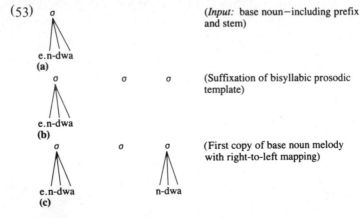

(53)

(Input: base noun—including prefix and stem)

(a)

(Suffixation of bisyllabic prosodic template)

(b)

(First copy of base noun melody with right-to-left mapping)

(c)

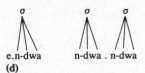

(d)

Output: e.n-dwa . n-dwa . n-dwa

(e)

Finally, in Kinande, nominal reduplication is blocked if a noun stem exceeds a disyllabic foot. This shows that the Template Satisfaction Condition must be met but not at the expense of what Hyman and Mutaka call the Morpheme Integrity Condition. In satisfying the prosodic template, a reduplicative process must use up all the segments representing the base morpheme, or none at all. Hence the reduplication of the nouns with polysyllabic stems in (54) is blocked:

(54)

o.mú-herukì	'bride'	(no reduplication)
o.tu-gotseri	'sleepiness'	(no reduplication)
e.bí-nyurúugúnzù	'butterflies'	(no reduplication)
e.ki-témbekalì	'kind of tree'	(no reduplication)

The Morpheme Integrity Condition which has an inhibiting role in Kinande reduplication is by no means universal. As we saw in (35) above, there are languages, such as Diyari, which pursue the setting up of minimal bases for morphological purposes with no regard for morpheme integrity. Words are parsed and melodies for reduplicative affixes are obtained without sparing a thought for the residue that is left. Thus the morpheme *ṭilparku* (which is divisible in the syllables *ṭil.par.ku*) is split to obtain the prefix melody. Furthermore, the second syllable is split: copying the initial foot in its entirety would give **ṭilpar-ñilparku* instead of the correct *ṭilpa-ṭilparku*. The template of the reduplicative prefix is simply CVC(C)V.

This completes the outline of the principles of the Prosodic Morphology model. We shall end the chapter by returning to the recalcitrant problems raised by Arabic broken plurals which defied earlier Template Morphology theories.

4.4 Melodic overwriting
Normally, in melody to template mapping of the type found in the Arabic verb system the consonantism is mapped onto empty C slots and the vocalism onto empty V slots (cf. (7) above). Such

mapping is easily handled using the standard Mapping Principles of autosegmental phonology.

However, broken plurals cannot be dealt with in the same way and cause severe analytical difficulties as we have seen. Attempts to deal with them either in terms of direct melody mapping (in Section 2) or templatic transfer (in Section 3) were shown to meet with only a modest degree of success. The essence of the problem is that unlike the melodies of verbal *binyanim*, broken plural melodies are not mapped onto vacant skeletal positions. So, McCarthy and Prince (1986, 1990a) have proposed an alternative solution whereby the broken plural is treated as a process that *overwrites* or replaces the original melody. We shall now show in turn how each type of broken plural is analysed in their model.

Let us deal with quadrilateral plurals first. These plurals, which are exemplified by *sulṭaan/salaaṭiin* (pl.), are derived as follows:

(a) Take *sulṭaa*n 'sultan' and bracket off the first two moras. This gives the minimal bimoraic base B/Φ *sul* leaving behind the residue *ṭan*.

(b) Map *sul* on the first iambic foot (F1) of the plural template, with the form Cμ Cμμ. (Here μ represents a mora).

This gives (55):

(55)

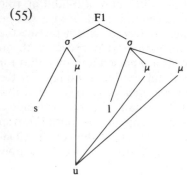

Mapping conventions associate consonants left-to-right with the C positions in the syllable onsets and the vowel *u* spreads to all available V positions in the foot.

Next the templatic vowel melody /a_i/ is linked to the V positions in the foot in (55) thereby replacing the *u* as seen in (56). When the first foot is concatenated with the residue, the V position(s) in the remnant of the word that lies outside the first foot gets associated

(56)

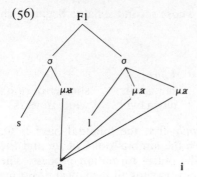

Note: V̆ = an overwritten vowel

with *i*, the second vowel of the templatic melody as shown in (57).
At no point are consonant associations in the original singular
form modified.

(57)

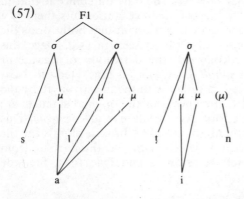

In the case of *jundub/janaadib* (pl.) 'locust' the derivation would
work in the same way. To begin with, the first two moras would be
parsed out, giving *jun*. The next operation would be to create an
iambic foot (CμC$\mu\mu$). Then the plural melody [a_i] would be
introduced. After that, the vowel *a* of the plural melody would take
over all the vowel positions in the first foot thereby overwriting the
original vowels of the singular to give *janaa*. Finally, the vowel *u* in
the residue would be replaced with *i*, the remaining vowel of the
melody, so that *dub* is changed to *dib*. Consonant associations
would remain unchanged throughout the derivation. When at the
end the two portions of the base are concatenated, we would get
the right output *janaadib*.

Let us now consider singulars whose second syllable begins with a CC sequence at the skeletal tier.

(58)

Singular	B/Φ	B:Φ	Plural	
šuʔbuub	šuʔ	buub	šaʔaabiib	'shower of rain'
nuwwaar	nuw	waar	nawaawiir	'white flowers'

In the case of *šuʔbuub* > *šaʔaabiib*, first the minimal base B/Φ, which is *šuʔ*, is factored out. Then the iambic foot CμCμμ and the melody [a_i] are introduced by the plural formation process. The vowel *a* of the plural melody then overwrites all the vowel positions in the iambic foot to yield *šaʔaa* from *šuʔ*. After that the *i* melody overwrites all the available V positions of the second foot changing *buub* to *biib*. When the two parts are joined together we get *šaʔaabiib*.

Mutatis mutandi, the broken plural *nawaawiir* is derived in the same way from the singular *nuwwar*. The only difference is that in this instance, instead of having two distinct consonants there is a single doubly linked, i.e. geminate *w* consonant that both forms the coda of B/Φ and the onset of B:Φ as seen in (58). Once this divalent nature of *w* is recognized, the derivation of *nawaawiir* progresses like that of *šaʔaabiib*. First, *nuwa* is bracketed off. Next an iambic foot is introduced, together with the melody [a_i], by the plural rule. Following that, the vowels of the original singular are replaced by *a* in the iambic foot. As a result, *nuw* gives *nawaa*. This solution deals with the difficulties caused by broken plurals for the Geminate Integrity Constraint which bars epenthesis rules from splitting true geminates (cf. Kenstowicz and Pyle 1973, Steriade 1982)):

(59)

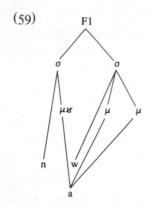

Then it is the turn of *waar* to have its vowels replaced to give *wiir*. Following this the two parts are finally concatenated. I have conflated the two processes in (60).

(60)

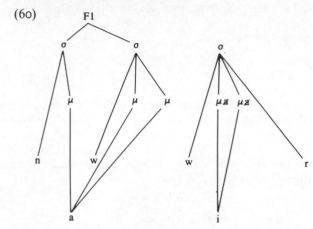

When the B/Φ and B:Φ parts are put together in (60), *w* which was a geminate ambisyllabic consonant functioning simultaneously as the onset of B:Φ and coda of B/Φ in (60) is now split into two segments attached to separate C positions in the onsets of their respective syllables in the derived representation.

The fact that broken plurals involve the bracketing off of the first two moras is most obvious in forms like *xaatam* 'signet ring' and *ǰaamus* 'buffalo'. In this type of noun which has only three root consonants, the initial iambic foot contains just one consonant. When the first two moras are bracketed off, we get $C\mu\mu$ (in the form of *xaa* and *ǰaa*). It is clear that such nouns fail to satisfy requirements of the broken plural template since the template has an iambic foot that contains two consonants. Remedial action is required if the Template Satisfaction Condition is to be met.

Note also that these nouns could also potentially raise problems related to syllable structure. Since the maximum number of moras per syllable is two, if the plural inserted an iambic foot with three moras where only a single consonant occurring in initial position was available, the result would be a disallowed $*C\mu\mu\mu$ sequence. Resyllabifying such a syllable as $C\mu.\ \mu\mu$, i.e. a first syllable with a short vowel followed by an onsetless long second syllable, with two moras, would not be permitted because syllables must obligatorily have onsets in Arabic (McCarthy 1979, McCarthy and Prince 1990a).

When the melody of a noun like *xataam* or *ǰaamus* is mapped onto the plural template, a solution to the twin problems identified above must be found. The solution offered by Arabic grammar is to insert a default *w* after the first mora, as shown in (61).

(61)   *Default consonant insertion*

$$\emptyset \rightarrow w/ \left\{ \begin{array}{l} V\rule{1em}{0.4pt}VV \\ VV\rule{1em}{0.4pt}V \end{array} \right\}$$

After the default consonant *w* has been inserted, it links to the second C position of the initial iambic foot of the plural template. As a result, instead of having a triconsonantal CvvCv(v)C sequence (as in *ǰaamus*) we now have a quadriliteral form with CvCvCv(v)C. The association can now proceed as it would if this, indeed, were a quadriliteral plural (see (55)–(57) above).

(62)

Singular	B/Φ	B:Φ	Plural	
ǰaamus	ǰaa	mus	ǰawaamiis	'buffalo'
xaatam	xaa	tam	xawaatim	'signet ring'

Melodic overwriting ensures that all the V positions of the first foot are associated with the vowel *a*. The residue has either a long or short vowel, depending on whether in the plural template there is just one V slot (as in *xawaatim*) or two V slots (as in *ǰawaamiis*) for the melody *i* to be associated with.

Another class of problem broken plurals also involves triconsonantal nouns. This group need to have a consonant epenthesized at the beginning of the residue (rather than at the beginning of the second syllable of the iambic foot as in *ǰawaamiis*) in order for them to satisfy the requirements of the quadriliteral broken plural template. This is exemplified by the following forms:

(63)

Singular	B/Φ	B:Φ	Plural	
saḥaab(-at)	saḥa	ab	saḥaaʔib	'cloud'
ǰaziir(-at)	ǰazi	ir	ǰazaaʔir	'island'

These nouns clearly show that the parsing is prosodically driven and that it is done in terms of moras rather than syllables. What the parsing rule that brackets off B/Φ requires is a bimoraic foot. In the data considered until now, B/Φ has fortuitously been identical with the first syllable of the world. What is different about (63) is that in this case B/Φ is obtained by taking the first syllable, plus one mora of the second syllable which happens to have a long vowel.

But this parsing of the bimoraic initial foot leaves us a problem. On its own B : Φ, the remnant of the base, is not a syllable since, as we mentioned above, in Arabic onsetless syllables are impermissible as we saw above. So something has to be done to make the residue pronounceable. The problem is solved by applying rule (61) which inserts the default consonant w. In this environment w surfaces phonetically as [ʔ]. The rest of the derivation is similar to that of the words in (62).

Finally, we will consider triconsonantal nouns with a singular CvC(v)C shape which clearly need considerable modification in order for them to satisfy the CVCVVCV(V)C plural template:

(64)

Singular	B / Φ	B : Φ	Plural	
nafs	naf	s	nufuus	'soul'
qidħ	qid	ħ	qidaaħ	'arrow'
ħukm	ħuk	m	/ħakaam/ [ʔaħkaam]	'judgement'
farx	far	x	/faraax/ [ʔafraax]	'young bird'
qadam	qada	m	qadaam [ʔaqdaam]	'foot'

Nouns whose singular shape is CvC(v)C form their plural essentially in the same way as quadriliteral *sulṭaan* above. The base is factored as shown in (64) (cf. *qada – m*) and an iambic first foot CσCσσ is introduced by the plural operation. The vowel *a* of the melody /a_i/ overwrites all V positions of the first foot. This gives *qadaa-*. The final consonant *m* is extrametrical at the point when melody mapping takes place and so it is ignored. Although *m* is associated morphologically with a C position, it is not integrated in the syllable structure at this stage. The *i* of the /a_i/ melody is left floundering, unable to be licensed by any syllable. So, the Stray Erasure convention removes this *i*. Finally, at a very late stage, the final consonant becomes visible and attaches to *qadaa-* to give *qadaam*.

A further complication which has not been pointed out so far is due to metathesis which applies in the first syllable in this group of plurals changing **Ca** to **aC**, thereby creating an onsetless syllable which is disallowed. To fix this ill-formed representation, another rule inserts the default consonant /w/ which functions as the obligatory onset of what is now a vowel-commencing syllable. Subsequently, /w/ is changed to [ʔ] by a lower level rule. So, the derivation of a plural like [ʔaqdaam] includes these stages: / qadaam/ → *aqdaam* → *waqdaam*

→ [ʔaqdaam]. Melody mapping applies before metathesis and therefore metathesis has no implications for melody mapping.

One thing that is lexically determined and unpredictable is the melody a particular noun in this group takes. There is considerable diversity in the melodies found in these short triliteral plurals. In addition to /a_i/ we find /u/ and /i_a/as seen in (64).

5   Conclusion

Following McCarthy and Prince, we have argued in this chapter that many morphological rules apply, not in arbitrary phonological domains defined in terms of CV slots on the skeletal tier and segments that are mapped onto them, but rather in domains that constitute genuine units of the prosodic hierarchy such as the mora, the syllable and the foot, all of which involve the skeletal tier.

Further, we have shown that many morphological and phonological processes apply not to an entire base, but to a portion of it that constitutes a prosodically circumscribed minimal base. Prosodic circumscription may be positive, in which case it is the kernel returned by the parsing function Φ that undergoes the phonological or morphological operation (as in Arabic or Ulwa). Or, alternatively, prosodic circumscription may be negative, in which case it is the residue left by the parsing that is subject to a phonological or morphological operation (as in Latin stress assignment). Negative prosodic circumscription is also referred to as extrametricality.

The discussion has concentrated on a number of reduplication processes in various languages, and on the broken plurals of Arabic. These two types of phenomena have been scrutinized because they pose serious theoretical challenges for any model of how phonological representations interact with morphological representations. They call for an account that shows that underneath the surface diversity in the phonological realization of morphological representations there exists a degree of phonological coherence. In Arabic broken plurals, it is intuitively clear that phonological aspects of the singular noun carry over in the plural. But it is difficult to specify explicitly the nature of the carrying over. Likewise, in (modified) reduplication, the reduplicative affix carries over some properties of the base. Again the task of the linguist is to state explicitly how the carrying over is done.

It has been shown that in the Prosodic Morphology solution, broken plurals must commence with an iambic first foot (CvCvv +) and their second foot must be Cv(v)C. The broken plural as a whole has a CVCVVCV(V)C template. The plural is derived from the singular by getting the plural template and associated melody to overwrite the singular. The Template Satisfaction Condition ensures that all positions in the plural template are properly filled. It may be necessary to insert or delete segments in order to satisfy the template. Likewise, in reduplication, instead of operating on individual elements of the skeletal tier, rules of morphology affect authentic prosodic units like moras, syllables and feet.

Thus Prosodic Morphology offers interesting answers to the questions with which this chapter started concerning the relationship between phonology and morphology, and in particular the role of units of the prosodic hierarchy in phonology in specifying the phonological domains required by morphological operations.

Acknowledgements

I am indebted to John McCarthy and Jacques Durand for numerous helpful comments on an earlier version of this chapter which enabled me to correct factual errors and make many theoretical, analytical and presentational improvements. I have also benefited from comments by Latifa al Sulaiti, Saleh el Khatib and Salah Elhassan. Of course, I am responsible for any shortcomings that remain.

PART 3

DERIVATIONS

Chapter 8

Universalism in phonology: atoms, structures and derivations

Jacques Durand

1 Introduction

In the history of linguistics, phonology has played an important role and, at various points, has been seen as providing the key concepts for the analysis of language as a whole. After the Second World War, for instance, the work of phonologists such as Trubetz-koy and Jakobson was seen by many scholars as providing a model of precision that should be emulated in the social sciences: for instance, the structural anthropology of Lévi-Strauss was explicitly based on the achievements of structural phonology (see Dosse 1991). In recent years, however, many of the claims concerning the nature of the theory of language would appear to have come from syntax, semantics and pragmatics. While in terms of volume of production, the place of phonology within an account of linguistic structure seems unassailable, there are wide differences in the field as to the role, nature and structure of a phonological component. The purpose of this chapter is to offer a brief rational reconstruction of aspects of the theory of phonology. While the discussion here is framed within the Chomskyan paradigm of linguistic structure, I will take as little for granted as possible. Inevitably, there are many short-cuts and the reader is asked to exercise some charity in filling in the gaps at various points of the discussion.

2 Does phonology fall outside the theory of grammar?

In the Chomskyan tradition, which in this respect is Jakobsonian, the association of language and speech is assumed to be natural and innate. Spoken languages are acquired without special instruction as a normal part of the process of maturation and socialization, whereas this is not true of written languages. It has also been pointed out by various specialists that children are biologically equipped to produce and recognize certain classes of speech sounds (cf. Mehler 1981; Darwin 1987). If one accepts that the syntactic and semantic structure of human languages is narrowly constrained by a species-specific, innate faculty, as Chomsky has argued, we might seem to be justified in concluding that it is spoken language as such, if not the whole of speech, that is innately determined by the principles of universal grammar. Yet John Lyons (1991: 7) points out:

> On present evidence, this [i.e. the idea that the association between language and speech is innately determined, JD] would be a hasty conclusion to draw. In my view, it is quite possible that the language-faculty and the predisposition to vocalize are biologically independent and only contingently associated in speech.

What John Lyons is arguing is that the language-faculty should not be tied in an absolute manner to a realization in the spoken medium – a position that I would fully endorse. After all, the expressive power of the sign languages of the deaf is in no way inferior to spoken languages and there is no doubt, in my mind, that as human beings we come into the world with an ability to produce and understand signs which is not restricted to a particular medium. It may still be true, however, that in human beings not suffering from a speech/hearing impairment the predisposition to vocalize is severely constrained by species-specific mechanisms. Still, we have to accept that it is logically and empirically possible that the association between language and speech is a contingent one. If this is so we should not be surprised if phonology were to obey quite different principles from morphology, syntax or semantics.

A position along these lines has been advocated by a variety of phonologists and phoneticians over the years and most trenchantly by Geoffrey Sampson in his *Schools of Linguistics. Competition and Evolution* (1980). In this book, Sampson offers a severe critique of classical generative phonology arguing, *inter alia*, that the putatively universal distinctive features inherited from Jakobson have changed over the years, that they are not particularly adequate, that notions such as markedness require no account within phonology (e.g. [y] being more complex than [i] and [u] follows straightforwardly from facts about the vocal tract and requires no postulation of innate principles), and that the postulation of universal distinctive features is aprioristic and of doubtful empirical status (cf. Sampson 1980:

118–25, 189–98). After surveying a number of aspects of work in generative phonology, Sampson (1980: 198) concludes:

> I infer that this strand of generative-phonological thought is wholly bankrupt, and that, where a phonetic parameter is physically capable of taking a large range of values, the number and identity of the parameter-values which are used distinctively is quite likely to differ unpredictably from one language to another. There is no 'universal phonetic alphabet' in men's minds; the only physical constraints on human language are those set by the physical facts of vocal-tract anatomy.

If we push this position to its limits we should not be surprised if there is no need for phonology and this is in fact what Sampson ends up claiming:

> At least one leading theoretician (Vennemann 1974) has come to the view that we store our vocabulary, not in terms of underlying phonetic forms of roots, but simply in terms of the surface pronunciations of words, with separate entries for each of their various derivational and inflexional forms. This new trend is sometimes called 'Natural Generative Phonology', making it sound as if it incorporated some novel theoretical insight. A better name might be 'Commonsense Phonology'; it boils down to the view that the true theory of phonology is that there is virtually no 'theory of phonology' (p. 208).

This set of assumptions will be labelled here 'Level 0 Universality' and is summarized in (1) below.

(1)   *Level 0* Universality

The sound-component of language is language-specific and determined by facts of anatomy or acoustics; the only phonological representations are phonetic ones; the lexicon is a vast inventory of fully specified forms.

3   Some problems with Level 0 Universality

Before we turn to the issue of distinctive features, let us examine briefly the thesis that phonological representations should be limited to phonetic forms listed in the lexicon. In a sense, the vast majority of modern articles on phonology – starting from work based on the phoneme – offer a demonstration of the opposite thesis. To capture various generalizations concerning the sound-systems of human languages we need to move away from surface phonetics. But, since the virtue of such approaches might be

claimed to be in the eyes of the beholder only, it is worth noting
that 'external' evidence (as provided by language acquisition, speech
pathology, language games, speech errors, etc.) provides support
for the idea that a level more abstract than surface phones has
psychological reality.

Victoria Fromkin has been a particularly stout defender of the
idea that in certain types of common speech errors, usually referred
to as spoonerisms, the targeted allophones do not occur as such
when disordered. Consider the following examples (cf. Fromkin
1971, 1973, 1988 from whom these examples are borrowed):

(2)

(a)	rank order	→	rand order
	[ræ̃ŋk ɔrdər]	→	[rænd ɔrkər]
(b)	Bing Crosby	→	Big Cronsby
	[bɪŋ krɔsbi]	→	[bɪg krɔ̃nsbi]
(c)	Stan Kenton	→	Skan Tenton
	[stæn kʰɛ̃ntən]	→	[skæn tʰɛ̃ntən]

We would predict that if mental representations were based on
sequences of allophones we should regularly find interchanges of
surface phonetic segments as part of the output of a disordered
sequence. Thus, in (2c) we might expect [skʰæn tɛ̃ntən] – a type of
error which is not reported. In (2b), we would not expect to find a
[g] which is not part of the input string. And in (2a), we would not
expect the input [ŋ] to be affected by the speech error.

In the face of these observations, some strategy can always be
deployed to account for the realizations on the right-hand side of
(2). To deal with (2a), for instance, we can claim that starting from
the string on the left as the underlying string, the [k] and the [d]
interchange places. And, as a result, the [ŋ] is automatically converted into a velar [n] to agree with the place of articulation of the
following [d]. But note a paradox here: so-called concrete phonology becomes abstract. We have to assume that a matrix of distinctive features is being altered – that is, rules with full transformational powers have to be assumed which make the phonology non-
monotonic (see Coleman, this volume, for the terminology and the
associated concepts and Sections 4–5 below).

By contrast, let us assume that phonological representations are
more abstract than allophones. Let us say, for the sake of the
argument, that the contrastive segments of a language – the phonemes – are represented as bundles of distinctive features which
abstract away from the surface realization and let us also allow for
the possibility of archisegments in certain contexts (e.g. cases of

neutralization). Starting then from /ræNk ɔrdər/ as our (abbreviated) input string held by the speaker in his/her mind at some processing stage, the disordered sequence on the right hand side of (2a) is easy to account for: we simply have to posit a k ↔ d interchange. The presence of an alveolar [n] is independently predictable by a simple filling in of the matrix of the archisegment /N/ which is unspecified for place of articulation. There is no need to assume any change of feature-structures: default values merely get instantiated at the relevant processing stage.

The other two examples in (2) could be similarly analysed to show that so-called surface phonetics won't do! A full rebuttal of the 'common sense' position with respect to levels of representation would require much more space than is available here, but, in any case, we should note that the notion of 'surface pronunciation of words' is highly problematic. Sampson seems to assume that there is a notion of phonetic representation which is clearly isolatable from phonological theory. But nothing could be further from the truth. There are no theory-free observation reports, and this is as true of phonetics as of the classical physical sciences (see Feyerabend 1958; Losee 1980: 190–2). Unless one believes that allophonic representations just mirror attested acoustic patterns – a position which is ultimately meaningless since at the level of tokens every sequence of sounds is unique – one has to constrain somehow the nature of phonetic representations, either on the basis of the kinds of distinctions which can be encoded in the signal or in cognitive terms (cf. the insightful discussion in Lindsey and Harris, 1990). Let us therefore turn our attention to the status of distinctive features.

I assume that the universality of distinctive features is not a logical necessity and that, in the absence of any direct evidence that there are receptors in the brain corresponding to distinctive features, the supposition of universality in this domain requires careful examination (see too Durand 1990a: 59–61).

First of all, it is a common observation made by phoneticians that the dimensions along which sound-systems are structured are *recurrent* and *finite*. As pointed out in Durand (1990a: 39), even a phonetician like Catford (1977: 14) who 'refrain(s) from positing a set of positive, fixed, parametric values that constitute *the* universal set of distinctive phonetic features' recognizes that 'in descriptive linguistic phonetics we seem to have reached a point of diminishing returns: it is only occasionally that some totally new and unknown phonetic phenomenon turns up'.

The recurrence of a small set of phonetic parameters cannot be taken for granted. Ladefoged (1992), in discussing the interfaces between phonology and phonetics, does point out in connection

with the attested vowel systems that they do not stray in random
and unpredictable ways: no less than 20 per cent of Maddieson's
(1984) vowel inventories have segments something like [i, e, a, o, u].
As Ladefoged observes:

> As a minimum estimate we can say that there are about 50 broadly
> distinct vowels that languages might have chosen as the vocalic elements
> of their segmental inventory. The likelihood of the same five being chosen
> so frequently is therefore comparable with the likelihood of playing
> poker and finding that one hand in five always had the Ace, King, Queen,
> Jack, and Ten of Spades (1992: 167).

A similar point is echoed in Kaye (1989: 21) who notes that, on
the assumption that a typical phonological inventory consists of 33
members, the number of possible bifurcations of such a system is
given by the formula $2^n - 1$, where n is the number of segments in
the inventory. The result is approximately 8.6 billion potential
bifurcations for an average phonological system. So, as Kaye adds,
if the game is not rigged and the units are unanalysable, the
chances of the same bifurcation turning up with respect to a
particular phonological phenomenon are about 1 in 8.6 billion.
Yet, it is quite easy to show that various groupings (e.g. labiality or
coronality) keep recurring across unrelated languages.

It is unlikely that presented with such arguments the committed
sceptic (if this is not an oxymoron!) will give up the battle. He/she
will tell us that these recurrences are hardly surprising if we look at
the vocal tract. This latter is not some undifferentiated continuum,
we might be told, but, actually, made up of discontinuities: thus
the lips can surely be distinguished from the teeth; the latter are
clearly different from the alveolar ridge which is convex; on the
other hand, the palate is concave; the palate itself is bony then
becomes fleshy, and so on and so forth. But are the 'quanta'
derivable from the anatomy of the vocal tract so self-evident?
Consider again the structure of vowel systems. *A priori* there are
many other organizations of the vowel system than the ones classi-
cally envisaged in phonological work. For instance, Catford (1977:
184–7) presents an alternative classificatory system – which he calls
a 'polar co-ordinate' vowel diagram (see Figure 8.1) – which would
appear to be nearer articulatory 'reality', with the further advantages of using the same terminology for vowels and consonants
and elucidating the aerodynamics of vowel production better than
diagrams based on Jones' Cardinal Vowels.

However, Catford immediately proceeds to observe that 'some
curious difficulties' arise in attempting to use this seemingly more
'rational' schema. First of all, 'it seems easier to slide the tongue as

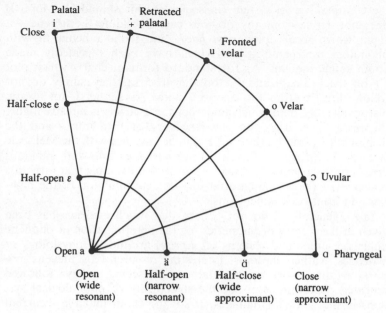

FIGURE 8.1

a whole vertically or horizontally, rather than along the radii of the polar co-ordinate system; assessment of the relationship of vowels to Cardinal Vowels is thus easier using the traditional figure'. Second, the traditional quadrilateral (or indeed triangular representations) seems more appropriate than the polar co-ordinate system for the display of attested vowel systems. Catford then points out that there are two reasons for the inadequacy of the classification in Figure 8.1: acoustically, a plotting of the cardinal vowels with F_1 on the vertical axis and F_2 on the horizontal axis yields a chart which is closer to traditional articulatory classification; physiologically, the movements of the tongue on the high-low and front-back axis correspond to muscle actions which 'feel' more like natural classes (see Catford 1977: 186).

The lack of fit between the polar co-ordinate system and the attested vowel systems in the languages of the world is in fact the crucial argument. The vowel space is not there – to be read off in any direct manner – in the oral cavity or in the world of sounds. It is through the evidence of vowel systems, phonological processes (both synchronic and diachronic), the acquisition or loss of sound-systems, that we can validate dimensions such as height, rounding, retraction, advanced tongue root or whatever. The advantage of the Cardinal Vowel system (in so far as this should be adopted) does not derive from any obvious ease in sliding the tongue – a claim which seems quite *post hoc* – but from a better fit with phonological generalizations which have been repeatedly made about sound systems. As for standard formant charts which plot F_1 on the ordinate and F_2 on the abscissa, they surely do not follow directly from the acoustic data. As far as I am aware, historically, the data which underlies these charts is already highly theorized – i.e. based on the discovery of formants – and the displays of F_1 and F_2 (but not F_3) in accordance with the Mel scale (see e.g. Ladefoged 1982: ch. 8) are *post hoc*: following standard descriptions of sound systems we can see for example that formants higher than F_2 can be ignored for the determination of the high-low and front-back dimensions.

More generally, I do not believe that much evidence has been given in the history of phonetics for the determination of phonetic dimensions of sound systems on *a priori* grounds of physiology or acoustics. Rather, the most interesting research (e.g. Stevens' important (1972) work on quantal vowels) seems to have followed repeated observations about the structuring of phonological systems in the world's languages. If so, the claim that the recurrent nature of a small number of dimensions falls out from the nature of the speech apparatus (or the auditory system) turns out to be less convincing than might have appeared at first sight.

In any case, even if it turned out that the nature of phonological primes derived from optimal properties of the speech apparatus, some further assumptions would have to be made about the decoding system of human beings. In particular, it would have to be assumed that our perceptual system is wired up to respond optimally to the natural resonance properties of the vocal tract – an assumption which does not appear to be biologically necessary. Moreover, given our previous claim that phonetics has had difficulties in establishing classificatory dimensions ahead of work on phonological systems, a universalist enterprise – *pace* Sampson – would still be the best strategy to discover the putatively natural properties of the vocal apparatus.

Let us now examine the claim that the postulation of universal distinctive features is not a genuinely empirical hypothesis. Any survey of competing proposals concerning distinctive features would in fact demonstrate the opposite. To begin with, the formal functioning of distinctive features (e.g. whether they are unary, binary, scalar, etc.) can be tested by careful investigation of phonological phenomena (cf. the essays by Harris and Lindsey, van der Hulst, and Pulleyblank this volume). And the alternative feature-sets themselves make different predictions concerning phonological regularities. For instance, the I-A-U systems defended in Dependency Phonology (cf. Anderson and Ewen 1987; Durand 1990a, b, van der Hulst 1989) and in Government Phonology (Kaye et al. 1985, 1990) can be invalidated by displaying phenomena where the notion [+ / − high] plays a crucial role (cf. Kenstowicz 1990 and Durand 1990b, and see Harris and Lindsey this volume). Unwittingly, Sampson (1980: 191) gives evidence that reasoning about the adequacy of feature-sets is possible since he argues that the classification of 'place of articulation' in terms of the Jakobsonian features 'diffuse' and 'grave' is not borne out by the behaviour of plosives in Slavonic languages. Given the following cross-classification:

(3) *Jakobsonian classification*

	p	t	k	c
diffuse	+	+	−	−
grave	+	−	+	−

Sampson observes that, if [t] is to [c] as [p] is to [k], then we would predict that, in environments where [t] is replaced by [c], [p] ought always or usually to be replaced by [k]; but he claims that this never happens. Whether Sampson is ultimately correct with respect to the Slavonic data is not essential in this context. What is important is the fact that empirical evidence can be brought to bear on the choice of particular phonetic parameters.

It is also worth pointing out that while much remains to be learned about the psycho-physical basis of phonology, there is reasonable evidence that sounds in language are not all on the same footing. For instances, various studies (cf. Blumstein and Cooper 1972, 1974; van Lancker and Fromkin 1973) point to a non-parallel treatment of intonation and tone (both based on pitch) in a tonal language like Thai: there is clear left-ear supremacy in the processing of intonation as opposed to right-ear dominance in the processing of tones. While the observations they report do not demonstrate the existence of a set of innate phonetic parameters, they are suggestive of a special neural basis for the distinctive sounds of language.

We have presented a set of arguments in favour of a universalist position concerning the atoms of phonology. There are important differences between competing models of phonological description. Thus, the elements of Government Phonology (cf. Harris and Lindsey this volume) and the components of Dependency Phonology (cf. Anderson and Ewen 1987, Durand 1990a) are not fully equatable with classical distinctive features such as those advocated in Chomsky and Halle's *The Sound Pattern of English* (hereafter SPE). But the main point is the common assumption of a small, universal inventory of primitives from which each language draws a subset to mark distinctions at various points of phonological structure.

4 Level 1 Universality

If we leave distinctive features aside, it is well known that the phonological paradigm embodied in Chomsky and Halle's SPE made the assumptions that (a) phonological representations were strings of phoneme-sized units (made up of simultaneously occurring features) delimited by boundaries; (b) the mapping between phonological and phonetic representations is the result of the application of extrinsically ordered rules (which are local transformations).

For a good number of years now, the first assumption has been under severe scrutiny. The development of so-called 'Non-Linear Phonology' has been predicated on the assumption that phonological representations should be seen as the interfacing of various types of information: e.g. that there are timing or weight units which relate information about features, syllable structure, stress, with the possibility that certain features might be autosegmental or prosodic. Again, while there are substantive differences between various approaches (compare the essays by Bickmore, Brockhaus, Katamba, Zec, and other contributors to this volume), there is general agreement that phonological representations cannot be seen as the simple concatenation of bundles of distinctive features.

The second assumption has also been under close examination. Particularly, as a result of the work done on Autosegmental Phonology, the types of operation to be countenanced in phonology have been claimed to be severely limited and there has been a move away from what has been perceived as the arbitrariness and excessive power of phonological rules *à la* SPE. In many respects, phonologists have moved closer to the work of syntacticians or morphologists, who, for a number of years, have dropped the assumption that extrinsically ordered transformations were needed to capture well-formedness at the syntactic or morphological level. However, in an important article published in the late 1980s, Bromberer and Halle (1989: 53) have attempted to argue that there was a fundamental distinction between phonology and syntax. If I may quote them at length, Bromberger and Halle make the following unequivocal statement:

(4)
Phonology . . . is primarily concerned with the connections between
surface forms that can serve as input to our articulatory machinery
(and to our auditory machinery) and the abstract underlying forms in
which words are stored in memory. Whereas syntax is concerned with
the relations among representations that encode different types of
information requiring different types of notation, phonology is
concerned with the relationship between representations that encode
the same type of information – phonetic information – but do so in
ways which serve distinct functions: articulation and audition, on the
one hand, and memory, on the other. Whereas phonetic surface
representations are generated only when a word figures in an actual
utterance, there is a clear and theoretically significant sense in which
underlying representations are prior to surface representations, a sense
that justifies thinking of the surface form as "derived" from the
underlying form. This fact in turn brings up the question of the
manner in which surface representations are derived from underlying
representations. The answer clearly is to be decided by looking at the
actual contingent evidence rather than by reflecting on *a priori* logical
or methodological necessities. In particular, there is no *a priori* reason
to hold that the derivations must be subject to a theory formally
similar to the theory appropriate for syntax/semantics.

The claim made by Bromberger and Halle is that in phonology
extrinsically ordered transformations are required if we want to
capture simple generalizations and that to try and make phonology
mirror syntax is fundamentally erroneous. The view of phonology
advocated by these authors will be described here as 'Level I
Universality', which is summarized in (5).

(5)   *Level I Universality*

Phonological representations are based on a universal inventory
of distinctive features. Representations within the phonological
module are related by local transformations which are extrinsically ordered.

The evidence cited by Bromberger and Halle in favour of Level I
Universality is both synchronic and diachronic. Starting with the
synchronic evidence, Bromberger and Halle rehearse an old claim
(see Chomsky 1964 and Chomsky and Halle 1968: 342, both
based on Joos 1942) that many varieties of Canadian English fall
into two sets with respect to the phenomena commonly known
as 'Canadian Raising' and 'Flapping'. Flapping refers to the neutralization of the /t/ – /d/ intervocalic contrast exemplified by
riding [rayDɪŋ] – *writing* [rayDɪŋ] and can be informally stated as
in (6).

(6) *Flapping*

$$\{t, d\} \longrightarrow D \; / \left[\begin{array}{c} -cons \\ +stress \end{array} \right] \quad \text{——} \quad \left[\begin{array}{c} -cons \\ -stress \end{array} \right]$$

Canadian Raising refers to the adjustment of diphthong quality (ay → ʌj, aw → ʌw) in the context of a voiceless consonant as exemplified in *rise* [rayz] – *rice* [rʌys] and *cloud* [klawd] – *clout* [klʌwt]. This process can be informally summarized as in (7).

(7) *Raising*

$$a \longrightarrow \text{ʌ} \; / \; \text{—} \quad \text{——} \; \{y, w\} \; [\text{-voiced}]$$

Dialects of Canadian English are claimed to fall into two groups, traditionally referred to as Dialect A and Dialect B, for which representative data is given below.

(8) *Dialect A*

rise	[rayz]	rice	[rʌys]
tribe	[trayb]	tripe	[trʌyp]
riding	[rayDɪŋ]	writing	[rʌyDɪŋ]
rouse	[rawz]	mouse	[mʌws]
cloud	[klawd]	clout	[klʌwt]
clouded	[klawDɪd]	shouted	[šawDɪd]

(9) *Dialect B*

rise	[rayz]	rice	[rʌys]
tribe	[trayb]	tripe	[trʌyp]
riding	[rayDɪŋ]	writing	[rayDɪŋ]
rouse	[rawz]	mouse	[mʌws]
cloud	[klawd]	clout	[klʌwt]
clouded	[klawDɪd]	shouted	[šawDɪd]

In Dialect A, Raising applies to words with underlying /t/, but not to words with underlying /d/. We can predict this if Raising is ordered before Flapping (counter-feeding order). On the other hand, in Dialect B, while both processes are active, the pronunciation of *riding* and *writing* is the same. This can be predicted if in such dialects, Flapping is ordered before Raising (feeding order).

The second type of evidence in favour of the extrinsic ordering of phonological rules adduced by Bromberger and Halle comes from the diachronic field. If we assume that one of the mechanisms of phonological change is the addition of phonological rules to the battery of rules internalized by speakers of a language, then it can be shown that some sound changes will have to be incorporated in a way which requires a stipulated ordering. Thus, if we consider Grimm's law, this will be seen to have two parts. First, voiceless stops became continuants (except after obstruents): compare Sanskrit 'tray' with Germanic 'θre' (Eng. three). Second, non-aspirated stops became voiced: compare Sanskrit 'duva' with Germanic 'two' (Eng.). Bromberger and Halle argue in favour of the likelihood that these two sub-parts of Grimm's law became ordered in the synchronic phonology of Germanic speakers. And while they acknowledge that they could formally have applied simultaneously in a synchronic grammar of Germanic, they believe that Verner's law (the voicing of continuants after unstressed vowels which entered the language after the first sub-part of Grimm's law) provides 'conclusive evidence' that sound laws are the effect of the addition of rules, some of which will require extrinsic ordering in synchronic grammars.

Bromberger and Halle make other assumptions about the nature of rule application: notions such as disjunctive ordering, cyclic ordering and stratal ordering will also be part of the 'principles' of grammar. What will concern us here, however, is not the nature of these auxiliary assumptions but the conclusions reached by these authors: given that the subject matter of phonology is 'intrinsically different from that of syntax' and that phonological rules (ordered transformations) are required by the data, 'to construct phonology so that it mimics syntax is to miss a major result of the work of the last twenty years, namely that syntax and phonology are essentially different' (1989: 69).

5   Level 1 Universality under fire

The arguments put forward by Bromberger and Halle are familiar. In the light of current concerns within linguistic theory, they do, however, raise a number of problems.

First of all, it is clearly the case that many treatments of a variety of phenomena, which were claimed to require extrinsic rule-ordering have been recast in recent years within frameworks which do not appeal to stipulated rule-ordering *without any clear loss of generality*. The loss of generality has been a standard argument against frameworks such as Natural Generative Phonology, which in the 1970s and early 1980s barred extrinsic rule ordering. But, in many cases, the new accounts have only made reference to general – inevitably tentative – principles or parameters rather than language particular rules (cf. among many examples Encrevé's 1988 comprehensive treatment of French liaison).

The second difficulty is that in empirical terms the piece of

synchronic evidence which is adduced by Bromberger and Halle –
i.e. Canadian Raising – is not an ironcast argument in favour of
rule-ordering. On the assumption that the data is correct, Coleman
(this volume) argues that other ways of dealing with them are
possible. But, Jonathan Kaye in a recent article on the matter
(Kaye 1990b, this volume) points out that, surprisingly for a
phenomenon which has been at the centre of phonological theoriz-
ing, the sum total of what is known about dialects A and B is a
couple of short paragraphs in Joos (1942: 141–4) 'A phonological
dilemma in Canadian English'. Dialect A does not pose a problem
but when one attempts to track down speakers of Dialect B they
simply seem to evaporate – an odd fact given that Canada is far
from inaccessible. Kaye notes that, even Chambers (1973), the
modern authority on Canadian raising, just quotes Joos and claims
that in the early 1970s there were no remaining speakers of Dialect
B. Yet, from the observations in Joos' article, the speakers of
Dialect B, a group of Ontario public-school children, should have
been about 50 in 1972. As Kaye points out, it is unbelievable that
in 1972 not a single speaker of Dialect B should remain. How is it
possible that so much theoretical conflict should have taken place
around a single datum: Joos' transcription of the word 'typewriter'?

There is, of course, the historical evidence provided by the
interaction of the subparts of Grimm's law and Verner's law. But,
as observed by Bromberger and Halle themselves (1989: note 13,
p. 65), the argument rests on the assumption that at some point
these rules coexisted side by side and were actively present in a past
synchronic state of Germanic. While some brief observations are
presented in favour of this assumption, it does seem to the author
of these lines that too little is known about the remote synchronic
grammars of Germanic to base an argument engaging the whole of
phonology on it. In any case, the argument in favour of rules being
at the core of phonological change is somewhat circular: if phonological change is, in fact, the result of parameter settings and re-
settings by learners and speakers of a language, as is assumed in
much recent Chomskyan theory, then the historical 'facts' have to
be looked at again in that light.

A third point (well discussed in Lindsey and Harris 1990: 358,
passim) which is worth emphasizing is that the conception of
phonology as an encoding device seems to involve some confusion
between a theory of competence and a theory of performance.
Recall the claim made as part of (4) that 'Whereas phonetic surface
representations are generated only when a word figures in an
actual utterance, there is a clear and theoretically significant sense
in which underlying representations are prior to surface representa-

tions, a sense that justifies thinking of the surface form as "derived" from the underlying form.' Phonology – within the Chomskyan paradigm that Bromberger and Halle follow – is a sub-module of a cognitive system and does not deal with 'tokens' but with 'types'. If we were to adopt the same reasoning that these authors follow with respect to syntax and semantics, we would also be driven to the position that these modules (and representations within them) also need to be ordered and (arguably) related by transformations: one might well claim that, since speaking involves converting a proposition into a surface form, semantic representations must be ordered first and progressively transformed into a surface syntactic marker. Since such a position involves a misunderstanding of the goals of Chomskyan generative grammar, it needs to be shown why phonology, as part of a competence system, should be fundamentally different.

A fourth difficulty in adopting Bromberger and Halle's approach is that a belief that phonology is based on transformational rules seriously weakens the claim made here that distinctive features are empirically based and as such part of cycles of 'conjecture and refutation'. Consider, for example, the treatment of vowel height in the SPE tradition. As is well known, only three degrees of vowel height are allowed in SPE: i.e. [+high, −low], [−high, −low], [−high, +low], the fourth combination *[+high, +low] being ruled out for physiological reasons. Now, since at the phonetic level SPE accepts that many features are non-binary, we can assume that the features [high] and [low] will be mapped onto a single scalar feature (since if we take the auditory correlate of this feature to be linked to the inverse relation between F_1 and F_2 we are clearly not dealing with two sub-scales but a single parameter). Let us assume we come across a language which seems to present more than three degrees of vowel height. If so, given that the inventory of distinctive features can potentially characterize many more sounds than the segments to be found in natural languages, there will always be available feature-values lying around which allow us to classify the sounds in question without modifying our initial assumption. At some point in a transformational derivation there will be nothing preventing us from converting a set of features, say, [+AVAILABLE, −high, +low], into [1 high − low]. Much care has been devoted within generative work to justifying hypotheses and perhaps such derivations will be seen as absurd. But the fact is that, as a model of grammar, the transformational approach is simply not restrictive enough.

This last point brings us naturally to the general view that it is

not an accident that generative grammar in its early transformational variant virtually passed away in the 1970s. As noted in
Gazdar (1987: 125):

> That fact is almost certainly causally linked to what has come to be
> known as the Peters–Ritchie result. At the beginning of the decade, in
> a classic series of mathematical papers, Peters and Ritchie (e.g. 1973)
> had shown that 1960s-style transformational grammars were equivalent
> to Turing machines. This meant that the claim that natural languages
> had transformational grammars essentially amounted to the claim that
> they could be characterized mathematically. Beyond this, the claim has
> no content.

There has been some debate as to the precise significance and
interpretation of the Peters–Ritchie result. It may be, as Chomsky
(1980: 122 and note 47, p. 273) suggests, that the work of Peters
and Ritchie does not inevitably lead to the conclusion that within a
linguistically motivated transformational grammar 'anything goes'.
But it is difficult to see how the kinds of SPE-like derivations
defended by Halle and Bromberger can constitute a theory of
phonological structure restrictive enough to stand alongside other
modules of linguistic description which have long abandoned the
types of mechanism which are claimed to be necessary in
phonology.

6 Structural analogy and Level 2 Universality

The preceding Section has argued against the opinion that phonology was intrinsically different from other grammatical modules. If
we look at the way that phonology is structured, the correspondence between phonology and syntax, for example, is rather striking.
Let us consider a few aspects of the 'mirroring' between these two
components of linguistic description.

In both cases, the primitives are not atomic categories such as
'phoneme' (in phonology) or 'noun/verb/etc.,' (in syntax). There is
agreement that such traditional categories need to be split into
smaller components or features. In the wake of Chomsky's *Aspects
of the Theory of Syntax* (1965: 82) and 'Remarks on nominalization'
(1970) there is now a long tradition of work analysing syntactic
categories as sets of primitive syntactic features. Various frameworks (Government and Binding, Generalized Phrase Structure
Grammar, etc.) assume that syntactic representations are built
around the notion of projections from heads (X-bar syntax) and
that these projections are based on primitives of the following type
(Chomsky and Lasnik 1993: section 3.1):

(10)

(a) N = [+N, +V]
(b) V = [+N, +V]
(c) A = [+N, +V]
(d) P = [−N, −V]

If we turn to suprasegmental representations, many accounts of phonological structure have defended the concept of syllable and also argued that, like the sentence, the syllable was a projection from a head into 'phrases' of progressively increasing size. There are many slightly different versions of this idea in syntax and phonology but, essentially, there is a strong correspondence between the splitting of the syllable into two major constituents (onset + rhyme) and the structure of sentences. On the one hand, the syntactic head and its subcategorized complements (the internal arguments), which are somehow together in what used to be referred to as a VP, can be equated with the syllabic and its right-hand side dependents (the rhyme). On the other hand, the subject NP (the external argument) can be put in correspondence with the onset of the syllable (see e.g. Michaels 1992).

In recent work, the correspondence between phonology and syntax has been pushed much further within various frameworks. To make a striking example, Government Phonology has explored a variety of concepts, principles and conditions – e.g. government, the empty category principle, the projection principle, the minimality condition – which are related to fundamental assumptions of the syntactic approach often referred to as Government and Binding (see Kaye this volume and Brockhaus this volume; see also the programme described in Michaels 1992). In this context, the work of John Anderson within Dependency Phonology seems to be exemplary. In a number of publications, Anderson has attempted to defend the Structural Analogy assumption which is spelled out in (11) below.

(11)   *Structural analogy* (Anderson 1986: 85)

Putative structural properties which are unique to a particular plane
are illegitimate, unless they follow from the relationship between that
plane and others; such properties which are unique to a particular level
within a plane are also illegitimate, unless they follow from the
relationship between that level and others.

Again, as part of this assumption, John Anderson tries to demonstrate that, while the atoms of syntax are not the atoms of phonology, the formal nature of these atoms is identical in both cases.

Within Dependency Phonology the basic primitives are unary components which can occur on their own, enter into simple combinations or be related by dependency. Thus, taking the I and the A primitives (also characterized in Harris and Lindsey this volume), we can combine them as in (12) which corresponds to the maximum set of vowel height distinctions:

(12)

/i/	/e/	/ɛ/	/æ/	/a/
{I}	{I; A}	{I : A}	{A; I}	{A}

In (12), which corresponds to a scale of frontness, the two extreme points /i/ and /a/ are characterized by the components I and A alone. In between them, /e/ and /æ/ are mixtures of I and A, which differ as to which component preponderates. The middle point /ɛ/ is one in which the two components are mutually dependent (neither preponderates over the other). In the same way, in syntax, it is argued by Anderson (1989, 1990) that major word classes can be differentiated in terms of combinations of the notional features P (predication) and N (nominality). Some suggested classes are given in (13):

(13)

P	P; N	P: N	N; P	N
finite	non-finite	adjectives	common	names
verbs	verbs		nouns	

with functors corresponding to a null combination. More complex categories (e.g. gerunds) can be obtained by second-order combinations of features. Moving now to the suprasegmental level, representations in syntax, morphology and phonology are assumed to be based on dependency stemmata which are projections from heads (see too Durand 1990a: ch. 8). But what is particularly interesting in Anderson's programme is the explicit effort to demonstrate that many properties which, at first sight, appear to characterize one domain only turn out to be equally applicable to the other components of linguistic description. To limit ourselves to a single example, it has frequently been suggested in phonology that in building suprasegmental representations a stray argument convention was in operation. Consider the dependency representation in Figure 8.2 (Anderson 1986: 88) below.

In Figure 8.2, *i* is successively the head of the rhyme with *d* as dependent, of the syllable with *w* as dependent and of the 'supersyllable' which is formed by attaching the extrametrical -*th* to the syllable. By the same token, we can assume that within syntax,

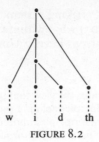

w   i   d   th

FIGURE 8.2

circumstantials are in some sense 'stray arguments' which are 'extra-clausal' as in Figure 8.3 below (Anderson 1986: 88).

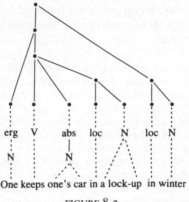

erg   V   abs   loc   N   loc   N

N   N

One keeps one's car in a lock-up in winter

FIGURE 8.3

In Figure 8.3 the verb is successively the head of the VP with the *abs(olute)* and the first *loc(ative)* as dependents, and of the clause with the *erg(ative)* element as dependent. The circumstantial *in winter* which is not part of the subcategorization frame of the verb *keep* is extra-clausal and attached to the preceding clause by a *stray argument convention* which explicitly mirrors the *stray segment convention* of phonology.

In considering such examples it is not essential to agree with the details of each analysis. What is important is the range of evidence supporting the overall claim that the different modules of linguistic description are not accidentally related to one another but share essential properties. This mirroring between syntax and phonology brings us back in a natural way to the derivational question. As was mentioned in the previous section, there is now a growing body of phonological work which explicitly rejects a rule-based approach. One of the most striking statements of such a position is that of Kaye et al. (1985: 305) who, within Government Phonology, state explicitly what I refer to as Level 2 Universality:

(16)   *Level 2 Universality*

> [Our] programme incorporates the view that phonology is to be regarded as a system of universal principles defining the class of human phonological systems. These principles underdetermine given phonologies in certain specific areas. A complete phonological system consists, then, of these principles along with sets of parameter values. Taken together, the principles and language-specific parameter settings give a complete characterisation of the phonological component. In this model, a phonological system contains no rule component.

In derivational terms, the approach advocated by Bromberger and Halle is rejected as too unconstrained. As pointed out by Lindsey and Harris (1990: 362):

> In contrast, the Government approach we adopt here incorporates a radically pared-down theory of phonological activity. Only two types of phonological activity are countenanced: composition, in which material from one segment spreads onto a neighbouring segment, and decomposition, in which material is lost from the internal structure of a segment. When linked to a strictly privative system in which oppositions are uniformly expressed in terms of univalent elements, this impoverished model of phonological processing generates an extremely small set of possible decomposition operations. The number of decomposition processes which a given segment can potentially undergo is logically limited by the number of elements of which it is composed.

Does this mean, however, that no more questions should be asked and that the path ahead is clearly set for all phonologists to follow? John Coleman's Chapter 10 in this volume is a salutary reminder that there are still important issues worth debating. In particular, Coleman argues that despite disclaimers to the contrary, Government Phonology analyses (and, by implication other contemporary analyses which adopt a similar stance) are still transformational. As formulated in writings within Government Phonology, there are derivations which are not merely assemblages of well-formedness constraints. In that respect, the Government Phonology stress on 'phonological processes' would seem to connote a procedural approach to phonology which is not in line with the purely declarative stance that Coleman argues is correct. According to Coleman, operations such as the loss of elements, the delinking of constituents, shortenings-lengthenings, the arbitrary insertion of elements ('ambient' elements postulated in addition to spreading mechanisms) 'conspire to make Government Phonology (as most other contemporary phonological formalisms) equivalent to an unrestricted rewrite system'.

Whether Coleman is fully correct can be debated (see Kaye this volume). First of all, it is probably the case that a number of operations postulated by Government Phonology (e.g. ambient elements) should not be countenanced. Their arbitrariness is at least apparent whereas arbitrary insertions/deletions are the norm in the classical SPE framework. It may also be the case that, under the trigger of universal conditions, the loss of elements between underlying and surface representations given the paucity of available solutions does not lead to the explosion of interpretations that was characteristic of less constrained approaches. It is also likely that the 'process' vocabulary adopted in much Government Phonology writing will progressively be abandoned in favour of a notion of interpretation which does not require us to think in terms of changes between underlying and surface structures. It has to be admitted, though, that as Coleman stresses, no mathematical demonstration of the non-transformational nature of contemporary theories of phonology has yet been offered.

At this point, it is worth noting that the debate is taking us in new directions. What is at issue is no longer whether phonology mirrors other linguistic modules – a point which secures the agreement of Coleman and Kaye, among others – but the nature of linguistic constructs and of the link between linguistic objects (the derivational issue). As is well known, the formal nature of grammars does not receive a single answer from, on the one hand, unification-based approaches (such as Head-driven Phrase Structure Grammar (HPSG), for instance) and, on the other, the Principles and Parameters approach advocated in the new Chomskyan tradition. In many versions the Principles and Parameters approach has countenanced a limited transformational solution to the link between certain linguistic objects – a position strongly rejected by unification-based approaches. It is not the purpose of this chapter to offer a definitive answer to this question. The parallelism between phonology and other linguistic components is strong enough to warrant an adoption of Level 2 Universality. The precise nature of Level 2 Universality in terms of atoms, structures and derivations depends on where one stands on the nature of linguistic theory.

7   Conclusion

In this chapter, it has been argued that phonology is not different from other domains of linguistic structure. Whether it be in terms of atoms, structures or derivations, there are strong arguments (both methodological and empirical) for defending the idea that the various modules making up the language faculty mirror one another in fundamental ways. The precise nature of the mirroring depends on which version of linguistic theory one subscribes to, but, as far as the derivational issue is concerned, a position advocating that phonology should have transformational power in the classical sense seems quite unwarranted.

Acknowledgements

This chapter is the final version of a paper entitled 'Universalism in phonology: is it just fashion?' which I have given in a number of universities (Oxford, Oslo, University College London, Paris VIII, Lancaster). In all these places, I have received useful comments and encouragements. Special thanks go to John Anderson, Jean-Luc Azra, Monik Charette, John Coleman, David Cram, John Harris, Francis Katamba, Jonathan Kaye, Marc Klein, Bernard Laks, Chantal Lyche, for advice and feedback. My colleague, Leo Hickey, saved me from a number of errors and infelicities. All the remaining errors are mine.

Chapter 9

Derivations and interfaces

Jonathan Kaye

Introduction

In this chapter I will discuss the notion of derivation within the framework of *Government Phonology* (GP).[1] I will consider the lexical representation of phonological strings, how they are treated by the phonology, and their relationship to the speech signal. Such considerations inevitably lead us to the study of interfaces. I will present a proposal, first formulated by Jean-Roger Vergnaud and me (Kaye and Vergnaud (1990)), for a phonological-lexical interface. I will then argue that there is no phonological-phonetic interface for the simple reason that there is no linguistically significant level of phonetics as distinct from phonology.

A number of different proposals concerning the nature of phonological derivations will be considered. In particular, there is the mainstream view as found in Bromberger and Halle (1989) (see Durand this volume, Coleman this volume). They argue for language-specific rule ordering as a property of phonological systems. It has also been claimed by proponents of one or another version of *lexical phonology* that phonological processes may apply at different morphological strata. Once again, where a process applies within a stratum with respect to other processes and to what stratum (or strata) a process is assigned, is a language-specific matter. There are also certain claims made by proponents of the notational system or 'framework' known as *constraint-based phonology or declarative phonology*.[2] I will briefly show that these claims are largely irrelevant to our discussion and contain little if any empirical content.

I will be arguing for a reasonably simple view of phonological derivations. My view can be summed up by the minimalist hypothesis formulated in Kaye (1992: 141), 'Processes apply whenever the conditions that trigger them are satisfied.' GP does not allow for *phonological* processes applying at different levels of a derivation. Derivations are assumed to be 'blind' in the sense that no process is aware of the history nor the future of any derivation in which it is involved. The view expressed here is to be distinguished from the Bromberger and Halle (1989: 58–9) position:

> Phonological rules are ordered with respect to one another. A phonological rule R does not apply necessarily to the underlying representation; rather, R applies to the derived representation that results from the application of each applicable rule preceding R in the order of the rules.

While I agree with Bromberger and Halle (hereafter B&H) that a phonological *process* (to use a more neutral term than their *rule*)[3] need not apply to an underlying representation, the sense of the minimalist hypothesis is that no process may be prevented from applying to a string by virtue of its position in a putative ordering relationship.

A view which, at first glance, appears radically different from the B&H position, is that of declarative phonology (see, e.g. Coleman this volume). The position of this group with respect to derivations is expressed by Coleman as follows (p. 335):

> All rules *R* that alter representations in a way that gives rise to derivations, so that applying *R* before some other rule *R'* brings about a different result from applying *R after R'* are to be prohibited. Such a grammar thus attempts to characterise the set of surface forms of utterances directly, not via representation-altering rules from lexical entries which differ from the surface.

In a later Section I will discuss to what extent Coleman's position differs from that of B&H.

To summarise, we have here three positions with respect to phonological derivations:

(a) The B&H position, which allows free interplay amongst the phonological processes.

(b) The Declarative Phonology position, which allows no derivations at all.

(c) The Government Phonology position, which states that processes take place whenever the conditions for their application are satisfied.

It remains to be seen what the empirical and logical consequences are of each view.

1 Derivations in Government Phonology

In this Section I will discuss how phonological derivations work within the theory of Government Phonology. As has been stated above, I am assuming a minimalist hypothesis repeated in (1) below.

(1)

Processes apply whenever the conditions that trigger them are satisfied.

Consider a process whereby the element I° in the nuclear head position is shared by the preceding onset which contains the elements R° and h°.[4] What (2) indicates is that any sequence of onset-

(2)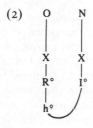

nucleus containing I° as the head of the nucleus must share this element with the preceding onset containing the expression . . . h° • R°. This will be true for lexical forms as it will be for any such configuration encountered in the course of a derivation. My intention here is to give a neutral interpretation to this event. It may be viewed as a static constraint on well-formed lexical items, or it may be considered in a process model usually called spreading. I will discuss this in greater detail in a later section. A phonological derivation takes us from the lexicon, through the phonology and eventually brings us to signal. In order to provide a complete account of derivations within GP I will have to follow this trail. This implies that derivations cannot be discussed without also discussing the phonological interfaces. To begin this discussion, let me present a fundamental claim of GP: the Uniformity Principle.

1.1 The Uniformity Principle

Simply stated the uniformity principle claims that phonological representations are the same type of object at every linguistically significant level. To clarify this point let us consider a theoretical approach that does not respect the uniformity principle: Classical Generative Phonology (CGP). In CGP lexical representation consisted of two-dimensional feature matrices whose cells could be marked with *m*, +, or −; or they could be left unmarked. Before entering the phonology lexical forms underwent a series of marking conventions that replaced the cells containing *m*'s or nothing, with +'s and −'s. Thus, lexical representation differs *in kind* from phonological representation. The former contains *m* or nothing, + or −; the latter is restricted to +'s and −'s. At the end of a phonological derivation, after the last rule has applied, at least some +'s and −'s are converted to scalar values: 1, 2, 3, etc. These scalar values along with some +'s and −'s constitute the form of *phonetic representation*: a set of instructions to the articulatory apparatus for the production of speech sounds.

As we have seen in the preceding paragraph, CGP does not have uniform representations across linguistic levels. To a greater or lesser extent current theories also violate the uniformity principle. The various flavours of 'underspecification' theory are obvious cases in point. At the level of lexical representation and continuing into some arbitrary and language-specific point within the phonology, representations may be 'underspecified', i.e. not directly interpretable. Eventually incompletely specified matrices are 'filled in' by rules and we arrive again at the level of phonetic representation. At this level all representations are fully specified.

The above considerations lead us to the following formulation of the uniformity condition:

(3)   *The Uniformity Condition*

Phonological representations are directly interpretable at every level.

One implication of (3) is that there is no linguistically significant level of phonetic representation. We simply come to the end of a phonological derivation. The kinds of changes that take place in the course of these derivations do not involve any fundamental difference in the type of representation involved. The notion *interpretable* in (3) means mappable to and from signal. Phonological representations are as interpretable at the beginning of a derivation as they are at the end of one.

The view expressed here is completely incompatible with any

notion of 'underspecification'. In fact, nothing corresponding to underspecification is even expressible in GP. This follows from the privative nature of phonological expressions.[5] Phonological expressions are combinations of one or more of a set of elements (including an identity element).[6] These elements are not features; they have no values. They are present in or absent from phonological expressions. Consider the following two expressions:

(4)   (a) I° (= 'i')(b) A⁺ • I° (= 'e')

There is no sense that (4a) is or could be more or less specified than (4b). Both (4a) and (4b) are interpretable as they stand. Nothing is lacking. It makes no sense to say that 'i' is an underspecified 'e'. Both are complete theoretical objects. It does make sense to say that I° is less complex (contains fewer elements) than A⁺ • I°. This property is exploited by the theory. Thus, the privative nature of the representational system of GP precludes any form of underdetermination of phonological expressions. The above discussion should provide a general idea of the force of the uniformity condition.

We see that no fundamental changes occur in the course of a phonological derivation. I will continue the discussion with the issue of phonological constituent structure. The key notion here is the *projection principle* which limits derivational changes relating to constituent structure.

1.2 The Projection Principle

Changes in or indeed creation of constituent (syllable) structure within a phonological derivation is a property of many current theories of phonology.[7] In contrast, GP denies this possibility completely. This injunction against any sort of structural changes is formulated in Kaye et al. (1990: 221) under the heading of the *projection principle.*

(5)   Governing relations are defined at the level of lexical representation and remain constant throughout a phonological derivation.

The projection principle excludes any form of resyllabification. Onsets remain onsets and nuclei remain nuclei. A 'coda' (nonexistent in GP *qua* constituent but may be a synonym for a postnuclear rhymal position) may not change to an onset, or vice versa. Codas are governed and licensed by following onsets.[8] An onset is licensed by a following nucleus. Shifting between onsets and codas clearly violates the projection principle.

There is some latitude in how we are to interpret (5). I do not believe that we can claim that *all* governing relations are defined at the level of lexical representation. I have in mind many instances of phenomena associated with the nuclear projection such as stress, tonal phenomena and harmonic effects. Inter-onset government[9] would be another dubious case of a governing relation being set at the level of lexical representation. The simplest approach might be to understand governing relations as applying at the P_0 projection, i.e. the projection on which all string positions are present. This covers both constituent and transconstituent government. These are the relations involved in questions of syllable structure and resyllabification. Be that as it may, changes of constituent structure, so prominent in other current phonological theories, are excluded from GP.

To sum up, we have seen that GP recognizes no distinct level of phonetic representation. Phonological representations are uniform in kind throughout derivations. Constituent structure does not change in the course of a derivation. Phonological events take place in accordance with the minimalist hypothesis – there are no language-specific 'rule' ordering statements. All these points are at variance with the claims of other modern phonological theories. It might be well to ponder as to how such fundamentally different approaches could emerge. I believe that the principal reasons for these profound differences lie in two areas:

1. the theory of empty categories
2. the phonology-morphology interface.

I will discuss (1) in the following Section. Topic (2) will be the subject matter of Section 2.

1.3 Empty categories and derivations

Much theoretical discussion about phonological derivations involves so-called epenthesis or syncope phenomena. Such phenomena are 'accounted for' by means of arbitrary rules and/or syllable or sonority constraints which are typically language-specific. Discussion of these types of events frequently brings in notions of resyllabification subsequent to the application of such processes. Typical data calling for the invocation of epenthesis or syncope are the following:

(6)

French	amɛn	'brings'	amøne	'to bring'
	apɛl	'calls'	apøle	'to call'
Yawelmani	'a:milhin	'helped'	'amlit	'was helped'
	logiwhin	'pulverize'	logwit	'was pulverized'

Polish	cukier	'sugar'	cukru	'sugar' (gen.sg.)
	koper	'dill'	kopru	'dill' (gen.sg.)
Arabic	kt + b	'he writes'	k + tbu	'they write'
	šr + b	'he drinks'	š + rbu	'they drink'

In GP these data are manifestations of the phonological ECP.[10] The relevant definitions are found below.

(7) *The Phonological ECP*:

A p-licensed (empty) category receives no phonetic interpretation

P-licensing: 1. domain-final (empty) categories are p-licensed (parameterized)
2. properly governed (empty) nuclei are p-licensed
3. a nucleus within an inter-onset domain [11]

Proper government:
α properly governs β if:
1. α and β are adjacent on the relevant projection,
2. α is *not itself* licensed, and
3. no governing domain separates α from β

Consider the first line of French data in (6) above. The following structures are involved. Epenthesis or syncope effects involve the

(8) (a) amène

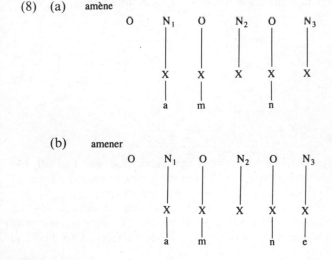

(b) amener

interpretation of N_2 in (8a) and (8b) above. In (8a) N_3 the potential proper governor of N_2 is itself licensed since all domain-final empty nuclei are licensed in French. Since N_2 is not P-licensed it must receive phonetic interpretation according to the ECP. If nothing further is said, this is strictly a case of *interpretation* and does not involve any change in representation. This is to say that

(9)   N

      X

the same object (e.g. (g)), is either interpreted as silence (if it is licensed) or as some phonological expression. This is determined by the Empty Category Principle (ECP). An unlicensed empty nucleus is normally interpreted as [ɨ] which is what the identity element sounds like. An unlicensed empty nucleus is realized as such in Arabic, (European) Portuguese and Korean. What is crucial here, is that in such languages, the representation of (9) does not vary whether or not it is audible. Its interpretation, as stated above, is a matter for the ECP.

In French we do need to add a representational change. The empty nucleus N_2 of (8a) is the head of its domain (it bears primary stress). In French, an empty position cannot serve as a domain head. An empty position acting as domain head receives the phonological expression $A^+ \bullet I^\circ$.[12] This is shown in (10).

(10)   O N_1 O N_2 O N_3

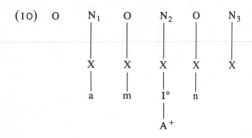

Two things need to be said about this derivation. First of all, the phonological expression $A^+ \bullet I^\circ$ cannot be viewed as some form of 'underspecified' or 'default' vowel. An empty position and one filled by the expression $A^+ \bullet I^\circ$ are two distinct theoretical objects. An empty position will display ECP effects, i.e. alternations with zero. The expression $A^+ \bullet I^\circ$ shows no such effects. This point is illustrated in (11).

(11)   (a)   *Empty position*
              apɛl   'calls'   aple   'to call'

(b) $A^+ \bullet I°$
        sɛl   'saddle'   sɛle [13]   'to saddle'

Second, the presence or absence of an audible nucleus between 'm' and 'n' does not involve any change of constituent structure. If we compare (8a) and (8b) we see that their structures are identical. There is no reason to take the derivation any further. The ECP and the French-specific fact about domain-heads suffices to give the correct interpretation to (8a).

The Yawelmani data in (6) give a further example of how derivations involving rules and rule ordering in standard approaches, require no such treatment in GP. Let us reconsider these data repeated in (12).

(12)

'aːmilhin   'helped'   'amlit   'was helped'
logiwhin   'pulverize'   logwit   'was pulverized'

Notice that the vowel length in the first example is sensitive to licensed status of the following empty nucleus. It remains long when the following empty nucleus is unlicensed hence audible and shortens when followed by a licensed empty nucleus.

(13)   (a) 'aːmilhin

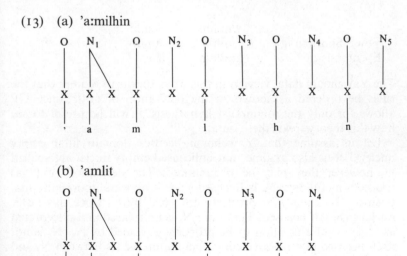

       (b) 'amlit

The comparison of (13a) and (13b) shows the interplay of vowel shortening and the appearance or non-appearance of the following nucleus. The standard account of the Yawelmani data is to posit two rules: one of vowel shortening in closed syllables and the other of epenthesis. The two rules may be expressed as follows:

(14)

  (a) *Epenthesis*
     $\emptyset \rightarrow$ i / C_C{C,#}
  (b) *Vowel shortening*
     v → v̌ / _C$ (where $ is a syllable boundary)

Applying these two rules to the Yawelmani forms yields the following traditional derivations:

(15)

	'a:mlhin	'a:mlit
Epenthesis	'a:milhin	n.a. (= not applicable)
Vowel Shortening	n.a.	'amlit

If we were to reverse the order of application of these two rules, or allow each to apply to the initial representation the results would change for the worse.

(16)

	'a:mlhin	'a:mlit
Vowel Shortening	'amlhin	'amlit
Epenthesis	'amilhin	n.a.

The Yawelmani data, viewed in this way, appear to require that the rules be ordered as shown in the derivation of (15). Since GP allows for only the minimalist hypothesis, it will be useful to see how this theory treats these data.

Let us assume that Yawelmani licenses domain final empty nuclei. Let us also assume that unlicensed empty nuclei are spelled 'i', however they may be pronounced. The derivation of (13a) proceeds as follows: N_5 is licensed since it appears in domain final position. N_4 cannot be properly governed by N_5 since this latter nucleus is itself licensed. Therefore N_4 is unlicensed and interpreted as 'i'. N_3 is in a position to be properly governed by N_4. N_4 is not itself licensed and no governing domain intervenes between N_3 and N_4. Thus, N_3 is P-licensed through proper government. This brings us to N_2, the so-called epenthetic vowel of traditional treatments. N_2's potential proper governor, N_3 is P-licensed via proper government. Thus, N_3 is not a proper governor for N_2 and N_2 remains unlicensed appearing as 'i'.

Before turning to the issue of vowel shortening, let us review the derivation of *a:mlit* whose structure is given in (13b) above. N_4 is domain-final and hence licensed. N_3 lacks a proper governor (N_4 is itself licensed) and is, accordingly unlicensed. Being unlicensed N_3 can serve as a proper governor for N_2. Therefore N_2 is P-licensed and receives no interpretation. These derivations show that no rule of epenthesis is required. The interpretation of N_2, the nucleus in question, is dealt with by a principle of UG: the ECP, along with the parameter settings appropriate to Yawelmani. Let us now turn to the question of vowel length.

Charette (1990) has shown that governors must be licensed in order to govern. She calls this effect 'government-licensing'. In the French word, [rɛstorã] 'restaurant', the nucleus containing 'o' government-licenses the onset 't' to govern the preceding 's'. Properly governed nuclei are not government-licensers in French. Thus, a word like margØritØ 'marguerite' 'daisy' must be pronounced [margərit] are not *[margrit]. The empty nucleus located between the 'g' and the 'r' cannot be properly governed since it is required to government-license the 'g' to govern the preceding 'r'. In French, the conflict between proper government and government-licensing is resolved in favour of government-licensing.

In a recent article Yoshida has proposed that branching nuclei are also subject to government-licensing parameters. In such languages the head of a branching nucleus must be government-licensed to govern the weak member of the constituent. This proposal is schematized in (17) below.

(17)   Government licensing

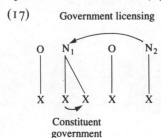

In (17) above, N_2 is the government-licenser. Yoshida states that N_2 cannot be P-licensed and still government-license N_1. The head of the branching nucleus N_1 is unable to govern its weak position. It has not received the license to do so. The weak position cannot receive its phonological content from the head of N_1. It is inaudible and N_1 gives the impression of being a short vowel. One of Yoshida's arguments for this position is that if branching nuclei require government licensing in some languages, then domain-final long vowels should be impossible in precisely those languages. This appears to be the case. Yawelmani has no domain-final long vowels. Contrast this situation with English where branching nuclei occur freely before licensed empty nuclei as in 'keep' or 'teamster' and domain-final branching nuclei occur equally freely as in 'see' or 'day'. Thus, the apparent length of N_1 in (13a) and (13b) is dependent on the status of N_2. N_1 receives a government license from N_2 if N_2 is not P-licensed. If N_2 is P-licensed, then N_1 receives no license to govern its weak position and the vowel is interpreted as short. The situation is schematized in (18).

(18)

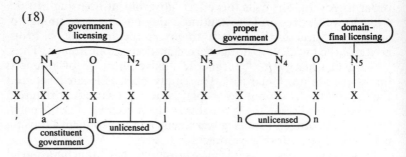

(a) Derivation of 'a:milhin

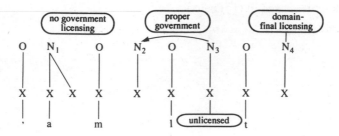

(b) Derivation of 'amlit

The derivations of (18a) and (18b) clearly show the difference in approach between GP and rule-based systems. The phonological ECP takes care of the interpretation of empty nuclei. What we need to know about Yawelmani is that heads of branching nuclei must be government licensed and that unlicensed empty nuclei are spelled out as 'i'. It does not really matter if one considers these devices as processes or conditions of well-formedness of phonological structure. Events take place where they must and the Yawelmani results follow from the principles and parameters approach illustrated here. The above discussion was designed to give a taste of phonological derivations in GP. Nevertheless, the story is incomplete without a discussion of the organization of the lexicon, methods of lexical access, and the interface between the lexicon and the phonology. These matters will be discussed in the following Section.

2 Phonology, morphology and the lexicon[14]

A number of issues need to be addressed when discussing the phonology-morphology interface. To what extent is morphological structure visible to the phonology? How is morphological structure represented in the phonology (if at all)? Are all lexically related forms derived phonologically from the same source? Are phonological events sensitive to morphological structure? I will lead off the discussion with the question of the visibility of morphological structure in the phonology.

2.1 Morphological effects in the phonology
The simplest hypothesis regarding the visibility of morphological information in the phonology, is that there is none. Accepting this hypothesis would entail the prediction that there should be no correlations between phonological representations and morphological structure. This being the case, it is easy to show that this hypothesis is false. To take but two examples, first consider the distribution of the English pseudo-cluster[15] 'mz' as in 'dreams'. Notice that 'dreams' is morphologically complex consisting of a stem plus a suffix. If morphology were totally invisible to the phonology there would be no reason to expect that all such forms are morphologically complex. And yet, this is exactly the case.[16]

In French we find differences between 'son ami' [sɔ̃nami] 'his friend' vs. 'bon ami' [bɔnami] 'good friend'. This same distinction is found in forms with 'non-', 'not, non'.[17] Cf. 'non-attraction' [nɔ̃natraksjɔ̃] 'non-attraction' vs. 'nonobstant' [nɔnɔpstã] 'notwithstanding'. Now many French words that are morphologically simplex contain a sequence of an oral vowel followed by a nasal consonant such as [ɔn] in 'sonate' [sɔnat] 'sonata'. However, forms containing a nasal vowel nasal consonant sequence such as [ɔ̃n] are nearly always morphologically or syntactically complex. These types of correlations, which are quite common, are at odds with the hypothesis that all morphological structure is invisible to the phonology.

We must conclude then that some morphological structure is visible to the phonology. I will now try to define precisely exactly what that structure is and what form it takes in the phonology. I will conclude that morphological structure has two effects on the phonology: little and none. These two interactions are called *analytic* and *non-analytic*.

2.2   Analytic and non-analytic morphology
We have established above that there is some interplay between morphology and phonology. I will argue that this interplay is minimal and is confined to a subset of morphological structures. I will show that some morphology is invisible to the phonology; forms displaying this kind of structure are indistinguishable from morphologically simplex forms. I will begin with morphology that is visible to the phonology.

2.2.1   Analytic morphology
It has been noted above that a form like 'dreams' which displays the 'mz' pseudo-cluster is invariably morphologically complex. A more extreme example is the form 'sixths' with the pseudo-cluster [ksθs]. Why are these bizarre 'clusters' correlated with morphological complexity? What does this tell us about morphological penetration into the phonology? Suppose we assume that only morphological domains can be represented in the phonology. To take the simplest case, a compound like 'blackboard' would have the following structure:

(19)   [[black][board]]

In (19) we see three pairs of brackets. I will use brackets to enclose a phonological domain. The form in (19) has three domains: *black*, *board* and *blackboard*. How are we to interpret these brackets? In fact the brackets are not objects in themselves but rather represent instructions as to how the phonological string is to be processed. To explain what I mean let me define two functions: *concat* which takes two arguments which are strings and returns the string which results from concatening the second argument to the first. For example, concat('abc','def') = 'abcdef'. The second function is φ. This function has one argument, a phonological string, and returns the application of the phonology to its argument, also a phonological string.[18] The expression $\varphi(X)$ means, 'apply phonology to the string X'. $\varphi(X)$ returns the phonological string which results from the application of phonology to its argument.

We now have the necessary tools to give an exact definition to (19) above. This is shown in (20).

(20) $\varphi(concat(\varphi(black),\varphi(board)))$

In plain language (20) means, 'apply phonology to "black" and to "board"; concatenate the results to form a string and apply phonology to that string'. The brackets that are found in the representation of (19) are not part of phonological representation. There are no 'boundaries'. The brackets delimit phonological domains which are arguments to functions like *concat* and φ.

The presence of a stress bearing nucleus (among other things) is symptomatic of domainhood. This is due to the Licensing Principle given below.

(21)   *The Licensing Principle*

All positions in a phonological domain must be licensed save one: the head of the domain.

Metrical structure can be viewed as a form of licensing at the level of nuclear projection. The one unlicensed position of a domain will receive the main stress of that domain. In addition to (21), domains impact on the phonology by virtue of the fact that domain-final empty nuclei are licensed in a number of languages including English. Thus, each domain of *blackboard* will end in a licensed (hence inaudible) empty nucleus.

(22)

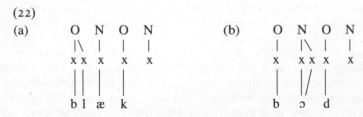

The domains of both (22a) and (22b) end with an empty nucleus. Both of the empty nuclei are licensed and hence the nuclei following the 'k' and the 'd' of *blackboard* are inaudible.

The above illustrates one type of structure involving morphologically complex forms. Given two morphemes, A and B, we can incorporate them into a structure of the form [[A][B]]. This was the case for *blackboard* as it is for most English compounds. This does not, however, exhaust the possibilities. There is a second type of structure involving two morphemes but which only involves two, and not three, domains. This structure is [[A]B]. It involves the domains A and AB but not B. The interpretation of this structure is given in (22, 23).

(23) $\varphi(\text{concat}(\varphi(A),B))$

What (22, 23) means is, 'do phonology on A and concatenate the result with B; then do phonology on the result of the concatenation'. This kind of structure occurs in the bulk of English regular inflexional morphology. It is also associated with many derivational suffixes such as '-ness' ('darkness') and '-ment' ('enlargement'). Consider the regular past tense of an English verb like 'seep', viz. 'seeped'. Its structure is [[seep]ed]. The details are given in (24).

(24)

Once again, an empty nucleus is found at the end of each of the two domains. They will both be licensed for the reasons discussed above. Notice that the first syllable is open and not closed. It has an onset followed by an empty nucleus as required by *coda licensing*.[19] In such circumstances there is no reason not to expect a branching nucleus in this situation and indeed the length of the stem vowel is constant. The English champion of this type of morphology is probably *sixths* which has the structure [[[sɪks Ø]θ Ø]s Ø]. Each of the domain-final empty nuclei are licensed being domain-final. Although the constituent structure of a form like *sixths* looks impressive, it is rather pedestrian containing only the rhymal-onset sequence *ks*. Analytic morphology has an interesting property in English. The distribution of empty nuclei is very restricted in English (in contrast with languages like (European) Portuguese, Polish, Arabic or French). It is found almost exclusively at the ends of domains and rarely elsewhere.[20] Thus, detection of empty nuclei presents us with a fairly reliable parsing cue. A form like *dreams* gives us two indications that the 'mz' sequence is a spurious one (i.e. the consonants are separated by an empty nucleus): first, the vowel length is maintained which would be impossible if 'mz' were a true transconstituent cluster, and second, there is a lack of homorganicity between 'm' and 'z'. This is impossible for true clusters. Hence much of analytic morphology is phonologically parsable.

Up to this point we have looked at structure of the form:

1. [[A][B]]
2. [[A]B]

for two morphemes, A and B. The question arises as to whether the third possible structure, viz. [A[B]] is attested as well. In fact this type of structure does not appear to be attested. Analytic prefixes such as English 'un-' show the type of structure in (i). Consider a form like *unclip*.

(25)

The empty nucleus N_2 is licensed by virtue of its domain-final position. The first nucleus of *clip* could not be its proper governor because of the intervening governing domain: the branching onset *cl*. This excludes the structure in (26) as a possible source for *unclip*.

(26)

In (26) there are only two domains: *clip* and *unclip*. *un* does not constitute a domain in itself. Since N_2 is not domain-final in (26), it can only be licensed by a following proper governor. This is not possible for the reasons stated above. Thus, (26) cannot be the structure of *unclip*. We conclude that for two morpheme combinations, analytic morphology provides only the possibilities shown in (1) and (2) above. The pair, *superman* and *postman*, provide a clear contrast in Southern British English. Note the stress and the assigned structures.

(27) superman [[súper][màn]] postman [[póst]măn]

The *man* in *superman* is a domain and accordingly is stressed. In contrast the *man* in *postman* is not a domain and thus remains unstressed.

Finally, let us return to the form *seeped*. Its structure is given in (28) below.

(28)

The past tense suffix *-ed* does not form a domain by itself. There is still another reason to affirm this. The suffix consists of two positions: an onset position and a nuclear position. Both positions are licensed. The onset position is licensed by its following nucleus and the nuclear position is (p-)licensed by virtue of its domain final position.[21] If *-ed* were a domain, this would be in violation of the licensing principle which states that a phonological domain must have one unlicensed position, viz. its head.

In this Section we have seen the sort of morphology that impacts on the phonology in the form of domains. I have illustrated two modes of combining two morphemes, A and B in an analytic fashion:

(29) (a) [[A][B][[A][B]]
      (b) [[A] B]
      (c) *[A[B]]

(29a) and (29b) are commonly found but (29c) is not attested. As a final point let us consider Prunet's analysis of French *son ami* vs. *bon ami*. The facts follow directly if we assume that *son* and *ami* occupy separate domains in the former example but are only found in the same domain in the latter. Prunet (1986) follows an idea of Vergnaud's (1980) concerning French liaison consonants. He assumes that they are floating. Thus, *son* and *bon* will have the structures given in (30) below.

(30)

(a) <u>son</u>   O N   (b) <u>bon</u>   O N
                      | | | |
                      x x   x x
                      | | | |
                      s o n   b o n

The structures in question are shown in (31).

(31)

(a) <u>son ami</u>

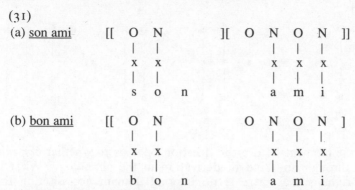

(b) <u>bon ami</u>

Crucially *son ami* contains internal domains while *bon ami* does not.[22] Taking the derivation of *son ami* we must apply the phonology to the internal domain (30a). The floating *n* has no available onset to which it can associate. Therefore it must associate to the preceding nucleus as shown below.

(32)

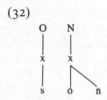

When phonology is done on the external domain, an empty onset is available for the *n*. However, the principle of *strict cyclicity*[23] states that the association created in the inner domain cannot be undone in an external domain. The association remains and the *n* also links to the available onset as shown below.

(33)

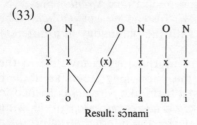

Result: sõnami

Let us turn now to the derivation of *bon ami* whose structure is shown in (34a) below. There are no internal domains so there is no point at which an available onset is not accessible to the floating *n*. Therefore, the *n* never attaches to the preceding nucleus as we see below.

(34)

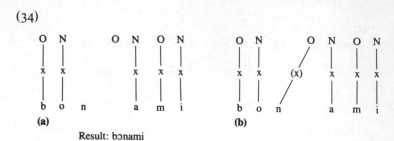

(a)

Result: bɔnami

(b)

For the moment I leave the question open as to whether *bon ami* goes through any kind of derivation in the phonology. What is important is that there is no internal domain necessitating the association of the floating *n* to the preceding nucleus. Let us leave analytic morphology for the moment and turn our attention to the second type of morphological interaction with the phonology: non-analytic morphology.

2.2.2 Non-analytic Morphology

In the previous Section we saw that morphology could have an impact on the phonology to the extent that morphological structure was present in the form of domains. These domains have the effect of respecting the integrity of the internal domains. Consider an analytic verbal suffix like -*ing* in English. Its stricture is of the form [[V]ing] where *V* is a verb stem. To pronounce such a form one simply pronounces the stem on its own and appends the suffix. The pronunciation of *V* on its own and *V* in the structure [[V]ing] are pretty much identical. This is what I mean about 'preserving the integrity' of the internal domains. This procedure does not apply in all forms of morphology. Consider two derivations of the word *parent*: *parenthood* and *parental*. The former does respect the integrity of the internal domains. The pronunciation: *párĕnt* is preserved in *párĕnthòod* but not in **párĕntăl*. Instead we get *păréntăl*. The morphology of -*al* is interacting with the phonology in a different way than that of -*hood*.

I will claim that the -*al* type of morphology is invisible to the phonology. That is to say that the phonology reacts as if there were no morphology at all. Thus, a form like *parental* is treated in exactly the same way as a form like *agenda* or *advantage*. Following our earlier model, we can characterize the internal structure of a form like *parental* as follows:

(35)   [A B]

Morphology which does not carry domains to the phonology will be referred to as *non-analytic morphology*. Since the only effect that morphology can have on the phonology is the presence of internal domains and since non-analytic morphology has no internal domains, it follows that non-analytic morphology should be invisible to the phonology. This is indeed the case. To sharpen the analytic–non-analytic distinction, let us compare two negative suffixes in English: *un-* which is analytic, and *in-*, which is not.

These prefixes have rather different properties. For one thing *un-* is completely insensitive to what consonant follows it. Indeed it can be followed by any onset expression of English. In particular, it can be followed by *r* or *l* as in *unreal* or *unlawful*. This property follows from its analytic morphology. Since the prefix final *n* is not adjacent to the following onset, there is no reason to expect any phonotactic restrictions on what follows it.

(36)   [[ʌn ∅   ][riːl ∅   ]]

As we see in (36) above, the *n* and the following *r* are not adjacent. They are separated by an empty nucleus. This is consistent with *un*'s status as an analytic prefix. In fact, *nl* and *nr* are not possible true sequences (sequences not separated by an empty nucleus). A nasal cannot be the head of a branching onset because of its neutral charm and *nl* and *nr* are not transconstituent sequences because both *l* and *r* are less complex than *n* and therefore cannot govern it – a requirement for a transconstituent sequence. Given the distribution of empty nuclei in English, sequences like *n ∅ l* and *n ∅ r* are phonologically parsable. Thus, the analytic forms *unreal* and *unlawful* are immediately analysable as *un-real* and *un-lawful*.

The situation is quite different with respect to the non-analytic prefix *in-*. There are no internal domains so appending *in-* to a stem must yield a well-formed phonological domain. Using the notational system described above, a non-analytic combination of two morphemes is interpreted as follows:

(37)   φ(concat(A,B))

That is, concatenate the two strings, A and B, and perform phonology on the result. Consider the formation of *irrational*. Concatenation of the strings *in* and *rational* yields *inrational*. But *inrational* is not a well-formed string for the reason stated above. The cluster *nr* is not possible in any language. Accordingly, the *n* is dropped from the string and we have *irrational*, which is a possible domain. The same applies to the formation of *illogical* from *in* and *logical*: *nl* is impossible and once again the *n* is dropped to form the word.

To recapitulate, non-analytic morphology is completely invisible to the phonology. It contains no internal domains nor any other phonological indication that it is a morphologically complex form. Non-analytic forms are not phonologically parsable. They have exactly the same phonological properties as any simplex form. I will assume that any form manifesting non-analytic morphology is listed in the lexicon. The discussion of a form like *irrational* does not reflect a phonological derivation but rather a strategy for the formation of a lexical representation. To drive home this point it will be interesting to consider the difference between regular and irregular English verbal inflectional morphology.

2.3   Regular and irregular morphology

We have stated above that English regular verbal inflectional morphology is analytic in nature. A past tense form like *seeped* shows this clearly. Notice that the vowel length is maintained before the pseudo-cluster 'pt' indicating that these two segments are never adjacent. The form is phonologically parsable as [[*seep*]*ed*]. Consider what makes this form parsable: *pt* is a possible transconstituent cluster in English (cf. *inept*, *apt*, *adopt* and so forth). Thus, it is the fact that there is a long vowel before *pt* that reveals its status as a pseudo-cluster. The *p* must be in the onset since the binarity theorem excludes a branching nucleus within a branching rhyme.

Let us now consider an irregular past tense form similar to *seep*, viz. *keep*. The past tense form is *kept*. What is striking about this form, is that its very irregularity involves its vowel length. As we have just seen, the vowel length of regular verbs is crucial for their parsability. The form *kept* could be a simplex English word just like *apt* or *adopt*. Thus, this irregular past tense form is not phonologically parsable. There is no phonological hint of its complex morphological structure. Let us follow this line with some other irregular verbs. Compare the regular verb *grieve* with irregular *weave* and *leave*. The regular past tense *grieved* is parsable for two reasons: first, the vowel length requires that *v* be in an onset position. This onset is followed by a licensed empty nucleus. The only p-licensing condition that could be met in this case is the domain final one. Second, the pseudo-sequence *vd* is not a possible transconstituent sequence. No morphologically simplex forms in English contain this pseudo-sequence. Thus, both the vowel length and the pseudo-sequence *vd* are parsing cues yielding the analysis [[gri:v Ø]d Ø]. Now consider the two irregular verbs, *weave* and *leave*. If we are right about the irregular strategy being to render irregular forms unparsable, then both these cues must be dealt with somehow. We can make the following prediction about the ultimate lexical representations of irregular forms: they will not contain a detectable pseudo-sequence,[24] and a long vowel will not be followed by a pseudo-sequence. In the case of *weave* the vowel length is maintained. Therefore the pseudo-cluster must go. There is a random vowel change and the resulting form is *wove*. The strategy has been followed: *wove* is indistinguishable from a simplex form like *clove* or *stove*. Notice that since non-analytic forms are listed in the lexicon, there is no particular reason to keep any trace of past tense morphology. This is the case for *wove*.

An alternative strategy is possible, to wit create a true cluster and shorten the preceding vowel. This will have the effect of masking the morphological complexity of the form and making it appear like a normal, simplex English word. But *vd* is not a possible true cluster. The closest sequence to *vd* that is, is *ft* (cf. *soft*, *rift*, etc.). This strategy is used to form the past tense of *leave*. Given the strategy just described, the predicted outcome for this verb should be *l*ft*, where '*' represents some randomly selected short vowel. In fact we get *left* confirming our prediction.

One final example which does not involve a branching nucleus will be instructive here. Consider the verb *wing* (as in 'She winged her way home'). The regular past tense is phonologically parsable because the pseudo-cluster *ŋd* involves a non-homorganic sequence of nasal plus stop. True sequences of nasal plus stop are always homorganic. Thus, *winged* could only be analysed as [[wing Ø]d Ø] with the two domain-final empty nuclei being licensed. If we take an irregular verb like *sing*, vowel length is not an issue but the resulting final pseudo-sequence is. Accordingly, we expect no remnant of past tense morphology in the past tense form. In fact only a random vowel change takes place and the lexical representation is *sang*, a possible simplex form along the lines of *bang* or *fang*.

Summing up these observations we come to the following conclusion:

(38) 'Irregular' morphology is always non-analytic.

What this means is that irregular morphology always hides its own morphological complexity.[25] The difference between morphologically regular forms like *seeped* and morphologically irregular forms like *kept* is that the former is phonologically parsable, i.e. identifiable on inspection as morphologically complex, while the latter is not. Its morphology has been rendered completely invisible. Why should this be so? Suppose that there are two ways of dealing with morphologically complex forms: (a) computation and (b) lookup. In the first case a phonological parse is done yielding, say, *seep* and *-ed*. The meaning of *seeped* is then computed on the basis of these components resulting in something like 'past governs seep'.

In the latter case, *kept*, the user is invited to simply look up the form, the way she would deal with *boy* or *go*. The relevant information concerning the morphological structure will be found in the lexical entry for *kept*. The form is 'precomputed' as it were, and the results are stored in the lexicon. This model has important implications for the nature of phonological derivations. Note that *keep* and *kept* are distinct lexical entries. As such they do not necessarily share a common phonological representation. It has been commonly assumed that *kept* is derived from a form that shares the same stem as *keep*; something like *keep + t*. The vowel must be shortened before two final consonants *pt*. The shortening rule will bleed the rule of 'vowel shift' which converts long ε: to i:. Notice that ordering vowel shortening before vowel shift is crucial in order to block the derivation of **kipt*.

In our model there is no direct phonological relationship between *keep* and *kept*.[26] The latter form is a well-formed English word exactly like *adopt* or *apt*. Since non-analytic morphology involves separate lexical items much of the argumentation used to support extrinsic rule ordering or level ordering as in lexical phonology, simply vanishes. Alternations like vowel shift, velar softening (as in *electric-electricity*), trisyllabic laxing (as in *opaque-opacity*) are simply not reflections of phonological events. This is all to the good since GP is incapable of expressing any of these processes. Phonological events involve fusion or fission of phonological elements. It further requires that there be a non-arbitrary association between an event and the context in which the event occurs. In fact, GP predicts that the so-called rules cited above could not occur in the phonology. This prediction is rich in empirical content – it need not be true. Consider the analytic verbal suffix *-ing*.[27] We are obliged to claim that neither velar softening nor trisyllabic laxing could be triggered by *-ing*. This is correct: *back-backing*, **back-bassing*; *teeter-teetering*, **teeter-tittering*.

With respect to English verbal inflectional morphology we have the following picture: the regular morphology is analytic while the irregular morphology is non-analytic. I have suggested that the strategy of masking the morphological structure of irregular forms constitutes an invitation to look up rather than to compute the ultimate meaning. Since verbal irregularity is an arbitrary lexical property,[28] it follows that which past tense forms are analytic and which are not is also an arbitrary lexical property. Indeed, if we look at compounds whose second member is *metre* we see the amount of variation that can exist.

(39)

Compounds in *metre*

	Analytic		Non-analytic
millimetre	[[millĭ][mètrĕ]]	thermometer	[thĕrmómĕtĕr]
kilometre	[[kilŏ][mètrĕ]]	kilometre	[kĭlómĕtrĕ]
altimeter	[[áltĭ][mètĕr]] (British)	altimeter	[àltímĕtĕr] (American)

As we can see from the data in (39) some *metre* compounds are analytic, some are non-analytic. Sometimes this division spans the English-speaking world (*millimetre* vs. *thermometer*); sometimes it varies with the individual (*kilometre*); and sometimes it is subject to dialect variation (*altimeter*). Although the analytic–non-analytic distinction is largely lexically arbitrary, it is correlated with compositionality. Consider the former English compound *cupboard*. Today its meaning is far removed from 'a board for cups'. We find that its former analytic morphology, [[cup][board]] has been lost. Phonologically *cupboard* behaves like an ordinary word with no internal structure (cf. *mustard, custard*). The pseudo-cluster *pb* has been eliminated as has the compound type stress *cúpbòard*, in favour of *cúpbŏard*.

In French[29] *mon oncle* [mɔ̃nɔ̃kl] displays its internal domains. Its meaning is compositional: *mon* 'my', *oncle* 'uncle', *mon oncle* 'my uncle'. In Quebec French the historical possessive pronoun *mon* has been absorbed into the word for 'uncle' itself. So 'uncle' is *mononcle* and 'my uncle' is *mon mononcle*; 'your uncle' is *ton mononcle*, and so on. It is not surprising that Quebec French *mononcle* has lost its internal domains. It is no longer phonologically parsable and appears as [mɔnɔ̃kl] and not *[mɔ̃nɔ̃kl]. There is no invitation to parse Quebec French *mononcle* as [[mon][oncle]].

One of the most important results of the model proposed here is that *morphologically related forms which resemble each other phonologically are not necessarily derived from a common source*. The pair *electric–electricity* is not prima facie evidence for the existence of a process of velar softening. The pair *opaque–opacity* does not, in itself, offer evidence for vowel shift or trisyllabic laxing. In providing evidence for a theory of phonological derivations, it is crucial to take into account the assumptions that are made about the phonology-morphology interface. It is equally important to know which portions of the available phonological data are to be derived from a common source and accordingly, provide information on the phonological events involved in their derivation.

Let us take a final look at some derivations that crucially involve the analytic–non-analytic distinction. These derivations are from Polish and revolve around the analysis of Polish *yer* (i.e. the Polish empty nucleus). Polish yers behave in exactly the same way as Yawelmani empty nuclei discussed above. If yers are p-licensed in Polish, they are inaudible. If the yers are not p-licensed they surface as ε (spelled 'e' in Polish orthography). Nothing further need be said about the basic facts. Derivations involving yers respect the minimalist hypothesis. No rule ordering nor complex interactions between the morphology and the phonology are required.

In contrast, Rubach (1984a) gives a rule-based account that appears to require both rule ordering and distinctive types or rule application (cyclic vs. postcyclic). Both these devices are at variance with the minimalist hypothesis. Let us compare these two approaches and see how their different initial assumptions give very different views of derivations.[30]

Rubach suggests that yers are underlying lax high vowels. He posits two of them: one which is [− back] and causes palatalization and the other, which is [+ back] and does not. There are also two rules involved in the derivations. A cyclic rule of lowering which converts both yers to ε and rule of yer deletion that removes all unlowered yers. This rule applies post-cyclically. The rules are given in (40).

(40)

Lower (cyclic)
$[+ \text{syll}, + \text{high}, - \text{tense}] \rightarrow [- \text{high}]/\_\_\_\_C_0[+ \text{syll}, + \text{high}, - \text{tense}]$
Yer Deletion (postcyclic)
$[+ \text{syll}, + \text{high}, - \text{tense}] \rightarrow \emptyset$

The rule of Lower converts a yer to ε when the following vowel is another yer. The rule of Yer Deletion then removes all unlowered yers. Sample derivations follow in (41).

(41)

	pi☺s☺	pi☺sa 'dog (nom.sg., gen.sg)'
lower	pies☺	n/a
yer deletion	pies	psa

	pi☺s☺cz☺k☺	'dog (double diminutive)'
lower	pieseczek☺	
yer deletion	pieseczek	

In (41) the symbol '☺' represents a yer. In the nominative singular *pies* Rubach must stipulate that this form takes a nominative singular suffix which contains a yer. The stem yer is lowered before the suffix yer. The suffix yer, not being followed by another yer is not lowered. It must be deleted and *pies* is derived. The genitive singular suffix is -*a*, not a yer. Therefore, the stem yer is not lowered and must be deleted by the rule of yer lowering. This yields *psa*. Rubach does not wish the lowering rule to apply to non-derived forms (note that this move is impossible if we respect the minimality hypothesis). The rule is stipulated as being cyclic and thus does not apply to non-derived forms.

In the derivation of the double diminutive of 'dog', we have a sequence of four consecutive yers. The rule Lower will lower all but the final one, which in turn will be removed by the Yer Deletion rule. This yields *pieseczek*. I have already stated that this analysis violates the minimalist hypothesis, not to mention the projection principle.[31] It is interesting to note that by assuming that the Polish yers are empty nuclei we can derive all the Polish forms without any recourse to rule ordering or stipulations about cyclic/post-cyclic rule application. The minimalist hypothesis remains: events occur when their conditions are satisfied.

Let us consider how these Polish forms are derived in GP. We use the same mechanisms discussed above in the Yawelmani example. The phonological ECP is applied to the structures below. All we need to know is that Polish unlicensed empty nuclei are realized as ε and domain-final empty nuclei are licensed in Polish.

(42)

(a)
```
    O   N₂   O   N₁
    |   |    |   |
    x   x    x   x
    |        |
    p        s
```

(b)
```
    O   N₂   O   N₁
    |   |    |   |
    x   x    x   x
    |        |   |
    p        s   a
```

In the nominative form (42a) the domain-final nucleus, N_1 is licensed. As such it cannot serve as a proper governor for N_2. This latter nucleus is unlicensed and accordingly is realized as ε as per the Polish parameter settings.[32] In (42b) the domain-final nucleus is non-empty. In fact it is -*a* the genitive singular suffix. It is unlicensed and can p-license the preceding empty nucleus N_2. The diminutive form of 'dog' presents an interesting problem. Note the pairs of forms below.

(43)

(a) pies – psa   'dog: nom.sg./gen.sg.'
(b) pies – piesek   'dog: nom.sg./dim.'

In (43a) the stem yer is licensed by the genitive singular suffix. In
(43b) the stem yer is not licensed by the initial nucleus of the
diminutive suffix. This vowel is itself a yer as we shall see anon.
Nevertheless, it is unlicensed and therefore a potential proper
governor for the stem yer. What is going on? In reality (43a,b)
simply illustrate the analytic–non-analytic division. The genitive
suffix -*a* is non-analytic whereas the diminutive suffix -Øk Ø
is analytic.[33] The derivation of *piesek* is now straightforward.
The structure of *piesek* is [[p Øs Ø] Øk Ø]. Following the model de
scribed above, we must perform phonology on the internal domain
[p Øs Ø].

(44)

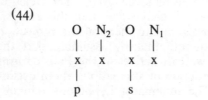

N_1 is licensed being domain-final. N_2 has no proper governor and
remains unlicensed. The unlicensed N_2 is realized as ε.

(45)

```
O  N₂  O  N₁
|  |   |  |
x  x   x  x
|  |   |
p  ε   s
```

The structure in (45) is now concatenated with the diminutive
suffix and phonology is performed again.

(46)

```
O  N₂  O  N₁  O  N₄  O  N₃
|  |   |  |      |   |  |
x  x   x  x      x   x  x
|  |   |             |
p  ε   s             k
```

Note that the domain-final licensed empty nucleus is now immediately followed by an empty onset and then by a following nucleus.
The structure in question is shown below.

(47)

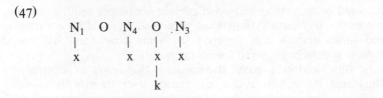

In a phonological string an empty nuclear position can never be immediately followed by another nuclear position (empty or filled). In such cases the first nuclear position is removed from the structure along with the following onset. This is not a special fact about Polish but rather a universal constraint on phonological strings. It is the one case where the skeletal content of a string may be changed. This constraint is seen to operate in familiar cases such as French definite article behaviour, $l\emptyset$ *ami* is realized as *lami*. The structure (46) has now become (48).

(48)

$$
\begin{array}{cccccc}
O & N_2 & O & N_4 & O & N_3 \\
| & | & | & | & | & | \\
x & x & x & x & x & x \\
| & | & | & & | & \\
p & \varepsilon & s & & k &
\end{array}
$$

Phonology now applies to the result of concatenation. N_3 is licensed being domain final. N_4 is not followed by a proper governor (N_3 being licensed cannot do the job) and so remains unlicensed and we derive *piesek*. Note that although N_4 is now a possible proper governor, N_2 is not empty and does not fall under the ECP.

Deriving the double diminutive follows along exactly these lines. The structure is $[[[p s \emptyset] \emptyset k \emptyset] \emptyset k \emptyset]$. Using the methods discussed above, we successively derive *pies*, *piesek* and finally, *pieseczek*.[34] Thus, the difference in behaviour of the genitive singular suffix and the diminutive suffix is directly attributable to the difference in their analytic–non-analytic status. We have no need of Rubach's cyclic and post-cyclic rules. We adhere strictly to the minimalist hypothesis. Obviously, it is possible to present fragments of data that superficially appear to require something less restrictive than the model proposed here. The point I have been trying to make, with the help of the Polish data, is that it is difficult to evaluate fragmentary data because of the crucial role of the analytic–non-analytic distinction. A fairly rich array of data have already been successfully understood using this model without recourse to such devices as rule ordering or complex interactions with the morphology.

It would be surprising indeed if certain languages require a richer expressive framework than that presented here. If rule ordering and other devices are required for some languages, we would expect them to be required for all languages.

In this Section I have shown how the types of derivations illustrated in Section 1 can be carried over to morphologically complex cases. We have seen that the morphology interacts with the phonology in two ways: its domains are visible to the phonology – analytic morphology, or its domains are invisible to the phonology – non-analytic morphology. With this division we can still maintain the minimalist hypothesis of phonological derivations: events occur when their conditions are satisfied. In the following Section I will compare this view with two competing views.

3   Other approaches to phonological derivations

In the preceding Sections I have illustrated the notion of derivation within GP. The key aspect of these derivations is that they respect the minimalist hypothesis. There is no need to say anything more about phonological events than that they occur. There are no ordering statements. Certain events are not labelled as being restricted to a certain level of phonological structure. Events have no notion of the history of a derivation nor of its future outcome. If an event's conditions are satisfied, it takes place; if they are not, it does not. The minimalist hypothesis is bolstered by a theory of the phonology-morphology interface. Non-analytic morphology is invisible to the phonology. It involves separate listings in the psychological lexicon. Forms related by non-analytic morphology do not necessarily share common stems. They are proximate in the psychological lexicon but they do not have a common source. They are subject to lexically arbitrary, random alternations such as *write-wrote, ring-rang-rung, bring-brought*, etc.

This position is at variance with both the Bromberger and Halle (1989) (B&H) position and that of Declarative or Constraint-Based Phonology. In this Section I will argue that the GP view of phonological derivations is the most empirically adequate of this group. I will begin with a discussion of some of the arguments presented by B&H to support their view that phonological systems must include language-specific rule ordering statements.

3.1   Mainstream phonology: the B&H position
B&H's (1989) arguments presuppose a number of theory-internal assumptions. They are presented without justification and may be

assumed to constitute the central dogma of mainstream phonology. Some of these assumptions are listed below.

(49)

 (a) 'The phonological surface representation must encode how a word is pronounced.' (p. 53)

 (b) '... the representations required for the articulation of different words are given in the form of stipulations of discrete sound segments concatenated in the order in which they must be produced' (p. 53f.)

 (c) '... speech sounds are composite entities constituted by complexes of binary phonetic features.' (p. 54)[35]

 (d) '... speakers represent words in their memory by means of a code that is directly related to ways of producing linguistic sounds and that words are stored in memory as sequences of items in such a code.' (p. 56)

 (e) '... the symbols in memory stand in a direct relation to the production of sounds.' (p. 56)

 (f) 'Not all of the information required for producing a word phonetically is needed by speakers for storing the word in memory and for retrieving it when the occasion arises, because a significant fraction of that information is predictable through general rules and principles that govern the pronunciation of English.' (p. 56)

 (g) '... memory storage and search time are at a premium in the case of language' (p. 56)

These assumptions are presented without supporting arguments. If one accepts them, it is reasonable that one will arrive at the same conclusions as B&H concerning the nature of phonological derivations. It is important to note, however, that none of them are *a priori* truths. Any or all of them could be wrong. I happen to believe that all the assumptions of (49) are incorrect. It is not surprising then, that I arrive at different conclusions concerning phonological derivations. The claim that the phonetic representation of a form is a set of instructions as to how it is pronounced may seem to be a truism, not requiring justification. I remain unconvinced. Consider the tune of a song that we know. Is it stored as a series of instructions to the vocal folds requiring them to tense or lax to such and such a degree? This seems to be far from the most obvious hypothesis. Be that as it may, it is not my intention to enter into speculations on the form of word or song storage. I only wish to suggest that B&H's assumptions presented in (49) above are not *a priori* true. Since they are unaccompanied by any form ot argumentation I feel justified in dismissing them. I will concentrate on the more substantive arguments presented in B&H.

B&H offer the interaction of rules for syllabification and rules for stress assignment in English to support their view that rules must be applied in a definite order. Since English stress assignment depends crucially on syllable structure it follows that stress rules must apply after rules of syllabification. There are a number of things that can be said about this example. Strictly speaking, it is not incompatible with the minimalist hypothesis. Any rule assigning stress that is sensitive to syllable structure will not apply to forms which contain no specifications for this structure. That the rule of stress follows the rule of syllabification follows from the fact that the former rule refers to the output of the latter, but not vice versa. This example is instructive on other grounds. B&H argue for a rule of syllabification of the basis of two claims both of which I believe to be false: (i) 'the syllable structure of an English word ... is totally predictable from the sounds that compose the word' (p. 57) and (ii) 'both syllable structure and stress are predictable: therefore they do not appear in the underlying representation' (p. 57).

B&H offer no support for these two claims. They are far from obvious. Consider the English words *beat* and *bit*. We may say that they consist of the sounds, 'b', 'i', and 't'. Since both words contain the same sounds, if B&H are correct they must have the same syllable structure, since the latter is 'totally predictable' from the former. Yet *beat* contains a branching nucleus while *bit* does not. It could be argued that the vowel of *beat* is tense while that of *bit* is lax. Therefore they do not contain the same 'sounds' and so their syllable structure need not be the same. But the tenseness of these vowels is equally predictable; the tense vowel occurs in branching nuclei while the lax one occurs in non-branching nuclei. B&H's claim (ii) states that if something is predictable it does not appear in underlying representation. Therefore *beat* and *bit* do have the same sounds, and so on. It is clear that B&H need to make a choice: is the tenseness a function of syllable structure? or is syllable structure a function of tenseness? B&H offer us no insights on this issue.

Indeed things get worse if we take claim (i) beyond English. Consider French *watt* 'watt' and *oiseau* 'bird'. Their initial portion is pronounced identically, [wa]. If claim (a) is applied to French then their initial portion ought to have the same syllable structure. It does not, cf. *le watt* vs. *l'oiseau* and *les watts* vs. *les oiseaux*. Consider also Italian pairs such as *fato* 'fate' vs. *fatto* 'fact'. Both contain the sounds 'f', 'a', 't', and 'o'. The first syllable of *fato* is open, while that of *fatto* is closed. Such examples could be easily multiplied. Is it B&H's position that syllable structure is present in underlying representations in some languages but not in others? At best their claim is controversial and cannot be accepted in the absence of compelling arguments.

B&H's second claim is that anything which is predictable is not contained in the underlying (lexical) representation of a form. Once again this claim is not a truism: it could be false. In fact claim (b) can be viewed as the modern version of the phonemic principle which seeks to eliminate predictable/'redundant' aspects of initial phonological representations. Phonological 'contrast' was and is a crucial component of this type of view. This view is certainly the traditional one and one adhered to by a large number of practising phonologists. However, it is a view that could be erroneous and hence requires some form of justification. This is to say that other views are also possible. For example, Vergnaud and I (Kaye and Vergnaud 1990) have expressed the view that phonological representations do not form part of lexical representations as such but are rather the addressing system for lexical access. A phonological representation is the address of a lexical entry.[36] Lexical items that are phonologically similar are physically proximate in the psychological lexicon. What does 'phonologically similar' mean? We suggest that nuclear constituents play a very different role in lexical access from non-nuclear constituents. Non-nuclear constituents play a major role in lexical access while nuclei play a very minor role. The consonantal melody may be viewed as a major factor in locating a lexical form. Constituent (syllable) structure also plays a major role in this process. *Quality* and *equality* share a consonantal melody but are not involved in a lexical relationship. If constituent structure is part of a lexical addressing system then clearly it must be present in lexical representation. This view, which I have sketched in a very cursory fashion, would need considerable justification. But this is equally true of B&H's claim (b). My point is that claim (b) cannot be accepted on the face of it. In the absence of justification it cannot be used as support for the view of phonological derivations that B&H wish us to accept.

In fact, the best possible case to support B&H's view of language-specific rule ordering would be a case of two identical rules found in two languages or two dialects of one language. In dialect A the rules would apply in a given order and in dialect B they would apply in the reverse order. Indeed, B&H provide just such an example: the case of Canadian English. It is important to note that this example is the one piece of empirical evidence supplied by B&H to support their view of derivations. The state of affairs described by them (pp. 58-9) is completely incompatible

with the minimalist hypothesis and the view of derivations that I
have presented in the preceding Sections. GP must predict that
examples such as that of Canadian English cannot exist. This is
part of the empirical content of the theory.

Briefly, the Canadian English example goes like this: a rule turns
an intervocalic stop [t] or [d] into a voiced flapped stop.[37] A second
rule raises the nuclei [ay] and [aw] to [ʌy] and [ʌw] before a
voiceless consonant. B&H show that in most Canadian dialects the
derivation proceeds as follows:

(50)

	r[ay]t	r[ay]d	r[ay]ting	r[ay]ding
raising	r[ʌy]t	r[ay]d	r[ʌy]ting	r[ay]ding
flapping	r[ʌy]t	r[ay]d	r[ʌyD]ing	r[ayD]ing

B&H claim that there are Canadian dialects in which the rules
apply in the opposite order as shown below.

(51)

	r[ay]t	r[ay]d	r[ay]ting	r[ay]ding
flapping	r[ʌy]t	r[ay]d	r[ayD]ing	r[ayD]ing
raising	r[ʌy]t	r[ay]d	r[ayD]ing	r[ayD]ing

The following quotation (B&H, p. 59) accompanies this example.[38]

> It is worth noting that Principle (7) was not needed to account for the
> order in which the rules of syllabification and stress assignment are
> applied in English. That ordering did not need to be explicitly stipulated.
> It could be achieved by the simple proviso that a rule applies whenever
> conditions for its application are satisfied. Principle (7) is needed if
> conditions for the application of more than one rule are satisfied
> simultaneously. The order of application then – as the Canadian example
> ˜hows – becomes a language-specific matter.

The theoretical stakes are clearly stated in this quotation. The
existence of dialectal 'minimal pairs' such as the Canadian English
example described above, are certainly indicative of the correctness
of B&H's position on phonological derivations. The absence of
these sorts of examples swings the pendulum in favour of 'the
simple proviso' which corresponds to the minimalist hypothesis
discussed in this article. It is important to note that the Canadian
English example is the sole piece of empirical synchronic evidence
advanced by B&H to support their position. In fact the data are
false. There are no two dialects of Canadian English now and it is
highly unlikely that the dialect exemplified in (51) ever existed.[39]

We must conclude, then, that B&H have presented no synchronic evidence to support their Principle (7). They do have another section where they claim to have diachronic evidence to support their position.

The structure of B&H's diachronic evidence for rule ordering is very simple. They make the assumption that sound changes enter the grammar as phonological rules. They show that the order in which these rules are applied in the resulting grammar is significant. Therefore, we must assume the 'psychological reality of ordered rules' (p. 61). They offer no evidence for their claim that all sound changes enter grammar as phonological rules. This is simply an assumption. There is no apparent reason why it must be true.

Their example involves the sound change known as Grimm's Law. They note that it is 'surely one of the most securely established of all "sound laws"' (p. 61). This is not to say that it is one of the most securely established phonological rules of some stage of Proto-Germanic. Grimm's law converts: p → f, t → θ, k → x except after an obstruent.⁴⁰ So, all cases of earlier 'p' are converted into Proto-Germanic 'f'. But is this a phonological rule? Will a Germanic child hearing 'foːt' analyse this form as /poːt/ in lexical representation and apply Grimm's Law *qua* phonological rule to derive the Germanic form? B&H do not explain why the Germanic child would not simply set up 'fot' as the lexical representation. There are no Germanic alternations involving p ~ f.⁴¹ It could be argued that the Germanic system would have an 'f' but no 'p' and for this reason the child would be led to posit an underlying 'p'. Notice that Arabic has exactly this type of situation: 'f's are realized but there is no Arabic 'p'. To my knowledge no one has proposed deriving Arabic *foq* 'on top of' from /poq/. Perhaps there are arguments that indicate that Grimm's Law was indeed incorporated into the synchronic grammar of Germanic as a phonological rule. B&H offer none. Indeed, they do not even mention the possibility that Grimm's Law is simply a change in lexical representations. Since B&H present no evidence that Grimm's Law was incorporated into Germanic as a phonological rule, none of their ensuing discussion is relevant to the issue of the nature of phonological derivations. Principle (7) remains without empirical support, neither synchronic nor diachronic.

The phonological literature abounds with examples purporting to show the necessity of language-specific rule ordering. By and large the authors of these examples accept without question or evidence B&H's assumptions in (49). In addition, little attention is paid to the analytic–non-analytic morphological division. We have seen above that this division is essential for an understanding of how morphology interacts with the phonology. Standard scientific practice dictates that we accept that simplest hypothesis that enjoys reasonable empirical success. Those wishing to argue for an expressively richer system must show that the simpler model is in principle incapable of treating a significant set of well-understood analyses. These analyses, of course, must be based on assumptions that are justified and justifiable. B&H do not meet these standards and I am unaware of cases in the phonological literature that do. Principle (7) remains an unjustifiable complication to phonological theory.

In this Subsection I have criticized an approach that allows for greater expressive freedom than the minimalist hypothesis adopted by GP. GP is subject to the criticism that it itself is too unrestricted and that it even approaches mainstream phonology in its (potential) expressive power. I will discuss and evaluate these claims in the following Subsection.

3.2 Declarative or Constraint-based Phonology

Phonology is an empirical science. That is to say, phonology is designed to make statements about the material world. Phonological theories may be evaluated on the basis of the empirical content of their claims. To the extent that the claims of a given theory coincide with experimental results, this theory may be deemed to be successful. Such empirical success may be positive: what the theory says may occur does indeed occur, or negative: what the theory says may not occur is not attested.

In like manner a theory may be criticized for being too constrained: it cannot, *in principle*, express events that are known to occur. Likewise, a theory may be criticized for being too unconstrained: unattested events are expressible within the formalism in question. Coleman's contribution to this volume (Chapter 10) contains a number of criticisms of the latter sort directed towards GP. Coleman's conclusion is that 'Government Phonology is therefore as unconstrained as the models it seeks to replace (see p. 344). This is a serious charge and it is surely worth investigating the evidence on which it is based. If GP is too unconstrained then one would expect a list of phonological phenomena permitted by GP that can be shown to be impossible or, at least unlikely, components of a phonological system. For example, a binary feature system containing twenty features allows for 2^{20} or 1,048,576 segments. This number can be reduced if certain feature values cannot co-occur. For example, if the features [HIGH] and [LOW] are members of the feature list and no matrix can contain the values [+ HIGH, + LOW], then we can reduce the number of segments by one-quarter to 786,432.

In a GP theory of phonological representations where 10 elements are assumed, H and L do not cooccur in a phonological expression and ATR, H and L cannot be heads, 2,304 phonological expressions can be generated. This number is still too high and recent work in GP has sought to reduce the number of expressions by reducing the number of elements.[42] It is clear that the GP representational scheme is more constrained than the feature based system described above.

These are the kinds of arguments that one would expect from Coleman to support his claims concerning the relative restrictiveness of the theories he considers. No such arguments are forthcoming. Indeed Coleman attempts to reduce GP's unary element-based system to a binary feature system. Unfortunately, Coleman's portrayal of element theory is quite inaccurate. Among other things, he equates 'charm', a property of elements, with an SPE-type feature. Charm and elements are different theoretical types as defined in GP. Coleman is of course free to define any theory he wishes, but his version of GP bears little resemblance to anything that has been proposed. Coleman's discussion contains no reference to the identity element of GP (the 'cold vowel' of early formulations). It is unclear how this would be translated into his feature theory. Similarly, the head-operator distinction is difficult to reproduce in a feature-based framework. There are phenomena involving 'head alignment' where expressions become empty headed when preceded or followed by other empty headed expressions. Once more, Coleman offers no suggestion as to how a feature-based system would express these events.

In fact, these differences between feature theory and element theory could have constituted the basis for a substantive discussion of differing theoretical claims. GP countenances head alignment while feature theory (apparently) does not. Coleman's feature-based system (see p. 357) allows for the expression of [-NASAL] as a linguistically significant class of objects; GP recognizes no such class. Sadly, Coleman does not appear to address such issues.

Much of Coleman's discussion is concerned with the weak generative power of GP. His conclusion is that GP's formal properties 'constitute a rewrite-rule formalism with a weak generative capacity at least equal to the SPE formalism,' (see p. 344). Coleman provides no examples of the nefarious effects of this purported excessive generative power. He makes much of the alleged derivational nature of GP although it is not clear what exactly would change if some of the procedural language in some GP formulations were replaced by declarative ones. Coleman lists a number of 'structural configurations and constraints' but appears unaware of any restraining properties they may have on the expressive power of a phonological theory. This is surely a crucial issue when one is discussing theoretical restrictedness. Two of the 'structural configurations and constraints' mentioned by Coleman, are the phonological ECP and Coda Licensing. Let me try to show how these constraints make strong empirical claims about the nature of phonological events.

In earlier sections I discussed Polish yers and the ECP in some detail. Rule-based systems such as Rubach's require rules (or their declarative counterparts) as in (40) repeated below.

(52)
Lower (cyclic)
$[+ \text{syll}, + \text{high}, - \text{tense}] \rightarrow [- \text{high}]/\underline{\quad} C_0 [+ \text{syll}, + \text{high}, - \text{tense}]$
Yer Deletion (postcyclic)
$[+ \text{syll}, + \text{high}, - \text{tense}) \rightarrow \emptyset$

The Lower rule converts a yer to [ɛ] when followed by another yer. Yer Deletion removes all unlowered yers. Now consider the Polish alternations *pies* 'dog nom.sg.'; *psa* 'gen.sg.' and *dno* 'bottom nom.sg.'; *den* 'gen.pl.' Rubach's analysis requires that the forms in question be represented as: p☺s☺ – p☺sa; d☺no – d☺n☺, respectively. Since yer is a vowel and since Rubach's theory is not constrained by a principle like Coda Licensing, he is required to stipulate that one of the forms of the nominative singular and the genitive plural is a yer. This means that it is a *contingent* fact that these suffixes behave the way they do. Notice that it just so happens that the nominative singular and genitive plural are all and only the apparently empty suffixes in nominal paradigms. For Rubach this must be an accident. His theory predicts the possibility of some truly empty suffix that does not contain a yer. In such a case we would have p☺s yielding *ps* alongside of p☺s☺ which yields *pies*. This, of course, does not happen. The Phonological ECP and Coda Licensing combine to make the Polish facts *necessary* rather than *contingent*. Coda licensing excludes p☺s as a possible form. It requires p☺s☺. Since yers are really empty categories the ECP will then provide the correct interpretation of these representations. The only contingent aspect of the analysis is how Polish realizes unlicensed empty nuclei.

It seems to me that these are the types of issues that one needs to consider in evaluating theoretical restrictiveness. They are conspicuously lacking in Coleman's discussion. Since I am concerned principally with derivations here, it would be worth comparing Coleman's view of rule-ordering effects with that of GP. I discussed the Canadian English example cited by B&H as evidence for language-specific rule ordering. I noted that GP could not accommodate the data cited by B&H. That is, if the Canadian English facts stand as

correct, there is a serious flaw in the underlying principle of GP. It
was this concern that led me to investigate the status of these 'data'
and conclude that they are flawed. Since Coleman's contention is
that GP is much less constrained than non-derivational models, it
would be interesting to see if his approach has any difficulty
'accounting for' the spurious Canadian English data. The relevant
'data' given above in (50) and (51) are repeated below for convenience of reference.

(53)

	r[ay]t	r[ay]d	r[ay]ting	r[ay]ding
raising	r[ʌy]t	r[ay]d	r[ʌy]ting	r[ay]ding
flapping	r[ʌy]t	r[ay]d	r[ʌyD]ing	r[ayD]ing

(54)

	r[ay]t	r[ay]d	r[ay]ting	r[ay]ding
flapping	r[ʌy]t	r[ay]d	r[ayD]ing	r[ayD]ing
raising	r[ʌy]t	r[ay]d	r[ayD]ing	r[ayD]ing

(53) and (54) are given with their rule-based derivations. Traditionally, (53) is called 'Dialect A', and (54), 'Dialect B'. Coleman (see
pp. 362–3) unfortunately reverses the usual nomenclature and calls
(53) 'Dialect B' and (54), 'Dialect A'. I will simply refer to them by
their example numbers for clarity. In speaking of (54) Coleman
states, 'it is claimed, there is a rule ("flapping") which transforms
intervocalic /t/ and /d/ into [ɾ] [our "D"/JK]. Thus, both "writing"
and "riding" are pronounced [rayɾiŋ].' Coleman then concludes
(see pp. 362–3), 'Firstly, since in dialect A [sic] raising is not
manifested, there is no evidence at all that the rule even exists in
the grammars of speakers of this dialect.'

A cursory inspection of the first two columns of (53) and (54)
shows that Coleman's conclusion is far from apparent. It is difficult
to speak with assurance about a dialect which never existed but
Joos' original claim was that the behaviour of speakers of the two
dialects converged in all cases where /t/ did not undergo 'flapping'.
So the mythical speakers of (54) did distinguish 'right' r[ʌy]t from
'ride' r[ay]d. Furthermore the 'manifestation' of raising was completely general when the voiceless consonant following the diphthong was not /t/. Thus, 'type' = [tʌyp], 'typing' = [tʌypiŋ],
'bribe' = br[ay]b and 'bribing' = [braybiŋ]. These forms are all
valid for Central Canadian English and would be valid for (54) if
that dialect existed. Thus, we must conclude that Coleman's conclusion is false or his phrase 'raising is not manifested' has an unusual
interpretation.

Coleman's difficulty with phonological data aside, it is apparent that his theory of derivations is not constrained in any real sense. That is, it makes no empirical claims about the material world. This impression is reinforced as one reads further into Coleman's work. Our old SPE friends 'Tri-syllabic shortening', 'Velar softening', '-ic- shortening', etc. all find a home in Coleman's non-derivational theory. Alternations, the likes of which have not been seen since Lightner's time reappear: *'drink* vs. *drench, church* vs. *kirk, bridge* vs. *brig'* (see p. 376). All these alternations are grist for Coleman's non-derivational mill. In sum, calling a theory 'truly restrictive' does not make it so. If one searches Coleman for specific empirical claims about what may or may not be a phonological event, one searches in vain.

Coleman may have some inkling of the situation when he states, 'Accepting that my proposals in this area may be less than convincing than my criticisms, however, I should point out from the start that the criticisms do not stand or fall by the success or failure of my attempt to propose an alternative' (see p. 336). I fully agree that GP, like any other serious theory, could be significantly improved. I hope that I would be the first to applaud such an improvement by Coleman or anyone else. It is my conviction, however, that Coleman's criticisms are hard to accept since they offer no indications as to how any phonological theory could be improved. Indeed, Declarative Lexical Phonology – as far as one can ascertain from Coleman's contribution to this volume – does not appear to offer any fundamentally new insights into the nature of phonological phenomena. Coleman states that 'It is a matter of speculation and belief as to whether these principles [of GP/JK] combine to define the phonology of even a single language' (see p. 344). There is no need for speculation. GP is not a complete theory. There remains work to be done. There exists no definition of even a single language. This is hardly surprising nor a peculiar property of GP. I am unaware of any definition of even a single language in any theoretical framework. Work in Government Phonology will continue. There are a wide range of interesting and unresolved problems that await treatment. I remain confident that our knowledge of phonological phenomena will increase. I hope this Chapter is a step in this direction.

Notes

1. For discussions of this theoretical approach see Kaye et al. (1985, 1990), Charette (1991), Kaye (1990a) and the references therein.
2. See, for example, Coleman (this volume).

3. In fact I would prefer the term *event* rather than rule or process. The use of this term here would make the comparison of positions somewhat more awkward to express. I use *process* but attach no theoretical importance to it.
4. I am assuming familiarity with the theory of elements used in GP. The reader is referred to the article by Harris and Lindsey in this volume for further information.
5. See Harris and Lindsey (this volume) for details of GP representations.
6. See Charette and Kaye (in preparation) for a revised version of element theory. The original version is found in Kaye et al. (1985).
7. For a particularly spectacular example of 'resyllabification' see Mohanan (1989).
8. See Kaye (1990a), KLV (1990), Brockhaus (this volume) for discussion.
9. See Cyran (1992), Gibb (1992), Heo (in preparation) for examples of this phenomenon in Irish, Finnish and Korean, respectively.
10. See Charette (1991), Kaye (1990b), Gussmann and Kaye (1992) among others for discussion of the phonological ECP.
11. By 'inter-onset domain' I have the following structure in mind. The nucleus sandwiched between the onsets is p-licensed.

12. This process may well take place in the lexicon as part of the generative process of word formation. I will return to this point in Section 2.
13. *Le Petit Robert* offers **sɛle** rather than **sɛle** as the pronunciation of the infinitive. Many French speakers use the pronunciation presented here. There is general agreement on **sɛl** as the pronunciation of 'selle'.
14. The following Section presents work done jointly with Jean-Roger Verngaud. An oral version of this theory was presented in Kaye and Vergnaud (1990). I follow the basic tenets of that presentation although I may differ somewhat from it in detail. Nothing momentous hangs on these differences.
15. That is, a sequence of onsets with an intervening licensed empty nucleus.

16. Aside from some proper names such as 'Sims', etc.
17. See Prunet (1986: 148ff.) for details.

18. Strictly speaking φ is not a function but a family of functions. A function should return a unique result but given that some phonological processes are optional, the application of φ does not always return a unique result. It is therefore not a function in the mathematical sense. Rather it represents a family of functions φ', φ'', φ''', etc. where each φ represents a unique solution.

19. See Kaye (1990a).

20. In fact, empty nuclei are found between flanking onsets that may contract a governing relation where the first onset could govern the second. Empty nuclei occur in forms like, *bæt Øl* 'battle', *kæt Øn* 'cotton', *æt Øləs* 'atlas', etc. See Heo (in preparation) for similar effects in Korean.

21. The domain in question is *seeped* and not *-ed*.

22. See Prunet (1986) for arguments.

23. I mean *strict cyclicity* in its original sense as proposed by Chomsky (1973) and applied to phonology by Kean (1974). It has subsequently been used in a very different sense, for example, in lexical phonology.

24. A detectable pseudo-sequence is one that could not be analysed as a rhymal consonant followed by an onset. *vd* is a detectable pseudo-sequence; *ft* is not a detectable pseudo-sequence (cf. *bluffed* and *soft*). Note that any sequence following a branching nucleus is a detectable pseudo-sequence. The binarity theorem requires such a form to be analysed as $v{:}C_1 \: ØC_2$.

25. In fact, (38) is not 100 per cent true. There are analytic past tense forms like *sold*, *told* and *dreamt*. Interestingly, all these forms correspond to words with no obvious internal morphological structure. Alongside of *sold* and *told*, we have *old* and *gold*; *dreamt* is phonologically similar to *unkempt* and has a frequent regular past tense, *dreamed*. See Harris (1990c) for discussion of the *sold-told* type cases.

26. The fact that *keep* and *kept* have a certain phonological resemblance does not mean that they are derived from a common source; *write* and *wrote* also resemble each other and yet one rarely claims that they are derived from the same stem. In the Kaye–Vergnaud model of lexical access, there is a reason for these forms to be similar. We claim that phonological representations are *addresses* for lexical items (or perhaps addresses for pointers to lexical items). We assume that phonologically similar forms are physically proximate in the psychological lexicon. With these assumptions it is possible to develop a model whereby it is advantageous for morphologically related forms like *keep-kept* to be phonologically similar. It should be kept in mind that this similarity is *not* based on derivations from a common stem.

27. We know this suffix is analytic because of the behaviour of the velar nasal, ŋ. Within a domain, English ŋ can never be followed by anything other than a velar stop: *k* or *g* if the following nucleus is not p-licensed. Cf. *fiŋger* (which has no internal domains) vs. *siŋger*, which does ([[sing Ø]er Ø]). We know that *-ing* is analytic because of *siŋgin* and not * *siŋgiŋ*

28. Not entirely arbitrary, of course. If we assume that look-up is more efficient, in some sense than computing and if we assume that morphological irregularity does have some overhead, e.g. learning the forms, then it follows that we would expect the morphologically irregular forms to be relatively frequent to exploit their greater computational efficiency.

29. This example is taken from Prunet (1986).

30. This discussion is taken from Gussmann and Kaye (1992). See that article for more detailed discussion of the Polish facts and analysis.

31. This analysis can be criticised on a number of other grounds. See Gussmann and Kaye (1992) for discussion.

32. In fact the nominative singular form of 'dog' is *pies* and not *pes*. The analysis of Polish palatalization appears in Gussmann and Kaye (in preparation).

33. Polish also has a non-analytic diminutive suffix, *-ik*, as in *tomik* 'little volume'. See Gussmann and Kaye (1992) for a discussion of these two suffixes.

34. The realization of *k* as *cz* (= č) does not concern us here. See Gussmann and Kaye (in preparation) for discussion.

35. This may represent a departure from the SPE position (Chomsky and Halle (1968)). 'The distinction between the phonological and phonetic matrices must be kept clearly in mind. In the case of the phonetic matrix, each row corresponds to a phonetic feature, physically defined, from a predetermined initial set. The entry occupying a particular square of the matrix will be *an integer specifying the degree to which the segment in question is characterized by the corresponding property.*' [emphasis mine/JK] Chomsky and Halle (1968: 165). Thus, phonetic features are not considered binary in SPE.

36. Or perhaps, the address of a pointer to that entry.

37. I make no claims for the accuracy of B&H's description. Indeed, it is inaccurate. See Chambers (1973) for details. It will be seen that their description faces more important problems than just accuracy.

38. The principle (7) referred to in the quotation below is the one quoted on page 1 above. It states,

> Phonological rules are ordered with respect to one another. A phonological rule R does not apply necessarily to the underlying representation; rather, R applies to the derived representation that results from the application of each applicable rule preceding R in the order of the rules.

39. Arguments against the existence of the two Canadian English dialects are found in Kaye (1990). The dialect whose data are found in (51) is based on a single report in 1942. Doubt as to its existence is based on the fact that all speakers of this dialect would have died out before the age of 60.

40. B&H express this as an arbitrary fact. In GP terms, Grimm's Law does not take place when the segment in question is a governor of an

obstruent. See Harris and Kaye (1990) for discussion of a similar case in Modern English.
41. Proto-Germanic 'p' did not occur following an obstruent.
42. This is the objective of Charette and Kaye, in preparation.

Chapter 10

Declarative lexical phonology

John Coleman

1 Constraining phonological theory

The many generative phonological theories which have arisen in
the wake of *The Sound Pattern of English* (SPE) (Chomsky and
Halle 1968), several of which are discussed in the other chapters to
this volume, share three fundamental assumptions:

First, each attempts to allow only the phonologies of natural
human languages to be defined. In other words, there are some
languages, which linguists call unnatural or impossible human
languages, which the theories aim to exclude. The inclusion of a
particular phonology among the set of natural human phonologies
is characterized by the use of constraints of one kind or another, a
phonological rule being a common way of expressing such
constraints.

Second, each posits the existence of lexical representations of
words which are distinct from their surface form. The surface
forms of words are related to their lexical encoding by certain
alterations to phonological representations: insertion, deletion, or
substitution of individual features or entire segments.

Third, the phonological rules which define these operations may
be cascaded, that is, applied in a particular sequence one after the
other, possibly more than once, as exemplified in Table 10.1. Such
cascading of rules gives rise to the notion of the *derivation* or
derivational history of the surface form of an utterance from the
lexical forms of the words in the utterance.

These three characteristics of generative phonology are the historical remains of a theory of grammar that has been largely super-
seded, the 'Standard' or 'Aspects' theory. Its pretensions to psycholinguistic plausibility have been questioned and found wanting.

TABLE 10.1:   Ordering of rules after Halle and Mohanan (1985).

MORPHOPHONOLOGICAL RULES

Stratum 1:	*Examples:*
Stress rules	
CiV Lengthening (57)	Caucăsus ⇒ Caucāsian
s-Voicing (111)	Malthu/s/ ⇒ Malthu[z]ian
Shortening rules (56)	(56a) Trisyllabic shortening: divīne ⇒ divĭnity
and (110)	(56b) Cluster shortening: crucifȳ ⇒ crucifixion
	(56c) -ic shortening: cōne ⇒ cŏnic
	(110) i-Shortening: revīse ⇒ revīsion
Stratum 2:	
Velar Softening (64)	electri/k/ ⇒ electri[s]ity
	analo/g/ue ⇒ analo[ǰ]y
Nasal assimilation (11)	/ng/ ⇒ [ŋ]
Prenasal g-deletion	si/g/n(ature) ⇒ [sain]
(106a)	
n-Deletion (106b)	hym/n/(al) ⇒ [him]
Noncoronal deletion	bom/b/(ard) ⇒ bo[m], long/ŋg/(est) ⇒ lo[ŋ]
(106c)	
Vowel shift (61)	div/i/n(ity) ⇒ div[ai]ne, ser/e/n(ity) ⇒
	ser[i:]ine, s/a/n(ity) ⇒ s[ei]ne
⋮	⋮

ALLOPHONIC RULES

Diphthongization (62)	ser/i:/ne ⇒ ser[iy]ne
Vowel Reduction	the/æ/tr(ical) ⇒ the[ə]tre
Vowel Tensing	Nonfinal Tensing: th/ɪ/atre ⇒ th[i]atre
(dialects A, B) (74)	Stem-final Tensing: happ/ɪ/(ly) ⇒
	happ[ī], caf/ɛ/ ⇒ caf[ē]
	hind/ʊ/ ⇒ hind[ū], Mexic/o/ ⇒ Mexic[ō]

Stratum 3	
Vowel Tensing	cit/ɪ/(hall) ⇒ cit[i]
(dialect C) (2)	
Stem-final lengthening	cit/ī] ⇒ cit[iy]
(9)	

Stratum 4	
l-Resyllabification (21)	[σsea/l/]σ ⇒ sea[σlo]σffice

Postlexical stratum	
ɔ-Unrounding (GA) (43)	verb/ɔ/sity ⇒ verb[a]sity
⋮	⋮
l-Velarization (19)	be/l/ ⇒ be[ɫ]

⇒ SYSTEMATIC PHONETIC REPRESENTATIONS

Its self-declared aim to provide a learnable, workable mechanism for relating one end of a derivation to the other has been investigated by mathematicians and found not to have been met. Working phonologists, perhaps sometimes unaware of the undercurrents of change in other areas of generative grammar, have independently found it necessary to introduce significant changes to the original transformational theory of generative phonology. The notation of generative phonology has changed, certainly. Notions such as syllable and foot are now explicitly incorporated in the grammar. Various special principles, such as Strict Cyclicity, the Obligatory Contour Principle (OCP), the No Crossing Condition, and others, have been proposed to restrict the class of languages defined by generative phonological theories, so that that class more closely approximates the class of observed human languages.

But these changes do not achieve their goal. They are merely superficial adjustments to the underlying transformational mechanism. The new phonological theories may *look* more natural, but they still allow both natural and unnatural languages to be defined. In short, as I shall demonstrate in more detail below, phonological theories are still far too unconstrained. A new, bolder strategy is required to define a more restricted class of grammars than hitherto.

Inspired by the success of non-transformational, non-derivational syntactic theories (such as Lexical-Functional Grammar and Generalized Phrase Structure Grammar) in challenging, matching and improving on transformational, derivational syntactic theory, a number of phonologists (including myself) are examining the applicability of *non-derivational* grammar formalisms to the phonological domain. The strategy offered by non-derivational phonology to the problem of excessive power is to drop the notion of derivation from the characterization of the surface form of words. All rules R that alter representations in a way that gives rise to derivations, so that applying R before some other rule R' brings about a different result from applying R *after* R', are to be prohibited. Such a grammar attempts to characterize the set of surface forms of utterances directly, not via representation-altering rules from lexical entries which differ from the surface.

In a pre-emptive defence of derivational phonology, Bromberger and Halle (1989) argue that derivational analyses are unavoidable in phonology if undue complexity is to be avoided, and generalizations and parsimony retained. I shall examine below many of the examples which they propose in support of derivational analysis, and show that non-derivational accounts of the same set of phenomena are possible and, given that they can be expressed using a more constrained grammar formalism, to be preferred. I examine a number of other potential problems for non-derivational, phonological formalisms, and show that all of these phenomena may be given elegant and explanatory analyses in a non-derivational phonological formalism.

In a series of papers, Kaye, Lowenstamm, Vergnaud and others have proposed a 'principle-based', 'rule-free' yet still derivational phonological theory, Government Phonology. Government Phonologists argue that phonological theories which use general constraints and principles of derivation are more restrictive and constrained than theories which employ orthodox, context-sensitive rewrite rules of the form $A \rightarrow B/C\_\_D$ of the sort employed in the SPE phonological formalism. Because Government Phonology rightly recognizes the problem of excessive power, and seeks to overcome it, I examine this framework in detail. However, contrary to the claims of Government Phonologists, I shall show that all the arbitrary derivational operations which can be expressed using rewrite rules in SPE phonology are also available in Government Phonology. I shall argue that although such principle-based theories are indeed constrained (by stipulation), it has not been demonstrated that such constraints reduce the class of languages which can be described. I shall show that some possible constraints do so, and others do not. It is therefore incumbent on proponents of principle-based theories to *prove*, rather than assert, that their theories are more restrictive than SPE.

Since I aim to be both constructive as well as critical, I shall conclude by outlining a linguistic formalism which may offer phonologists who desire a truly restrictive, principle-based theory a formally sounder basis than the derivational approach. Accepting that my proposals in this area may be less convincing than my criticisms, however, I should point out from the start that the criticisms do not stand or fall by the success or failure of my attempt to propose an alternative.

True transformational rules are quite rare in phonological theory, but context-sensitive rewrite rules are commonplace. If it can be shown that they are unnecessary, however, they should be dropped, so that the rule component of phonological theory is constrained as much as possible. In this chapter, I shall argue that it is possible to apply the techniques of Unification-based Grammars to phonological theory, and thereby do without transformational or context-sensitive rewriting rules – in fact, without any rules at all, in the traditional sense.

2 The excessive power of transformational phonology

Although it is widely accepted that SPE phonology is too unconstrained, the precise nature of this excessive power is not widely understood. Although the failure of SPE to provide insightful accounts of such phenomena as tonal stability, rhythmic alternation of syllable prominence and compensatory lengthening can be appreciated at a practical level, the deeper formal problems with SPE are generally unappreciated. In addition, it seems not to be generally recognized that the new formal devices proposed in Autosegmental and Metrical phonology, while rectifying some of the empirically based problems of SPE phonology, do little or nothing to address the formal problems of excessive power, since the new theories retain the transformational and derivational resources of SPE phonology. It is wise to begin, then, with a brief review of the concept of formal restrictiveness in generative grammar.

In 'Syntactic Structures' (Chomsky 1957) and other writings of that period, Chomsky established that not all sets of strings ('formal languages') are equally complex. Some types of grammar ('more restrictive') define *proper subsets* of some other types of grammar ('less restrictive'), because the rules allowed in the more restrictive types of grammar were a sub-type of the rules of the less restrictive types. He expressed this result in the form of a hierarchy of languages and grammar types which has come to be known as The Chomsky Hierarchy, illustrated in Table 10.2. (V_T is the set of terminal symbols, e.g. surface segments, V_N is the set of non-terminal symbols, e.g. prosodic constituent categories and lexical segments, X^+ denotes one or more occurrences of X, X^* denotes zero or more occurrences of X, and $|X|$ denotes the length of string X. For further explanation of the Chomsky hierarchy, consult, e.g. Partee et al. 1990: 451–2 and 562–3.)

TABLE 10.2: The Chomsky Hierarchy of grammars. Rule formats of equivalent weak generative capacity are assigned to the same Type.

Type	Conditions on Rules	Name
0	$A \rightarrow B, A \in (V_T \cup V_N)^+, B \in (V_T \cup V_N)^*$	Unrestricted
1	$A \rightarrow B, |A| \leqslant |B|, A, B \in (V_T \cup V_N)^+$	Monotonic
	$A \rightarrow B/C\_\_D, A \in V_N, B \in (V_T \cup V_N)^+,$	Context
	$C, D \in (V_T \cup V_N)^*$	Sensitive
2	$A \rightarrow B, A \in V_N, B \in (V_T \cup V_N)^*$	Context Free
3	$A \rightarrow aB, A \in V_N, B \in (V_N \cup \{\emptyset\}), a \in V_T$	Right linear
	$A \rightarrow Ba, A \in V_N, B \in (V_N \cup \{\emptyset\}), a \in V_T$	Left linear

Type 0 rules are completely unrestricted rewrite rules of the form A → B, where A and B are any strings whatsoever. Rules of this form are usually called Unrestricted Rewrite Rules. These grammars are therefore called Unrestricted Rewrite Systems, or *Transformational Grammars*. The languages defined by type 0 grammars are called Recursively Enumerable (RE) languages. If Church's hypothesis is correct (see Partee et al. 1990: 517), any language which can be recognized using some algorithm is RE. Since it is widely accepted that human languages can be recognized by some algorithm, the use of Unrestricted Rewrite Systems constitutes the weakest hypothesis regarding the grammar of natural languages.

Type 1 rules are the same as type 0 rules, but with the further constraint that B must be no shorter than A. Rules of this form are usually called Non Length-Decreasing Rules or Monotonic Rules. I shall call grammars of this type *Monotonic Grammars*. A derivation in such a grammar consists of an ordered sequence of strings which at each step grow longer or stay the same length. I shall argue below that the kind of formal devices employed by phonologists should be no more powerful than a monotonic grammar.

Chomsky (1959, 1963: 363) proved that the set of languages which can be defined by grammars in which all rules are of the form A → B/C__D, where A is a single symbol and B, C, and D are non-empty strings, is identical to the set of languages defined by type 1 grammars. Consequently, type 1 grammars are more commonly called Context Sensitive Grammars, because they allow the application of a step in a derivation to be sensitive to the context of the rewritten substring. The languages defined by type 1 grammars are called Context Sensitive (CS) or Monotonic Languages. Though the term *'context sensitive'* is used more commonly than *'monotonic'*, I shall avoid it for two reasons. First, *all* rules of the form A → B/C__D (not just those subject to the conditions in Table 10.2) are also usually called context sensitive, though without these conditions they may in fact define an unrestricted rewrite system. Second, dependencies between a constituent and its left- and right-hand neighbours do not require the use of a type 1 grammar. Less powerful grammars are often adequate to model such dependencies. The term 'context sensitive' is therefore unfortunately rather misleading.

Because type 1 rules are a special, constrained case of type 0 rules, all Context Sensitive Languages (CSLs) are also Recursively Enumerable (RE), but not all RE languages are CS. Some RE languages are not CS. These are called Strictly RE Languages.

Type 2 rules are the same as type 1 rules with the added constraint that A is a single symbol. Such grammars are called

Context Free Grammars (CFGs). Bar-Hillel et al. (1961) proved that CFGs including rules of the form A → B where A is a single symbol and B is the *empty string* ø also define CF languages. Consequently, it is possible to include empty rules, or context free deletions, in a CFG without affecting the restrictiveness of CFGs. However, this is not true of Context Sensitive Grammars, where the inclusion of empty rules renders the resulting grammar type 0, i.e. as unrestrictive as Unrestrictive Rewrite Systems. In all other respects, though, CF rules are a special case of context-sensitive rules, and consequently, all CFGs are also CSGs and all CFLs are also CSLs, but not vice-versa. CSGs and CSLs which are not CFGs and CFLs respectively are called Strictly CSGs and Strictly CSLs.

Type 3 rules are the same as type 2 rules except that they are subject to the further constraint that all rules are of the form A → b or A → B b, where A and B are single symbols, and B is a terminal symbol (i.e. one which cannot be rewritten). These systems are collectively called Linear, Regular, or Finite State (FS) Grammars.

FSLs are a proper subset of CFLs, CFLs are a proper subset of CSLs, and CSLs are a proper subset of RELs. The existence of languages which are strictly context free, strictly monotonic and strictly recursively enumerable establishes that these grammar formalisms are non-trivially different from each other, and that the constraints on the form of their rules are indeed true constraints on their weak generative capacity.

It is the addition of deletion rules to monotonic grammars which brings about the principal formal problem of excessive power in grammars employing rules of the form A → B/C__D. Note that the formal definition of monotonic grammars prohibits such deletion rules, since they are length-reducing. It is possible to mathematically prove that the addition of such deletion rules to monotonic grammars renders them equivalent to unrestricted rewriting systems, i.e. unconstrained transformational grammars.[1]

In addition, grammars made with context sensitive rules of this type (i.e. including the possibility of deletion) may sometimes happen to be (contingently) quite restricted. For instance, if the rules do not contain integer-valued features, and are applied in a fixed order without reapplication, they are no more powerful than a finite-state transducer (Johnson 1972). But this result should not be taken to mean that SPE-type rules are acceptable, for there is nothing in the formalism of generative phonology to prevent reapplication of rules – in fact, cyclicity and resyllabification depend crucially on such reapplication – and in general there is no guarantee that lexical representations are

recoverable from their surface manifestation by any possible computations in the SPE formalism, whether artificial or natural.

3 Solving the problem of excessive power

Faced with difficulties in the formalism of transformational phonology, the reaction of phonologists in the main has been to seek
empirical, i.e. *substantive*, constraints on generative phonological
formalisms. At the same time, generative phonologists have added
new formal resources to their repertoire. Thus, along with inser-
tions, deletion and replacement, new resources such as delinking
and tier conflation have been adopted without regard for the
formal consequences of adopting such operations.

Substantive constraints, while desirable in themselves in order to
choose between grammars of equivalent formal complexity, are
insufficient to resolve the problem of excessive power of SPE
phonology. While it is almost universally accepted that theories of
grammar should be maximally constrained, in order to account for
the facts of language acquisition, it is easy to demonstrate that
there are some constraints which reduce the generative capacity
of a grammar and there are other so-called 'constraints' (pseudo-
constraints) which do not. This is an important observation, because constraints are often presented in the literature with an *a
priori* assumption that they reduce the class of languages defined
by the particular theory in which they are proposed, an assumption
which is demonstrably wrong. Simply adding a restriction to the
form of rules or representations is not sufficient to ensure that the
class of languages which is defined by the thus-'constrained' grammar formalism is actually a subset of the unconstrained case. Some
examples in support of this claim are given in the following subsections, where I present a number of cases which demonstrate that
formal constraints help make a theory *restrictive*, whereas substantive constraints simply make a theory *restricted* – which may or
may not be restrictive.

3.1 Restricting part of a grammar is insufficient
When Peters and Ritchie (1973) proved that classical Transformational Grammars are capable of defining any recursively enumerable language, they considered the effect of constraining the base
component of transformational grammars to be regular, not context sensitive, as in Chomsky (1965), the standard theory of transformational grammar at that time. Although regular grammars are
indeed more restrictive than context sensitive grammars, Peters and
Ritchie showed that transformational grammars with a regular

base are *not* more restrictive than transformational grammars with a context sensitive base. The moral of this example is that constraining one component of a theory of grammar does not necessarily constrain the grammar as a whole.

3.2 Prohibiting empty rewrites

I stated above that Context Free Grammars, unlike Context Sensitive Grammars, may contain empty rewrites (deletion rules) of the form $A \rightarrow \emptyset$. Since the prohibition of deletion rules from context sensitive systems turns them from transformational grammars into monotonic grammars, we might wonder whether the elimination of such rules from Context Free Grammars might result in a more restrictive theory of grammar. It does not: the grammars which result (called *ø-free context free grammars*) are still strictly context free. In short, prohibition of empty rewrites makes CF grammars more constrained, but not more restrictive (constraining). Such a constraint would thus be more apparent than real, since it would not reduce the class of languages that linguistic theory defines.

3.3 Prohibiting left- and right-hand contexts

According to the Chomsky hierarchy, eliminating the left- and right-hand contexts from the rules of a context sensitive grammar results in a context free grammar. Prohibition of 'horizontal' contexts is thus genuinely restrictive, a true constraint on grammars. However, while the addition of left- and right-hand contexts to CFGs turns them into CSGs, the addition of 'vertical' constraints on context and boolean constraints on domination in analysis trees does not weaken context free grammars (Joshi and Levy 1977).

The representations generated by the grammars of the Chomsky hierarchy are all strings. Since phonological theory now countenances more complicated representations than strings, it is relevant to consider whether this constraint still holds if the representations are, say, graphs?[2] The answer is no. Levy and Yueh (1977) have proved that elimination of contexts from the rules of Context Sensitive Graph Grammars does not constrain them any further, or conversely, addition of contexts to the rules of Context Free Graph Grammars does not make them any less restrictive. Context Sensitive and Context Free Graph Grammars are, it turns out, weakly equivalent, a perhaps surprising and counter-intuitive result.

3.4 Constraining the form of rules

Suppose we insisted that CFGs were restricted in the following ways:

(a) All rules must be of the form $A \rightarrow a\ B$, where a is a terminal symbol, and B a (possibly null) string of terminals and/or non-terminals.

(b) All rules must be binary branching with non-terminal daughters, or non-branching with a terminal daughter (i.e. of the form A → B C or A → b).

It might be intuitively assumed that restrictions of this kind on the form of rules would constrain the class of languages defined by the theory. But such is not the case: CF grammars adhering to (a) and (b) remain context free, and all CFLs can be defined by CFGs whose rules are of form (a) or (b). Forms (a) and (b) are called *Greibach Normal Form* and *Chomsky Normal Form* respectively. The very existence of Normal Forms should serve to warn linguists against assuming that proposing constraints on rules or the form of representations is sufficient to constrain the class of languages defined by their grammars, for Normal Forms are simply constrained ways of writing down grammars without affecting the class of languages that can be defined by that class of grammars.

3.5 Requiring strings to conform to a regular template

A number of phonological theories require all of the strings of a language to conform to a syllable structure template. A very strong example of this is the claim of Government Phonology that (a) strings are a sequence of onset and rhyme constituents; (b) rhymes consist of a nucleus and possibly a rhymal complement; (c) the occurrence of segments at each syllable terminal position is controlled by the value of the feature 'charm' at that position (see Brockhaus this volume).

It is easy to encode such template-based constraints using regular rules, as follows. Suppose L(G) is the set of strings defined by all the other rules of grammar, i.e. excluding the template-based constraints. Now, consider the following right-linear regular grammar F:

$$\sigma \rightarrow O\,R$$
$$\sigma \rightarrow O\,R_+$$
$$R_+ \rightarrow R\,\sigma$$

The symbol R_+ is to be interpreted as 'R and all following syllables'. σ denotes 'syllable(s)', and is the start symbol. The regular grammar F defines sequences of one or more occurrences of the syllabic template O R. If we want to take into account the internal structure of the onset or rhyme, we could augment the grammar further, yet still remain regular.[3] Likewise, the particular sequential pattern of charmed, uncharmed and charmless segments in the syllable would require the grammar to be expanded, but not beyond the regular.[4] It might appear, then, that a phonological theory which includes such a set of constraints on phonotactic structure is very constrained indeed: so constrained as to be a regular grammar, the most constrained kind of grammar in the Chomsky hierarchy.

The logic of such an assumption is appealing, but greatly mistaken. An utterance u is well-formed with respect to both the syllable template as defined by F, and all the other constraints and rules of the phonology, G, if and only if u is a member of both L(F) and L(G): in other words, if u is a member of the intersection of L(F) and L(G). But the weak generative capacity of the intersection of a regular language L(F) and an additional language L(G) does not depend on F, but on the weak generative capacity of G, the other (non-template-defining) rules. If G is also regular, then all will be well: L(F) ∩ L(G) would indeed then be very constrained indeed. If, however, G contains context sensitive rules with or without deletion, L(F) ∩ L(G) will be monotonic or transformational respectively: the highly constrained syllable templates do not reduce the power of the formalism. Unfortunately for Government Phonology, the G part of the theory includes deletion rules in left- and right-hand contexts, just as in SPE. The net result is that Government Phonology turns out to be no less powerful than SPE. I consider this matter in more detail in the next Section.

4 Government Phonology

I said earlier that some phonologists, at least, have rightly recognized the problem of excessive power in the SPE system, though the solutions they have proposed – strict cyclicity, syllable templates, the Obligatory Contour Principle (OCP), etc. – are formally inadequate to rectify the initial problem. The proponents of Government Phonology, for instance, claim that theirs is a 'rule-free' theory of phonology, completely different from the SPE framework. Kaye et al. (henceforth KLV) (1985: 305) state: 'In this model, a phonological system contains no rule system.' The claim has often been repeated:

> This sort of account is not available within Government Phonology, which lacks *anything equivalent* to traditional rule formalism . . . This leads to an extremely restrictive theory of phonological processing. In fact, only two types of operation are possible: composition (the fusion of elements from neighbouring segments) and decomposition (the loss of elements). There is no operation of substitution, in which any element

could be randomly replaced by any other element not locally present in the representation. (Harris and Kaye 1990: 251–2, emphasis added)

Government Phonology is, nevertheless, a derivational model, as its proponents acknowledge. That is, systematic phonetic representations are derived from the lexical representations after the operation of such derivational changes and alterations as autosegmental spreading, element 'depletion' (i.e. deletion), delinking, and the OCP. These derivational processes are both triggered and circumscribed by various structural configurations and constraints, such as the Projection Principle (Harris and Kaye 1990: 259, Harris 1990b: 272, KLV 1990: 221–4), the 'Coda' Licensing Principle (Harris and Kaye 1990: 259, Harris 1990b: 272, Kaye 1990, Charette 1991: 26), the Complexity Condition (KLV 1990: 219, Harris 1990b: 274, Harris and Kaye 1990: 267), the Empty Category Principle (Lowenstamm and Kaye 1986: 115, KLV 1990: 219, Kaye 1990a: 313), the Prosodic Government Principle (Lowenstamm and Kaye 1986: 115, Charette 1989: 161), and the Minimality Condition (Charette 1989, KLV 1990: 225). It is a matter of speculation and belief whether these principles combine to define the phonology of even a single language.

The rhetoric of this 'rule-free', 'extremely restrictive' theory is not matched by the details of the Government Phonology formalism. Far from being a rule free theory completely unlike the SPE model, as its proponents claim, Government-based phonological analyses employ various derivational devices which are transformational rules in all but name. Examination of these devices from the perspective of formal language theory shows them to constitute a rewrite-rule formalism with a weak generative capacity at least equal to the SPE formalism. Government Phonology is therefore as unconstrained as the models it seeks to replace.

4.1 Government-based phonological representations

There are two established types of formal equivalence between different grammars. First, two grammars are said to be weakly equivalent if they define the same language. By extension, we can say that two grammar formalisms are weakly equivalent if they define the same class of languages. Second, two grammars are said to be strongly equivalent if they define the same language, and furthermore assign the same or isomorphic structural analyses to the expressions of that language. By extension, we can say that two grammar formalisms are strongly equivalent if they define the same class of languages and furthermore assign the same or isomorphic structural analyses to the expressions of those languages.

The phonological representations of Government Phonology include aspects of the constituent structure of syllables not found in the phonological representations of SPE phonology, so that Government Phonology and SPE phonology are not strongly equivalent phonological formalisms. If we compare the sets of *languages* which can be defined by SPE and Government Phonology, what do we find? If the sets of languages which can be defined by the two theories are equal, the two theories are (weakly) equivalent. If, on the other hand, the set of languages produced by one theory (A) is a proper subset of the other (B), it is said that theory A is more restrictive (i.e. constraining) than theory B. Provided that theory B is not *over*-constrained, established assumptions about language acquisition require theory B to be preferred over theory A.

The set of *languages* defined by a phonological theory is the set of systematic phonetic representations of sentences. In both SPE phonology and Government Phonology, the systematic phonetic representations of sentences are derived from the syntactically bracketed concatenation of lexical entries (the output of the syntactic component) after the operation of the language-specific rules and/or the parameterized, principle-driven derivational steps sanctioned by the theory.

By this definition, the languages defined by Government Phonology differ from those of SPE phonology in two ways. First, Government Phonology imposes syllable structure, a form of metrical structure, and a set of government relations over the segments in the strings. Second, Government Phonology regards segments as being constructed from a set of fundamental subsegmental units that is different from the SPE distinctive features. Specifically, Government Phonology regards a small set of segments, including [ʊ], [ɪ], [ɨ], [a], [ɨ], [ɾ][ʔ], [h] and [ŋ], as more basic (in particular, less marked) than all other segments, since they may be characterized by at most one marked SPE feature ([ɪ] is the segment which has no marked features). These segments are thus represented as a set of fundamental phonological units called *elements*, and are assigned the phonological symbols U°, I°, Ɨ°, A⁺, v°, R°, ʔ°, h° and N⁺ respectively. (In addition, there are two tone/voicing elements H⁻ and L⁻. Other elements may prove to be necessary in future.) The marked phonetic property which each of these elements represents is labiality, frontness, tongue root advancement, non-highness, nothing, coronality, stoppedness, stridency, and nasality, respectively. Every other segment is analysed as being the *fusion* of two or more elements. The fusion of an element A with an element or derived segment B (denoted A • B) is computed by combining the single marked feature f of A with all of the marked features of B except for f. For example, the segment [m] can be defined as the fusion of U° with N⁺, that is, it has all the same features as [ŋ], except that instead of being [− labial] it bears the marked feature of U°, i.e. [+ labial]. (For further examples, see KLV 1985, 1990, and Harris 1990b.) Every element, therefore, functions in isolation as a complete segment, or, in combination with other elements, as contributing a single marked property to a derived segmental category.

The segments in the output of the Government framework are convertible to SPE-type segments by the following relations. First, single elements correspond to marked values of SPE features (and thus to segments which bear only a single marked feature), as follows:

Elements ↔ features
U° ↔ [+ lab] ([+ rnd] in KLV 85)
I° ↔ [− back]
Ɨ⁺ ↔ [+ atr]
A⁺ ↔ [− high]
v° ↔ [ ]
R° ↔ [+ cor]
ʔ° ↔ [− cnt]
h° ↔ [+ str]
N⁺ ↔ [+ nas]
H⁻ ↔ [+ stiff v.c.]
L⁻ ↔ [+ slack v.c.]

Second, since the elements of Government Phonology are unary, privative objects, the *absence* of an element (called here a *gap*) is also an informative part of a phonological representation. A correspondence between gaps and unmarked values of SPE features can be tabulated as follows:

Absence of elements (gaps) ↔ features
absence of U° ↔ [− lab] ([− rnd] in KLV 85)
absence of I° ↔ [+ back]
absence of Ɨ⁺ ↔ [− atr]
absence of A⁺ ↔ [+ high]
absence of v° ↔ [ ]
absence of R° ↔ [− cor]
absence of ʔ° ↔ [+ cnt]
absence of h° ↔ [− str]
absence of N⁺ ↔ [− nas]
absence of H⁻ ↔ [− stiff v.c.]
absence of L⁻ ↔ [− slack v.c.]

Finally, expressions such as $(I° \bullet (U° \bullet A^+))$, denoting combinations of fused elements, can be converted to SPE segments according to the following definition:

$A \bullet B \leftrightarrow [f;v](B')$ where $A \leftrightarrow [f;v]$, $B \leftrightarrow B'$ and $[f;v](B') =_{def}$ for $[f;x] \in B'$, Bx/v

In other words, the featural interpretation of $A \bullet B$ can be written $[f;v](B')$, where the element A corresponds to the feature-value pair $[f;v]$, the expression B corresponds to the feature-value structure B', and $[f;v](B')$ is obtained by replacing the value x of feature f in B' by the value v, that is, by replacing $[f;x]$ by $[f;v]$.

Despite these equivalences, the alphabet of Government Phonology is a subset of the alphabet of SPE phonology, because charm theory prohibits like-charmed elements from being combined. However, since the set of features of SPE-type phonology is substantively, not formally, fixed, there is nothing in the *formalism* of SPE phonology to preclude the adoption of the new 'charm' feature. The charm feature and the restrictions on the distribution of charm are substantive, not formal components of Government Phonology. The association between each marked feature and the charm property found in each element of Government Phonology is indeed a formal, not substantive, aspect of Government Phonology, but without the substantive constraints on charm distribution and combination, the coupling of a charm value with each element is not formally constraining. Furthermore, whether an element is plus-charmed, minus-charmed or uncharmed is a substantive, not formal aspect of the theory. Consequently, charm does not *formally* constrain the alphabet of Government Phonology, which is thus formally completely equivalent to the alphabet of SPE phonology. And as I argued above, formal constraints are more important than substantive constraints in ensuring that a generative theory is not excessively unconstrained.

4.2 Arbitrary transformations in Government Phonology

Consider the class of processes that can be defined using SPE-type rules. Generally speaking, rewrite rules can change a string or a segment in only two ways: addition and/or deletion of material. In strings, addition of a segment is insertion (e.g. epenthesis). In segments, addition of (a) feature(s) is termed by Gazdar et al. (1985: 26) extension. In strings, deletion of a segment is elision. In segments, deletion of a feature is lenition or dearticulation. Addition and deletion can also be combined in a single operation. Removal of a segment or feature combined with addition of a different segment or feature at the same place constitutes replacement, or feature-changing. Removal of a segment or feature combined with addition of the same segment or feature at a *different* place constitutes movement.

Government Phonologists rightly recognize that the power and arbitrariness of SPE rules is undesirable, and claim that their model is much more restrictive. As the following quotations indicate, the only processes which Government Phonologists allow are spreading (after the fashion of Autosegmental Phonology), and element depletion, i.e. the deletion of single elements:

> within the Government framework, phonological events are restricted to the operations of composition or, as in this case, decomposition. There is no operation of substitution. (Harris 1990b: 268)

However, Government Phonologists in fact make use of a large number of operations other than 'composition and decomposition' that are as arbitrary as any in SPE-type analyses. Furthermore, even 'composition and decomposition' are no less constrained than segmental operations in SPE phonology. Government Phonologists might respond that, whatever the force of the formal argument developed here, the processes of spreading and element depletion are subject to substantive constraints. My response is to invite Government Phonologists to formally prove that the substantive constraints which they propose actually do reduce the class of languages which can be defined by the theory to less than un-restricted rewriting systems.

Let us first consider insertion of features. Each element of Government Phonology bears a single marked feature. According to the correspondences noted above, unmarked features are present in all segments, even empty slots (i.e. the 'cold vowel'). So although only marked features may spread, unmarked features are omni-present anyway. Insertion of an unmarked feature can thus be modelled by deletion of the marked value of that feature (see the discussion of deletion below) and insertion of a marked feature can be modelled by insertion or spreading of an element. It will be objected that arbitrary insertion of elements is an operation not listed in the Government Phonologists' enumeration of valid processes, but it is an operation which Kaye (1990c: 179) employs:

> It should be noted that three vowel systems involving /i, u, a/ need not have ATR-ness specified as part of the lexical representation. Assuming such systems have the charm parameter specified as requiring only positively charmed segments in nuclei, then *i* and *u* need only be specified as I° and U°, respectively. The ATR element I^+ can be added to satisfy this charm requirement.

So, addition of elements which are not already in the lexical representation (and hence not available for a 'spreading' analysis) is quite all right in Government phonology, providing that it is needed to get the surface string right – exactly the same criterion for arbitrary insertion that obtains in the SPE formalism! On this subject, Harris and Kaye (1990: 252, n. 1) state:

> it is necessary to recognise the existence of 'ambient' elements. These are elements which are not distinctively present in lexical representations but which, in a language-specific manner, spontaneously appear in certain positions during a derivation.

They offer no restrictions on the insertion of ambient elements. In the face of these examples, therefore, it is clear that contrary to the proclaimed tenets of Government Phonology, arbitrary insertion of elements is allowed.[5]

I have thus shown that arbitrary insertion of a marked or unmarked feature, or of a segment, is formally possible in Government Phonology. Let us now consider different sorts of arbitrary deletion. First arbitrary deletion of an unmarked feature is completely equivalent to arbitrary insertion of the corresponding marked value of that feature, a process which I discussed above. Arbitrary deletion of a marked feature in Government Phonology would be arbitrary deletion of an element. There are numerous precedents for such arbitrary deletions. For example:

> Kpokolo has alternations which appear to involve the 'unrounding' of non-final rounded vowels . . . We see that 'unrounding' results from the disassociation of U – . . . Unrounding involves loss of the U element . . . In each case of unrounding, the U – element on the BACK/ ROUND line is detached and the cold vowel v – appears in its place. (KLV 1985: 317–9)

KLV (1985: 324) state that the disassociation of U – arises through deletion of the skeletal position to which it was attached. Note that such deletion is a violation of the Projection Principle.[6] Overleaf are three more examples of arbitrary (i.e. rule-stipulated) deletion. An element must be governed to be deleted, it is true, but all segments bar one in a string are governed one way or another.

Arbitrary deletion of the cold segment is effected in Government Phonology by appeal to the OCP:

> Under the OCP, the empty nucleus deletes next to a filled nucleus. (Harris and Kaye 1990: 264)

t-<u>lenition</u> — stage 1

(Harris 1990b: 292)

t-<u>lenition</u> — stage 2

Context: O   N
              | |
              x   x
              |
              R°
              |
              ʔ°

Process:

		N empty	N filled
London, Fife:	R° → Ø	√	√
NYC:	ʔ° → Ø	*	√

(Harris 1990b: 292)

<u>Glottalling/tapping</u>

Input: N   O   N
            | | |
            x   x   x
                / \
               ʔ° R°

Output:

		N empty	N filled
London:	R° → Ø	√	√
NYC:	ʔ° → Ø	*	√

(Harris and Kaye 1990: 263)

Deletion of a segment with some marked features can thus be effected in Government Phonology by deleting each of its elements in turn (as above), which leaves the cold segment, which can then be removed by OCP. Another, quite arbitrary, mechanism for deletion is exemplified by the following remark:

> The plural suffix is − *I*. It typically causes thę deletion of the final stem vowel that immediately precedes it. (KLV 1985: 317)

As in SPE, replacement of one segment or feature by another can be implemented by a combined deletion and insertion operation. Besides arbitrary deletion, insertion, and by combining them, replacement, Government Phonologists employ various other operations, of which the following are a selection:

Breaking (e.g. affrication)
We will appropriate the traditional term *breaking* to refer to processes of this type which involve decomposition without element loss:

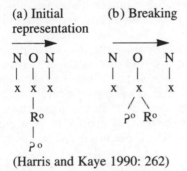

(a) Initial representation

(b) Breaking

(Harris and Kaye 1990: 262)

Delinking
Delinking is employed in many Government Phonological analyses, though it is neither composition nor decomposition. Cf. Kaye and Lowenstamm (1985: 228–31). 'Unrounding' in KLV (1985: 318), mentioned above, is claimed to arise through the disassociation of U − from its skeletal position, as a result of the deletion of that position. Charette (1989: 181) employs delinking and reassociation in an analysis of complete assimilation in Cordoba Spanish. Yoshida (1990: 339) also employs delinking, accompanied by the admission that 'it remains to be explained why the nasal element delinks from the onset'. Delinking is again invoked by Yoshida (1990: 344) to bring about a process called *Nuclear Fusion*.

Shortening

Shortening of nuclei (Kaye 1990a) is another structure-changing transformation of syllable structure which arises from deletion of a nuclear position, with concomitant delinking. Although the English examples of shortening (Kaye 1990a: 312) might be interpreted as complementary possibilities, rather than as in a derivational relation, the derivational status of shortening in the Government Phonology analysis of Turkish is explicit on p. 311, example (20), where the derivation [ʔilet] < /ʔileːt/ is given.

Even without the rich repertoire of arbitrary transformations in Government Phonology, the combination of left- and right-hand context to rules and the possibility of deletion suffices to make Government Phonology (as most other contemporary phonological formalisms) equivalent to an unrestricted rewriting system.

5 Derivational, nonderivational and declarative phonology

The solution to the problem of excessive power, then, lies not in the adoption of yet more substantive constraints, which is quite tangential to the issue at hand. That is the strategy offered by most contemporary phonological theories. Because the restrictive power of proposed constraints cannot be assessed intuitively, it is necessary to adopt a formalism that is *proved* to be more constrained than the old derivational, polystratal rewriting systems. In this Section I shall propose that the new declarative, monostratal, monotonic, non-transformational theories of syntax offer a rich vein of new formal techniques from which phonological theory can benefit.

The view of grammar proposed by grammarians in the declarative approach is concisely described by Ladusaw (1986) as follows:

> The view of filtering that I adopt here is one which views a grammár as a whole as a filter. A grammar for a language defines a predicate *grammatical*. The statement of a grammar is a statement of a number of necessary conditions on grammaticality . . . Theories which define grammaticality as in (1) give independent characterizations of syntactic and semantic well-formedness.
>
> 1. grammatical(ϕ) = $_{def}$ Syn(ϕ) & Sem(ϕ)

The input to the filter, in this conception of grammar, is the free concatenation of all words in the grammar, that is, the set of all possible arrangements of words. The task of the grammar is to pick out those sequences of words that are grammatical.

Importantly, in declarative approaches, the well-formedness constraints which constitute the definition of the predicate *grammatical* characterize the surface structure ϕ directly, not via transformations of a deep structure distinct from the surface structure. These well-formedness constraints are of several kinds:

1. The syntactic (constituent structure) rules of the surface grammar. These are usually context free, or no more than mildly context sensitive, and the nodes are usually labelled with feature-structures, rather than atomic symbols.

2. Constraints on feature-structures, such as logical constraints on what features may or may not cooccur, and which features are predictable on the basis of which others. Feature propagation constraints (a form of feature cooccurrence constraint holding between different nodes of the syntactic structure) may be regarded in like manner.

3. Feature-structure defaults. This is a challenging area in declarative grammatical research, since defaults may introduce nonmonotonicity into the semantics of the grammar formalism, which gives rise to some technical difficulties, though they do not necessarily make the grammar itself (i.e. the syntax) nonmonotonic.

4. Constraints on the linear order of sister constituents.

5. The lexical entries of words, containing information about their category, and the categories of the phrases they subcategorize for. Lexical entries may be regarded as highly informative and specific feature-structures which contribute information to the surface representation. Such information is complementary to the more general information contributed by the other grammatical constraints.

6. Rules for productively generating new lexical descriptions from lexical entries, such as productive active-passive morphosyntactic relations. Since these are implications of the form 'if X is well-formed, then Y is well-formed', these too are simply logical constraints on well-formed surface structures.

7. Principles for the semantic interpretation of well-formed syntactic structures: usually, some form of function for combining the semantic interpretation of the parts of a well-formed syntactic structure to form the semantic interpretation of the larger structure (compositional semantics).

In an analogous manner, a theory of phonology can be developed in which a well-formed phonological representation is one that satisfies various independent kinds of constraints:

1. Structural constraints (phase structure rules): syllable structure constraints (rather than procedural 'syllabification rules'), metrical structure constraints, lexical structure constraints (see examples below), and morpheme structure constraints. These rules may be language-specific or universal (cf. Coleman 1991b for an example of universal constraints in declarative metrical phonology.)

2. Constraints on the linear order of sister constituents, as in parametric metrical theory (cf. Coleman 1991b).

3. Constraints on the set of phonological objects, such as feature cooccurrence restrictions, and specification implications (redundancy rules).

4. Principles of compositional phonetic interpretation (see Coleman 1992). Existence of an interpretation (pronounceability) is a constraint on the semantics of the phonological formalism. (In syntactic theory, such a constraint is called 'semantic filtering'.)

The various kinds of constraints in a declarative grammar can be regarded as directly contributing information to the surface structure in the following way. Consider the rule $\sigma \rightarrow$ O R, encoding the constraint that a syllable consists of an onset and a rhyme. If this were to be interpreted like the context sensitive rewrite rules of generative phonology, it would mean something like 'any occurrence of the symbol σ may be replaced by the sequence of symbols O R'. In fact, that is how context free grammars were originally presented (see Chomsky 1957: 27). However, that is not how context free rules are usually interpreted. The normal interpretation is 'one of the constraints which characterize a given syntactic structure as well-formed is: a constituent labelled σ may be composed of two constituents, one of which is labelled O and the other of which is labelled R.' From this perspective, every constraint in the grammar can be regarded as either licensing, contributing, or actually *being* a piece of well-formed surface structure. A surface structure is well-formed if all the pieces fit together, like a jigsaw puzzle, to form a well-formed whole. In order to make this technique work, however, it is necessary to define some general operation which can be used to fit all the pieces of the puzzle together.

5.1 Unification

One such general operation is *unification*. Unification is already familiar to phonologists, in the shape of *matching* in SPE rule application:[7] we say a rule $A \to B/C\_\_D$ may be applied to a string of the form VWXYZ, where V and Z are (possibly empty) strings and W, X and Y are (possibly empty) segments, if and only if CAD *matches* WXY. We do not require that CAD be *equal to* WXY, because A, C and D need not be complete segmental specifications: a few features will suffice. Yet being objects in a phonological string, W, X and Y *must* be complete segmental specifications. Thus, matching is not equality. Neither is matching the same thing as the subset relation. For example, the feature-structure

$$F = \begin{bmatrix} +\text{back} \\ +\text{rnd} \end{bmatrix}$$

matches the segmental specification

$$G = \begin{bmatrix} +\text{cns} \\ -\text{son} \\ -\text{syll} \\ +\text{high} \\ +\text{back} \\ -\text{ant} \\ -\text{cor} \\ -\text{nas} \\ -\text{cnt} \end{bmatrix}$$

even though the features of F are not a subset of the features of G. All that matters is that the features of F *do not conflict with* the features of G. If this is the case, we say that F *is unifiable with* or *can unify with* G. If F is unifiable with G, then we can join F and G together to form a new object:

$$H = F \sqcup G = \begin{bmatrix} +\text{cns} \\ -\text{son} \\ -\text{syll} \\ +\text{high} \\ +\text{back} \\ +\text{rnd} \\ -\text{ant} \\ -\text{cor} \\ -\text{nas} \\ -\text{cnt} \end{bmatrix}$$

Note that H is still a well-formed phonological object. The unification operation ⊔ has the property (unlike union of sets of features, for instance) that it preserves well-formedness of feature-structures. Objects such as

$$\begin{bmatrix} +\text{rnd} \\ -\text{rnd} \end{bmatrix}$$

cannot arise in unification-based grammars, since they are not well-formed primitive objects, and neither can they be created by unification of two well-formed primitive objects [+rnd] and [−rnd]. (For more technical discussion the reader is referred to Shieber 1986 and Pollard and Sag 1987: 27–50.)

If each constraint is a partial description of a possible surface structure, a complete surface structure will be well-formed if and only if it can be constructed by amalgamating the different substructures licensed or contributed by the constraints of the grammar. For instance, the disyllabic structure in Figure 10.1 could be analysed as the unification of the substructures in Figure 10.2.

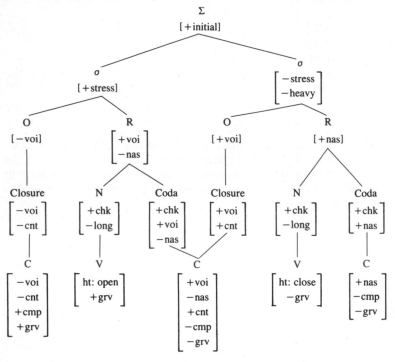

FIGURE 10.1

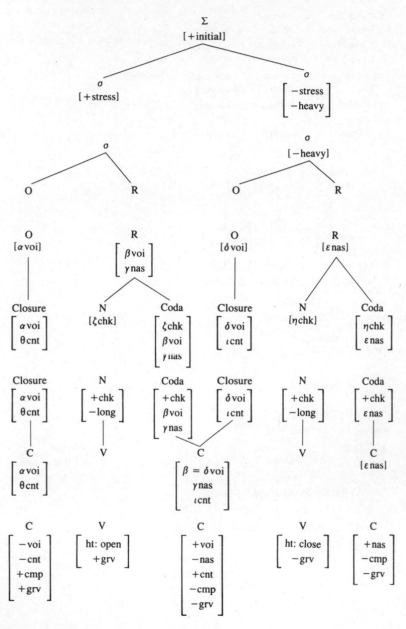

FIGURE 10.2

Word   →   Word   Inflection   Inflection e.g. cat + s
[+inflected]   [−inflected]

Word   →   Word   Word   Compounding e.g. black + bird
[−inflected]   [−inflected]   [−inflected]

Word   →   Prefix*   Word   Suffix*
[−Latinate]   [−Latinate]   [−inflected]   [−Latinate]

Word   →   Stress   Morphology   o denotes coanalysis
[+Latinate]   [+Latinate]o   [+Latinate]

$$\text{Stress} \atop [+\text{Latinate}] \; \rightarrow \; \left(\Sigma \atop [+\text{initial}] \right) \; {\Sigma* \atop [-\text{final}]} \; \Sigma$$

$$\Sigma \rightarrow \begin{bmatrix} \sigma \\ +\text{stress} \\ +\text{heavy} \end{bmatrix} \left(\begin{bmatrix} \sigma \\ -\text{stress} \\ -\text{heavy} \end{bmatrix} \right)$$

$$\Sigma \rightarrow {\sigma \atop [+\text{stress}]} \begin{bmatrix} \sigma \\ -\text{stress} \\ -\text{heavy} \end{bmatrix} \begin{bmatrix} \sigma \\ -\text{stress} \\ -\text{heavy} \end{bmatrix}$$

Morphology   →   Prefix*   Stem   Suffix*
[+Latinate]   [+Latinate]   [+Latinate]   [+Latinate]

$${\sigma \atop [\alpha\text{heavy}]} \rightarrow (O) \; {R \atop [\alpha\text{heavy}]}$$

$${O \atop [\alpha\text{voi}]} \rightarrow {\text{Affricate} \atop [\alpha\text{voi}]}$$

$${O \atop [-\text{voi}]} \rightarrow \text{Aspirate}$$

$${O \atop [\alpha\text{voi}]} \rightarrow \left(\text{Obstruence} \atop [-\text{voi}] \right) (\text{Glide})$$

Obstruence   → ([s]), Closure   (Either order)
  [αvoi]

Constraint: in onsets, [s] < Closure

$${R \atop [\alpha\text{heavy}]} \rightarrow {N \atop [\alpha\text{heavy}]} \left(\text{Coda} \atop [\alpha\text{heavy}] \right)$$

N → Peak   Offglide

                                                                    etc. etc.

FIGURE 10.3

The structure of the complete representation, then, is the unification of its parts. Since the unification operation is monotonic, i.e. it does not delete any features or change the values of any features, it does not matter what order the unifications are performed in. This is because unification is an associative operation: $P \sqcup (Q \sqcup R) = (P \sqcup Q) \sqcup R$. In a declarative phonological theory, then, rules (declarative constraints) can be applied in any order, and the same surface structure results, though it may be that there is sometimes only one consistent order in which all the constraints may be applied. (A fragment of such a unification-based grammar is illustrated in Figure 10.3.) The essence of a declarative theory, then, is to enforce strict structure preservation (not the watered-down versions employed in Lexical Phonology and Government Phonology), and employ structure-building rules only. Since the constituent structure rules are context free, a limited kind of deletion, namely empty terminal symbols, is possible.

In a non-declarative theory, such as SPE phonology, an ordered sequence of non-monotonic rules may yield different results depending on the order of application. The question arises, then, as to whether such power is needed once the techniques of declarative approaches to grammar are adopted. I address this question in the remainder of the chapter.

5.2 Structure-changing and structure-building
Structure changing rules introduce derivations into phonology, because a structure-changing rule may destroy the conditions under which some other rule in the grammar may apply. Thus applying one structure-changing rule sc_2 to a string *after* applying some other structure-changing rule sc_1 to a string may yield a different result from applying sc_1 after sc_2, since if sc_2 removes part of the structural conditions of sc_1 from the string, it will not be possible to apply sc_1 after sc_2, even though it is possible to apply sc_2 after sc_1.

With structure-building rules this circumstance never arises, though in derivational phonology different orders of application of structure-building rules may still produce different results. For instance, if sb_1 relies on sb_2 to *create* part of its structural description, sb_1 will fail to apply before sb_2, though it will succeed in applying after sb_2.

We can overcome this case of order-dependence in structure-building rules, however. In the derivational scenario, if sb_1 is extrinsically ordered before sb_2, attempting to apply sb_1 to any input will fail, so sb_1 is passed over and its input passes, unchanged, to sb_2. The derivational model thus embodies a mechanism for what to do if a rule fails to apply: proceed to the next rule. This is not the only mechanism for coping with failure to apply, however. In declarative systems the rules can be regarded as applying simultaneously. If the additional (reasonable) constraint is enforced that all rules applicable to a surface form must do some work in the grammar, the only possible order of application is sb_2, sb_1. In derivational phonology, conjunctive application of rules is always implemented by stepwise application, and simultaneous application of rules is only permitted for disjunctions of rules. It is not necessary that conjunctive, sequential and disjunctive, simultaneous application be bound together in this way, as in the SPE framework. It is equally possible to have conjunctive, simultaneous application of rules (the 'blackboard' metaphor of computation; see Gelertner 1989: 56 for an elementary description) or disjunctive, sequential application (trying one possibility after another). The relevant dimension for determining the manner of rule interaction is whether they are conjunctive or disjunctive, and this does not make any commitments regarding the implementation of those computations: that is an independent issue. Logical dependencies between rules, such as feeding or bleeding relations, do not have to be defined in terms of sequential ordering of rules.

Many standard examples of structure-changing operations can be reanalysed as purely structure-building. Analyses employing a resyllabification operation (such as Borowsky 1984), which removes a consonant from coda position and attaches it to the onset node of the following syllable, can be replaced by an analysis in which the coda consonant is shared with the onset of the following syllable (ambisyllabicity). Such an analysis has the merit that it does not require deletion and is consistent with declarative principles. It must be constrained so that the number of mothers a constituent may have does not get out of hand, or the resulting system will be equivalent to an unrestricted rewriting system, but this is easily done (a limit of two mothers seems to be sufficient), and preferable to structure-changing rules.

6 Is phonology different?

In an apparently pre-emptive strike on declarative phonology, Bromberger and Halle (1989: 57) argue

> that derivations based on ordered rules (that is, external ordering) and incorporating intermediate structures are *essential* to phonology – in other words, that they represent an *uneliminable* aspect of linguistic knowledge.

Bromberger and Halle's attempt to establish this claim is seriously weakened by the fact that the partial phonological analyses they adduce in support of their claim are susceptible to elegant non-derivational analyses, and therefore, in these cases at least, intermediate structures are *in*essential and *eliminable*.

6.1 Argument 1: stress, syllable weight and lexical representations

Bromberger and Halle's first argument concerns the ordered application of syllabification and stress rules to lexical representations. They state (1989: 57):

> Since stress assignment thus depends on whether or not certain syllables have a branching core, stress cannot be assigned *until* the word has been syllabified . . . the stress rules must apply *after* the rule of syllable structure assignment since the stress rule requires information that is not present until syllable structure has been assigned.

This is not a sound argument for the necessity of intermediate representations, derivations and sequential rule application. In fact the contemporary view of stress assignment and syllable structure assignment is essentially a context-free analysis which can be implemented by simultaneous application of independent foot- and syllable-structure context free rules. The precise details of the rules in question are open to debate, but the following analysis will illustrate the feasibility (and preferability) of a non-derivational account. First, there are metrical structure rules for two kinds of syllables, those that have a branching rhyme (heavy syllables), and those whose rhymes do not branch (light syllables):

$$\sigma \longrightarrow O \qquad R$$
$$[\alpha\text{heavy}] \qquad [\alpha\text{heavy}]$$
$$R \longrightarrow X \quad X$$
$$[+\text{heavy}]$$
$$R \longrightarrow X$$
$$[-\text{heavy}]$$

Second, there are metrical structure rules for various kinds of feet. The following three disjoint cases can be identified.[8]

$$\Sigma \longrightarrow \sigma$$
$$[+\text{heavy}]$$

$$\Sigma \longrightarrow \sigma \qquad \sigma$$
$$[+\text{heavy}] \quad [-\text{heavy}]$$

$$\Sigma \longrightarrow \sigma \qquad \sigma$$
$$[-\text{heavy}] \quad [-\text{heavy}]$$

To encode the fact that the foot which is the main stress domain comes at the right-hand edge of the word, the following word-level[9] metrical phrase structure is sufficient:

$$\omega \longrightarrow (\Sigma_w^{'}) \quad \Sigma_s$$

The optional non-final feet have the following structure: [10]

$$\Sigma_w^{'} \longrightarrow (\sigma^L (\sigma^L)) \quad \Sigma *$$

Finally, in words of only one or two light syllables (which will not satisfy the above word rule for want of the appropriate syllables to form even a normal binary foot), the first is stressed:

$$\omega \longrightarrow \sigma_s^L \quad (\sigma_w^L)$$

The way in which these rules are applied need not be regarded derivationally. In fact, it is not normal to think of a set of phrase structure rules as a sequence of mappings from strings to strings which apply in sequence. The same selection of phrase structure rules can be applied top-down, bottom-up, left-to-right, right-to-left, outside-in, inside-out, breadth-first, depth-first or even head-first to yield the same set of hierarchical phrase structure relations (see Coleman 1991a: 146–7 for an illustration of this). In the words of Booij (1988: 69), syllable structure rules are 'anywhere' rules available at all times in the construction of phonological representations.

6.2 Argument 2: flapping and raising in Canadian and American English

Bromberger and Halle (1989: 58–9) reiterate an old argument[11] for necessary rule ordering in two dialects of Canadian English. In one dialect (A), it is claimed, there is a rule ('flapping') which transforms intervocalic /t/ and /d/ into [ɾ]. Thus, both 'writing' and 'riding' are pronounced [ray ɾ ɪŋ]. In another dialect (B), a certain rule ('raising') transforms /ay/ into [ʌy] before voiceless consonants. Flapping also occurs in this dialect, but raising must take place before flapping, since flapping destroys the environment to which raising is sensitive, and yet the word 'writing' surfaces with both a raised vowel and a flap: [rʌy ɾ ɪŋ]. The argument for rule ordering has two parts: first, in dialect B, raising must be ordered before flapping; and second, the fact that raising is not manifested in words like 'writing' in dialect A can be accounted for by postulating that flapping *precedes* raising.

There are simple alternatives to both parts of this argument which do not make reference to rule ordering, and which therefore undermine the motivation for rule ordering. First, since in dialect

A raising is not manifested, there is no evidence at all that the B-dialect raising rule even exists in the grammars of speakers of this dialect. It is equally possible, and by Occam's razor preferable, to infer that speakers of dialect A simply lack the B-dialect rule. The proposal that two dialects may differ in terms of a rule is quite orthodox. So now we only have to address the issue of rule ordering within a single dialect.

An alternative analysis of dialect B is that both flapping and raising are rules of phonetic interpretation, that do not alter the phonological structure. The interpretive raising rule /áy/ → [ʌɪ] / __ / [−voiced]/is to be understood as '/áy/ is phonetically interpreted as [ʌɪ] when it (i.e. /áy/) occurs before a /[−voiced]/ phonological unit'. The interpretive flapping rule /t,d/ → [ɾ]//V́/__/V/ is to be understood as '/t/and /d/after a stressed vowel and before an unstressed vowel are interpreted as [ɾ]'. Since rules of this kind non-destructively *interpret* phonological representations, i.e. map them onto phonetic representations, rather than *alter* the phonological representations, raising does not need to be applied before flapping, since it is not the *output* of raising which is the *input* to flapping. Raising and flapping are performed simultaneously, in parallel, on the same phonological representation. Thus both raising and flapping apply to /raytɪŋ/, resulting in the phonetic interpretation [rʌɪɾɪŋ], whereas the representation /raydɪŋ/ does not satisfy the structural description of raising, so only flapping occurs. Thus this case presents no evidence for the *existence* of rule ordering, let alone for its necessity.

Bromberger and Halle pursue their argument for rule ordering by appealing to cyclicity, as in metrical structure assignment, and the existence of strata in Lexical Phonology. Neither of these concepts is unique to a phonological theory with ordered rule application. For example, in his celebrated argument that English metrical structure assignment is cyclic, Kiparsky (1979) points out that in Liberman and Prince (1977), structure is erected and then deleted on each cycle. Consequently, in the Liberman–Prince analysis, stress might as well have been assigned only once, on the final cycle. So at least one metrical analysis of English stress is amenable to a non-derivational treatment. Since metrical theory employs context-free constituent structures for its representations, it is one of the easiest areas of phonology to model using purely declarative resources (see Coleman 1991b and the discussion below). Neither cyclicity nor the concept of strata in Lexical Phonology need to be analysed transformationally, as Church (1985) and Cole and Coleman (forthcoming) show. Church (1985) proposed a non-transformational, context-free model for the organization of morphemes into sublexical 'levels'. The grammar which he proposed:

    word → level3 regular-inflection *
    level3 → level3-prefix * level2 level3-suffix *
    level2 → level2-prefix * level1 level2-suffix *
    level1 → level1-prefix * syll level1-suffix *

imposes a stratified structure on the arrangement of morphemes within words. This structure, as several morphologists have noted previously, enforces the affix ordering generalization that in words containing both Latinate and Germanic affixes, all of the Latinate affixes occur inside all of the Germanic affixes (cf. Selkirk 1984a: 75–82).

Selkirk's and Church's structural accounts of lexical levels also provide the domains within which phonological rules are constrained to operate in Lexical Phonology. Sproat and Brunson (1987) combined a structure-based implementation of Lexical Phonology similar to Church's with a structural characterization of vowel harmony domains in Warlpiri. The analysis trees which their grammar of Warlpiri defined, and which their parser computed, encoded both lexical constituency and vowel harmony domains.

I shall not examine Halle and Bromberger's final argument for rule ordering, which concerns Grimm's Law and Verner's Law, due to its diachronic nature. The relevance of such arguments to synchronic phonology is highly controversial, and thus no basis on which to evaluate the transformational hypothesis.

7 Declarative Lexical Phonology

In the preceding Sections I have presented a detailed critique of derivational phonology that is matched only programmatically by the declarative alternative. To give real substance to the declarative approach, I shall conclude this chapter by examining several of the rules in Halle and Mohanan's (henceforth H&M's) (1985) Lexical Phonology of English in some detail, proposing specific declarative alternatives.[12]

H&M's rules (see Table 10.1 and H&M's example 119) can be roughly divided into two main groups: morphophonologically motivated rules (i.e. those which accompany a morphological affixation or other category-changing operation), from the stress rules to the Centering Diphthong Rule (72), and allophonic 'detail' rules from Diphthongization (62) to the end. All of the rules convert relatively more abstract representations corresponding more closely to lexical forms to relatively more concrete representations corresponding more closely to systematic phonetic forms. Nasal Assimilation, y-

Insertion and y-Deletion are somewhat out of place among the morphophonological rules, in that they simply adjust the output of one set of rules in order to match the input to another set of rules without any particular morphophonological consequence. Nevertheless, the approximate divisibility of the rule sequence in this fashion surely cannot be accidental, yet the theory in which H&M's analysis is cast does not predict or account for this partition. Indeed, given the difficulty of determining the particular rule ordering with maximal exploitation of the potential for feeding, bleeding and parsimony, it is not obvious how it comes about that such a rule ordering can be naturally partitioned in this way. The twofold division is natural in a non-derivational model, however, in which there are two levels: a morphophonological ('syntactic') level, at which morphophonological alternations are represented, and a phonetic ('semantic') level, at which non-functional, phonetic details are described.[13]

Cross-cutting the division into lexical strata and the morphophonological/allophonic partition, the rules can be grouped into functionally related blocks on the basis of their effects and structural conditions:

1. Parsing of metrical structure, including syllable structure, e.g. the stress rules and the rules of Prenasal g-Deletion, n-Deletion, Non-coronal Deletion, and l-Resyllabification.
2. Phonetic interpretation of metrical structure, e.g. the rules of CiV Lengthening, s-Voicing, Shortening rules, Vowel Reduction, Vowel Tensing, and Stem-final Lengthening.
3. Vowel shift, e.g. the rules of Vowel Shift, ɨ-Lowering, Centering Diphthong Rule and Diphthongization.
4. Palatal assimilation, e.g. the rules of Velar Softening, ɨ-Lengthening, Spirantization, y-Insertion, Palatalization, y-Vocalization and y-Deletion.
5. Phonetic interpretation of syllable structure, e.g. Nasal Assimilation, æ-Tensing and l-Velarization.

H&M's derivational analysis can be recast non-derivationally, while retaining an analysis which is no less parsimonious and elegant than theirs, a justified failing of the 'straw man' non-derivational analyses which Halle and Bromberger put forward. Furthermore, in my non-derivational alternative, the functional relations between what are disparate rules in H&M's analysis will be more transparent by virtue of the fact that they are cooperative constraints. The strategy of my reanalysis can be summarized as follows:

1. The group of rules which I have labelled 'parsing of metrical
   structure, including syllable structure', can be replaced by
   context-free Metrical Structure Rules. Being context free, these
   yield the same result however they are applied.

2. The group of rules which I have labelled 'phonetic interpretation of metrical structure' are akin to redundancy rules, in
   which the presence of (a) particular feature(s) not present in
   the lexical representation is predictable on the basis of the
   metrical structure. These rules can be recast as implicational
   constraints on feature specification, or in some cases as prosodic features supplied by the metrical structure rules.

3. The group of rules which I have listed under the common
   label as 'Palatal Assimilation' rules will be replaced by a
   metrical version of the autosegmental analysis of the spread
   of a 'high, front' feature specification from the syllable nucleus
   to the onset. The variety of phenomena expressed in H&M's
   various rules will be shown to be the consequences of palatal
   assimilation in conjunction with implicational constraints on
   feature specification and the application of Feature Specification Defaults.

4. The group of rules which I have labelled 'phonetic interpretation of syllable structure', are, like 'phonetic interpretation of
   metrical structure' (of which syllable structure is a part), those
   in which the presence of (a) particular feature(s) not present in
   the lexical representation is predictable on the basis of the
   syllable structure. These rules will be recast as implicational
   constraints on feature specification, or in some cases as prosodic features supplied by the syllable structure rules.

In every case, structure-changing rules will be avoided, and an
unordered set of cooperative structure-building rules developed
instead. Space does not permit a consideration of all of H&M's
rules, so I shall focus on a number of illustrative examples from
stratum 1, and Velar Softening, a stratum 2 rule. For examples of
how allophonic phenomena are treated, see e.g. Coleman (1992).

7.1 Stratum 1
7.1.1 Stress rules
Stress rules are placed at the beginning of H&M's rules. This is
because the metrical structures which stress rules assign to lexical
representations feed other rules, starting with H&M's first rule,
CiV Lengthening. Placing stress rules at the beginning of stratum 1
implies that only stratum 1 constituents of words have a metrical

structure, which is not the case: stratum 1 stress placement may have attracted most attention from phonologists, due to the apparent intricacies of its movable nature, but morphological constructions at strata 2–4 also have an associated metrical structure. A declarative version of metrical theory was described above, in Section 6.1. Further details of this account of English stress and parametric variation between stress systems may be found in Coleman (1991a: 266–76, 420–35; 1991b).

7.1.2 CiV Lengthening (57)

CiV Lengthening is the rule which derives words such as *Caucāsian*, *Horātian*, *Lillipūtian*, *custōdial* and *colōnial* from *Caucăsus*, *Horăce*, *Lillipŭt*, *custŏdy* respectively. H&M formulate the rule as follows: [14]

$$
\begin{array}{ccc}
\text{Rhyme} & \text{Rhyme} \\
| & / \ \backslash \\
\text{X} & \rightarrow & \text{X} \quad \text{X} \\
| & \backslash \ / \\
\text{[-cons]} & \text{[-cons]}
\end{array}
\Bigg/ \left[\underline{\quad\quad} \atop \text{-high} \right] C_1^1
\left[\begin{array}{c} \text{+high} \\ \text{-cons} \\ \text{-stress} \\ \text{-back} \end{array} \right] V
$$

The 'rewrite' part of this rule (i.e., excluding the contextual restriction) is not by itself structure-changing, but because vowel length affects syllable weight, which in turn affects metrical structure, the analysis is nevertheless one in which the metrical structure of lexically underived forms is *changed* to produce derived forms. It is consequently a structure-changing analysis and therefore not immediately amenable to reinterpretation in an entirely structure-building framework. Despite this, a structure-building analysis is available, which I shall now describe.

First, note that H&M's analysis is simply a pairing of a structural change with an *ad hoc* rule environment which neither determines nor follows from the form of the structural change itself. The form of CiV Lengthening is as arbitrary or as motivated as the precisely contrary rule:

$$
\begin{array}{ccc}
\text{Rhyme} & \text{Rhyme} \\
/ \ \backslash & | \\
\text{X} \quad \text{X} & \rightarrow & \text{X} \\
\backslash \ / & | \\
\text{[-cons]} & \text{[-cons]}
\end{array}
\Bigg/ \left[\underline{\quad\quad} \atop \text{-high} \right] C_1^1
\left[\begin{array}{c} \text{+high} \\ \text{-cons} \\ \text{-stress} \\ \text{-back} \end{array} \right] V
$$

(This has the same structural change as H&M's Shortening Rule (56), discussed below.) The phenomenon of CiV Lengthening can be related to the fact that the lengthened vowel is also stressed. The relationship between vowel length and stress placement is non-arbitrary in the arboreal metrical theory. Let us therefore attempt to relate the lengthening phenomenon more directly to its metrical environment. The suffixes -*ian* and -*ial* in cases of CiV Lengthening may conservatively be analysed as metrically disyllabic. The placement of stress on the stem-final syllable follows from the fact that a polysyllabic word ending in two light syllables can only be metrically parsed as finishing with a word-final ternary foot. In this case, the first, stress-bearing syllable is the stem-final syllable. For CiV Lengthening to follow from stress placement, it is sufficient to propose that stressed syllables which are otherwise unspecified for weight are by default *heavy*:

(1)   Default: $\sigma_s \supseteq$ [weight: heavy]

In a Unification-based account of syllable weight, it seems convenient to regard light syllables as unmarked for weight for an independent reason. Recall that the rime is heavy if the nucleus is heavy (e.g. a long vowel or diphthong) or if the coda is heavy (e.g. an obstruent cluster). This can be expressed by the following pair of constraints:

(2)   N[weight: heavy] $\supseteq$ R[weight: heavy]

(3)   Coda[weight: heavy] $\supseteq$ R[weight: heavy]

But we also need to ensure that the rime is *only* heavy if either the nucleus or the coda is heavy, i.e. we want to rule out *R[weight: heavy] → N[weight: light] Coda[weight: light]. The two constraints above do not prevent this pattern of instantiations. Let us therefore strengthen the weight constraints to:

(4)   N[weight: heavy] ↔ R[weight: heavy]

(5)   Coda[weight: heavy] ↔ R[weight: heavy]

But this is too strong, because it implies that if the nucleus is heavy, the rime is heavy, and therefore (*wrongly!*) that the coda is heavy also. Likewise, if the coda is heavy, the nucleus must be heavy, which is also wrong. The following, Unification-based constraint does work, however, provided that light weight is unspecified (in other words, the feature [weight] is *privative*):

(6)   N: weight = R: weight = Coda: weight

To return to CiV Lengthening, the final syllable of a stem such as *Caucas-* is light, and thus unmarked for weight.[15] Metrical structure will locate stress on the stem-final syllable when *-ian* or *-ial* is suffixed, and since the weight of the stem-final syllable is unspecified, (1) marks it as heavy by default. The o˙ ˡᵛ way in which marked heaviness can be squared with the rest of thᵤ ˌyllable structure is for either the nucleus or the coda (or both) to branch. But geminate codas are prohibited in English, so it must be the nucleus that branches (structure-building). According to this analysis, CiV Lengthening is not the product of an *ad hoc* context-sensitive rewriting rule, but arises from the interaction of several independent principles of metrical structure. Contrary to H&M's extrinsic ordering of Stress Rules before CiV Lengthening, the construction of metrical structure and the phenomenon of CiV Lengthening are crucially intertwined.

This analysis suffers from an important set of counterexamples (as does the CiV Lengthening Rule): words with stem-final short vowels that fail to lengthen when *-ian* or *-ial* is added, e.g. *Circăssian*. Since there is no alternation in this form and others like it in the Unification-based analysis it suffices to lexically mark the last vowel of the stem as [weight: light]. (1) will then not apply. H&M's analysis, by contrast, fails to accommodate these counterexamples.

Even if the alternative analysis that I have just outlined proves untenable for some reason, there is a second possible declarative analysis available, which is closer in form to H&M's analysis, but which relates the lengthening directly to the lexical representation of the $\_C]_{m_1}i]_\sigma[_\sigma R]_\sigma]_{m_1}$ suffixation environment in which it occurs.[16] In this analysis, we include the long vowel and the final C of the stem which the suffix subcategorizes for in the lexical representation of the -iR suffixes which trigger presuffixal lengthening. For example, the lexical representation of *-ian* would be:

$$\begin{array}{ccccc} \text{X} & \text{X} & \text{X}]_{m_1} & \text{X} & \text{X} & \text{X} \\ \diagdown\diagup & & | & | & | & | \\ \text{[-cons]} & & \text{[+cons]} & i & a & n \end{array}$$

Unification of this representation with the representation of the stem $[_{m_1}Caucas]_{m_1}$ would not be prohibited whether the stem-final vowel is underspecified for length, or specified as short, as the structural representation of long vowels in Autosegmental phonology unifies with that of short vowels. The resulting unified representation would be:

```
X  X  X  X  X  X    X]mi  X  X  X
|   \ /  |   \ /      |    |  |  |
k   ɔ  k   a        s    i  a  n
```

7.1.3 s-Voicing (111)

s-Voicing is the name H&M give to alternations such as
Malthu[s] − *Malthu*[z]*ian*, *Cauca*[s]*us* − *Cauca*[z]*ian*, *preci*[s]*e* −
preci[z]*ion* and *re*[z]*ign*, *de*[z]*sign*, *re*[z]*ume*, *pre*[z]*ume*, *re*[z]*ist vs.*
con[s]*ign*, *con*[s]*ume*, *con*[s]*ist*. They account for these alternations
with the rule:[17]

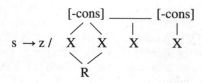

Whether the rule is structure-changing or not depends on the
representation of the voicing distinction (the rule does not resolve
this matter). If derivational 'voicing' is represented as [−voi] →
[+voi] it is clearly structure-changing. But if voicelessness is unmarked, 'voicing' could be treated as spread or addition of [+voi].

Since both voiced and voiceless forms occur in the alternation, it
is necessary to assume either that one particular value of [voi] is
underspecified, or that the domain-edge /s/ in this alternation is
lexically unspecified for [voi], i.e. it is represented archisegmentally
as, e.g., /S/. Descriptively, we want to enforce a single category-
building implication in two symmetrical environments:

/S/ ⊇ [+voi] in env.V́__]m₁V̆ or V̆[m₁__V́

Whether the accentuation of the Vs is a *condition* of this rule is not
clear, but since the phenomenon is triggered by the environment
V́__V̆ stem-finally, and V̆__V́ stem-initially, we cannot attribute s-
Voicing to stress placement. Neither can we attribute it to resyllabification (e.g. Mal. thus vs. Mal.th[uw].[z]ian), because in the stem-
initial s-Voicing cases there is no resyllabification (cf. [s]ign,
de.[z]ign). Length of the preceding vowel is not a necessary part of
the condition for some speakers, since pronunciations *fissile* −
fi[ž]*ion* are common.

Clearly, the crucial determinant of s-Voicing is its intervocalic
environment. A part of this is the absence of any other intervocalic
consonants, since s-Voicing is blocked in clusters. The only challenge which s-Voicing presents to a structure-building, implicational

account is how to formulate the environment and the affected category as the antecedent of a single implicational constraint. Such a formulation can be constructed by adding sufficient structure to the 'structural description' of the rule to create a context-free environment for the rule. This can be done if 'intervocalic consonant' is formalized as the category *Interlude*, a term originally proposed by Hockett and discussed more formally in Anderson and Jones (1974), Lass (1984: 266–8) and subsequent work in Dependency Phonology.[18]

A number of arguments against interludes (ambisyllabicity) have been raised in previous phonological analyses:

1. interlude clusters may involve tangling (Kahn 1976: 37);
2. interludes can be analysed derivationally as resyllabification (Kiparsky 1979);
3. interludes involve improper bracketing, which is not attested elsewhere in grammar (Harris and Kaye 1990: 253).

These are questionable, aesthetic judgements, however. First, the analyses of tangling to which Kahn alludes are both incorrect and inapplicable in this context: inapplicable, because s-Voicing only concerns a single consonant, not a cluster; incorrect, because ambisyllabic consonant clusters do *not* create tangling: the cluster as a whole may be ambisyllabic (Anderson and Jones 1974: 7). Second, as I argued above, enriching the class of representations is often preferable to employing a more powerful rule formalism than would otherwise be the case. If the price of a more constrained phonological formalism than the standard derivational model is ambisyllabicity, then it is formally well worth the price. Third, the claim that improper bracketing is not attested elsewhere is both theory-dependent, and even within orthodox contemporary phonological theory, incorrect: re-entrancy (i.e. being in two constituents at once) is also employed even in H&M's analysis to represent long vowels and consonants. In syntax, re-entrancy could be employed in the analysis of raising, as in Relational Grammar. Thus ambisyllabicity is not as unprecedented as some phonologists argue.

Given the existence of ambisyllabic interludes, s-Voicing can be formulated declaratively as:[19]

[interlude: S] $\supseteq$ [+ voi]

where S abbreviates the category of archisegmental /S/. If s-Voicing is indeed restricted to foot-internal occurrence after long vowels, the constraint could be tightened to:

$$\left[\Sigma: \begin{bmatrix} \sigma_s: & \left[R: \begin{bmatrix} X_1: & \text{[-cons]}_{\boxed{1}} \\ X_2: & \text{[-cons]}_{\boxed{1}} \end{bmatrix}\right] \\ \sigma_w: & [O: [X:S]] \end{bmatrix}\right] \supseteq [\Sigma: [\sigma_w: [O: [X: \text{[+voi]}]]]]$$

Finally, a note on the ordering. s-Voicing must follow CiV Lengthening in H&M's account because it applies not just to lexically long vowels, but also to long vowels derived by CiV Lengthening (metrically long vowels). Therefore, according to H&M, 'the presuffixal syllable *must* underlyingly be short' (my emphasis). Although this fact *can* be accounted for derivationally, it is not the case that it *must* be accounted for derivationally. It can be expressed declaratively by simultaneously *conjoining* the declarative formulation of the CiV Lengthening and s-Voicing constraints. The definition of phonological well-formedness will then look like:

well formed(ϕ) $\leftrightarrow$ . . . CiV Lengthening(ϕ) & s-Voicing(ϕ) . . .

By conjoining the constraints in this way, examples such as *Malthusian* which satisfy the antecedents of both constraints must satisfy both constraints for the representation to be well formed. Examples such as *Lilliputian*, which satisfies the antecedent (structural description) of CiV Lengthening but not the antecedent of s-Voicing will be well-formed provided that the consequent (structural change) of CiV Lengthening obtains, which it satisfies, and provided that the consequent of s-Voicing does *not* obtain, which it does not satisfy. Examples such as *resign* satisfy the antecedent of the s-Voicing constraint, and must therefore also satisfy the consequent, but since they do not satisfy the antecedent of CiV Lengthening, that constraint simply does not obtain. Examples such as *cretinous*, which do not satisfy the antecedent of CiV Lengthening or of s-Voicing are not required to satisfy the consequents, so the result is well-formed. In simple terms, the two constraints (and possibly others) apply together, and a representation is only well-formed if it adheres to every constraint which actually applies to it.

7.1.4   Shortening Rules (56) and (110)

H&M conclude stratum 1 with two rules (56 and 110) that together describe four vowel shortening phenomena: Trisyllabic Shortening (56a), Cluster Shortening (56b), -*ic*-Shortening (56c) and *i*-Shortening (110), which in SPE was a subcase of (what is now called) Trisyllabic Shortening.

I shall discuss rule (56) in two parts: the structural change itself, and the disjunction of environments in which it occurs.

Structural change:

$$\text{Rhyme} \qquad \text{Rhyme}$$

X X $\rightarrow$ X

[-cons] [-cons]

Environments:

(a.) Trisyllabic shortening: ____ [-stress] | σ   σ

(b.) Cluster shortening: ____ X X

R

(c.) -*ic*-Shortening: ____ -*ic*, -*id*, etc.

The structural change is exactly the opposite of the structural change of CiV Lengthening. Furthermore, since it deletes structural information, it appears superficially to challenge the possibility of an entirely non-derivational analysis. There is nevertheless a possible non-derivational analysis of shortening, which I shall now discuss.

Suppose that in addition to the branching vs. non-branching representation of length, a binary length feature is employed. This would not be an unnecessary redundancy, since such a feature would allow syllable weight to be defined by a context-free grammar. If [+long] is left unspecified, shortening could be characterized as the incremental, category-building addition of [−long] to nuclei in the three environments. Parallel to the declarative analysis of CiV Lengthening, then, the lexical representation of Trisyllabic Shortening triggers such as -*ity* would be:

$[-\text{long}]([+\text{cons}])]_{m_1}\text{ity}$

In effect this proposes that Trisyllabic Shortening is a property of specific affixes. If a more general statement is required, the above pattern could be generalized to:

$[-\text{long}]([+\text{cons}])]_{m_1}\sigma_w\sigma_w$

and regarded as a special case of the ternary foot metrical structure rule (however that is expressed).

Alternatively, we might regard 'shortening' and 'lengthening' as simply non-derivational alternations between different instantiations of metrical structure. The account of shortening given in Myers (1987) is very similar in spirit to this declarative proposal.[20] Note that H&M's discussion about the relative order of CiV Lengthening and Shortening is internally contradictory. They defend the SPE analysis in which forms such as *devotion, deletion* and *integration* first undergo Trisyllabic Shortening and then CiV Lengthening, i.e. devōte ⇒ devŏtion ⇒ devōtion (p. 83). Then they propose the alternative ordering, which would be plausible within the terms of the derivational model if some form produced by CiV Lengthening was subsequently shortened (p. 97). Let us examine the possibility of a CiV-lengthened form being subjected to one of the three shortening rules. All forms which undergo CiV Lengthening will contain a substring of the form V V CiV. Consider

$$\underset{[\text{-high}]}{V \, V} \, CiV$$

Trisyllabic Shortening first. V V matches the left-hand side of

$$\underset{[\text{-high}]}{V \, V}$$

the Shortening rule, Ci could match $\sigma_{[-\text{stress}]}$, and the final V could match the final σ of the Trisyllabic Shortening environment. So Trisyllabic Shortening should apply to CiV-lengthened words such as *Caucasian* to produce *Caucăsian*, which is the wrong output. Now consider Cluster Shortening. For Cluster Shortening to apply to a form which is subject to CiV Lengthening, the C in the environment of the CiV Lengthening rule must be C^2, not C^1 as I stated in fn 14. The input must thus contain a 'superheavy' rime consisting of a long vowel and a consonant cluster. CiV Lengthening and Cluster Shortening have complementary environments, so need not be ordered with respect to each other, but can be applied concurrently. Finally, consider -*ic* shortening. The statement of that rule is inexplicit about the range of morphemes such as -*ic* which trigger -*ic* shortening. The two which are listed in H&M, -*ic* and -*id*, do not unify with the iV part of the environment for CiV Lengthening, and thus there is no reason to suppose CiV lengthening and -*ic* shortening to be applied in any particular order, since they are complementary rules which could be applied concurrently.

I have shown, then, that the seemingly complex phenomena of stratum 1 phonology are susceptible to a declarative analysis that is as elegant (parsimonious, etc.) as, yet more restrictive than, H&M's derivational account. Furthermore, the declarative account makes crucial reference to aspects of the structure of phonological representations that in H&M's account are not considered, e.g. metrical structure. The declarative account is thus less arbitrary than H&M's derivational analysis.

7.2 Stratum 2 'derivation': velar softening

The velar softening rule is a classical transformational statement of the paradigmatic alternation exemplified by pairs of forms such as *electric ~ electricity*. While it might be questioned whether the phonology of these forms is indeed productive and therefore requiring expression in the grammar, I shall nevertheless show that by dividing the description of the velar softening relation into several sub-constraints, a more motivated, non-destructive, structure-building analysis is possible.

H&M's statement of velar softening is:

(7)

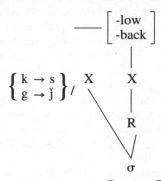

The feature-structure $\begin{bmatrix} -low \\ -back \end{bmatrix}$ describes the class of segments {i, ɪ, e, ɛ, y}. Note that the structural change and environments of Spirantization and Palatalization (H&M's rules 85 and 80) are similar to the structural changes[21] and environments of Velar Softening. A number of potential generalizations are therefore not captured in H&M's account, because their derivational theory requires them to place these three rules at non-adjacent positions in the derivation. I shall show that if the necessity of a specific derivational sequence of rule application does not hold, then the component 'palatalization', 'coronalization' and 'lenition' phenomena of Velar Softening, Spirantization and Palatalization can be expressed with greater generality.

First, the disjunction $\begin{Bmatrix} k \to s \\ g \to \check{j} \end{Bmatrix}$ can be eliminated and the analysis thus improved[22] by abstracting the description of 'palatalization' from 'voiceless softening' thus:

$\begin{Bmatrix} k \to \check{c} \\ g \to \check{j} \end{Bmatrix}$ and č → s. The disjunction can then be eliminated by generalizing over [± voice]. The first conjunct, *'palataling'* is an independently motivated phenomenon which is exemplified in other environments, e.g. *drink* vs. *drench, church* vs. *kirk, bridge* vs. *brig*. The lenition relation expressed by č → s can also be broken up into two conjuncts: č → š and š → s. The first conjunct here, 'deaffrication/palatal spirantization' is also exemplified by the non-productive alternations *Frenč ~ Frenš, Welš ~ Welč*. The third sub-process involved in velar softening, š → s is the (dissimilatory) inverse of the sharpening process s → š, as in *a[sj]ume ~ a[š]ume*. A declarative relation š ~ s captures both š → s and s → š in a unitary fashion. I shall now show how the three 'subderivations' of palataling, palatal spirantization and depalatalization can be expressed declaratively, and how the specific environments of velar softening phenomena can be accounted for non-derivationally.

Viewed derivationally, *palataling* is a change in place and manner of articulation of certain velar stops which makes them palatal affricates in a palatal environment. The putative change in *manner* of articulation is unproblematic for a declarative analysis, because affrication is a predictable property of palatal closure. We can thus break palataling down into two sub-relations: (informally) [velar] → [palatal] and [(palatal) stop] → [affricate]. We might very plausibly analyse the English affricates /č/ and /ǰ/ as 'strident stops', as Jakobson et al. (1952: 24–5, 43–4) suggest, and describe the process [(palatal) stop] → [(palatal) affricate] with the structure-building implication [+ palatal] ⊇ [+ str]. Equivalent formulations of this implication can be given in the manner of SPE (e.g. [+ palatal] ⊇ [+ del rel]) or Autosegmental/Metrical Phonology:

$$
\text{(e.g.} \qquad \underset{\text{[+palatal]}}{\text{C}} \qquad \supseteq \qquad \overset{\overset{\text{C}}{\text{[+palatal]}}}{\diagup \diagdown} \qquad \text{)}.
$$
$$
\qquad\qquad\qquad\qquad\qquad \text{[-cnt]} \quad \text{[+cnt]}
$$

A structure-building representation of the 'change' in place of articulation from velar to palatal is readily afforded by feature geometry and underspecification theory. In forms which exemplify the velar ~ palatal alternation, the lexical representation of the place of articulation could be simply [+ dorsal], i.e. not specified further as velar or palatal. Bearing in mind that the voiceless instantiation of velar softening k → s involves a further 'change' to coronal place of articulation, this proposal needs to be generalized a little further so that the lexical representation in these forms is simply [+lingual], a category proposed by Anderson and Ewen (1980: 32) and further motivated in Lass (1984: 285–9). Since the chain of relations k ⇒ č ⇒ š̬ ⇒ s must involve *addition* of features in a declarative account, I shall propose that in the lexical entry, the specification [+lingual] suffices to define both place and manner of articulation, the addition of [−velar] (or [−grv] or $\begin{bmatrix} -\text{low} \\ -\text{back} \end{bmatrix}$) to [+lingual] suffices to restrict the class {k, č, š, s} to {č̬, š, s}, the addition of [+cnt] restricts it further to {š, s}, and the addition of [+cor] restricts it further to {s}. I shall consequently analyse the apparently derivational train of *alterations* k ⇒ č ⇒ š̬ ⇒ s as a non-derivational accretion of features determined by context and defaults. The [−velar] (or [−grv] or $\begin{bmatrix} -\text{low} \\ -\text{back} \end{bmatrix}$) feature added to [+lingual] is an assimilatory feature(-structure) which spreads from the following nucleus to the onset:

(8) *Palatal assimilation*

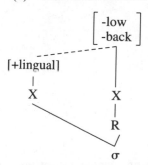

Why this assimilation constraint holds is not explained by this analysis, but at least the form which it takes lays the foundation for a motivated explanation.

For the further definition of velar place and stop manner of articulation in the interpretation of unmodified [+lingual] in the cases without $\begin{bmatrix} -\text{low} \\ -\text{back} \end{bmatrix}$, there are two possibilities: either the phonetic interpretation function is sensitive to the fact that [+lingual] is unaccompanied by other place and manner features, and therefore we can reliably interpret unadorned [+lingual] as 'velar stop', or defaults such as [+lingual] ⊇ [+velar] and [−cnt] might be proposed. As described above, the affrication of palatal closure is predictable and can be expressed by a structure-building implicational constraint.

In the voiceless case of velar softening, it must be ensured that the palatal specification $\begin{bmatrix} -\text{low} \\ -\text{back} \end{bmatrix}$ is subject to the application of further structure-building constraints. Specifically, constraints are needed that will ensure the obligatory constructions č → $_{sb}$š and š → $_{sb}$s. In terms of the features employed in the analysis so far, this conjunction of constructions is: [23]

$$
\begin{bmatrix} -\text{voi} \\ +\text{lingual} \\ -\text{velar} \end{bmatrix} \Rightarrow \text{sb} \begin{bmatrix} -\text{voi} \\ +\text{lingual} \\ -\text{velar} \\ +\text{cnt} \end{bmatrix} \quad \& \quad \begin{bmatrix} -\text{voi} \\ +\text{lingual} \\ -\text{velar} \\ +\text{cnt} \end{bmatrix} \Rightarrow \text{sb} \begin{bmatrix} -\text{voi} \\ +\text{lingual} \\ -\text{velar} \\ +\text{cor} \\ +\text{cnt} \end{bmatrix}
$$

The first of these conjuncts must also be specifically restricted to the same context as the first component of velar softening, palataling, except that the description of the contextual nucleus, rhyme and syllable structure need not be stated again:

(9)   *Palatal softening*

$$
\begin{bmatrix} -\text{low} \\ -\text{back} \end{bmatrix}
$$
$$
\big|
$$
$$
\begin{bmatrix} +\text{lingual} \\ -\text{voi} \end{bmatrix} \supseteq [+\text{cnt}]
$$

The second conjunct in velar softening, 'depalatalization' or 'coronalization', may be described in terms of the addition of coronality, rather than deletion of palatality:

(10)   *blah blah*

$$
\begin{bmatrix} +\text{lingual} \\ -\text{velar} \\ -\text{voi} \end{bmatrix} \supseteq [+\text{cor}]
$$

To summarize this discussion of the sub-constraints involved in 'velar softening', see Table 10.3. The five constraints listed in this table are applied concurrently, not sequentially.

TABLE 10.3: Subconstraints in 'velar softening'.

	Alternating forms				Non-alternating forms	
	electric(al)	analog(ous)	electricity	analogy	indicate	delegate
Lexical rep.:	$\begin{bmatrix} + \text{ling} \\ - \text{voi} \end{bmatrix}$	$\begin{bmatrix} + \text{ling} \\ + \text{voi} \end{bmatrix}$	$\begin{bmatrix} + \text{ling} \\ - \text{voi} \end{bmatrix}$	$\begin{bmatrix} + \text{ling} \\ + \text{voi} \end{bmatrix}$	$\begin{bmatrix} + \text{ling} \\ + \text{velar} \\ - \text{voi} \\ - \text{cnt} \end{bmatrix}$	$\begin{bmatrix} + \text{ling} \\ + \text{velar} \\ + \text{voi} \\ - \text{cnt} \end{bmatrix}$
Palatal place assimilation:	—	—	[− velar]	[− velar]	—	—
Palatal affrication:	—	—	[+ str]	[+ str]	—	—
Voiceless palatal softening:	—	—	[+ cnt]	—	—	—
Voiceless coronalisation:	—	—	[+ cor]	—	—	—
Phonetic interpretation:	[k]	[g]	[s]	[ǰ]	[k]	[g]

H&M (p. 79) argue that Velar Softening must precede Vowel Shift:

> If Velar Softening is ordered after Vowel Shift, the statement of its environment becomes much more complex

because Velar Softening applies before *shifted* /i/ and /e/ (e.g. *criticīze, matricēs*) as well as unshifted /i/ and /e/ (e.g. *medicĭne, intelligĕnt(sia)*). Because they fail to consider the possibility of an analysis in which Velar Softening and Vowel Shift apply *simultaneously*, their argument for placing the two rules in a derivational sequence is rather weaker than might at first appear.

8 Conclusion

I have examined in some detail a number of different kinds of rules from H&M's derivational analysis, along with their arguments in support of particular rule ordering proposals. I have argued, by proposing specific alternative analyses, that neither structure-changing rules, nor particular rule ordering proposals, are actually necessary. Structure-building rules, applied according to simultaneous constraint-based considerations, are adequate in these cases, as well as in the other rules, not examined in this chapter, which H&M have proposed.

I have shown that both the standard derivational-transformational approach to phonology, and the supposedly principle-based alternative proposed in Government Phonology, are excessively powerful.

This excessive power is eliminable, however, if a more constrained formalism, such as unification-based context-free phrase structure grammar, is applied to the expression of phonological analyses. In some cases I have shown the declarative alternatives to be not only less unconstrained, but more general in appropriate ways.

I shall conclude by briefly reiterating some references to the steadily growing body of papers and dissertations on declarative approaches to phonology. For the reader who wishes to learn more about this approach, I suggest Coleman (1991b) and the other chapters from the same volume, Coleman (1992), Cole and Coleman (forthcoming), and Bird et al. (forthcoming), and references therein. This sample of studies covers a broad variety of phonological issues, including cyclic rule application, universals of metrical structure (e.g. a declarative version of the parameter setting theory), and the interfaces to articulatory and acoustic phonetics.

Notes and Acknowledgements

Parts of this chapter were presented at the First UK Workshop on Computation and Phonology, York, 1990, and at the XVth International Congress of Linguists, Quebec, 9th–14th August 1992. I am grateful to Ted Briscoe, Wiebke Brockhaus, Jacques Durand, Francis Katamba, John Local, Janet Pierrehumbert, Pete Whitelock, Richard Wiese and Sheila Williams for their helpful comments. All faults in this chapter are mine.

1. Such a proof is given in Coleman (1991a: 128–30). See also Salomaa (1973: 83), Levelt (1976: 243), Lapointe (1977: 228) and Berwick and Weinberg (1984: 127).
2. Networks of points linked by lines, as in Autosegmental Phonology, for instance.
3. Of course, I am not proposing that the grammar of syllable structure in human linguistic competence is like *F*. Context-free rules, or equivalent hierarchical constraints on structure are more natural for the description of syllables. *F* is only proposed as a demonstration that the weak generative capacity of sequences of syllable templates is equivalent to a regular grammar.
4. The grammar of syllable structures in any language is trivially regular, since in every language the length of syllables is always subject to some finite upper-bound.
5. Even if this mechanism were to be prohibited, spreading might be employed as an insertion mechanism. It will be objected that spreading only permits *existing*, not *new*, material to be added to a segment, but the existence of floating autosegments allows arbitrary element insertion:

   Up to this point, we have assumed deletion of a skeletal position in plural forms, which leads to a floating U −. While floating, the U −

is unable to govern (in this case spread to) the preceding vowel . . .
The reader will recall that we refrained from claiming that the U –
element was lost. In the derivations given above it simply floated,
not being attached to any skeletal point. (KLV 1985: 324)

There are numerous examples in the Autosegmental literature of
floating segments or autosegments, of course. We can then attach the
floating segment to the desired insertion site by creating or coopting a
slot for it, and then spreading its elements one-by-one to that slot. The
proliferation of empty syllable positions in Government Phonology
facilitates this possibility.

6. Kaye (1990a: 328 n. 19), considering such violations, states

It is worth considering whether the loss of a nuclear point in the
course of a phonological derivation is in violation of the projection
principle. Notice that such a loss does not involve changing the nature
of governing relations. The head of the nucleus remains the head (on
the assumption that it is the governed member of the nucleus that is
lost). No formerly governed position is elevated to the status of
governor.

True enough: but since the governee has been deleted, one of the
governor-governee relations that makes up the set of government
relations pertinent to the projection principle has been removed, an
alteration which is in violation of the principle.

7. Janet Pierrehumbert, in Bird et al. (forthcoming), points out that
'matching' is defined in SPE in two different ways: on p. 391 as
containment, and on pp. 336–7 as non-distinctness. The latter conception of matching is most similar to unification.

8. The first two rules can be collapsed to $\Sigma \rightarrow \begin{smallmatrix}\sigma \\ [+\text{heavy}]\end{smallmatrix} \left(\begin{smallmatrix}\sigma \\ [-\text{heavy}]\end{smallmatrix} \right)$.

The third case, the ternary foot rule, is given a degree of internal
structure by some phonologists (e.g. Liberman and Prince 1977,
Kiparsky 1979), which can be expressed: $\Sigma_{\text{ternary}} \rightarrow \Sigma_{\text{binary}} \begin{smallmatrix}\sigma \\ [-\text{heavy}]\end{smallmatrix}$,
where Σ_{binary} is expanded as in the second foot rule below.

9. In fact, this will refer to the constituents called α-constituents in Selkirk
(1982a), Class 1 words in Siegel (1974), level 1 in Church (1985), etc.

10. The superscript $^\text{L}$ abbreviates the feature [– heavy].

11. After Chomsky and Halle (1968: 342).

12. The principal omissions in my analysis are the Vowel Shift and associated rules. A declarative analysis of this part of English phonology is
given in Coleman (1991a: 382–6). The contentious status of vowel shift
rules in the synchronic phonology is discussed in several papers in
Phonology Yearbook vol. 3. One aspect of Halle and Mohanan's
analysis – its postulation of *four* rule strata – is widely regarded as
something of an oddity. However, that detail is not consequential to
this discussion. The merit of their analysis is that, as in Chomsky and
Halle (1968), an attempt is made to explicitly formulate a more-or-less

complete set of rules. This fact alone makes their analysis a worthy exemplar of derivational phonological theory. Note that the declarative reanalysis of Halle and Mohanan's rules is offered only for exemplification.

13. The point in the sequence of rules which divides morphophonological from allophonic rules may be considered as constituting a level of representation which corresponds quite closely to the traditional phonemic level. Kiparsky (1985: 113) compares the classical phonemic level with the Lexical/Postlexical division. Note, however, that the morphophonological/allophonic division of rules in fact falls well before the Lexical/Postlexical division.

14. In fact, for some reason, H&M's formulation of this rule does *not* include C_1^i or V in the environment of the rule (cf. Rubach 1984b: 40, examples 35, 36, SPE p. 181). I cannot see how the rule could work without them, and assuming the absence to be an oversight, have inserted them here.

15. Since there is a length alternation in these examples, it could be argued that the lexical representation of the stem is unmarked for length, which is then determined by the context in which the stem occurs. Underspecification of length is impossible with the autosegmental approach to the representation of length as branching, prompting H&M to note: 'the presuffixal syllable *must* underlyingly be short' (my emphasis). The '*must*' rests on a theory-internal assumption, however.

16. As in Coleman (1992), the subscript m_1 denotes the lexical domain of level 1 morphophonology.

17. This rule misses an important characteristic of the examples, however: it is limited to /s/es which are at the edge of the domain (i.e. stem-initial or -final).

18. It might be questioned whether the $\check{V}z\acute{V}$ cases of stem-initial s-Voicing such as *resign*, *resist* and *consist* are interludes, since they are not foot-internal.

19. In Old English (according to Sweet 1882: 3), all fricatives were redundantly voiced intervocalically. Distinctively voiced fricatives are from later sources, a fact which is still reflected in the different distributions of voiced and voiceless fricatives in the synchronic grammar of English. For example, voiced fricatives do not occur in onset consonant clusters. Perhaps it is the cases of intervocalic fricatives which *fail* to become voiced intervocalically which require special explanation.

20. Though Myers's analysis is couched in derivational terms, it is like much work in Metrical phonology declarative in orientation, and can be recast in purely declarative terms without extensive modification.

21. Note that (7) is actually an abbreviation for a disjunction of two rules with identical environments.

22. Manaster-Ramer and Zadrozny (1990) argue for the elimination of disjunctions in cases such as this: 'disjunction is not forbidden, but when it occurs, it implies the factual claim about the referents of the disjuncts are distinct linguistic phenomena' (p. 196).

23. Ignoring possible segment-internal feature geometry.

REFERENCES

AKINLABI, A. (1992) 'Underspecification and the phonology of Yoruba /r/', *Linguistic Inquiry* **24**: 139–60.

ANDERSEN, H. (1972) 'Diphthongization', *Language* **48**: 11–50.

ANDERSEN, H. (1974) 'Towards a typology of change: bifurcating changes and binary relations.' In ANDERSON, J. M. and JONES, C. (eds) *Historical Linguistics II: Theory and Description in Phonology. Proceedings of the First International Congress on Historical Linguistics, Edinburgh 1973*, North Holland, pp. 17–60.

ANDERSON, J. M. (1969) 'Syllabic or non-syllabic phonology?', *Journal of Linguistics* **5**: 136–42.

ANDERSON, J. M. (1986) 'Structural analogy and case grammar', *Lingua* **70**: 79–129.

ANDERSON, J. M. (1987) 'Structural analogy and Dependency Phonology.' In ANDERSON, J. M. and DURAND, J. (eds) *Explorations in Dependency Phonology*. Foris: Dordrecht, pp. 15–48.

ANDERSON, J. M. (1989) 'Reflexions on notional grammar, with some remarks on its relevance to issues in the analysis of English and its history.' In ARNOLD, D., ATKINSON, M., DURAND, J., GROVER, C. and SADLER, L. (eds) *Essays on Grammatical Theory and Universal Grammar*. Oxford: Oxford University Press, pp. 13–36.

ANDERSON, J. M. (1990) 'On the status of auxiliaries in notional grammar', *Journal of Linguistics* **26**: 341–62.

ANDERSON, J. M. and DURAND, J. (eds) (1987) *Explorations in Dependency Phonology*. Foris: Dordrecht.

ANDERSON, J. M. and DURAND, J. (1988) 'Vowel harmony and non-specification in Nez Perce.' In HULST, H. G. VAN DER and SMITH, N. (eds) *Features, Segmental Structure and Harmony Processes, Part II*. Foris: Dordrecht, pp. 2–17.

ANDERSON, J. and EWEN, C. (1980) 'Introduction: A sketch of dependency, phonology.' In ANDERSON, J. and EWEN, C. (eds) 'Studies in dependency phonology', *Ludwigsburg Studies in Language and Linguistics* **4**: 9–40.

ANDERSON, J. M. and EWEN, C. J. (1981) 'The representation of neutralisation in universal phonology.' In DRESSLER, W. U., PFEIFFER, O. E. and RENNISON, J. R. (eds) *Phonologica 1980*. Innsbrucker Beiträge zur Sprachwissenschaft: Innsbruck, pp. 15–22.

ANDERSON, J. M. and EWEN, C. J. (1987) *Principles of Dependency Phonology*. Cambridge University Press: Cambridge.

ANDERSON, J. M. and JONES, C. (1974) 'Three theses concerning phonological representations', *Journal of Linguistics* 10: 1–26.

ANDERSON, J. M. and JONES, C. (1977) *Phonological Structure and the History of English*. North-Holland: Amsterdam.

ANTELL, S. A., CHERONO, G., HALL, B. L., HALL, R. M. R., MYERS, A. and PAM, M. (1973) 'Nilo-Saharan vowel harmony from the vantage point of Kalenjin', *Research Notes from the Department of Linguistics and Nigerian Languages* 6: 1–58. University of Ibadan.

ARCHANGELI, D. (1983) 'The root CV-template as a property of the affix: evidence from Yawelmani', *Natural Language and Linguistic Theory* 1: 387–84.

ARCHANGELI, D. (1984) *Underspecification in Yawelmani Phonology and Morphology*. MIT, PhD dissertation. Published 1988, Garland: New York.

ARCHANGELI, D. (1988) 'Aspects of underspecification theory', *Phonology* 5: 183–205.

ARCHANGELI, D. (1991) 'Syllabification and prosodic templates in Yawelmani', *Natural Language and Linguistic Theory* 9: 231–84.

ARCHANGELI, D. and PULLEYBLANK, D. (1989) 'Yoruba vowel harmony', *Linguistic Inquiry* 20: 173–217.

ARCHANGELI, D. and PULLEYBLANK, D. (1994) *Grounded Phonology*. MIT Press: Cambridge, Mass.

ARNOLD, D., ATKINSON, M., DURAND, J., GROVER, C. and SADLER, L. (eds) (1989) *Essays on Grammatical Theory and Universal Grammar*. Oxford University Press: Oxford.

ARONOFF, M. and OEHRLE, R. (eds) (1984) *Language Sound Structure: Studies in Phonology Presented to Morris Halle by his Teacher and Students*. MIT Press: Cambridge, Mass.

AUSTIN, P. (1981) *A Grammar of Diyari, South Australia*. Cambridge University Press: Cambridge.

AVERY, P. and RICE, K. (1989) 'Segment structure and coronal underspecification', *Phonology* 6: 179–200.

BACKLEY, P. (1993) 'Coronal: the undesirable element', *UCL Working Papers in Linguistics* 5: 301–23.

BAO, Z. (1990) 'Fanqie languages and reduplication', *Linguistic Inquiry* 21: 317–50.

BAO, Z. (1991) 'On the nature of tone.' Unpublished PhD dissertation, MIT.

BAR-HILLEL, Y., PERLES, M. and SHAMIR, E. (1961) 'On formal properties of simple phrase structure grammars', *Zeitschrift für Phonetik, Sprachwissenschaft und Kommunikationsforschung* 14: 143–72.

BASBØLL, H. (1977) 'The structure of the syllable and proposed hierarchy of phonological features.' In DRESSLER, W. U. et al. (eds) *Phonologica*

1976. Innsbrucker Beiträge zur Sprachwissenschaft. Innsbruck, pp. 143–8.

BENDER, B. W. (1969) *Spoken Marshallese*. University of Hawaii Press, Honolulu.

BERWICK, R. C. and WEINBERG, A. S. (1984) *The Grammatical Basis of Linguistic Performance: Language Use and Acquisition*. MIT Press: Cambridge, Mass.

BHAT, D. N. S. (1974) 'The phonology of liquid consonants', *Working Papers on Language Universals* **16**: 73–104.

BICKMORE, L. (1991) 'Compensatory lengthening in Kinyambo.' In KATAMBA, F. (ed.) *Studies in Inter-lacustrine Bantu Phonology*. Afrikanistische Arbeitspapiere: Cologne, pp. 75–103.

BIRD, S., COLEMAN, J., PIERREHUMBERT, J. and SCOBBIE, J. (forthcoming) 'Declarative phonology.' To appear in *Proceedings of the XVth International Congress of Linguists*, 9–14 August 1992, Laval University, Quebec.

BLAKE, B. J. (1979) 'Pitta-Pitta.' In DIXON, R. M. W. and BLAKE, B. J. *Handbook of Australian Languages*. John Benjamins: Amsterdam.

BLUMSTEIN, S. and COOPER, W. (1972) 'Identification versus discrimination of distinctive features in speech perception', *Quarterly Journal of Experimental Psychology* **24**: 207–14.

BLUMSTEIN, S. and COOPER, W. (1974) 'Hemispheric processing of intonation contours', *Cortex* **10**: 146–58.

BLUMSTEIN, S. E. and STEVENS, K. N. (1981) 'Phonetic features and acoustic invariance in speech', *Cognition* **10**: 25–32.

BOGORAS, W. (1922) 'Chukchee'. In BOAS, F. (ed.) *Handbook of American Indian Languages*, Part II, Smithsonian Institution, Washington D.C., Bureau of American Ethnology, Bulletin 40. (Reprinted 1969 by Anthropological Publications. Oosterhout N.B., The Netherlands), pp. 631–903.

BOOIJ, G. (1988) 'On the relation between lexical and prosodic phonology.' In BERTINETTO, P. M. and LOPORCARO, M. (eds) *Certamen Phonologicum: Papers from the 1987 Cortona Phonology Meeting*. Rosenberg and Sellier: Turin.

BOROWSKY, T. (1984) 'On resyllabification in English.' In COBLER, M., MACKAYE, S. and WESTCOAT, M. T. (eds) *Proceedings of the West Coast Conference on Formal Linguistics*. Vol. **3**. Stanford Linguistics Association. 1–5.

BOROWSKY, T. (1986) Topics in the lexical phonology of English. Unpublished PhD dissertation, University of Massachusetts.

BOROWSKY, T. (1989) 'Structure preservation and the syllable coda in English', *Natural Language and Linguistic Theory* **7**: 145–66.

BOYCE, S. E., KRAKOW, R. A. and BELL-BERTI, F. (1991) 'Phonological underspecification and speech motor organisation', *Phonology* **8**: 219–36.

BRAINE, M. D. S. (1974) 'On what might constitute learnable phonology', *Language* **50**: 270–99.

BROCKHAUS, W. G. (1992) 'Final devoicing: principles and parameters.' Unpublished PhD dissertation, University College London.

BROMBERGER, S. and HALLE, M. (1989) 'Why phonology is different', *Linguistic Inquiry* **20**: 51–70.

BROSELOW, E. (1983) 'Salish double reduplication: subjacency in morphology', *Natural Language and Linguistic Theory* **1**: 347–84.

BROSELOW, E. and MCCARTHY, J. (1983) 'A theory of internal reduplication', *The Linguistic Review* **3**, 25–88.

BROWMAN, C. P. and GOLDSTEIN, L. (1989) 'Articulatory gestures as phonological units', *Phonology* **6**: 201–52.

BROWN, C. (1994) 'The feature geometry of lateral approximants and lateral fricatives.' In Hulst, H. G. van der and Weijer, J. van der (eds.) (1994) *HIL Phonology Papers I*. HIL Publications no I. Holland Academic Graphics: Leiden.

BRUCK, A., FOX, R. A. and LA GALY, M. W. (eds) (1974) *Papers from the Parasession on Natural Phonology*. Chicago Linguistic Society: Chicago.

CARRIER-DUNCAN, J. (1984) 'Some problems with prosodic accounts of reduplication.' In ARONOFF, M. and OEHRLE, R. (eds), pp. 260–86. *Language Sound Structure: Studies in Phonology Presented to Morris Halle by his Teacher and Students*. Cambridge, Mass.: MIT Press.

CATFORD, J. C. (1977) *Fundamental Problems in Phonetics*. Edinburgh University Press: Edinburgh.

CHAMBERS, J. K. (1973) 'Canadian raising', *Canadian Journal of Linguistics* **18**: 113–35.

CHARETTE, M. (1988) Some constraints on governing relations in phonology. PhD dissertation, McGill University.

CHARETTE, M. (1989) 'The minimality condition in phonology', *Journal of Linguistics* **25**: 159–87.

CHARETTE, M. (1990) 'Licence to govern', *Phonology* **7**: 233–53.

CHARETTE, M. (1991) *Conditions on Phonological Government*. Cambridge University Press: Cambridge.

CHARETTE, M. (1992) 'Mongolian and Polish meet government-licensing', *SOAS Working Papers in Linguistics and Phonetics* **2**: 275–91.

CHARETTE, M. and KAYE, J. (1993) 'The death of ATR.' MS, School of Oriental and African Languages.

CHARETTE, M. and KAYE, J. (in preparation) 'A revised theory of phonological elements.' MS. School of Oriental and African Studies, University of London (SOAS).

CHO, Y. Y. (1990) 'Parameters of consonantal assimilation.' Unpublished PhD dissertation, Stanford University.

CHO, Y. Y. (1991a) 'Voicing is not relevant for sonority.' *Proceedings of the Berkeley Linguistic Society*, Berkeley Linguistic Society (BLS) 17.

CHO, Y. Y. (1991b) '"Voiceless" sonorants are aspirates.' Paper presented at the annual Linguistic Society of America (LSA) meeting.

CHOMSKY, N. (1957) *Syntactic Structures*. Mouton: The Hague.

CHOMSKY, N. (1959) 'On certain formal properties of grammars', *Information and Control* **2**: 137–67.

CHOMSKY, N. (1963) 'Formal properties of grammars.' In LUCE, R. D., BUSH, R. R. and GALANTER, E. (eds) *Handbook of Mathematical Psychology*, vol. 2, John Wiley: New York, pp. 323–418.

CHOMSKY, N. (1964) *Current Issues in Linguistics Theory*. Mouton: The Hague.
CHOMSKY, N. (1965) *Aspects of the Theory of Syntax*. MIT Press: Cambridge, Mass.
CHOMSKY, N. (1970) 'Remarks on nominalization.' In JACOBS, R. A. and ROSENBAUM, P. S. (eds) *Readings in English Transformational Grammar*. Ginn: Waltham, Mass., pp. 184–221.
CHOMSKY, N. (1973) 'Conditions on transformations.' In ANDERSON, S. and KIPARSKY, P. (eds) *A Festschrift for Morris Halle*. Holt, Reinhart & Winston: New York, pp. 232–86.
CHOMSKY, N. (1980) *Rules and Representations*. Basil Blackwell: Oxford.
CHOMSKY, N. and HALLE, M. (1968) *The Sound Pattern of English*. Harper & Row: New York.
CHOMSKY, N. and LASNIK, H. (1993) 'Principles and parameters theory.' In JACOBS, J. et al. (eds) *Syntax: an International Handbook of Contemporary Research*. Mouton de Gruyter: Berlin.
CHURCH, K. (1985) 'Stress assignment in letter to sound rules for speech synthesis.' In *Proceedings of the 23rd Annual Meeting of the Association for Computational Linguistics*. Association for Computational Linguistics: Bernardsville, NJ.
CLEMENTS, G. N. (1981) 'Akan vowel harmony: a nonlinear analysis.' In CLEMENTS, G. N. (ed.) *Harvard Studies in Phonology* 2: 108–77.
CLEMENTS, G. N. (1985a) 'The geometry of phonological features', *Phonology Yearbook* 2: 225–52.
CLEMENTS, G. N. (1985b) 'The problem of transfer in nonlinear phonology', *Cornell Working Papers in Linguistics* 5: 38–73.
CLEMENTS, G. N. (1986) 'Compensatory lengthening and consonant gemination in LuGanda.' In WETZELS, L. and SEZER, E. (eds) *Studies in Compensatory Lengthening*. Foris: Dordrecht, pp. 37–77.
CLEMENTS, G. N. (1987) 'Toward a substantive theory of feature specification.' In *Proceedings of NELS 18*, Department of Linguistics, University of Massachusetts Press, Amherst, pp. 79–93.
CLEMENTS, G. N. (1990) 'The role of the sonority cycle in core syllabification.' In KINGSTON, J. and BECKMANN, M. (eds) *Papers in Laboratory Phonology, I. Between the Grammar and Physics of Speech*. Cambridge University Press: Cambridge, pp. 283–333.
CLEMENTS, G. N. (1991a) 'Vowel height assimilation in Bantu languages', *Working Papers of the Cornell Phonetics Laboratory* 5, 37–76.
CLEMENTS, G. N. (1991b) 'Place of articulation in consonants and vowels: a unified theory', *Working Papers of the Cornell Phonetics Laboratory* 5: 77–123.
CLEMENTS, G. N. (1992) 'Phonological primes: features or gestures?' Ms, Paris: Institut de Phonétique. To appear in *Phonetica*.
CLEMENTS, G. N. and Hume, E. (1994) 'Segment structure.' In GOLDSMITH, J. (ed.) *A Handbook of Phonology*. Blackwell: Oxford.
CLEMENTS, G. N. and FORD, K. (1979) 'Kikuyu tone shift and its synchronic consequences', *Linguistic Inquiry* 10: 179–210.
CLEMENTS, G. N. and HERTZ, S. R. (1991) 'Nonlinear phonology and acoustic

interpretation.' *Proceedings of the XIIth International Congress of Phonetic Sciences*, vol. 1/5, Université de Provence, pp. 364–73.

CLEMENTS, G. N. and KEYSER, S. J. (1983) *CV Phonology: a Generative Theory of the Syllable*. MIT Press: Cambridge, Mass.

COLE, J. (1987) 'Planar phonology and morphology.' Unpublished PhD dissertation, MIT.

COLE, J. S. and COLEMAN, J. S. (forthcoming) 'No need for cyclicity in generative phonology.' To appear in CANAKIS, C., CHAN, G. and DENTON, J. (eds) CLS 28-II: *Papers from the Parasession on The Cycle in Linguistic Theory*. Chicago Linguistic Society: Chicago.

COLEMAN, J. S. (1990a) 'Charm theory defines strange vowel sets', *Journal of Linguistics* 26: 165–74.

COLEMAN, J. S. (1990b) 'Vowel sets: a reply to Kaye', *Journal of Linguistics* 26: 183–7.

COLEMAN, J. S. (1991a) 'Phonological representations – their names, forms and powers.' Unpublished PhD dissertation, University of York.

COLEMAN, J. S. (1991b) 'Prosodic structure, parameter-setting and ID/LP Grammar.' In BIRD, S. (ed.) *Declarative Perspectives on Phonology*. Centre for Cognitive Science, University of Edinburgh.

COLEMAN, J. S. (1992) 'The phonetic interpretation of headed phonological structures containing overlapping constituents', *Phonology* 9: 1–44.

COLEMAN, J. S. and LOCAL, J. K. (1991) 'The "No crossing constraint" in autosegmental phonology', *Linguistics and Philosophy* 14: 295–338.

COOPER, F. S., DELATTRE, P. C., LIBERMAN, A. M., BORST, J. M. and GERSTMAN, L. J. (1952) 'Some experiments on the perception of synthetic speech sounds', *Journal of the Acoustical Society of America* 24: 597–606.

CYRAN, E. (1992) 'Irish "tense" sonorants and licensing of empty positions.' Paper presented at the Government Phonology Workshop, 7th International Phonology Meeting, Krems, Austria.

DARWIN, C. J. (1987) 'Speech perception and recognition.' In LYONS, J., COATES, R., DEUCHAR, M. and GAZDAR, G. (eds) *New Horizons in Linguistics: 2*. Penguin: Harmondsworth, pp. 59–81.

DAVENPORT, M. J. S. (1994) 'The characterisation of nasality in dependency phonology.' In Hulst, H. G. van der and Weijer, J. van der (eds.) *HIL Phonology Papers no 1*. Holland Academic Graphics: Leiden.

DAVENPORT, M. J. S. and STAUN, J. (1986) 'Sequence, segment and configuration: two problems for dependency phonology.' In DURAND, J. (ed.) *Dependency and Non-linear Phonology*. Croom Helm: London, pp. 135–59.

DAVIS, S. (1988) 'Syllable onsets as a factor in stress rules', *Phonology* 5: 1–20.

DAVY, J. I. M. and NURSE, D. (1982) 'Synchronic versions of Dahl's law: the multiple applications of a phonological dissimilation rule', *Journal of African Languages and Linguistics* 4: 157–95.

DICHABE, S. (in preparation) 'Vowel harmony in Setswana.' MA thesis, University of Ottawa.

DIKKEN, M. DEN and HULST, H. G. VAN DER (1988) 'Segmental hierarchitecture.' In HULST, VAN DER H. G. and SMITH, N. (eds) *Features, Segmental Structure and Harmony Processes, Part I*. Foris: Dordrecht, pp. 1–78.

DIXON, R. M. W. (1972) *The Dyirbal Language of North Queensland.* Cambridge University Press: Cambridge.

DIXON, R. M. W. (1977) *A Grammar of Yidin.* Cambridge University Press: Cambridge.

DIXON, R. M. W. and BLAKE, B. J. (1979) *Handbook of Australian Languages.* John Benjamins: Amsterdam.

DONEGAN (MILLER), P. J. (1978) 'On the natural phonology of vowels.' Unpublished PhD dissertation, Ohio State University.

DOSSE, F. (1991) *Histoire du structuralisme. Tome 1: le champ du signe.* Editions La Découverte: Paris.

DRESSLER, W. et al. (eds) (1992) *Phonologica 1988. Proceedings of the 6th International Phonology Meeting.* Cambridge University Press: Cambridge.

DUANMU, S. (1991) 'A formal study of syllable, tone, stress and domain in Chinese languages.' Unpublished PhD dissertation, MIT.

DURAND, J. (1986) 'French liaison, floating segments and other matters in a dependency framework.' In DURAND, J. (ed.) *Dependency and Non-Linear Phonology.* Croom Helm: London, pp. 161–201.

DURAND, J. (1990a) *Generative and Non-linear Phonology.* Longman: Harlow.

DURAND, J. (1990b) 'In defence of dependency phonology', *Rivista di Linguistica* 2(2): 87–102.

ENCREVÉ, P. (1988) *La liaison avec et sans enchaînement. Phonologie tridimensionnelle et usages du français.* Seuil: Paris.

EWEN, C. J. (1980) 'Aspects of phonological structure, with particular reference to English and Dutch.' Unpublished PhD dissertation, University of Edinburgh.

EWEN, C. J. (1986) 'Segmental and suprasegmental structure.' In DURAND, J. (ed.) *Dependency and Non-linear Phonology,* Croom Helm: London, pp. 203–22.

EWEN, C. J. (1994) 'Dependency relations in phonology.' In GOLDSMITH, J. A. (ed.) *A Handbook of Phonological Theory.* Basil Blackwell, Oxford.

EYNDE, K. VAN DEN (1968) *Éléments de grammaire yaka.* Université Lovanium, Kinshasa.

FAHS, VON A. (1985) 'Grammatik des Pali.' Verlag Enzyklopädie: Leipzig.

FARID, M. O. (1980) *Aspects of Malay Phonology and Morphology: a Generative Approach.* Universiti Kebangsaan Malaysia, Bangi.

FEYERABEND, P. K. (1958) 'An attempt at a realistic interpretation of experience', *Proceedings of the Aristotelian Society* 58: 160–62.

FOLKINS, J. W. and ZIMMERMAN, G. N. (1981) 'Jaw-muscle activity during speech with the mandible fixed', *Journal of the Acoustical Society of America* 69: 1441–4.

FROMKIN, V. (1971) 'The non-anomalous nature of anomalous utterances', *Language* 47: 27–54.

FROMKIN, V. (ed.) (1973) *Speech Errors as Linguistic Evidence.* Mouton: The Hague.

FROMKIN, V. (1988) 'Grammatical aspects of speech errors.' In NEWMEYER, F. J. (ed.) *Linguistics: the Cambridge Survey, Vol. II Linguistic theory: Extensions and Applications.* Cambridge University Press, Cambridge, pp. 117–38.

FUDGE, E. C. (1969) 'Syllables', *Journal of Linguistics* **5**: 253–86.

GAZDAR, G. (1987) 'Generative grammar.' In LYONS, J., COATES, R., DEU-CHAR, M. and GAZDAR, G. (eds) *New Horizons in Linguistics 2*. Penguin Books: Harmondsworth, pp. 122–51.

GAZDAR, G., KLEIN, E., PULLUM, G. and SAG, I. (1985) *Generalized Phrase. Structure Grammar*. Blackwell: Oxford.

GEIGER, W. (1968) *Pali Literature and Language*. Oriental Books Reprint Corporation: New Dehli.

GELERTNER, D. (1989) 'The metamorphosis of information management', *Scientific American*, August, 54–61.

GIBB, L. (1992) 'Domains in phonology: with evidence from Icelandic, Finnish and Kikuyu.' Unpublished PhD dissertation, University of Edinburgh.

GNANADESIKAN, A. (1991) 'Issues of sonority in Pali syllable structure.' Unpublished paper, University of Massachusetts.

GOLDSMITH, J. (1976) 'Autosegmental phonology.' PhD dissertation, MIT, Cambridge, Mass. Published 1979, Garland: New York.

GOLDSMITH, J. (1985) 'Vowel harmony in Khalkha Mongolian, Yaka, Finnish and Hungarian', *Phonology* **2**: 251–74.

GOLDSMITH, J. (1989) 'Licensing, inalterability and harmonic rule application.' *Papers from the Annual Regional Meeting, Chicago Linguistic Society* **25**: 145–57.

GOLDSMITH, J. (1990) *Autosegmental and Metrical Phonology*. Basil Blackwell: Oxford.

GORECKA, A. (1989) 'Phonology of articulation.' Unpublished PhD dissertation, MIT.

GREENBERG, J. H. (1970) 'Some generalizations concerning glottalic consonants, especially implosives', *International Journal of American Linguistics* **36**: 123–45.

GRUBER, J. (1964) 'The distinctive features of tone.' MS, MIT, Cambridge, Mass.

GUSSMANN, E. and KAYE, J. (1992) 'Polish note from a Dubrovnik café.' *The yers*, MS, School of Oriental and African Studies, University of London (SOAS).

HALE, K. and LACAYO BLANCO, A. (1988) Vocabulario preliminar del ULWA (sumu meridional). Centro de investigaciones y documentación de la Costa Atlantica, Karawala, Zelaya Sur, Nicaragua, and Center for Cognitive Science, MIT.

HALL, B. L. and HALL, R. M. R. (1980) 'Nez Perce vowel harmony: an Africanist explanation and some theoretical questions.' In VAGO, R. M. (ed.) *Issues in Vowel Harmony*. John Benjamins: Amsterdam, pp. 201–36.

HALLE, M. (1959) *The Sound Pattern of Russian*. Mouton: The Hague.

HALLE, M. and CLEMENTS, G. N. (1983) *Problem Book in Phonology*. MIT Press: Cambridge, Mass.

HALLE, M. and MOHANAN, K. P. (1985) 'Segmental phonology of modern English', *Linguistic Inquiry* **16**(1): 56–116.

HALLE, M. and STEVENS, K. (1971) 'A note on laryngeal features', *Quarterly*

Progress Report 101: 198–213. Research Laboratory of Electronics, MIT Press: Cambridge, Mass.

HALLE, M. and VERGNAUD, J.-R. (1980a) 'Three-dimensional phonology', *Journal of Linguistic Research* 1: 83–105.

HALLE, M. and VERGNAUD, J.-R. (1980b) 'Tiered phonology.' MS, MIT, Cambridge, Mass.

HALLE, M. and VERGNAUD, J.-R. (1981) 'Harmony processes.' In KLEIN, W. and LEVELT, W. (eds) *Crossing the Boundaries in Linguistics.* Reidel: Dordrecht, pp. 1–22.

HAMMOND, M. (1988) 'Template transfer in Arabic broken plurals', *Natural Language and Linguistic Theory* 6: 247–70.

HANKAMER, J. and AISSEN, J. (1974) 'The sonority hierarchy.' In BRUCK, A., FOX, R. A. and LA GALY, M. W. (eds) *Papers from the Parasession on Natural Phonology.* Chicago Linguistic Society: Chicago, pp. 131–45.

HARRIS, J. (1983) *Syllable Structure and Stress in Spanish.* MIT Press: Cambridge, Mass.

HARRIS, J. (1985) *Phonological Variation and Change: Studies in Hiberno-English.* Cambridge University Press: Cambridge.

HARRIS, J. (1990a) 'Reduction harmony.' Paper delivered to the GLOW Phonology Workshop, University of London.

HARRIS, J. (1990b) 'Segmental complexity and phonological government', *Phonology* 7: 255–300.

HARRIS, J. (1990c) 'Parameters in phonological acquisition.' Paper read at the University College London Linguistics Seminars.

HARRIS, J. (1992) 'Licensing inheritance', *UCL Working Papers in Linguistics* 4: 359–406.

HARRIS, J. and KAYE, J. (1990) 'A tale of two cities: London glottalling and New York City tapping', *The Linguistic Review* 7: 251–74.

HARRIS, J. and LINDSEY, G. (1991) 'Segmental decomposition and the signal.' Paper delivered to the London Phonology Seminar, University of London. In *Phonologica 1992: Proceedings of the 7th International Phonology Meeting, Krems, 1992.* Cambridge University Press: Cambridge.

HARRIS, J. and MOTO, F. (1989) 'Bantu height harmony.' Paper delivered at the 20th Annual Conference on African Linguistics, University of Illinois at Urbana-Champaign.

HAUDRICOURT, A. G. (1954) 'De l'origine des tons en vietnamien', *Journal Asiatique* 242: 68–82.

HAUGEN, E. (1956) 'The syllable in linguistic description.' In HALLE, M., LUNT, H. G., MCLEAN, H. and VAN SCHOONEVELD, C. H. (eds) *For Roman Jakobson: Essays on the Occasion of his Sixtieth Birthday.* Mouton: The Hague, pp. 213–21.

HAYES, B. (1981) 'A Metrical Theory of Stress Rules.' MIT PhD Dissertation. Distributed by Indiana University Linguistics Club, Bloomington, Indiana.

HAYES, B. (1982) 'Extrametricality and English stress', *Linguistic Inquiry* 13: 227–76.

HAYES, B. (1984) 'The phonetics and phonology of Russian voicing assimilation.' In ARONOFF, M. and OEHRLE, R. (eds) *Language Sound Structure*. MIT Press: Cambridge, Mass., pp. 318–28.

HAYES, B. (1986) 'Assimilation as spreading in Toba Batak', *Linguistic Inquiry* **17**: 467–99.

HAYES, B. (1988) Review of WETZELS, L. and SEZER, E. (eds) *Studies in Compensatory Lengthening*. *Linguistics* **26**: 167–73.

HAYES, B. (1989) 'Compensatory lengthening in moraic phonology', *Linguistic Inquiry* **20**: 253–306.

HAYWARD, R. (1984) *The Arbore Language: a First Investigation*. Helmut Buske, Hamburg.

HEGARTY, M. (1989) 'An investigation of laterals and continuancy.' MS, MIT, Cambridge, Mass.

HEO, Y. (in preparation) 'Empty categories in Korean phonology.' PhD Thesis, School of Oriental and African Studies, University of London (SOAS).

HOGG, R. M. and MCCULLY, C. B. (1987) *Metrical Phonology: a Coursebook*. Cambridge University Press: Cambridge.

HOOPER, J. B. (1976) *An Introduction to Natural Generative Phonology*. Academic Press: New York.

HULST, H. G. VAN DER (1988a) 'Phonological structure and the nonlinear analysis of vowel harmony.' Paper delivered to the Linguistics Association of Great Britain, University of Edinburgh.

HULST, H. G. VAN DER (1988b) 'The geometry of vocalic features.' In HULST, H. G. VAN DER and SMITH, N. S. H., *Features, Segmental Structure and Harmony Processes, Part II*. Foris: Dordrecht, pp. 77–125.

HULST, H. G. VAN DER (1989) 'Atoms of segmental structure: components, gestures and dependency', *Phonology* **6**: 253–84.

HULST, H. G. VAN DER (1993) 'Principles of Radical cv phonology.' MS, University of Leiden.

HULST, H. G. VAN DER (1994) 'Radical cv phonology: the locational gesture.' UCL working papers in Linguistics 6, 439–78.

HULST, H. G. VAN DER (in preparation), The segment – syllable connection. MS University of Leiden.

HULST, H. G. VAN DER (to appear) 'Introduction to Radical cv phonology.' Jn Shore, S (ed.) SKY 1994. Helsinki.

HULST, H. G. VAN DER and SMITH, N. (eds) (1982a) *The Structure of Phonological Representations, Part II*. Foris: Dordrecht.

HULST, H. G. VAN DER and SMITH, N. (eds) (1982b) Introduction. In HULST, H. G. VAN DER and SMITH, N. (1982a) *The Structure of Phonological Representations, Part II*. Foris: Dordrecht, pp. 1–45.

HULST, H. G. VAN DER and SMITH, N. (1985) 'Vowel features and umlaut in Djingili, Nyangumarda and Warlpiri', *Phonology* **2**: 275–302.

HULST, H. G. VAN DER and SMITH, N. (eds) (1988) *Features, Segmental Structure and Harmony Processes, Parts I, II*. Foris: Dordrecht.

HULST, H. G. VAN DER and SNIDER, K. L. (1993) 'Issues in the representation of tonal register.' In HULST, H. G. VAN DER and SNIDER, K. L. (eds) *The Phonology of Tone: the Representation of Tonal Register*. Mouton de Gruyter: Berlin, pp. 1–27.

HULST, H. G. VAN DER and WEIJER, J. M. VAN DE (1994) 'Nonlinear phonology 1982–1992.' In HULST, VAN DER H. G. and WEIJER, J. M. VAN DE (eds) (1994).

HULST, H. G. VAN DER and WEIJER, J. M. VAN DE (to appear) 'Vowel harmony.' To appear in GOLDSMITH, J. A. (ed.) *A Handbook of Phonological Theory*. Basil Blackwell: Oxford.

HULST, H. G. VAN DER and WEIJER, J. M. VAN DE (eds) (1994). Leiden in Last. HIL Phonology Papers 1. Academic Graphics. Holland HIL Publications no 1.

HYMAN, L. M. (1985) *A Theory of Phonological Weight*. Foris: Dordrecht.

HYMAN, L. M. (1993) 'Register tones and tonal geometry.' In HULST, H. G. VAN DER and SNIDER, K. L. (eds) *The Representation of Tonal Register*. Mouton de Gruyter: Berlin, 75–108.

HYMAN, L. M. and KATAMBA, F. (1992) 'Final vowel shortening in Luganda', *Studies in African Linguistics*. Vol. 21, pp. 1–59.

HYMAN, L. M. and KATAMBA, F. (1993) 'A new approach to tone in Luganda.' *Language* 69: 34–67.

HYMAN, L. M., KATAMBA, F. and WALUSIMBI, L. (1987) 'Luganda and the strict layer hypothesis', *Phonology Yearbook* 4: 87–108.

HYMAN, L. M. and MUTAKA, N. (1990) 'Syllables and morpheme integrity in Kinande reduplication', *Phonology* 7: 73–119.

INKELAS, S. (1989) 'The representation of invisibility.' Unpublished manuscript, Stanford University.

INKELAS, S. (1990) 'Prosodic constituency in the lexicon.' Unpublished PhD dissertation, Stanford University.

INKELAS, S., LEBEN, W. and COBLER, M. (1987) 'The phonology of intonation in Hausa.' *Proceedings of NELS* 17: 327–42. University of Massachusetts.

ITÔ, J. (1986) 'Syllable theory in prosodic phonology.' Unpublished PhD dissertation, University of Massachusetts.

ITÔ, J. (1989) 'A prosodic theory of epenthesis', *Natural Language and Linguistic Theory* 7: 217–59.

ITÔ, J. (1991) Prosodic minimality in Japanese. In DEATON, K., NOSKE, M. and ZIOLKOWSKI, M. (eds) CLS 22-11: *Papers from the Parasession on the Syllable in Phonetics and Phonology*. Chicago Linguistic Society, Chicago.

ITÔ, J. and MESTER, R. A. (1986) 'The phonology of voicing in Japanese: theoretical consequences for morphological accessibility', *Linguistic Inquiry* 17: 49–73.

ITÔ, J. and MESTER, A. (1992) 'Weak layering and word binarity.' Unpublished manuscript, University of California.

JAKOBSON, R. (1941/1968) *Kindersprache, Aphasie und allgemeine Lautgesetze*. Translated by KEILER, A., *Child Language, Aphasia and Phonological Universals*. Mouton: The Hague.

JAKOBSON, R., FANT, C. G. M. and HALLE, M. (1952) *Preliminaries to Speech Analysis – the Distinctive Features and their Correlates*, 2nd edn. MIT Press: Cambridge, Mass.

JOHNSON, C. D. (1972) *Formal Aspects of Phonological Description*. Mouton: The Hague.

394   REFERENCES

JONES, C. (1989) *A History of English Phonology*. Longman: Harlow.
JOOS, M. (1942) 'A phonological dilemma in Canadian English', *Language* **18**: 141–4.
JOSHI, A. K. and LEVY, L. S. (1977) 'Constraints on structural descriptions: local transformations', *SIAM Journal on Computing* **6**: 272–84.
JUNGHARE, I. Y. (1979) *Topics in Pali Historical Phonology*. Shri Jainendra Press: New Delhi.
KAHN, D. (1976) 'Syllable-based generalizations in English phonology.' PhD dissertation, MIT. Published 1980, Garland: New York.
KAISSE, E. (1985) *Connected Speech: the Interaction of Syntax and Phonology*. Academic Press: Orlando.
KAISSE, E. M. and SHAW, P. A. (1985) 'On the theory of lexical phonology', *Phonology Yearbook* **2**: 1–30.
KATAMBA, F. (1984) 'A nonlinear analysis of vowel harmony in Luganda', *Journal of Linguistics* **20**: 257–75.
KATAMBA, F. (1989) *An Introduction to Phonology*. Longman: London.
KATAMBA, F. (1993) *Morphology*. Macmillan: Basingstoke.
KAYE, J. (1987) 'Government in phonology: the case of Moroccan Arabic', *The Linguistic Review* **6**: 131–59.
KAYE, J. (1988) 'On the interaction of theories of lexical phonology and theories of phonological phenomena.' MS, School of Oriental and African Studies, University of London (SOAS).
KAYE, J. (1989) *Phonology: a Cognitive View*. Lawrence Erlbaum Associates: Hillsdale, New Jersey.
KAYE, J. (1990a) '"Coda" licensing', *Phonology* **7**: 301–30.
KAYE, J. (1990b) 'Whatever happened to dialect B?' In MASCARÓ, J. and NESPOR, M. (eds) *Grammar in Progress: GLOW Essays for Henk van Riejmsdijk*. Foris: Dordrecht, pp. 259–63.
KAYE, J. (1990c) 'The strange vowel sets of Charm theory: the question from top to bottom', *Journal of Linguistics* **26**: 175–81.
KAYE, J. (1991) 'Head projection and indexation: a theory of reduplication.' Paper presented at the GLOW colloqium, Leiden.
KAYE, J. (1992a) 'On the interaction of theories of lexical phonology and theories of phonological phenomena.' In DRESSLER, W., LUSCHÜTZKY, W. U., PFEIFFER, O. E. and RENNISON, J. R. (eds) *Phonologica 1988*. Cambridge University Press: Cambridge, pp. 141–55.
KAYE, J. (1992b) 'Do you believe in magic? The story of s + C sequences', School of Oriental and African Studies, University of London (SOAS), *Working Papers in Linguistics and Phonetics* **2**: 293–313.
KAYE, J. and LOWENSTAMM, J. (1984) 'De la syllabicité.' In DELL, F., HIRST, D. and VERGNAUD, J.-R. (eds) *Forme sonore du langage*. Hermann: Paris, pp. 123–59.
KAYE, J. and LOWENSTAMM, J. (1985) A non-linear treatment of Grassman's Law. In *Proceedings of the XVth meeting of the North Eastern Linguistics Society*. GSLA: Amherst, Mass., pp. 220–33.
KAYE, J., LOWENSTAMM, J. and VERGNAUD, J.-R. (1985) 'The internal structure of phonological representations: a theory of charm and government', *Phonology Yearbook* **2**: 305–28.

KAYE, J., LOWENSTAMM, J. and VERGNAUD, J.-R. (1989) 'Konstituentenstruktur und Rektion in der Phonologie', *Linguistische Berichte* **114**: 31–75.

KAYE, J., LOWENSTAMM, J. and VERGNAUD, J.-R. (1990) 'Constituent structure and government in phonology', *Phonology* **7**(2): 193–231.

KAYE, J. and VERGNAUD, J.-R. (1990) 'Phonology, morphology and the lexicon.' Paper presented at the 1990 GLOW colloquium, St John's College, Cambridge University.

KEAN, M.-L. (1974) 'The strict cycle in phonology', *Linguistic Inquiry* **5**: 179–204.

KEATING, P. A. (1988) 'Underspecification in phonetics', *Phonology* **5**: 275–92.

KENSTOWICZ, M. (1990) 'Stress and generative phonology', *Rivista di Linguistica*, Vol. 2, No. 2: 55–86.

KENSTOWICZ, M. and KISSEBERTH, C. (1979) *Generative Phonology: Description and Theory.* Academic Press: New York.

KENSTOWICZ, M. and PYLE, C. (1973) 'On the phonological integrity of geminate clusters.' In KENSTOWICZ, M. and KISSEBERTH, C. (eds) *Issues in Phonological Theory.* Mouton: The Hague.

KHABANYANE, K. E. (1991) 'The five phonemic vowel heights of southern Sotho: an acoustic and phonological analysis', *Working Papers of the Cornell Phonetics Laboratory* **5**: 1–36.

KINGSTON, J. and SOLNIT, D. (1988) 'The tones of consonants.' MS, Cornell University.

KIPARSKY, P. (1979) 'Metrical structure assignment is cyclic', *Linguistic Inquiry* **10**: 421–41.

KIPARSKY, P. (1982a) 'From cyclic phonology to lexical phonology.' In HULST, H. G. VAN DER and SMITH, N. (eds) *The Structure of Phonological Representations, Part 1.* Foris: Dordrecht, pp. 131–75.

KIPARSKY, P. (1982b) 'Lexical morphology and phonology.' In YANG, I.-S. (ed.) *Linguistics in the Morning Calm.* Hanshin: Seoul, pp. 3–91.

KIPARSKY, P. (1985) 'Some Consequences of Lexical Phonology', *Phonology Yearbook* **2**, 85–138.

KLATT, D. H. (1987) 'Review of selected models of speech perception.' In MARSLEN-WILSON, W. (ed.) *Lexical Representation and Process.* MIT Press: Cambridge, Mass., pp. 169–226.

KOHLER, K. J. (1966) 'Is the syllable a phonological universal?' *Journal of Linguistics* **2**: 207–8.

KUIPERS, A. E. (1967) *The Squamish Language.* Mouton: The Hague.

LACHARITÉ, D. (1993) 'The internal structure of the affricate.' Unpublished PhD dissertation, University of Ottawa.

LADEFOGED, P. (1971) *Preliminaries to Linguistic Phonetics.* University of Chicago Press: Chicago and London.

LADEFOGED, P. (1973) 'The features of the larynx', *Journal of Phonetics* **1**: 73–83.

LADEFOGED, P. (1982) *A Course in Phonetics*, 2nd edn. Harcourt, Brace, Jovanovich: New York and London.

LADEFOGED, P. (1989) 'Representing phonetic structure.' *UCLA Working Papers in Phonetics* **73**.

LADEFOGED, P. (1992) 'The many interfaces between phonetics and phonology.' In DRESSLER, et al. (eds) *Phonologica 1988. Proceedings of the 6th International Phonology Meeting.* Cambridge University Press: New York, pp. 165–79.

LADEFOGED, P., DECLERK, J., LINDAU, M. and PAPCUN, G. (1972) 'An auditory motor theory of speech production', *UCLA Phonetics Laboratory Working Papers in Phonetics* 22: 48–76.

LADEFOGED, P. and HALLE, M. (1988) 'Some major features of the International Phonetic Alphabet', *Language* 64: 577–82.

LADUSAW, W. A. (1986) 'Principles of semantic filtering.' In DALRYMPLE, M., GOLDBERG, J., HANSON, K., INMAN, M., PIÑON, C. and WECHSLER, S. (eds). *Proceedings of the West Coast Conference on formal linguistics.* Vol. 5. Stanford Linguistics Association, 129–141.

LAHIRI, A. and MARSLEN-WILSON, W. (1991) 'The mental representation of lexical form: a phonological approach to the recognition lexicon', *Cognition* 38: 245–94.

LAMONTAGNE, G. A. (1993) 'Syllabification and consonant cooccurrence conditions.' Unpublished PhD dissertation, University of Massachusetts.

LANCKER, D. VAN and FROMKIN, V. A. (1973) 'Hemispheric specialisation for pitch and tone: evidence from Thai', *Journal of Phonetics* 1: 101–9.

LAPOINTE, S. (1977) 'Recursiveness and deletion', *Linguistic Analysis* 3: 227–65.

LASS, R. (1976) *English Phonology and Phonological Theory.* Cambridge University Press: Cambridge.

LASS, R. (1984) *Phonology: an Introduction to Basic Concepts.* Cambridge University Press: Cambridge.

LASS, R. and ANDERSON, J. M. (1975) *Old English Phonology.* Cambridge University Press: Cambridge.

LAVER, J. (1980) *The Phonetic Description of Voice Quality.* Cambridge University Press: Cambridge.

LEBEN, W. (1980) 'A metrical analysis of length', *Linguistic Inquiry* 11: 497–509.

LEKACH, A. F. (1979) 'Phonological markedness and the sonority hierarchy.' In SAFIR, K. (ed.) *Papers on syllable structure, metrical structure and harmony processes. MIT Working Papers in Linguistics,* Vol. 1. MIT Press: Cambridge, Mass.

LEVELT, W. J. M. (1976) 'Formal grammars and the natural language user: a review.' In MARZOLLO, A. (ed.) *Topics in Artificial Intelligence, CISM Courses and Lecture Notes,* no. 256. Springer: Berlin.

LEVIN, J. (1985) 'A metrical theory of syllabicity.' Unpublished PhD dissertation, MIT.

LEVIN, J. (1988) 'A place for lateral in the feature geometry.' MS, University of Texas at Austin.

LEVY, L. S. and YUEH, K. (1977) 'On labelled graph grammars.' Private communication, cited in NAGL, M. (1979) 'A tutorial and bibliographical survey on graph grammars.' In CLAUS, V., EHRIG, H. and ROZENBERG, G. (eds) *Graph-Grammars and their Application to Computer Science and Biology.* Springer, Berlin, pp. 70–126.

LIBERMAN, M. and PRINCE, A. (1977) 'On stress and linguistic rhythm', *Linguistic Inquiry* 8: 249–336.

LINDAU, M. (1980) 'The story of /ɾ/', *UCLA Working Papers in Phonetics* **51**: 114–19.

LINDSEY, G. (1990) 'Quantity and quality in British and American vowel systems.' In RAMSARAN, S. (ed.) *Studies in the pronunciation of English: a Commemorative Volume in Honour of A. C. Gimson.* Routledge: London, 106–18.

LINDSEY, G. and HARRIS, J. (1990) 'Phonetic interpretation in generative grammar', *UCL Working Papers in Linguistics* **2**: 355–69.

LLORET, M.-R. (1992) 'The complexity of the Oromo glottal consonants.' Paper presented at the Seventh Phonology Meeting, Krems, Austria.

LOMBARDI, L. (1990) 'The nonlinear organization of the affricate', *Natural Language and Linguistic Theory* **8**: 375–425.

LOMBARDI, L. (1991) 'Laryngeal features and laryngeal neutralization.' Unpublished PhD dissertation, MIT, Cambridge, Mass.

LOMBARDI, L. (1993) 'Laryngeal features and privativity.' MS, University of Maryland.

LONGUET-HIGGINS, H. C., LYONS, J. and BROADBENT, D. A. (eds) (1981) *The Psychological Mechanisms of Language.* Royal Society and British Academy: London.

LOSEE, J. (1980) *A Historical Introduction to the Philosophy of Science*, 2nd edn. Oxford University Press: Oxford.

LOWENSTAMM, J. and KAYE, J. (1986) 'Compensatory lengthening in Tiberian Hebrew.' In WETZELS, L. and SEZER, E. (eds) *Studies in Compensatory Lengthening.* Foris: Dordrecht, pp. 97–132.

LOWENSTAMM, J. and PRUNET, J.-F. (1988) 'Tigre vowel harmonies.' Rapport Annuel du Groupe de Recherche sur la Linguistique Africaniste au CRSH 1987–88. Université du Québec à Montréal.

LYONS, J. (1991) *Natural Language and Universal Grammar: Essays in Linguistic Theory, Vol. 1.* Cambridge University Press: Cambridge.

MADDIESON, I. (1984) *Patterns of Sounds.* Cambridge University Press: Cambridge.

MADDIESON, I. and EMMORY, K. (1984) 'Is there a valid distinction between voiceless lateral approximants and fricatives?', *UCLA Working Papers in Phonetics* **59**: 77–84.

MANASTER-RAMER, A. and ZADROZNY, W. (1990) 'Expressive power of grammatical formalisms.' In KARLGREN, H. (ed.) *COLING-90. Papers Presented to the 13th International Conference on Computational Linguistics*, Vol. 3, pp. 195–200.

MARANTZ, A. (1982) 'Re-reduplication', *Linguistic Inquiry* **13**: 435–82.

MASCARÓ, J. (1983) 'Phonological levels and assimilatory processes.' MS, Universitat Autònoma de Barcelona.

MASCARÓ, J. (1987) 'A reduction theory of voicing and other sound effects.' MS, Universitat Autònoma de Barcelona.

MATISOFF, J. (1973) 'Tonogenesis in Southeast Asia.' In HYMAN, L. M. (ed.) *Consonant Types and Tone. Southern California Occasional Papers in Linguistics* **1**: 71–95.

MCCARTHY, J. (1979) 'Formal problems in Semitic phonology and morphology.' Unpublished PhD dissertation, MIT. (Distributed by Indiana University Linguistics Club.)

MCCARTHY, J. (1981) 'A prosodic theory of nonconcatenative morphology', *Linguistic Inquiry* **12**: 374–418.
MCCARTHY, J. (1982) 'Prosodic templates, morphemic templates, and morphemic tiers.' In HULST, H. G. VAN DER and SMITH, N. S. H. (eds) (1982a) *The Structure of Phonological Representations*, Part II. Foris: Dordrecht, pp. 191–223.
MCCARTHY, J. (1983) 'A prosodic analysis of Arabic broken plurals.' In DIHOFF, I. (ed.) *Current Trends in African Linguistics, 1*. Foris: Dordrecht, pp. 299–317.
MCCARTHY, J. J. (1984a) 'Theoretical consequences of Montañes vowel harmony', *Linguistic Inquiry* **15**: 291–318.
MCCARTHY, J. (1984b) 'Prosodic organisation in morphology.' In ARONOFF, M. and OEHRLE, R. (1984) *Language Sound Structure: Studies in Phonology Presented to Morris Halle by his Teacher and Students*. MIT Press: Cambridge, Mass.
MCCARTHY, J. J. (1986) 'OCP effects: gemination and antigemination', *Linguistic Inquiry* **17**: 207–63.
MCCARTHY, J. (1988) 'Feature geometry and dependency: a review', *Phonetica* **43**: 84–108.
MCCARTHY, J. (1991) 'The phonology of semitic pharyngeals.' MS, University of Massachusetts.
MCCARTHY, J. J. and PRINCE, A. S. (1986) 'Prosodic morphology.' MS, University of Massachusetts.
MCCARTHY, J. and PRINCE, A. S. (1988) 'Quantitative transfer in reduplicative and templatic morphology.' In Linguistic Society of Korea (ed.) *Linguistics in the morning calm, 2*. Hanshin Publishing Company: Seoul, pp. 3–35.
MCCARTHY, J. and PRINCE, A. (1990a) 'Foot and word in templatic morphology: The Arabic broken plural', *Natural Language and Linguistic Theory* **8**: 209–83.
MCCARTHY, J. and PRINCE, A. (1990b) 'Prosodic morphology and templatic morphology.' In EID, M. and MCCARTHY, J. (eds) *Perspectives on Arabic Linguistics: Papers from the Second Symposium*. John Benjamins, Amsterdam, pp. 1–54.
MCCARTHY, J. and PRINCE, A. (1993) 'Prosodic morphology 1. Constraint interaction and satisfaction.' Unpublished manuscript, University of Massachusetts, Amherst and Rutgers University.
MCCARTHY, J. and PRINCE, A. (forthcoming) *Prosodic Morphology*. MIT Press: Cambridge, Mass.
MEHLER, J. (1981) 'The role of syllables in speech processing.' In LONGUET-HIGGINS, H. C., LYONS, J. and BROADBENT, D. A. (eds) *The Psychological Mechanisms of Language*. Royal Society and British Academy: London, pp. 332–53.
MESTER, A. R. (1990) 'Patterns of truncation', *Linguistic Science* **21**, 478–85.
MESTER, R. A. and ITÔ, J. (1989) 'Feature predictability and underspecification: palatal prosody in Japanese mimetics', *Language* **65**: 258–93.
MICHAELS, D. (1992) 'Natural and unnatural phonology.' In DRESSLER et al. (eds) *Phonologica 1988. Proceedings of the 6th International Phonology Meeting*. Cambridge University Press: Cambridge, pp. 207–14.

MOHANAN, K. P. (1983) 'The structure of the melody.' MS, MIT.

MOHANAN, K. P. (1986) *The Theory of Lexical Phonology.* Reidel: Dordrecht.

MOHANAN, K. P. (1989) 'Syllable structure in Malayalam', *Linguistic Inquiry* **20**: 589–626.

MOHANAN, K. P. (1991) 'On the bases of radical underspecification theory', *Natural Language and Linguistic Theory* **9**: 285–325.

MORAVCSIK, E. A. (1978) 'Reduplicative constructions.' In GREENBERG, G. H. (ed.) *Universals of Human Language, vol. 3, Word Structure*, pp. 297–334.

MTENJE, A. D. (1985) 'Arguments for an autosegmental analysis of Chichewa vowel harmony', *Lingua* **66**: 21–52.

MURRAY, R. (1982) 'Consonant cluster developments in Pali', *Folia Linguistica Historica* **3**: 163–84.

MUTAKA, N. and HYMAN, L. (1990) 'Syllables and morpheme integrity in Kinande reduplication', *Phonology* **7**: 73–119.

MYERS, S. (1987) 'Vowel shortening in English', *Natural Language and Linguistic Theory* **5**: 485–518.

NASH, D. (1979) 'Yidin stress: a metrical account', *Cunyforum* **7/8**: 112–30.

NESPOR, M. and VOGEL, I. (1986) *Prosodic Phonology.* Foris: Dordrecht.

ODDEN, D. (1986) 'On the role of the obligatory contour principle in phonological theory', *Language* **62**: 353–83.

PADGETT, J. (1991) 'Stricture in feature geometry.' Unpublished PhD dissertation, University of Massachusetts.

PAGONI, S. (1993) 'Ancient Greek reduplication: a government phonology approach.' *Meletes ja tin Elliniki glossa: Praktika tis 13is etisias sinandisis tu Tomea Glossologias tis Philosophikis Scholis tu Aristoteliu Panepistimiu Thessalonikis, 7–9 May 1992.* Thessaloniki.

PAINTER, C. (1970) 'Gonja: a phonological and grammatical study.' *University Publications, African Series 1.* Indiana University: Bloomington.

PALMADA, FÉLEZ B. (1991) 'La fonologia del català i els principis actius.' Doctoral thesis, Universitat Autònoma de Barcelona.

PARADIS, C. and PRUNET, J.-F. (1991a) 'Introduction: asymmetry and visibility in consonant articulations.' In PARADIS, C. and PRUNET, J.-F. (eds) (1991b) *The Special Status of Coronals: Internal and External Evidence. Phonetics and Phonology, Vol. 2.* Academic Press: San Diego: pp. 1–28.

PARADIS, C. and PRUNET, J.-F. (eds) (1991b) *The Special Status of Coronals: Internal and External Evidence. Phonetics and Phonology, Vol. 2.* Academic Press: San Diego.

PARTEE, B. H., MEULEN, A. TER and WALL, R. E. (1990) *Mathematical Methods in Linguistics.* Kluwer: Dordrecht.

PENG, L. (1991) 'A phonological argument against privative voicing.' Paper presented at the West Coast Conference on Formal Linguistics (WCCFL) X, Arizona State University.

PETERS, P. S. and RITCHIE, R. W. (1973) 'On the generative power of transformational grammars', *Information Sciences* **6**: 49–83.

PETTERSON, T. and WOOD, S. (1987) 'Vowel reduction in Bulgarian and its implications for theories of vowel reduction: a review of the problem', *Folia Linguistica* **21**: 261–79.

PIERREHUMBERT, J. (forthcoming) Declarative phonology, generative phonology, and laboratory phonology. In BIRD, S., COLEMAN, J., PIERREHUMBERT, J. and SCOBBIE, J. (forthcoming) 'Declarative phonology.' In *Proceedings of the XVth International Congress of Linguists*, 9–14 August, 1992, Laval University, Quebec.

PIERREHUMBERT, J. and BECKMAN, M. (1988) *Japanese Tone Structure*. MIT Press: Cambridge, Mass.

PIGGOTT, G. L. (1990) 'The representation of sonorant features.' MS, McGill University.

PIGGOTT, G. L. (1992) 'Variability in feature dependency: the case of nasality', *Natural Language and Linguistic Theory* **10**: 33–37.

PLÉNAT, M. (1984) 'Toto, Fanfa, Totor et même Guiguitte sont des anars.' In DELL, F., HIRST, D. and VERGNAUD, J.-R. (eds) *Forme sonore du langage*. Hermann: Paris.

POLLARD, C. and SAG, I. A. (1987) 'Information-based syntax and semantics.' *CSLI Lecture Notes No. 13. Vol. 1: Fundamentals*. CSLI: Stanford University, Palo Alto, California.

POSER, W. (1982) 'Phonological representation and action-at-a-distance.' In HULST H. G. VAN DER and SMITH, N. S. H. (eds) *The Structure of Phonological Representations, Vol. 2*. Foris: Dordrecht, pp. 121–58.

POSER, W. (1990) 'Evidence for foot structure in Japanese.' *Language* **66**, 77–105.

PRINCE, A. (1980) 'A metrical theory of Estonian quantity.' *Linguistic Inquiry*, **11**, 511–62.

PRINCE, A. and SMOLENSKY, P. (1991) 'Connectionism and harmony theory in Linguistics.' Lecture notes and handouts from LSA Summer Institute, UCSC, Santa Cruz. *Technical Report CU-CS-533-91*. University of Colorado.

PRINCE, A. and SMOLENKSY, P. (1992) 'Optimality. Constraint interaction in generative grammar.' Revised and augmented handout of WCCFL talk, Brandeis University and University of Colorado.

PRINCE, A. and SMOLENSKY, P. (1993) 'Optimality theory. Constraint interaction in generative grammar.' Unpublished manuscript, Rutgers University and University of Colorado.

PRUNET, J.-F. (1986) 'Spreading and locality domains in phonology.' PhD thesis, McGill University.

PULLEYBLANK, D. (1986a) *Tone in Lexical Phonology*. Reidel: Dordrecht.

PULLEYBLANK, D. (1986b) 'Rule application on a non-cyclic stratum', *Linguistic Inquiry* **17**: 573–80.

PULLEYBLANK, D. (1988) 'Vocalic underspecification in Yoruba', *Linguistic Inquiry* **19**: 233–70.

PULLEYBLANK, E. G. (1989) 'The Role of Coronal in Articulator Based Features.' *Chicago Linguistic Society:* **25**, pp. 379–94.

RENNISON, J. (1984) 'On tridirectional feature systems for vowels.' *Wiener linguistische Gazette*. In DURAND, J. (ed.) *Dependency and Non-linear Phonology*. Croom Helm: London, pp. 281–303.

RENNISON, J. (1987) 'Vowel harmony and tridirectional vowel features', *Folia Linguistica* **21**: 337–54.

RENNISON, J. (1990) 'On the elements of phonological representations: the evidence from vowel systems and vowel processes', *Folia Linguistica* 24: 175–244.

RENNISON, J. R. (1992) 'Syllables, variable vowels, and empty categories.' Paper presented at the 7th International Phonology Meeting, Krems, Austria.

RICE, K. (1992) 'On deriving sonority: a structural account of sonority relationships', *Phonology* 9: 61–99.

RICE, K. D. and AVERY, P. (1989) 'On the interaction between sonorancy and voicing', *Toronto Working Papers in Linguistics* 10.

RICE, K. and AVERY, P. (1990) 'On the representation of voice', *Proceedings of NELS 20, Vol. 2*, GLSA, UMASS, Amhert, pp. 428–42.

RICE, K.D. and AVERY, P. (1991) 'On the relationship between laterality and coronality.' In PARADIS, C. and PRUNET, J-F. (eds) *The Special Status of Coronals: Internal and External Evidence*. Academic Press: San Diego.

RUBACH, J. (1984a) *Cyclic and Lexical Phonology: the Structure of Polish*. Foris: Dordrecht.

RUBACH, J. (1984b) 'Segmental rules of English and cyclic phonology', *Language* 60: 21–54.

SAGEY, E. (1986) 'The representation of features and relations in nonlinear phonology.' Unpublished PhD dissertation, MIT, Cambridge, Mass.

SAGEY, E. C. (1988) 'Degree of closure in complex segments.' In HULST, H. G. VAN DER and SMITH, N. (eds) *Features, Segmental Structure and Harmony Processes, Part I*. Foris: Dordrecht, pp. 169–208.

SALOMAA, A. (1973) *Formal Languages*. Academic Press: New York.

SAMPSON, G. (1980) *Schools of Linguistics. Competition and Evolution*. Hutchinson University Library: London.

SCHANE, S. S. (1984a) 'The fundamentals of Particle Phonology', *Phonology* 1: 129–56.

SCHANE, S. S. (1984b) 'Two English vowel movements: a particle analysis.' In ARONOFF, M. and OEHRLE, R. T. (eds) *Language Sound Structure: Studies in Phonology Presented to Morris Halle by his Teacher and Students*. MIT Press: Cambridge, Mass., pp. 32–51.

SCOBBIE, J. (1991) 'Attribute value phonology.' PhD dissertation, University of Edinburgh.

SEGUNDO, S. O. (1990) 'On empty nuclei and metrical structure in Brazilian Portuguese.' School of Oriental and African Studies, University of London, (*SOAS*) *Working Papers in Linguistics and Phonetics* 1: 39–51.

SELKIRK, E. O. (1978) 'On prosodic structure and its relation to syntactic structure.' In FRETHEIM, T. (ed.) *Nordic Prosody, Vol. II*. Tapir: Trondheim, pp. 111–40.

SELKIRK, E. O. (1982a) *The Syntax of Words*. MIT Press: Cambridge, Mass.

SELKIRK, E. O. (1982b) 'The syllable.' In HULST, H. G. VAN DER and SMITH, N. S. H. (eds) *The Structure of Phonological Representations, Part II*. Foris: Dordrecht, pp. 337–84.

SELKIRK, E. O. (1984a) *Phonology and Syntax: the Relation Between Sound and Structure*. MIT Press: Cambridge, Mass.

SELKIRK, E. O. (1984b) 'On the major class features and syllable theory.' In

ARONOFF, M. and OEHRLE, R. (eds) *Language Sound Structure*. MIT Press: Cambridge, Mass.

SENN, A. (1966) *Handbuch der litauischen Sprache. Band I. Grammatik*. Carl Winter: Heidelberg.

SHAW, P. A. (1990) 'On the phonological representation of laterals and affricates.' MS, University of British Columbia.

SHAW, P. A. (1991) 'Consonant harmony systems: the special status of coronal harmony.' In PARADIS, C. and PRUNET, J.-F. (eds) *Phonetics and Phonology: the Special Status of Coronals*. Academic Press: San Diego, pp. 125–57.

SHIEBER, S. M. (1986) 'An introduction to unification-based approaches to grammar.' Center for the Study of Language and Information (*CSLI*) *Lecture Notes No. 4*. CSLI: Stanford University.

SIEGEL, D. C. (1974) 'Topics in English morphology.' Unpublished PhD dissertation, Department of Linguistics and Philosophy, MIT.

SMITH, N. (1985) 'Spreading, reduplication and the default option in Miwok nonconcatenative morphology.' In HULST, H. G. VAN DER and SMITH, N. S. H. (eds) *Advances in Nonlinear Phonology*. Foris: Dordrecht, pp. 363–80.

SMITH, N. (1988) 'Consonant place features.' In HULST, H. G. VAN DER and SMITH, N. S. H. (eds) *Features, Segmental Structure and Harmony Processes*, Part I. Foris: Dordrecht, pp. 209–36.

SNIDER, K. L. (1988) 'Towards the representation of tone: a three-dimensional approach.' In HULST, H. G. VAN DER and SMITH, N. S. H. (eds) *Features, Segmental Structure and Harmony Processes, Part I*. Foris: Dordrecht, pp. 237–67.

SNIDER, K. L. (1991) 'Tonal upstep in Krachi: evidence for a register tier', *Language* **66**: 453–74.

SONG, J.-S. (1990) 'Vowel harmony in Nez Perce and Korean.' MA thesis, University of Ottawa.

SPROAT, R. and BRUNSON, B. (1987) Constituent-based morphological parsing: A new approach to the problem of word-recognition. *Proceedings of the 25th annual meeting of the Association for Computational Linguistics*. Morristown, NJ: Association for Computational Linguistics, pp. 65-72.

STEMBERGER, J. B. (1991) 'Radical underspecification in language production', *Phonology* **8**: 73–112.

STERIADE, D. (1982) 'Greek prosodies and the nature of syllabification.' Unpublished PhD dissertation, MIT.

STERIADE, D. (1987) 'Redundant values.' In BOSCH, A., NEED, B. and SCHILLER, E. (eds) *Parasession on Autosegmental and Metrical Phonology. Papers from the 23rd Annual Meeting of the Chicago Linguistics Society, Part 2*, University of Chicago Press: Chicago, pp. 339–62.

STERIADE, D. (1988) 'Reduplication and syllable transfer in Sanskrit and elsewhere', *Phonology* **5**: 73–155.

STERIADE, D. (1991) 'Closure, release and nasal contours.' MS, UCLA.

STEVENS, K. (1972) 'The quantal nature of speech.' In DAVID, E. E. and DENES, P. B. (eds) *Human Communication: a Unified View*. McGraw-Hill: New York.

STEVENS, K. N. and KEYSER, S. J. (1989) 'Primary features and their enhancement in consonants', *Language* **65**: 81–106.

STREET, J. C. (1963) *Khalkha structure. Uralic and Altaic Series, Vol. 24.* Bloomington, Indiana.

SWEET, H. (1877) *A Handbook of Phonetics.* Henry Frowde: Oxford.

SWEET, H. (1882) *Sweet's Anglo-Saxon Primer.* Oxford University Press.

THRÁINSSON, H. (1978) 'On the phonology of Icelandic preaspiration', *Nordic Journal of Linguistics* **1**: 3–54.

TRAILL, A. (1991) 'The feature geometry of clicks.' MS, University of the Witwatersrand.

TRANEL, B. (1991) 'CVC light syllables, geminates and Moraic Theory', *Phonology* **8**: 291–302.

TRANEL, B. (to appear) 'Final consonants and non-linear phonology.' In DURAND, J. and HINTZE, M.-A. (eds) *Words, Syllables, Morae,* special issue of *Lingua* on French phonology.

TRIGO, R. L. (1988) 'On the phonological derivation and behavior of nasal glides.' Unpublished PhD dissertation, MIT.

TRIGO, L. (1991) 'On pharynx-larynx interactions', *Phonology* **8**: 113–36.

VAGO, R. M. (1987) 'On the representation of length.' In DRESSLER, W. U., LUSCHÜTZKY, H. C., PFEIFFER, O. E. and RENNISON, J. R. (eds) *Phonologica 1984. Proceedings of the Fifth International Phonology Meeting, Eisenstadt, 25–28 June 1984.* Cambridge University Press, Cambridge, pp. 319–24.

VAGO, R. M. (1988) 'Underspecification in the height harmony system of Pasiego', *Phonology* **5**: 343–62.

VAUX, B. (1992) 'Gemination and syllabic integrity in Sanskrit', *The Journal of Indo-European Studies* **20**: 283–303.

VENNEMANN, T. (1968) 'German phonology.' Unpublished PhD dissertation, UCLA.

VENNEMANN, T. (1972) 'On the theory of syllabic phonology', *Linguistische Berichte* **18**: 1–18.

VENNEMANN, T. (1974) 'Words and syllables in natural generative grammar.' In BRUCK, A., FOX, R. A. and LA SALY, M. W. (eds) *Papers from the Parasession on Natural Phonology.* Chicago Linguistic Society: Chicago.

VENNEMANN, T. (1988) *Preference Laws for Syllable Structure and the Explanation of Sound Change.* Mouton de Gruyter: Berlin.

VERGNAUD, J.-R. (1982) 'On the foundations of phonology.' Paper presented at GLOW colloquium, Paris.

WEIJER VAN DE, J. M. (1993a) 'The manner-place dependency in complex segments', *Linguistics* **31**: 87–110.

WEIJER VAN DE, J. M. (1993b) 'Continuancy in obstruents and in liquids.' MS, University of Leiden.

WEIJER VAN DE, J. M. (1994) 'Segmental structure and complex segments.' HIL dissertations no. g. Holland Academic Graphics.

WEIJER, VAN DE J. M. and HULST, H. G. VAN DER (in preparation) 'Two-root complex segments.' MS, University of Leiden.

WETZELS, L. and HERMANS, B. (1985) 'Aspirated geminates in Pali.' In

404   REFERENCES

BENNIS, H. and BENKEMA, F. (eds) *Linguistics in the Netherlands.* Foris: Dordrecht, pp. 213–23.

WICKENS, G. M. (1980) *Arabic Grammar: A First Workbook.* Cambridge University Press: Cambridge.

WIESEMANN, U. (1972) *Die phonologische und grammatische Struktur der Kaingang Sprache.* Mouton: The Hague.

WILLIAMS, G. (1992) 'Automatic speech recognition: a government phonology approach.' Paper presented at the 7th International Phonology Meeting, Krems, Austria.

WILLIAMS, G. and BROCKHAUS, W. G. (1992) 'Automatic speech recognition: a principle-based approach.' *SOAS Working Papers in Linguistics and Phonetics* 2: 371–401.

WOOCK, E. B. and NOONAN, M. (1979) 'Vowel harmony in Lango.' In CLYNE, P., HANKS, W. and HOFBAUER, C. (eds) *Papers from the Fifteenth Regional Meeting: Chicago Linguistics Society,* University of Chicago: Chicago, Illinois, pp. 20–9.

WRIGHT, W. (1971) *A Grammar of the Arabic Language.* Cambridge: Cambridge University Press.

YIP, M. (1980) 'The tonal phonology of Chinese.' Unpublished PhD dissertation, MIT.

YIP, M. (1982) 'Reduplication and CV-skeleta in Chinese secret languages', *Linguistic Inquiry* 13: 637–61.

YIP, M. (1988a) 'The obligatory contour principle and phonological rules: a loss of identity', *Linguistic Inquiry* 19: 65–100.

YIP, M. (1988b) 'Template morphology and direction of association', *Natural Language and Linguistic Theory* 6: 551–77.

YIP, M. (1989) 'Contour tones', *Phonology* 6: 149–74.

YIP, M. (1993) 'Tonal register in East Asian languages.' In HULST, H. G. VAN DER and SNIDER, K. L. (eds) *The Representation of Tonal Register.* Mouton de Gruyter: Berlin, pp. 245–68.

YOSHIDA, S. (1990) 'A government-based analysis of the "mora" in Japanese.' *Phonology* 7: 331–51.

YOSHIDA, S. (1991) 'Some aspects of governing relations in Japanese phonology.' Unpublished PhD dissertation, School of Oriental and African Studies (SOAS), University of London.

YOSHIDA, S. (1992) 'Licensing of governing nuclear heads.' Paper presented at the Government Phonology Workshop, 7th International Phonology Meeting, Krems, Austria.

ZEC, D. (1988) 'Sonority constraints on prosodic structure.' Unpublished PhD dissertation, Stanford University.

ZEC, D. (1992) 'Coda constraints and conditions on syllable weight.' Unpublished MS, Cornell University.

ZEC, D. (1993) 'Sonority constraints on syllable structure.' Unpublished MS, Cornell University.

Languages Index

Subject Index